The Educated Mind

KIERAN EGAN

The Educated Mind

How Cognitive Tools Shape Our Understanding

THE UNIVERSITY OF CHICAGO PRESS *Chicago & London*

The University of Chicago Press gratefully acknowledges the
assistance of the Exxon Foundation in the publication of this book.

The University of Chicago Press, Chicago 60637
The University of Chicago Press, Ltd., London
© 1997 by The University of Chicago
All rights reserved. Published 1997
Paperback edition 1998
Printed in the United States of America
06 05 04 03 02 01 00 99 98   2345
ISBN: 0-226-19036-6 (cloth)
ISBN: 0-226-19039-0 (paperback)

Library of Congress Cataloging-in-Publication Data

Egan, Kieran.
    The educated mind : how cognitive tools shape our understanding /
Kieran Egan.
        p.   cm.
    Includes bibliographical references and index.
    ISBN 0-226-19036-6 (alk. paper)
    1. Education—Philosophy.   2. Cognition and culture.
3. Civilization, Western—History.   4. Educational anthropology.
5. Educational sociology.   6. Learning, Psychology of.   7. Teaching.
8. Psycholinguistics.   I. Title.
LB14.7.E53   1997
370'.1—dc20   96-42208
                                                                                  CIP

♾ The paper used in this publication meets the minimum requirements of
the American National Standard for Information Sciences—Permanence of
Paper for Printed Library Materials, ANSI Z39.48-1992

O beloved kids
Michael, Catherine, and David

c o n t e n t s

acknowledgments

I am most grateful to the many kind people who have read parts or all of this book in manuscript, whose suggestions, criticisms, abuse, and corrections have made this book better than it would otherwise have been. In particular I am grateful to John Willinsky of the University of British Columbia; Wendy Strachan of the Department of English at Simon Fraser University; Richard Wilkins of the Association for Christian Teachers in Great Britain; Hunter McEwan of the University of Hawaii; Joanne Buckley of the Department of English at University of Western Ontario; Merlin Donald of the Psychology Department at Queen's University; Avril Chalmers, Jennifer Jenson, and David Hammond, Ph.D. students in the Faculty of Education at Simon Fraser University; and Susanna Egan of the English Department at the University of British Columbia.

I have also benefited from comments on parts of the book from Alan Rudrum of the Department of English, Jerry Zaslove of the Institute for the Humanities, Sen Campbell and Peter Cole, Ph.D. students in the Faculty of Education, and Stephen Smith and Heesoon Bai of the Faculty of Education, all at Simon Fraser University. I am grateful to Miranda and Christopher Armstrong for permission to reprint the conversation that appears in chapter 4.

Eileen Mallory has typed the whole manuscript with her everyday supernatural speed, accuracy, and kindly good cheer. John Tryneski of the University of Chicago Press has been supportive and challenging, and the source of numerous insightful suggestions that have improved the book significantly; the compleat editor. I am also indebted to the editorial skills of Leslie Keros, which she applied to the manuscript with grace and wit, clarifying it considerably. One of the Press's reviewers, I discovered, was Howard Gardner of Harvard University; his incisive suggestions have had a significant effect on the manuscript, and I am pleased to be able to acknowledge his generosity and help.

Some paragraphs from chapters 1, 2, 3, 4, and 5 appeared in "The development of understanding," my article in *The Handbook of Education and Human Development* (David R. Olson and Nancy Torrance, eds.), Oxford: Blackwell Publishers, Ltd., 1966. I am grateful to the editors and publisher for permission to use these paragraphs here. During the writing of this book I have been the grateful beneficiary of a research grant from the Social Sciences and Humanities Research Council of Canada.

Introduction

Those of us who were around during the economic crisis of the late sixteenth century in Europe find some features of the current educational crisis oddly familiar. There is a major social puzzle, which touches and irritates nearly everyone, and lashings of blame fly in all directions. Today we are puzzled by the schools' difficulty in providing even the most rudimentary education to so many students, despite a decade or more of effort by expensive professionals. The costs of our educational crisis, in terms of social alienation, psychological rootlessness, and ignorance of the world and the possibilities of human experience within it, are incalculable and heartbreaking.

In the sixteenth century, average citizens saw prices for all commodities begin to rise rapidly. Most obvious were the increased amounts they had to pay for necessities like clothes. The citizens blamed the clothiers for greedily raising prices. The clothiers protested, blaming the merchants who were greedily demanding more for their cloth; the merchants in turn blamed the weavers, who blamed the wool merchants, who blamed the sheep farmers. The sheep farmers said they had to raise their prices to be able to buy the increasingly expensive clothes. And so it went round. Who was to blame?

It took some time, and much blaming, before Jean Bodin (1530–1596) worked out that none of the obvious candidates was at fault. Rather, the general rise in prices was connected with the import into Europe of Central and South American gold and silver and with the European monarchs' use of this bullion through their royal mints. That is, the monarchs increased the money supply and thus stimulated inflation. A development in economic theory resolved the central puzzle and laid a tenuous foundation for greater understanding and practical control of economic matters.

So who is responsible for our modern social puzzle, the educational ineffectiveness of our schools? (By "modern" I mean the period beginning with the late-nineteenth-century development of mass schooling.) For media pundits and professional educators, there is no shortage of blameworthy candidates: inadequately educated teachers, the absence of market incentives, the inequities of capitalist societies, the lack of local control over schools, the genetic intellectual incapacity of 85 percent of the population to benefit from instruction in more than basic literacy and skills, drugs, the breakdown of the nuclear family and family values, an irrelevant academic curriculum, a trivial curriculum filled only with the immediately relevant, short-sighted politicians demanding hopelessly crude achievement tests while grossly underfunding the education system, a lack of commitment to excellence, vacuous schools of education, mindless TV and other mass media, the failure to attend to some specific research results.

Along with the cacophony of blame comes a panoply of prescriptions: introduce market incentives, make the curriculum more "relevant" or more academic, reform teacher training, ensure students' active involvement in their learning, and so on. Back in the sixteenth century, a litany of cures for inflation also was proposed: restrain merchants' profits, introduce price controls, restrict the export of wool, introduce tariffs on imported cloth, and so on. We can now look back indulgently at those prescriptions and see that they were irrelevant to the real cause of the problem: They would have been ineffective in slowing inflation and would in most cases have brought about further economic damage. Similarly, we are likely to look back on the current list of prescriptions to cure education's ills as irrelevant because they, too, fail to identify the real cause of the problem.

The trouble is not caused by any of the usual suspects. Instead, as I intend to show, it stems from a fundamentally incoherent conception of education. I will try, first and briefly, to show the lack of coherence that marks most people's notions of what schools ought to be doing, and, second and less briefly, to propose an educational theory that can enable schools to become more effective—a theory that lays a foundation for greater understanding and practical control of educational matters.

Oh, dear—the problem has to do with one educational theory and the solution with another one? The comparison with sixteenth-century inflation suggested something more richly tangible, like gold from Eldorado. The promise of a new educational theory, however, has the magnetism of a newspaper headline like "Small Earthquake in Chile: Few Hurt."

Educational theorizing is generally dreary because we have only three significant educational ideas: that we must shape the young to the current norms and conventions of adult society, that we must teach them the knowledge that will ensure their thinking conforms with what is real and true about the world, and that we must encourage the development of each student's individual potential. These ideas have rolled together over the centuries into our currently dominant conception of education. There are just so many variants that one can play with so few ideas before terminal staleness sets in, and matters are made worse by most people's unawareness of the fundamental ideas that shape their thinking about education.

The good news, I suppose, is that there are indeed only three ideas to grasp. The bad news is that the three ideas are mutually incompatible—and this is the primary cause of our long-continuing educational crisis. My first task in chapter 1 is to elaborate those ideas a little, to show in what ways they are mutually incompatible and to show that this incompatibility is the root of our practical difficulties in education today. My second task in chapter 1 is to introduce the new educational theory and indicate why it might be a better bet than any other, or any combination of others, currently around.

One unfamiliar feature of this new theory is that it describes education in terms of a sequence of kinds of understanding. A further oddity is that it conceives of education as so intricately tied in with the life of society and its culture that it is also a theory about Western cultural development and its relationship to education in modern multicultural societies. I characterize Western cultural history, and education today, in terms of an unfolding sequence of somewhat distinctive kinds of understanding.

What kind of category is a "kind of understanding"? Perhaps by reflecting on the following piece of information, you will gain a preliminary sense of what I mean.

In 1949, at El Quantara railway station in the Suez Canal Zone, there were ten lavatories. Three were for officers—one for Europeans, one for Asiatics, and one for Coloreds; three were for warrant officers and sergeants, divided by race as for the senior officers; three were for other ranks, also divided like the others by race; and one was for women, regardless of rank, class, or race. One might respond with outrage to the injustice of such arrangements and to the injustice inherent in the society that these arrangements reflect. One might feel a simple tug of delight at accumulating such a piece of exotica. If one considers social class a prime determiner of consciousness, such lavatory arrangements will have a particular resonance; if race, another; and if gender, yet another. One might fit this information into a narrative of social amelioration between earlier unjust authoritarian regimes and later democratic systems. One might consider it dispassionately as reflecting one among a kaleidoscopic variety of social systems human beings have devised and those lavatory arrangements as no more or less bizarre than whatever today would be considered more just, proper, or "normal." One might consider the arrangements with relief, taking the perspective of the officers, or with resentment, taking that of the other ranks, or with mixed feelings, taking that of the women.

In each of these responses the information is understood in a somewhat different way. Today a response will rarely involve just one of these ways of understanding the facts; we commonly adopt a number of such perspectives, understanding the information as complex, polysemous.

My primary aim in this book is to unravel some of the major strands or layers of our typically polysemous understanding. I try to separate out a set of general and distinctive kinds of understanding and characterize each of them in detail; I distinguish five, which I call Somatic, Mythic, Romantic, Philosophic, and Ironic. I try to show, furthermore, that these kinds of understanding have developed in evolution and cultural history in a particular sequence, coalescing to a large extent (but not completely) as each successive kind has emerged. The modern mind thus is represented as a composite. This conception of the mind is a bit messy, but it tries to adhere to what systems theorists call the principle of requisite variety: that the model conform with the complexity of what it represents.

My second and related aim is to show that education can best be conceived as the individual's acquiring each of these kinds of understanding as fully as possible in the sequence in which each developed historically. Thus I construct a new recapitulation theory, distinct from those articulated in the late nineteenth century mainly in terms of *what is identified* as being recapitulated.

I try to show that each kind of understanding results from the development of particular intellectual tools that we acquire from the societies we grow up in. While these tools are varied, I will focus largely on those evident in language: the successive development of oral language, literacy, theoretic abstractions, and the extreme linguistic reflexiveness that yields irony. I explore the implications of being an oral-language user for the kind of (Mythic) understanding one can form of the world, and the kind of (Romantic) understanding that is an implication of growing into a particular literacy, and the kind of (Philosophic) understanding that is an implication of fitting into communities that use theoretic abstractions, and the kind of (Ironic) understanding that is an implication of self-conscious reflection about the language one uses.

Now "tools" is obviously an awkward word; I mean something like the "mediational means" the Russian psychologist, Lev Vygotsky (1896–1934), describes as the shapers of the kind of sense we make of the world. Vygotsky argued that intellectual development cannot adequately be understood in epistemological terms that focus on the kinds and quantities of knowledge accumulated or in psychological terms that focus on some supposed inner and spontaneous developmental process. Rather, he understood intellectual development in terms of the intellectual tools, like language, that we accumulate as we grow up in a society and that mediate the kind of understanding we can form or construct. In chapter 1 I try to show how the focus on mediating intellectual tools, rather than on forms of knowledge or on psychological processes, enables construction of a new educational idea. So, my gold from Eldorado that is designed to carry us past our present educational problem and transcend the ideological logjam at its core is a set of language-based intellectual tools that generate Somatic, Mythic, Romantic, Philosophic, and Ironic kinds of understanding.

By "language based" I mean that my focus is on more general cultural phenomena that nevertheless are fairly distinctly reflected in language use, and in each discussion it is with the language forms that I begin. Merlin Donald notes that "the uniqueness of humanity could be said to rest not so much in language as in our capacity for rapid cultural change. . . . [W]hat humans evolved was primarily a generalized capacity for cultural innovation" (1991, p. 10). The kinds of understanding are attempts to characterize a basic level of significant innovative changes in human cultural life, historically and in individual experience.

A working title for this book had been "The Body's Mind." Given my references to language, intellectual tools, and cultural innovations, one may ask why the body figures so prominently. We had, as a species, and have, as individuals, bodies before language. Language emerges from the body in the process of evolutionary and individual development, and it bears the ineluctable stamp of the body: Phrases and sentences, for example, are tied to the time we take to inhale and exhale—though when we speak we take in quick breaths and release them steadily (in a process Steven Pinker describes as syntax overriding carbon dioxide [1994, p. 164]); similarly, we use language to represent the world as it is disclosed by our particular scale and kind of organs of perception. In other words, our body is the most fundamental mediating tool that shapes our understanding. This is obvious, of course, and Somatic understanding refers to the understanding of the world that is possible for human beings given the kind of body we have. In the theory to be elaborated in the following chapters, each kind of understanding does not fade away to be replaced by the next, but rather each properly coalesces in significant degree with its predecessor. The developments in language uses and their intellectual implications that I explore are, then, always tied in 5 some degree to this embodied core of understanding. This becomes especially important when I sketch my conception of Ironic understanding and confront some common assumptions of postmodernism.

In chapters 2 through 5 I describe both the minting in Western cultural history of the five kinds of understanding and the forms they commonly take among students today. I also attempt to show that education can best be conceived as the process of developing each of these kinds of understanding as fully as possible. The first kind of understanding, the Somatic, I discuss in chapter 5 after the Ironic, for reasons that will be given there. Apart from that, in each chapter I characterize one kind of understanding, showing its emergence in Western cultural history, giving examples of its occurrence in various historical periods, and indicating perhaps surprising parallels between these historical occurrences and the lives and activities of students today. Among other things, these accounts offer new explanations of the nature of fantasy and why four- and five-year-olds commonly find it so engaging, of ten-year-olds' interest in the contents of *The Guinness Book of Records,* of eleven- and twelve-year-olds' emotional associations with pop singers or sports heroes, of academic sixteen-year-olds' interest in general ideas, metaphysical schemes, or ideologies, and so on. The unfamiliar category of "kinds of understanding" has at least the virtue of bringing into focus features of students' thinking and learning that are prominent and powerful in their lives but have been somewhat neglected in educational writing.

I realize that this talk of Western cultural development, intellectual tools, and kinds of understanding may not exactly quicken the pulse of those hoping to discover better ways of preparing our children for productive work and satisfying leisure. And the references to Western culture, along with the announcement I now warily make—that I will be constantly discussing and quoting ancient Greeks—may add a seal of hopelessness to this enterprise for more radical spirits. I think neither group should feel disappointed. One simple aim of this book is to show that the occasionally derided "basics" of education may be much more effectively attained than is now common; another is to establish as the appropriate aim of education a kind of Ironic understanding that is quite distinct from the traditionalist conception of the educated person.

Chapter 6 provides a chance to reflect on the theory and to clarify its unfamiliar features. This chapter deals with a range of political, ideological, pedagogical, methodological, moral, and other issues raised by the presentation of the theory to that point. I pretend there that I am answering questions from a varied and critical audience that has had the preternatural patience to sit through the preceding chapters; despite my best efforts at evenhandedness, the skeptical questioners may come off as waspish, bad tempered, obtuse, evil minded, and perhaps somewhat drunk, and the answerer as the essence of sweet reason. (Mind you, this Western "reason" is another prominent issue to be dealt with.)

Chapters 7 and 8 then explore the theory's implications for the curriculum and the classroom. The overall shape of the book, then, is a funnel that begins with general theoretical issues, moves through more concrete theory construction, and concludes with a somewhat detailed look at practical implications. Readers whose primary interest is in the theory's practical implications might find the earlier chapters hard going, so I sketch the implications fairly thoroughly in chapter 2 and, to a lesser degree, in the succeeding chapters, hoping that such readers will be able to manage the trek through to chapters 7 and 8 without further oxygen.

I have organized the book into two parts. The first deals primarily with modern people's recapitulation of the kinds of understanding developed in their cultural history. The second looks at implications of the theory for the curriculum and for teaching practice. This division is designed to alert the reader to the rather different styles of the two groups of chapters. It is not possible to discuss the social studies curriculum in eighth grade or the science curriculum in third grade in quite the same style as one can lay out the theoretical argument. In addition, I try to relate the theory's implications as closely as possible to current curricula and to everyday classroom practice. It might seem less glamorous than what the earlier discussion prepares one for, but I hope nevertheless that the genuine practical improvements that follow from the theory will be clear.

Unusually for a developmental scheme, the gains that come with each new set of intellectual tools are represented as entailing some loss of the understanding associated with the prior set. For example, when we become literate we do not cease to be oral-language users, but we do commonly lose some of the understanding that is a part of being exclusively an oral-language user. While this theory identifies cumulative aspects of understanding, it also represents education, and cultural history, as processes in which we can lose more by way of alienation and emotional as well as intellectual desiccation than we gain by way of understanding and aesthetic delight. Stand outside a public high school at the end of the school day and you will see this only too painfully. The educational trick is to maximize the gains while minimizing the losses. If we are unaware of the potential losses, we do little to minimize them.

This is not a book of new discoveries or of new knowledge generated by research. Rather, it simply reorganizes long-known ideas into a coherent scheme. My aim is not to present some exotic new conception of education, but rather to articulate a theory that is more adequate to what has long been meant by the word. We have lived with important but inadequate and mutu-

ally incompatible educational ideas for such a long time, and have even become comfortable with the discomforts they have caused and cause, that a
theory aiming to remove the discomforts must itself seem rather a nuisance.
In his own work in economics, John Maynard Keynes expressed the problem
succinctly:

The composition of this book has been for the author a long struggle of escape, and so
must the reading of it be for most readers if the author's assault upon them is to be
successful,—a struggle of escape from habitual modes of thought and expression. The
ideas which are here expressed so laboriously are extremely simple and should be obvious. The difficulty lies, not in the new ideas, but in escaping from the old ones, which
ramify, for those brought up as most of us have been, into every corner of our minds.
(1936, p. xxiii)

chapter 1

Three Old Ideas and a New One

INTRODUCTION

Education is one of the greatest consumers of public money in the Western world, and it employs a larger workforce than almost any other social agency. The goals of the education system—to enhance the competitiveness of nations and the self-fulfillment of citizens—are supposed to justify the immense investment of money and energy. School—that business of sitting at a desk among thirty or so others, being talked at, mostly boringly, and doing exercises, tests, and worksheets, mostly boring, for years and years and years—is the instrument designed to deliver these expensive benefits. Despite, or because of, the vast expenditures of money and energy, finding anyone inside or outside the education system who is content with its performance is difficult. Many task forces, commissions, and reports have documented the inadequacies of schools throughout the Western world and have proposed even more numerous remedies. The diagnoses of illness are so many and the recommended remedies so varied that politicians and educational authorities cannot address the evident deficiencies with much confidence of success or of general support.

Consider the community school along with other major institutions that developed into their modern forms in the latter part of the nineteenth century. The factory, the hospital, the prison, and the school have become prominent and integral components of twentieth century societies in the West. The factory and the hospital are generally accepted as successful institutions. There may be arguments about whether American, Scandinavian, or Japanese styles of manufacturing are more efficient or socially desirable, or about iatrogenic diseases and "spiraling health care costs," but generally these institutions are viewed as being well designed to achieve their proper aims. Prisons are more problematic. They were developed in the West to achieve two aims—to punish and to rehabilitate. The problem is, these aims are not entirely compatible; the more a conscientious civil servant tries to achieve one, the more difficult it is to do the other.

In the case of the modern school, three distinctive aims have attended its development. It is expected to serve as a significant agency in socializing the young, to teach particular forms of knowledge that will bring about a realistic and rational view of the world, and to help realize the unique potential of each child. These goals are generally taken to be consistent with one another, somewhat overlapping, and mutually supportive. As shown later in this chapter, however, each of these aims is incompatible in profound ways with the other two. As with prisons' aims to punish and to rehabilitate, the more we work to achieve one of the schools' aims, the more difficult it becomes to achieve the others.

THE THREE OLD IDEAS

The First Idea: Socialization

Central to any educational scheme is initiation of the young into the knowledge, skills, values, and commitments common to the adult members of the society. Oral cultures long ago invented techniques to ensure that the young would efficiently learn and remember the social group's store of knowledge and would also take on the values that sustain the structure of the society and establish the sense of identity of its individual members.

Prominent among these techniques was the use of rhyme, rhythm, meter, and vivid images. Perhaps the most powerful technique invented, and the greatest of all social inventions, was the "coding" of lore into stories. This had the dual effect of making the contents more easily remembered—crucial in cultures where all knowledge had to be preserved in living memories—and of shaping the hearers' emotional commitment to those contents. One could ensure greater cohesiveness within the social group by coding the lore that was vital to one's society into stories—be it proper kinship relations and appropriate behavior, economic activities, property rights, class status, or medical knowledge and its application.

The young have a remarkable plasticity to adapt to an indeterminate range of cultural forms, beliefs, and patterns of behavior. The central task of socialization is to inculcate a restricted set of norms and beliefs—the set that constitutes the adult society the child will grow into. Societies can survive and maintain their sense of identity only if a certain degree of homogeneity is achieved in shaping its members; "education perpetuates and reinforces this homogeneity by fixing in the child, from the beginning, the essential similarities that collective life demands" (Durkheim, 1956, p. 70).

Whoever governs the initiation process—the storytellers or the ministry of education and the school board—acts to promote the norms and values that are dominant in the society at large. Their job is to perform the homogenizing task Durkheim refers to. If a school today in Cuba or Iran routinely graduated liberal, capitalist entrepreneurs, it would be considered a disaster. In Winnipeg, Wigan, Wabash, or Wollongong, this would not be considered so bad. Indeed, what would be considered outrageous in Iran is a deliberate aim of Wollongong schools.

The process of socialization is central to the mandate of schools today. Our schools have the duty to ensure that students graduate with an understanding of their society and of their place and possibilities within it, that they have the skills required for its perpetuation, and that they hold its values and commitments. While we might not feel comfortable with the term, we accept that a prominent aim of schools is the homogenization of children.

The spokespersons of governments, taxpayers, and businesses that require the schools to produce a skilled workforce of good citizens today echo those who learned long ago the techniques for reproducing in the young the values and beliefs, the skills and lore, that best contribute to the untroubled perpetuation of the tribe. The public voices that associate education primarily with jobs, the economy, and the production of good citizens reflect a predominantly socializing emphasis.

The very structure of modern schools in the West, with its age cohorts, class groupings, team sports, and so on, encourages conformity to modern Western social norms. Such structures can accommodate only a very limited range of nonconformity. Students learn, more or less, to fit in for their own good. We need not see this process of socialization and homogenization as the de-humanizing, right-wing conspiracy it was "exposed" to be by 1960s romantic radical writers on education (e.g., Goodman, 1962; Kozol, 1967; Roszak, 1969; Young, 1971). Of course, pushed to extremes—which is where the radicals consider the typical public school to be—the socially necessary homogenizing process can become totalitarian in its demands for conformity. But most pluralistic Western societies try to build defences

11

against those who are most eager to censor children's reading or restrict their behavior and shape their beliefs excessively.

The socialization of the young is also evident in the efforts to promote "useful" knowledge and skills through courses on consumer education, anti–drug use, and automobile maintenance. Sometimes the proponents argue that schools graduate students only when they are equipped to do a job. I have kept an old letter, published in an Ann Landers column, from someone who signed, sadly, as Too soon old—too late smart. The letter expresses frustration with schools in which "our children are subjected to 12 years of 'education' without learning how to conduct themselves in real-life situations" and suggests that schools introduce a course on the consequences of shoplifting, that several days a week be devoted to the subject of the hazards of cigarette smoke, that there be instruction in the dangers of alcoholism, that sex education be a "must" in every school, and that there be courses on "life," with how-to instructions on settling arguments, expressing anger and hostility, handling competitive feelings involving brothers and sisters, coping with alcoholic parents, and dealing with "funny uncles" and passes made by homosexual peers. The writer acknowledges the importance of algebra and geometry in the curriculum but argues that information on how to handle one's life should take precedence.

Too soon old—too late smart expresses very clearly how the curriculum would be changed if socializing were made more prominent in the schools' mandate. Those who share this view see the school as primarily a social agency that should accommodate society's changing needs. Recently their voices have been prominent in demands that students become familiar with computers and their range of applications. They support counseling programs and like to see school counselors working along with parents to help students adjust to the strains and challenges of modern society. Sports, travel, exchanges, visits to monuments and courts and government buildings, and social studies activities that help students understand their local environment all tend to be supported as helping to socialize the young. The teacher is seen as an important social worker, primarily valuable as a role model who exemplifies the values, beliefs, and norms of the dominant society; knowledge of subject matter cannot substitute for "character," wholesomeness, and easy and open communication with students.

The Second Idea: Plato and the Truth about Reality

Plato (c. 428–347 B.C.E.) had a radically different idea about how people should be educated. He wrote *The Republic* as a kind of elaborate prospectus for his Academy. Not conforming with the best modern advertising practice, he laid out his ideas in a manner that involved constantly arguing the inadequacy of the forms of education offered by his competitors. Plato wanted to show that the worldly wise, well-socialized, practical person equipped with all the skills of a good and effective citizen was not only an educationally inadequate ideal but actually a contemptible one. The assertive and confident Thrasymachus of *The Republic* and the worldly wise Callicles of the *Gorgias* are shown to be other than the masters of affairs they seem; in fact, they are slaves of conventional ideas. In contrast, the ability to reflect on ideas, to pull them this way and that until some bedrock of truth and certainty is established, was the promised result of the curriculum described in *The Republic* and offered in Plato's Academy. Plato certainly wanted the graduates of his school to be politically active and to change the world, but first they had to understand it.

Plato's revolutionary idea was that education should not be concerned primarily with equipping students to develop the knowledge and skills best suited to ensuring their success as citizens and sharing the norms and values of their peers. Rather, education was to be a process of learning those forms of knowledge that would give students a privileged, rational view of reality. Only by disciplined study of increasingly abstract forms of knowledge, guided by a kind of spiritual commitment, could the mind transcend the conventional beliefs, prejudices, and stereotypes of the time and come to see reality clearly.

Now this hasn't been everyone's cup of tea by any means. But Plato succeeded in expressing his central idea with such clarity, force, vividness, and imaginative wit that everyone who has written about education in the West has been profoundly influenced by it. Who, after all, wants to live and die a prisoner to conventional prejudices and stereotypes, never seeing the world as it really is? And how can one know when one is dealing with reality rather than with illusions and stereotypes? Plato's claim that his "academic" curriculum alone can carry the mind to rationality and a secure access to reality has been so influential that we can hardly imagine a conception of education without it.

Indeed, nearly everyone today takes it for granted that schools should attend to the intellectual cultivation of the young in ways that are not justified simply in terms of social utility. We include in the curriculum a range of subject matter that we assume will do something valuable for students' minds and give them a more realistic grasp of the world. We consider it important to teach them that Saturn is a planet that orbits the sun rather than have them believe it is a wandering star erratically orbiting the earth and influencing their daily fortune by its association with other stars. We teach division of fractions, algebra, drama, ancient history, and much else for 13 which most students will never have a practical need. The place of such topics in the curriculum is usually justified in vague terms such as "educational value." In Plato's idea, the mind is what it learns, so selecting the content of the curriculum is vital.

How, then, is the Platonic idea of education represented today? One prominent conception can be introduced through an image suggested by astronomer Carl Sagan. Sagan has been a prominent organizer of the search for signs of extraterrestrial intelligence with radio telescopes. This program assumes a vividly romantic picture of a conversation among intelligent beings in our galaxy, which we are just now developing the technology to enter. By plugging in, we might suddenly have access to a conversation of unimaginable richness and wonder. In a more immediately possible sense, modern proponents of the Platonic idea of education suggest that accessing a transcendent conversation is precisely what education does for the individual. Michael Oakeshott (1991), for example, represents education as entry into a conversation that began long ago in the jungles and plains of Africa, gathered further voices, perspectives, and varied experience in the ancient kingdoms of the East, added distinctive voices and experience in ancient Greece and Rome, and continues to accumulate value to the present. The conversation is now one of immense richness, wonder, and diversity.

An individual can live and die happily, be socialized harmoniously in her or his special milieu, but remain almost entirely ignorant of this great cultural conversation as we will likely do with regard to Sagan's imagined galactic interchange. But if it were really there in radio waves across the galaxy and we had the means to join it, would we not be foolish to ignore it? Would we not be impoverishing our experience? The task of education, in this view, is to connect children with the great cultural conversation that very definitely is there and that transcends politics, special milieus, local experiences, and conventional sets of norms and values. To pass up the chance to engage in this conversation is to be like Proust's dog in the library—possibly content, but ignorant of the potential riches around us.

Those who want the schools to connect children to this great cultural conversation, and to serve as bastions of civilization against the cretinizing mindlessness of pop culture (these are the kind of terms they like), who want students to be engaged by the disinterested pursuit of truth through the hard academic disciplines that will make them knowledgeable, discriminating, and skeptical, give new voice to the idea Plato bequeathed to us. These are people who value Plato's idea more highly than the other two ideas. For these people, school is properly a place apart from society: a place dedicated to knowledge, skills, and activities that are of "persisting value," transcending the requirements of current social life. Indeed, what students learn is to establish the grounds from which they can judge the appropriateness of the values, norms, beliefs, and practices of society. Schools dominated by this idea consequently tend to be called elitist. Knowledge is valued less for its social utility than for its presumed benefit to the mind of the student; thus, Latin has a higher status than automobile maintenance. Modern, neoconservative promoters of the Platonic idea (whose slogan is "excellence in education") direct their outrage particularly at students' ignorance of their cultural heritage (cf. the British Black Papers on Education during the 1960s and 1970s; Hirsch, 1987; Ravitch and Finn, 1987) and downplay programs that do not serve a specific academic purpose. Teachers tend to occupy a more distant, authoritative, and even authoritarian role because they properly embody the authority that comes from being an expert in the relevant subject matter.

The Third Idea: Rousseau and Nature's Guidance

Jean-Jacques Rousseau (1712–1778) viewed current educational practice as disastrous. He was happy to acknowledge that Plato's *Republic* "is the finest treatise on education ever written," but he concluded that when dull pedagogues took hold of Plato's idea, they took the forms of knowledge that made up the curriculum, organized those into what seemed the best logical order, then beat them into the students. The typical result was misery, violence, and frustration: a syndrome not unknown today, though we may mark some success, influenced by Rousseau, at reducing the physical violence inflicted on children in the name of education.

Pedagogues, Rousseau observed, "are always looking for the man in the child, without considering what he is before he becomes a man" (Rousseau, 1911, p. 1). In *Émile*, he focused attention instead on the nature of the developing child, concentrating less on what ought to be learned and more on what children at different ages are capable of learning and on how learning might proceed most effectively. He saw his book, *Émile*, as a kind of supplement to *The Republic*, rectifying its major omission and updating the master's work. But, as we'll see, *Émile* was built on assumptions profoundly at odds with Plato's.

"The internal development of our faculties and organs is the education of nature," Rousseau wrote. "The use we learn to make of this development is the education of men" (p. 11). So, to be able to educate, we must first understand that internal development process. The most important area of educational study, then, is the nature of students' development, learning, and 15 motivation. The more we know about these, the more efficient and humane we can make the educational process. The key is that underlying natural development: "Fix your eye on nature, follow the path traced by her" (p. 14).

As nature was to be our guide, and Rousseau clearly believed the nature of males and females to be significantly different, nature dictated a quite different education for Sophie from that of Émile—an education that encouraged the "domination and violation of women" (Darling and Van de Pijpekamp, 1994).)

Émile, published in 1762, was promptly ordered to be burned in Paris and Geneva. This no doubt helped sales considerably, as it went from printing to printing. The sentimental image of the child likely helped the book's popularity, too (Warner, 1940), even while Rousseau himself was dispatching his own unwanted children to foundling hospitals. But the rhetorical force of *Émile* carried Rousseau's ideas across Europe. In more recent times, John Dewey and Jean Piaget have been profoundly influenced by Rousseau, and the degree to which their ideas have affected practice is one index of his continuing influence.

Careful observation and study of students, recognition of the distinctive forms of learning and sense-making that characterize different ages, construction of methods of teaching that engage students' distinctive forms of learning, emphasis on individual differences among learners, the encouragement of active rather than passive learning, the insistence that a student's own discovery is vastly more effective than the tutor's "words, words, words," are all features of Rousseau's educational scheme. While it would be false to claim him as the originator of all these ideas, he did bring them together into a powerful and coherent conception of education.

These are ideas that have become a part of the "common sense," taken-for-granted folklore of so many educators today. It would now be considered strange not to recognize the importance of students' varying learning styles, the value of methods of teaching that encourage students' active inquiry, and the significant differences among students at different ages.

The modern voices that encourage schools to focus on fulfilling the individual potential of each student, that emphasize that students should "learn how to learn" as a higher priority than amassing academic knowledge, that support programs in "critical thinking," that evaluate educational success not in terms of what knowledge students have acquired so much as in terms of what they can do with what they know, reflect this third educational idea. Here, the focus of education is the experience of the child. The construction of a common core curriculum for all children therefore is not simply undesirable but actually impossible. Each child's experience, even of the same curriculum content, is necessarily different. We should recognize this, and

16

let the unique experience and needs of each child be the determiner of the curriculum, even to the radical point of making the curriculum a response to the questions students raise (Postman and Weingartner, 1969). The educator's attention should be focused on the individual development of each child and on the provision of the experiences that can optimally further this development.

The commonest expression of this idea today combines the variously interpreted progressivism of John Dewey (Kleibard, 1986) with Piaget's developmentalism and the psychologizing of the study of children—the modern form of discovering their "nature" that Rousseau recommended. In the classroom, and outside it, "discovery learning" is valued, manipulables and museums are recommended for students' exploration, discussion is encouraged, project work by individuals or groups is provided for. Careful attention is given to the results of empirical studies of children's learning, development, and motivation, and teaching and curricula are adjusted to conform with such "research findings." Teachers are not authorities so much as facilitators, providers of the best resources, shapers of the environment in which students will learn.

INCOMPATIBILITIES

Are these three ideas really incompatible? Can we not find a way of addressing these somewhat distinct aims for education without having them undermine one another? Why can we not socialize students to prevailing norms and values, ensure that they accumulate the kind of knowledge that will give a truer view of the world, and help them to fulfill their potential at each stage of development? A rigorous academic program surely does not conflict with society's needs, and facts about learning, development, and motivation surely can help us better implement both the academic program and socialization. At least, Plato's concern with the *what* of education does not seem to be at war with Rousseau's concern with the *how*. Don't they properly complement one another?

Looked at in sufficiently general and vague a manner, it may indeed seem that these distinctive ideas are not as incompatible as I have been suggesting. The everyday business of schooling in Western societies has been going ahead on the assumption that evident problems are caused by improper management, poor teaching, genetic constraints on students' abilities to learn, or flawed curriculum organization, not to some profound theoretical incompatibility. But I think the incompatibility is there, and it is at the 17 root of our practical problems. Let us consider each idea in turn with the others.

Plato and Socializing

The homogenizing aim of socialization, which is to reproduce in each student a particular set of beliefs, conventions, commitments, norms of behavior, and values, is necessarily at odds with a process that aims to show their hollowness and inadequacy. They do, after all, form the glue that holds society's foundations in place. If Socrates was Plato's ideal of the educated person, it is evident why the democratic citizens of Athens condemned him to death: the radical skepticism that his kind of education engendered threatened the foundations of society. He was condemned for corrupting the youth. What he was corrupting, or corroding, was their acceptance of the tenets of society. His fellow citizens saw his behavior as a kind of treason.

No one now believes that Plato's ideal aim of direct knowledge of the real, the true, the good, and the beautiful is attainable. What is attainable, though, is the skeptical, philosophical, informed mind that energetically inquires into the nature and meaning of things, that is unsatisfied by conventional answers, that repudiates belief in whatever cannot be adequately supported by good arguments or evidence, and that embodies the good-humored corrosive of Socratic irony. This kind of consciousness has not often been greatly valued by those who govern societies because it is a disruptive force. Everyday social life, particularly in complex modern economic systems, proceeds more smoothly and blandly without the irritant created by following Plato's educational prescription too closely. If people continually ask themselves "Is this really the best way to live?," they simply can't get on with day-to-day business in a single-minded, efficient manner.

Of course, we want the promised benefits of both educational ideas. We want the social harmony and the psychological stability that successful socialization encourages, but we also want the cultivation of the mind, the skepticism, and the dedication to rationality that Plato's program calls for. Designing schools to achieve either one is difficult. But our schools today are supposed to do both.

Rousseau and Plato

If we see Plato as dealing with the *what* of education and Rousseau with the *how*, then must the two ideas be considered incompatible? This common resolution of apparent conflicts would be fine were it not the case that it falsely represents both ideas. The above compromise, leaving Plato's descendants with the content and aims of education and Rousseau's with the methods, appeals to many as a neat division of labor. The educational philosophers can deal with content and aims, drawing on the knowledge generated by the educational psychologists about learning and development. It seems obvious that facts about students' development can blend with philosophers' research into the nature and structure of knowledge to yield a more easily understood math or history curriculum. It seems obvious that such collaboration should be common; the fact that we see so little of it suggests there is something preventing it from taking place.

One problem for the neat compromise is that, in the Rousseauian and Deweyan view, the means and ends of education are tied together. The means used in Rousseauian and Deweyan instruction are *parts* of their educational ends. They favor discovery procedures, for example, not because they are more efficient means to some distinct educational ends, but because they are a component of their educational ends. For example, in Rousseau's terms discovery procedures disclose nature and in so doing stimulate the development of a pure, uninfected reason. Or, as Dewey adapted the idea, discovery procedures mirror the scientific method whose acquisition by students is a crucial component of their education. We have incorporated this idea of intertwined means and ends into our currently dominant conception of education. Put crudely, we recognize the inappropriateness of beating children who have failed to memorize a text on compassion; we feel a bit uncomfortable about compelling attendance at institutions that try to teach the values of liberty and democracy; and it is increasingly clear that choice of teaching method is not a simple strategic matter disconnected from our educational ends. In our educational means are our ends; in our educational ends are our means.

Another problem follows from Plato and his descendants' having their own conception of educational development. Students progress, in Plato's scheme, from the stages of *eikasia,* to *pistis,* to *dianoia,* to *noesis.* But these stages are interestingly different from Rousseau's and Piaget's. Plato's stages represent greater clarity in understanding. Education, in Plato's view and in that of modern proponents of the academic idea, is marked by students' ability to master increasingly sophisticated knowledge, regardless of their supposed psychological development. For Rousseau and Piaget, the stages of psychological development are precisely what mark education and determine what kind of knowledge the student needs; as the development of the body proceeds almost regardless of the particular food it eats, so the mind will develop almost regardless of the particular knowledge it learns. For the Platonists, the only development of educational interest is the particular knowledge learned; the mind is not much else.

19

So Rousseau and his modern followers are not simply making methodological or procedural recommendations that might allow us to do the Platonic academic job more efficiently. They are actually recommending a different job. Rousseau's idea is not one that yields an easy accommodation with Plato's. These ideas conflict—most profoundly in identifying the cause and dynamic of the educational process. In the Platonic idea, learning particular forms of knowledge carries the educational process forward; knowledge drives development. In the Rousseauian idea, education results from an internal, developmental process unfolding within a supportive environment; development drives knowledge, determining what knowledge is learnable, meaningful, and relevant. For Plato education is a time-related, epistemological process; for Rousseau it is an age-related, psychological process.

We could design schools to implement either of these conceptions of education, but instead we require our schools to implement both. Our practical difficulties arise from accepting that both the Platonic and the Rousseauian ideas are *necessary* for education, but the more we try to implement one, the more we undermine the other.

The conflict between these two ideas has been the basis of the continuing struggles between "traditionalists" and "progressivists" during this century. One sees them at odds in almost every media account of educational issues—the Platonic forces argue for "basics" and a solid academic curriculum, and the Rousseauians argue for "relevance" and space for students' exploration and discovery. A key battleground now is the elementary social studies curriculum in North America. The progressivists are defending the "relevant" focus on families, neighborhoods, communities, and interactions among communities, and the traditionalists are pressuring for a reintroduction of history and geography as mainstays of the curriculum. The progressivist forces argue that history and geography require abstract concepts and are not "developmentally appropriate" for young children; the traditionalists respond that any content can be made comprehensible if presented sensibly.

Socializing and Rousseau

When socialization is the primary aim of education, we derive our priorities from society's norms and values. In the Rousseauian view, however, we should keep the child from contact with society's norms and values as long as possible because they are "one mass of folly and contradiction" (Rousseau, 1911, p. 46). If we want to let the nature of the child develop as fully as possible, we will constantly defend her or him against the shaping pressures of society. An aspect of this conflict is apparent today in many educators'

20

attitudes to the general influence of television on children. TV is a powerful instrument in shaping a set of prominent social norms and values, but educators resist much of this shaping in favor of activities that seem to them less likely to distort proper or "natural" development. "Natural" is not, of course, the term much used today, but it lurks around the various ways the Rousseauian position is restated, as in a number of books that appeal to a conception of a more natural kind of childhood that is being distorted or suppressed by current forms of socialization (e.g., Elkind, 1981; Postman, 1982). Some of the 1960s radicals were even plainer—Paul Goodman put it this way: "The purpose of elementary pedagogy, through age twelve, should be to delay socialization, to protect children's free growth. . . . We must drastically cut back formal schooling because the present extended tutelage is against nature and arrests growth" (1970, p. 86).

No one, of course, is simply on the side of Rousseau against socialization, or vice versa. We all recognize that any developmental process has to be shaped by a particular society. Our problem originates with the attraction of Rousseau's ideas about a kind of development that honors something within each individual, something uninfected by the compromises, corruptions, and constrictions that social life so commonly brings with it. We do not have to share Rousseau's own disgust with society (which returned him high regard and money) to recognize the attraction of his ideas.

There doesn't seem room for much compromise here. We can't sensibly aim to shape a child's development half from nature and half from society. To try to do so creates the same problems as half punishing and half rehabilitating a prisoner. Such treatments interfere with each other; by trying to compromise, we ensure only that neither is effective.

There are, of course, a number of ways of seeing this conflict that do not lead to the conclusion of incompatibility I am arguing. We can "solve" the problem by observing that our nature is indeterminately plastic in our early years and socialization is a condition of our nature being realized. We are, after all, social animals; there is no natural form that we will develop toward if we are kept apart from society. We can "solve" this conflict also by seeing it not as one between nature and society but, much more simply, as the kind of disagreement one must expect in a pluralistic society. But the incompatibility I am concerned with arises only within the conception of education, and seems to me unavoidable so long as people conceive of children as going through some regular, spontaneous process of intellectual development that can be optimized if we shape their learning environment to suit it. One cannot derive one's educational principles both from some conception of an ideal developmental process and from some current norms and values of adult society; they are bound to be incompatible unless one lives in a perfect   21 society. They are incompatible because socializing has a distinct end in view and is a shaping, homogenizing, narrowing process toward that end, whereas supporting the fullest development of student potential involves releasing students to explore and discover their uniqueness; this is an individualizing process that encourages distinctiveness even to the point of eccentricity, if necessary, and is expansive without predetermined ends.

Tidying Up

Some readers might consider "tidying up" a particularly unsuitable subheading on the grounds that the scheme presented so far is much too tidy: three neat ideas and three crisp incompatibilities. What it needs is roughing up; enormously complex processes cannot adequately be represented by such a simple scheme. Also it has long been recognized that "tensions" exist among competing values in education—between, say, the need to socialize and the academic curriculum. Clearly, when there is a conflict for curriculum time between consumer education or a new family life curriculum and drama or Latin, for example, no single criterion of educational value can be invoked to help us make a decision. These are "value issues," necessary tensions that follow from education's being one of those "essentially contested concepts"; ultimately such issues are reflections of large-scale political conflicts. So perhaps this talk of profound theoretical incompatibilities is simply an old truism dressed up in fancy language and made to look excessively dramatic?

In "tidying up" I mean to address objections like these, even if very briefly, and to summarize my point about the three ideas before I go on to introduce the fourth. Also, just before quitting the old ideas for the new, I will point out that each of the old ideas carries problems of its own for education, even beyond incompatibility.

Now nobody holds exclusively to any one of these ideas. Educational discourse during this century has been largely made up of arguments about which idea should be valued more highly. The persisting "traditionalist" vs. "progressivist," "subject centered" vs. "child centered" disputes may be reinterpreted in these terms as representing preferences for Plato's idea over Rousseau's or vice versa. Conflicts between those promoting vocationally oriented studies and those promoting more purely academic subjects may be seen as preferences for socializing over Plato's idea, or vice versa. Radicals, meanwhile, are identified by their simple solution of discarding two of the ideas. This does solve the theoretical problem, and does usually mean that they can speak with a clearer and more urgent voice, and so accumulate disciples, but at a harsh practical cost.

22

At the "chalk face" level of classrooms in the local school, the Plato-influenced teachers, who want to put in place more rigorous exams and to "stream" students so that learning disciplined knowledge can be maximized, come frequently into conflict with the Rousseau-influenced teachers, who want to remove exams and even grading and focus on opening up the range of exploratory opportunities for students. The former argue for a more structured curriculum, logically sequenced and including the canonical knowledge of Western "high" culture; the latter argue for activities that encourage students to explore the world around them and, in as far as they are willing to prespecify curriculum content, they propose knowledge relevant to students' present and likely future experience. The former are likely to prefer desks in neat rows and orderly lessons while the latter are likely to prefer varied work-centers, circled desks or no desks, and flexible interdisciplinary lessons.

Clearly few teachers adhere to one position to the exclusion of others; most teachers try to balance all of them in practice. So, for example, even Rousseau-inclined teachers tend to acknowledge the importance of the canonical content of the Plato-influenced curriculum; their compromise between incompatibles means that they feel it is important to "expose" students to the "high culture" curriculum content but they feel no imperative to persist with it for students who do not take to it. That is, each idea is allowed scope enough to undercut the other.

Most educational administrators feel pressure from groups who prefer one or another of the ideas; thus they seek to find a balance among them. This is the common-sense response to recognizing these competing "values" and it is the response that has given us the schools we have. They struggle to ensure a reasonably adequate socialization of students, provide a reasonable academic program, and enable as many students as seem suited to it to progress as far as possible, and attend to the different needs and potential of each student, allowing as much flexibility and choice among programs as resources allow.

Apologists for the general performance of schools in the West commonly point to the array of social ills that afflict the schools, arguing, reasonably, that given the circumstances schools are doing a heroic job. But such voices tend to be drowned by critics who argue that schools would do a much better job if only they would elevate one of the old ideas in importance over the others—put greater emphasis on developing the basic values and skills that will lead to good citizenship and economic productivity, or increase the time and conditions that will put greater pressure on students to master disciplined knowledge, or design curricula and teaching practices that are more relevant to students' experience. From a purely pragmatic 23 point of view, it seems extraordinarily unlikely that any of these emphases, or any combination, or any finer balance among them, will do the trick for us. The traditional social efficiency, liberal academic, and progressivist proposals have been tried and tried again; continuing to wobble from one to another will only exacerbate the confusion about schools' roles and perpetuate the blaming and the now stale and futile arguments about how to make things better. At best, schooling is a set of flaccid compromises among these three great and powerful ideas.

Great and powerful they undoubtedly are, but each carries baggage that creates problems for education even before we try sticking them together into an unworkable system. I want to dispense with some of the baggage these ideas come with and to *reconceive* education in a way that preserves adequate socialization, academic cultivation, and individual development disconnected from the educational ideas we have inherited. We have to hang onto the babies while tossing out their dirty old bathwater.

That there is bathwater to be thrown out seems to be generally acknowledged. Socialization to generally agreed norms and values that we have inherited is no longer straightforwardly viable in modern multicultural societies undergoing rapid technology-driven changes. The Platonic program comes with ideas about reaching a transcendent truth or privileged knowledge that is no longer credible. The conception of individual development we have inherited is built on a belief in some culture-neutral process that is no longer sustainable.

Yet a problem for any paradigm-shifting ambition to displace currently dominant ideas is that the new idea must initially be looked at through the perspectives it is trying to displace. What I must persuade you to do, if only provisionally, is to let go of the old ideas and consider what sense of education is generated by taking "kinds of understanding" as the primary category for thinking about education. In viewing education through this lens, children may be seen as picking up intellectual tools from society in an effort to make sense of the world. In the process, children become, willy-nilly, socialized. The criterion at work here, however, is not "What does the child need to learn in order to share the norms, values, and conventions of adult society?" but rather "What does the child need to learn to develop most fully each kind of understanding?" The former question, relatively straightforward for oral societies long ago and even for more homogeneous, class-based societies up to the mid-twentieth century, is problematic for modern multicultural societies undergoing rapid and seemingly accelerating change. What are the norms and conventions of adult life today? What are the values? How does the answer differ if asked of those whose prime educational criterion is the accumulation of disciplined knowledge? Tackling the latter question, however, is relatively straightforward and will involve the child developing the flexibility and "polysemousness" appropriate for modern social life. That is, while the old idea of socialization, and the criteria it brings with it, are dispensed with, adopting the new idea does not mean that socialization will not occur. If anything, its proper relevance to education will be exposed.

Now take the old academic disciplines idea. It has involved the belief that the accumulation of particular forms of knowledge, in sufficient breadth and depth, shapes the mind in desirable ways. Making "knowledge" the central building block of education creates the problem of determining what knowledge, and how much breadth and depth of that knowledge, is required to become adequately educated. It also leads to questions such as Herbert Spencer's "What knowledge is of most worth?," which has remained unanswered, and unanswerable in general terms, for more than a century. (The sense of the educated person being distinguished primarily by what the person knows has been criticized by progressivists as sterile and has been vulnerable to A. N. Whitehead's withering observation that the person who has accumulated lots of the appropriate kinds of knowledge may still be among the greatest bores on God's earth.) By displacing "knowledge" with the category of "kind of understanding," we will not be throwing knowledge overboard. The development of the various kinds of understanding requires particular kinds of knowledge. This new category also provides criteria for determining depth and breadth of knowledge; it enables us to answer Spencer's question—the knowledge that is of most worth will vary during the course of the individual's education and may be determined by the kind of understanding most actively being stimulated and developed. So academic disciplines and their knowledge are not being dispensed with; rather, the traditionalist curriculum—made up of attempts to answer what is the most privileged knowledge for best forming the rational mind and criteria for education derived from some image of an ideal epistemological condition or an ideally educated person—will disappear. The new category and its criterion will justify a richer curriculum that will require more knowledge and more varied forms of knowledge.

Yes, I know: promises, promises. I want only to indicate that pushing aside these old ideas will not mean that the insights they have brought to the process of education will be dumped. Some sense of socialization will persist in the process of developing kinds of understanding, but it is not a sense of socializing that brings along with it criteria that conflict with those that come from academic disciplines. Similarly, developing kinds of understanding will obviously involve the individual moving through layers or stages of psychological development. But the sense of development involved in this new   25 conception of education will yield categories quite different from those that have been pushed on education by proponents of theories like Piaget's, for example. And the development implicit in moving from one kind of understanding to another will not come into conflict with what remains of socialization or academic disciplines.

Again, of course this is too schematic to capture the huge complexity of educational ideas and practices. But it isn't obviously wrong or meaningless as a result. I think educational thinking *is* dominated by the three major ideas I have identified, and that they *are* incompatible in the ways I have indicated, and that these incompatibilities *are* at the root of many of the practical difficulties of schooling. The modern school has developed as a compromise among these three ideas, a compromise that shifts a little in one direction or another in response to social movements, or in response to particularly vivid and powerful articulations of the value of one or another of these ideas: socialization was somewhat more prominent in the 1950s in much of the Western world, Rousseau in the 1960s and early 1970s, and Plato made a pale comeback in some areas in the 1980s. The recognition of "tensions" and "value issues" in education is indeed a truism, but exposing their source isn't. And exposing their source is an important step to overcoming them. That is the task for the rest of the book.

So, while hardly providing all one needs to know about education, this sketch has had some heuristic value in grasping current disputes about education. Its value is to indicate why the proposals one sees in public media and in government reports for "solving the crisis in our schools" are unlikely to achieve that desirable end. They are captive to the ideas that are the problem. They propose more socializing and less Plato and Rousseau, or more Plato and less socializing and Rousseau, or more Rousseau and less socializing and Plato; the only difference decade by decade is the preferred terms, metaphors, and jargon. Giving a reason to believe that no shuffling of these ideas is likely to do us much good provides my route to introducing the new idea.

A New Idea

I mentioned in the introduction that the new conception of education to be elaborated below draws on nineteenth-century recapitulation theories and on Vygotsky, who died in 1936, so its main components are not exactly gleaming fresh from the mint. But blowing the dust off recapitulation theories and connecting them with an insight of Vygotsky's can, I think, lead to a new educational idea. The first trick, which earlier theories failed to pull off, is to identify the nature of the connection between cultural development in the past and educational development in the present. How can one locate a common element in the two processes and show a causal relationship between them? Exactly what is recapitulated in education? The second trick is to show that the theoretical solution implies practical curricula and teaching methods clearly appropriate to modern social conditions and requirements. I will try to perform the first trick in this section, and elaborate it, while performing the second trick, in the rest of the book.

In the latter part of the nineteenth century, after publication of Darwin's *The Origin of Species* (1859), recapitulation theories were formed to apply evolutionary ideas to processes other than those Darwin developed his theory to explain. Herbert Spencer (1820–1903) was one of the most energetic promoters of evolutionary ideas to explain pretty well everything in sight. He compactly expressed the basis for a cultural recapitulation theory of education in the following claim:

If there be an order in which the human race has mastered its various kinds of knowledge, there will arise in every child an aptitude to acquire these kinds of knowledge in the same order. . . . Education should be a repetition of civilization in little. (1861, p. 76)

At a sufficiently general level, all educational theories involve people recapitulating, repeating for themselves, the discoveries and inventions that have accumulated through the history of their culture. The five-year-old learning to write recapitulates an invention of a few thousand years ago. The student learning history recapitulates a kind of thinking, a way of making sense of experience, whose invention by the ancient Greeks we can trace in some detail. But recapitulation theories go further than this, claiming some precise causal connection between past cultural development and present educational development. Such theories propose ways in which the particular character of cultural development should shape the process of education.

The appeal of recapitulation to educators in the late nineteenth and early twentieth century lay in the promise that cultural history could guide the design of much more effective educational programs. G. Stanley Hall enthusiastically claimed that recapitulation, "when explored and utilized to its full extent will reveal pedagogic possibilities now undreamed of" (1904, 2:222). What it seemed to offer was a way of ordering the curriculum that corresponded with the way knowledge logically developed and/or with nature's own scheme of human development, both of which were to be exposed by the study of cultural development and either of which would ensure easier learning and secure understanding.

Two general kinds of recapitulation theories of education developed, which can be simply called logical and psychological. The first followed   27 from the observation that knowledge has developed gradually in cultural history and the "order in which the human race has mastered its various kinds of knowledge," to repeat Spencer's phrase, exposes a logic that in turn can be used in designing the curriculum. One only has to repeat that order in the curriculum and one has laid out a logical path that the mind of the developing child can follow with maximum ease and a guarantee of finishing up at the peak of human understanding.

The second, psychologically based recapitulation theories, tended to draw more directly from evolutionary theory (Gould, 1977). The recapitulation in these theories was assumed to be from the primitive psychological condition of savages to that of sophisticated Victorian adults. John Dewey supported such theories, at least to the degree that they broke the hold of the prevailing conventional schemes and provided "the first systematic attempts to base a course of study upon the actual unfolding of the psychology of child nature" (1911, p. 241). A more modern attempt to identify a common psychological basis to cultural and individual development is made by Hall-pike (1979), using Piaget's theory.

Commonly, aspects of logical and psychological theories were combined, with the usual problems. In Germany in particular, and in the United States, which was strongly influenced by German ideas, "culture epoch" curricula were developed with high hopes. These attempted to reflect in the curriculum the major epochs of cultural history, ensuring that children pass through them in logical sequence and at a pace suited to their psychological development. Dewey, though later dismissive of recapitulationism, expressed the kinds of observations that had an intuitive appeal for some people: "There is a sort of natural recurrence of the child mind to the typical activities of primitive people; witness the hut which the boy likes to build in the yard, playing hunt, with bows, arrows, spears and so on" (quoted in Gould, 1977, p. 154). But the high hopes faded quickly. The curricula seemed plausible when dealing with history and literature, beginning with the study of primitive people and folk tales and myth stories, but no amount of ingenuity (see, for example, Ziller's ideas in Seeley, 1906) could make recapitulation seem sensible when dealing with mathematics or science. If the logical principle was stumbling over how to avoid confusing children with a Ptolemaic view of the cosmos, the psychological principle was coming to grief as recapitulation ideas in biology, on which it had been based, were being abandoned (Gould, 1977).

One reason recapitulation theories failed and disappeared from the active educational scene was their inability to explain, to use Spencer's terms, how and why there should arise in modern children an aptitude to acquire knowledge in the order it was invented and discovered in cultural history.

Why not simply and sensibly begin, as the progressivists argued, with the immediate world around the child?

So, more significant in causing the disappearance of cultural recapitulation theories was the urgent task of equipping children entering the new mass schools with the basic knowledge, skills, and dispositions required by the rapidly developing industrial world. This was particularly so in the United States, where teachers also became the front-line troops in familiarizing huge numbers of immigrant children with contemporary American society. Educational schemes that were past-oriented and reached the present day only at the end of schooling could hardly be accommodated to meet such urgent social needs. Dewey finally dismissed the idea of recapitulation because its likely effect is "to make the . . . present a more or less futile imitation of the past" (1916, p. 75); as the purpose of progressive education is to "emancipate the young from the need of dwelling in an outgrown past" (p. 73), recapitulation has nothing to offer education. And that remains the most common, almost automatic, response of those educationalists today who have heard of recapitulation.

Vygotsky's idea can be stated very simply for present purposes. He argued that we make sense of the world by use of mediating intellectual tools that in turn profoundly influence the kind of sense we make. Our intellectual development, then, cannot adequately be understood in terms of the knowledge we accumulate or in terms of psychological stages like Piaget's but requires an understanding of the role played by the intellectual tools available in the society into which a person grows.

Intellectual tools, like oral language, that surround the child are gradually internalized as the child grows; intellectual tools, or sign systems, begin, to use Vygotsky's terms, as interpsychic processes and become intrapsychic within the child. That is, in Vygotsky's view, higher psychological processes —such as the dialogic question-and-answer structure—begin in interactions with others, as "external" social functions that were themselves invented perhaps long ago in cultural history, and then become internalized and transformed into psychological functions: "It is through this interiorization of historically determined and culturally organized ways of operating on information that the social nature of people comes to be their psychological nature as well" (Luria, 1979, p. 45). The process of intellectual development, then, is to be recognized in the individual's degree of mastery of tools and of sign systems such as language (Vygotsky, 1978). The development of intellectual tools leads to qualitatively different ways of making sense: *The system of signs restructures the whole psychological process*" (p. 35; emphasis in original). So the set of sign systems one internalizes from interactions with particular cultural groups, particular communities, will significantly inform the kind of understanding of the world that one can construct. "Vygotsky defined development in terms of the emergence or transformation of forms of mediation" (Wertsch, 1985, p. 15). So the mind is not an isolable thing like the brain inside its skull; it extends into and is constituted of its socio-cultural surroundings, and its kinds of understanding are products of the intellectual tools forged and used in those surroundings.

How does this help solve our theoretical problem about recapitulation? Well, we can identify what is recapitulated not in terms of knowledge or psychological processes but in terms of mediating intellectual tools and the kinds of understanding they generate. We can see, too, that Spencer posed the question wrongly; it is not that something that occurred in cultural history causes an aptitude in every child to acquire knowledge in the same order, but rather that by acquiring specific intellectual tools, the modern individual generates similar kinds of understanding as existed for people using those tools in the past. That is, the mistake of past recapitulation theorists was to look for some x in cultural history that causes some y in education today; rather we should look for some a—the mediating intellectual tools—that causes both x and y. So we can consider cultural and educational development as connected by the tools that generate common kinds of understanding in both processes.

Vygotsky focused largely on oral language in young children to work out his basic theories of culturally mediated action and development. I want to consider degrees of culturally accumulated complexity in language, beginning with oral language, then moving to literacy, then to the development of systematic, abstract, theoretic, linguistic forms, and finally to habitual highly reflexive uses of language. Each of these degrees of sophistication in language development restructures the kind of sense their users make of the world. I will investigate the implications of each of these degrees of linguistic development for kinds of understanding. Because the a of intellectual tools causes kinds of understanding common to the x of cultural history and the y of education today, I will consider both cultural and educational development together in the following four chapters.

It might reasonably be objected that this attempted marriage of Vygotsky and recapitulationism is improper as Vygotsky rejected recapitulation on the ground that ontogenesis involves the natural maturation of the brain, something that plays no part in the course of cultural history (Wertsch, 1991, p. 23). I have four responses. First, it is far from clear how the natural maturation of the brain affects individual's understanding compared with the acquisition of mediating tools, and one might reasonably argue that the influence of the tools is sufficient to explain the evident changes in kinds of understanding without resort to distinct influences from the maturation process. Second, Vygotsky and Luria distinguished between bifur-cated lines of development in the child, calling one "natural-psychological" and the other "cultural-psychological" and identifying in the latter the major reformulations of mental functioning (cf. Wertsh, 1985, p. 23), a move com-patible with the scheme to be outlined here. Third, ontogenesis, particularly during the early years, involves recapitulating patterns of maturation laid down in the process of evolutionary development, and while evolutionary influences diminish as the individual grows older, it is improper to suggest a sharp line at which the brain's physiological maturation escapes influence by such past cultural developments as language. Fourth, the conceptions of re-capitulation Vygotsky had in mind were those nineteenth-century kinds dis-missed above to which his objection would be destructive in a way that it isn't to what follows.

Now I could try to address in the abstract the many potential objections to this proposed project that will no doubt be thronging the minds of critical readers, but the objections and my responses might be made more pointed and concrete if I show first how one can characterize kinds of understanding as implications of intellectual tools. So let me put off the inquisition until chapter 6.

Conclusion

Our schools are not, in general, highly regarded today. The sense of their ineffectiveness is not, I have suggested, any specific group's fault. Yet when we have a general social unease, we tend to look for someone to blame. Much of the popular literature on education in the 1960s blamed the Platonists and an academic curriculum that was disconnected from students' experi-ence and irrelevant to their lives. The neoconservative critics of the 1980s blamed the Rousseauians, particularly John Dewey. The average schooling experience of students has not shown evident signs of improvement as a re-sult of these or earlier criticisms and the prescriptions that have followed from them.

Blaming Rousseau and Dewey for the condition of our schools, as do Bloom (1987) and Hirsch (1987), is akin to blaming merchants or sheep farmers for rising prices. Rousseau and Dewey have enriched our conception of education in important ways. We will not make educational progress by trying to cut away their contribution. The cause of our difficulties—our equivalent to sixteenth-century bullion imports—is, I have been arguing, the fact that the components of our conception of education are incompat-

31

ible with one another. The problem is not with the school necessarily but with the way we conceive what the school is supposed to do.

To practical people, such refined theoretical issues may seem remote from the activities of the school down the road. But I think there is something in John Maynard Keynes's famous, or infamous, conclusion to his *General Theory of Employment, Interest and Money* (1936) (I will change the words slightly to fit an educational rather than an economic context):

[T]he ideas of educational theorists, both when they are right and when they are wrong, are more powerful than is commonly understood. Indeed education is ruled by little else. Practical people, who believe themselves to be quite exempt from any intellectual influences, are usually the slaves of some defunct educational theorist. Mad people in authority, who hear voices in the air, are distilling their frenzy from some academic scribbler of a few years back. I am sure that the power of educational stakeholders is vastly exaggerated compared with the gradual encroachment of ideas. Not, indeed, immediately, but after a certain interval; for in the field of education there are not many who are influenced by new theories after they are twenty-five or thirty years of age, so the ideas which administrators and politicians and even teachers apply to current schooling are not likely to be the newest. But, soon or late, it is ideas, not "stakeholders," which are dangerous for good or ill.

What I will do in chapters 2 through 6 is offer one way of reconceiving education; in chapters 7 and 8 I will explore its implications in rather broad terms, but in sufficient detail, I hope, to show that the indispensable parts of our current conception of education are preserved. This reconceptualizing of education will have fairly radical implications for the curriculum and for teaching, but not so radical, I suspect, that they will not appear directly practical. If I do the job reasonably well, I will not seem to be sketching out some strange and new landscape, but drawing a picture that will seem recognizable and even familiar.

c h a p t e r

2

Mythic Understanding

INTRODUCTION

In a relatively brief period of time during the mid-Pleistocene era, evolutionary changes in the brain and in the larynx, pharynx, and jaw of our ancestors led to the development of language. An apparently universal consequence of elaborated language development was myth. As there have been no known mute human groups—having the potential for language but not realizing it—so there have been no preliterate groups without myth. Why should these odd stories be cultural universals?

While there is still "no monotony to complain of as regards the variety of opinions or the acrimony of the polemics" (Malinowski, 1954, p. 96) about the nature of mythic thinking, I want nevertheless to identify a set of its distinctive characteristics and to show that these are inevitable consequences of language development. I will try to show that they thus occur whenever people develop language, whether in oral societies throughout the world and throughout history or by children throughout the world as they grow into language-using environments.

Certainly the connection between language use in oral societies and mythic thinking has long been obvious, if puzzling. Herder (1744–1803), the proto-Romantic admirer of the vigor and purity of folk culture, proto-   33 evolutionary theorist, and great influence on Goethe, suggested that words must at first have appeared magical and their potency sacred; that is why, he suggested, in so many myths, gods or sacred ancestors created the world by naming the things in it, one by one, and why things named were thereby taken to have a numinous quality. The sense of the sacred and supernatural, too, is a cultural universal (cf. Brown, 1991). So it has been argued that the first languages must have been what the British rationalist Edward B. Tylor (1832–1917) called "a sounding pantheon," and their wild metaphoric connections and intellectually confused elaboration led to stories about potent gods born out of the earliest words. Max Müller (1823–1900) offered an alternative explanation of why "Mythology . . . is the power exercised by language on thought" (1873, p. 355). Müller considered mythology to be an inevitable "disease of language" resulting from languages' paronymia—their frequent cognate words, homonyms, similar sounding words borrowed from other languages, different words from the same root, and so on. He argued that the "infirm minds" of "primitive" people attempted to describe straightforward natural phenomena but became entangled in paronymial slippage, producing as a result those peculiar, irrational stories we call myths. Careful philological study, he tried to demonstrate, could untangle the confusions of these stories and so dispel "the dark shadow language throws upon thought" (353). For example, Müller interprets the Greek myth about Apollo's pursuit of Daphne, who escapes by turning into a laurel tree, as a confusion begun long ago in Sanskrit. Primitive people could not give simple rational accounts of the world, according to Müller; they expressed themselves instead in poetic metaphors. Thus, rather than observe that "the sun rises after the dawn each day" they would say, "Apollo pursues Daphne across the sky." Now "Daphne," Müller shows, derives from a Sanskrit word, a homonym whose other meaning is—you guessed it—"laurel tree." Long after, and far away, the Sanskrit homonym is lost and forgotten, but mythical elaboration, this disease of language, generates the story of Apollo and Daphne. All that Greek, Renaissance, and nineteenth-century European painting and sculpture of the two of them—she sprouting branches and leaves as he reaches out to touch her—a consequence of a simple paronymial slippage in Sanskrit!

These nineteenth-century attempts to connect language and myth were often ingenious. But none of the explanations accounted for all the features of myths, and their attempts to characterize the simple origins and evolution of language, using contemporary "primitive" languages for guidance, involved too much speculation and too little data. More recently it has become clear that there is no such thing as a "primitive" language; all languages give

34

evidence of equal complexity. This recognition has led to a new respect for the intellectual capacity of our earlier language-using ancestors and the sophistication of mythic thinking.

With the development of language, the mind "expanded its reach beyond the episodic perception of events, beyond the mimetic reconstruction of episodes, to a comprehensive modeling of the entire human universe. Causal explanation, prediction, control—myth constitutes an attempt at all three, and every aspect of life is permeated by myth. . . . [M]yth is the prototypal, fundamental, integrative mind-tool" (Donald, 1991, pp. 214–15). I want to consider some of the bits and pieces of this general mind-tool in this chapter; and because of myth's prototypal, fundamental, and integrative cognitive role I call this general kind of understanding Mythic.

Vygotsky presents an image of individual development in which "the beginnings of practical intelligence in the child . . . are independent of speech" (1978, p. 21). Donald describes prelinguistic "mimetic" thinking as "basically a talent for using the whole body as a communication device, for translating event perceptions into action. . . . It is the most basic human thought skill, and remains fundamentally independent of our truly linguistic modes of representation" (1993, p. 740). So while my focus in this chapter will be on the early forms of language use, I recognize that these are built on and develop alongside modes of sense-making that are independent of language.

Reference to a distinctive prelinguistic kind of understanding will appear odd to some readers, both to those who think of the human mind as something that comes into being only with the development of language, and to those who think of the human mind as "languaged" from the beginning. The latter, in particular, are growing in numbers rapidly, as Chomskian ideas are seen as increasingly compelling. They are impressed by accumulating evidence that even before birth babies attend to the rhythms of language and shortly after birth show a preference for the sounds of their mother tongue (Eimas et al., 1971; Mehler et al., 1988); the human baby is clearly a languaged animal *avant la lettre,* as it were. Even so, as I argue in chapter 5, until language is sufficiently deployed to structure our cognition we have a distinctively human but prelinguistic understanding of the world, and this Somatic understanding remains fundamental to our grasp on the world throughout our lives.

Language development in human beings is genetically determined, even if more fragilely so than such Somatic developments as learning to walk or attending to rhythms. So long as infants are fed and cared for physically they will develop those Somatic abilities, but language development requires 35 also the deliberate influence on the young child of a language-using society. That is, some features of Mythic understanding are evolutionarily coded into our genes but their adequate development requires deliberate adult intervention. There are endless jokes about how lucky it is that children do not need to be taught to walk as they need to be taught to read, or we would have continents full of incompetent staggerers. But we are robustly programmed to walk and robustly programmed to talk in an appropriately supportive environment. As we grow, however, we receive less precise genetic help and have to rely increasingly on a genetically encoded general learning capacity, which is not well differentiated for learning to read or to do mathematics. The educational trick is to make those kinds of learning easier and more effective by making them conform as well as possible to the weakening genetic dispositions still operative as we grow into childhood. That such genetic dispositions are operative may be inferred from the energetic development of language up to the age of seven; because development proceeds at a rate of word accumulation and sophistication of grammatical usage beyond what we achieve through teaching at any other period of life, it seems fair to assume some particular genetic influence is still active. So, the period of Mythic understanding is one during which weakening genetic influences merge with the increasing deployment of our undifferentiated learning capacity; learning consequently ceases to be effortless and begins to require deliberate work.

My purpose in this chapter, then, is to describe some distinctive characteristics of Mythic understanding and show how they can help make early education today more easy and effective. They will also help to redefine what constitutes early education.

Mythic understanding is typically predominant from the time grammatical language develops between the ages of two and three until about six, seven, or eight. The change to a somewhat distinct kind of understanding at about age seven is a result of the mind's ability to imcorporate literacy among the tools it deploys (and not a result of some Piagetian-style mental development spontaneously occurring, though some such development might be implicated in it). As Mythic understanding in significant degree incorporates and transforms some of the tools of Somatic understanding, so those of Mythic understanding are not things we leave behind as we become literate. They will remain in significant degree as transformed constituents of all further kinds of understanding. In the sense that Kolakowski calls myth "a permanent constitutive element of culture" (1989, p. x), Mythic understanding becomes a permanent constitutive element of our later understanding. It is still deployed, in perhaps transformed ways, by thee and me.

SOME CHARACTERISTICS OF MYTHIC UNDERSTANDING

As discussed below, each characteristic of Mythic understanding is a direct consequence of language development, and so can be found in both the mythic thinking of traditional oral societies and the everyday, spontaneous discourse of young children in modern literate cultures. Each of the following sections begins with a brief account of why language development should yield such characteristics in human thinking. Not all of these accounts are equally persuasive—in some cases there has been a lot of scholarly work to draw on, in others little—but the accumulation of evidence and plausibilities should build support for the new recapitulation theory. I have omitted some characteristics of Mythic understanding, such as lying (whose social and intellectual uses have been so engagingly explored by David Nyberg [1993]), because educational implications are perhaps a tad less evident than are those of, say, stories. Mind you, the inadequate distinction suggested there between lying and stories ("He's telling stories again!") brings to the fore the fact that the following characteristics overlap and interact intricately.

Binary Structuring

Let us begin by plunging into the "deep end" with binary structuring—dualisms, oppositions, whatever we choose to call this common proclivity in human thinking. This is a "deep end" characteristic because it has figured so prominently in postmodern and feminist writings as a kind of Western disease of language. Gender theorists, for example, have argued that "male/female," as the pair has been constructed in Western rationalist thought, are falsely dichotomous and their association with such further binary sets as culture/nature, rational/emotional, public/private, active/passive, dominant/subordinate, and so on (cf. Fox-Keller, 1986) sets in place a tool of hegemonic constructions that has been used to suppress and devalue women in Western cultures. In the most widely known fairy tales in the West, for example, the Grimms systematically represent women as exemplifying the latter of the above binary sets and so introduce young children to stereotyped gender roles.

Forming binary oppositions is a necessary consequence of using language; it is one tool of our sense-making. Tools can be used destructively, but they also can do useful, constructive work. I will return to the ideological arguments in chapter 6, but want to note here that destructive stereotyping and the pervasive set of gender associations in Western culture are contin-   37 gent. As such we can hope to deconstruct them; what we cannot hope to do is dispense with the use of binary oppositions as long as we use language. One effective procedure for deconstructing them is not, for example, to banish the Grimm fairy tales or to rewrite them to suit modern values but rather to make explicit the destructive associations they set up, leading to a fuller understanding of the tales and the culture that has bred and nourished them, while preserving their aesthetic (Hoogland, 1994) and psychological (Bettelheim, 1976) value.

The prime source of postmodern distrust of binary oppositions was Friedrich Nietzsche (1844–1900). He persistently attacked people's generation of oppositions in their thinking and language, asserting that people see phenomena in terms of oppositions that they invent and then assume the oppositions are a product of the phenomena rather than of their thinking. "There are no opposites: only from those of logic do we derive the concept of opposites—and falsely transfer it to things" (1968a, p. 298). Language, he insistently pointed out, is the source of oppositions whereas reality has only continua and infinite gradations of difference. So language falsifies the world to us, and our main intellectual task is to untangle the inadequate terms in which we represent the world, from the world itself. Nietzsche is wonderfully acute at pointing out "the misleading errors of language (and the fundamental fallacies of reason which have become petrified in it)" (1956, p. 178).

Nietzsche's observations, however, help prove my point: even if we regret particular uses of binary structuring and its simplification and falsification of un-binary reality, we cannot avoid doing so except by retreating into muteness. The use of fundamental binary oppositions, like male/female, black/white, natural/cultural, good/bad, is a cultural universal (Brown, 1991). Associations made with them may vary from culture to culture, but the fact that these and other binary oppositions are found in every culture suggest that they are not products of some particular contingencies of Western thinking but reflect something profound and common to all human beings.

Why should binary structuring be a necessary consequence of language development? Because "[l]ogically, we express . . . elementary differentiation in the form of contradictories, A and not-A, and it is certainly true that the ability to distinguish, together with the ability to perceive resemblances, is basic to all cognitive processes" (Hallpike, 1979, pp. 224–25). Vygotsky also notes the use of "elementary differentiation" in young children performing some basic tasks: "Association by contrast, rather than by similarity, guides the child in compiling a collection" (1962, p. 63). Edmund Leach makes the point similarly to Hallpike: "Binary oppositions are intrinsic to the process of human thought. Any description of the world must discriminate categories in the form 'p is what not-p is not'" (1967, p. 3). For present purposes I would prefer it if Leach's observation were not about opposition-construction being "intrinsic to human thought" but about its being an influence of language on thought, but it does seem that these languaged oppositions grow out of prior Somatic discriminations like self/other, figure/ground, face/not-face (cf. Banks and Salaparek, 1983).

This is a somewhat tricky topic, in that as soon as one begins looking for binary oppositions one sees them nearly everywhere. Whether this is a defect of the language we use or of the mind doing the looking seems to matter little since both support the notion that these logical constructs are at least very common. They seem to be fundamental to all languages; for example, categories that correspond to nouns (stasis) and verbs (change) (in whose differentiation syntax begins to emerge [Pinker, 1994, p. 268]) are found universally. It is hard to deny John Stuart Mill's regretful conclusion that any distinction tends to become an opposition; even if we don't find this true of our own thinking, it will no doubt be evident in that of others.

Binary structuring in the myths of traditional oral cultures has been demonstrated quite dramatically by Claude Lévi-Strauss (e.g., 1966, 1970, 1978). His work is controversial in this regard because of the large general claims he makes based on his somewhat limited data from American Indian myths. He has argued that binary structuring is basic to all myths and that the exposure of such a structure is the key to their proper interpretation. He has further suggested that binary oppositions occur so prominently in myths, and in modern thinking, because the human brain is innately "hard-wired" to build understanding on the basis of binary discriminations. Anthropologists may dispute the generalization of his findings beyond the large corpus of myths he has analyzed in his four-volume *Mythology,* but the underlying binary structure of those myths seems beyond dispute. Lévi-Strauss shows how a complex logical structure, which meaningfully orders the myth users' environment and lives, is constructed on otherwise arbitrarily opposed elements, such as honey and ashes. While Lévi-Strauss's is a debatable demonstration of uses of binary structuring in traditional oral cultures, it serves here as a slightly quirky addition to more routine observations about the universal use of such dualisms as male/female, permitted/forbidden, natural/cultural, bad/good. But one does find his basic observation about the ubiquitousness of oppositions constantly echoed: Joseph Needham's discussion of the simplicity of the Chinese Yin and Yang, and analogous oppositions in many cultures, leads Jack Goody to conclude that "such ideas seem intrinsic to human thought, to the use of language itself" (1977, p. 40).

That binary structuring is prominent in modern young children's thinking seems so obvious that it hardly needs pointing out. Anyone who attends to the structure of young children's thinking can observe what Bruno Bettelheim calls the "manner in which [children] can bring some order into [their] world by dividing everything into opposites" (1976, p. 74). The most evident structural feature of children's stories or self-generated narratives is that the surface content very commonly rests on such underlying binary sets as security/fear, good/bad, brave/cowardly, love/hate, happy/sad, poor/rich, health/sickness, permitted/forbidden. The story of Hansel and Gretel, for example, is articulated on a powerful security/fear structure.

Organizing one's conceptual grasp on the physical world by initially forming binary structures—hot/cold, big/little, soft/hard, crooked/straight, sweet/sour—allows an initial orientation over a range of otherwise bewilderingly complex phenomena: "When once an opposition is established and its principle understood, then either opposite, or any intermediate term, can be at once defined by opposition or by degree" (Ogden, 1976, p. 20). These oppositions are not necessarily, or even often, made up from genuine logical or empirical opposites; rather they are set up as opposites for conceptual purposes of orientation to complex phenomena, bringing them under some kind of initial conceptual control.

As Ogden points out, once an opposition is established and its principle understood, children not only grasp the oppositions but also use them to ascribe meaning to any intermediary terms. In a simple example I have used before, young children commonly begin conceptually to grasp the temperature continuum by establishing "hot" and "cold" as opposites. A logical and empirical necessity seems to underlie this opposition in that the first discriminable temperatures are things hotter than the child's body temperature and things colder. Intermediate terms, like "warm," thus become meaningful as a mediation between the oppositions already known. The child can continue to enlarge conceptual control over temperature by mediating between "warm" and "cold," for example, and grasping the concept "cool." Or this concept can be learned as a further intermediate term closer to "cold" than to "hot." This process seems to be widely deployed in making sense of the everyday physical world around the child. As I mentioned in the introduction, our bodies are our primary "mediators" of meaning, and some of the earliest discriminations we make are in terms of our bodies—so "wet" means wetter than my body and "dry" means drier than my body, "hard" means harder than my body and "soft" means softer than my body, "big" means bigger, "small" means smaller, and so on. These concepts are mediated in a literal dimension when children learn additional modifiers or comparisons —squishy, soft as a pillow, pretty soft, really soft, flabby, tender, cottony. They are also extended beyond the body by metaphor into other dimensions, so in/out may be extended from the body to a room or a house;

40

big/little may be extended by recognition that a small tree is often bigger than a big person.

There seems room for argument about much of the above: about how intensive or fundamental binary structuring is in any cultural group and among children, and about whether it is partly a result of "hard-wiring" in the brain or of the nature of language—not that language/brain is a discrimination easily to be sorted out. What is beyond argument is the fact that binary structuring is found universally among human groups and is commonly used by children today. If this much is granted, what is the educational point? Why the fuss?

I will later explore detailed educational implications, but it might help in this chapter to indicate how these rather abstract points can influence everyday teaching practice and the curriculum. The example of history in the curriculum should serve the purpose.

The early years of schooling include very little history, and what there is usually concerns local or regional facts that have affected the child's environment in some significant way. History has been emptied out of the early curriculum in response to the progressivist doctrine that we must begin exploring the world with what the child already knows and experiences, and we must expand understanding gradually from their everyday environments. Progressivism has also encouraged the removal from the curriculum of content that children cannot actively engage, because early learning is most profoundly of "how to do" (Dewey, 1966, p. 184), and practical, hands-on experience of historical events is clearly impossible. Dewey further argued that the "true starting point of history is always some present situation with its problems" (p. 214). The diminution or exclusion of history has been further supported by Piagetian research, which demonstrated that certain concepts crucial to historical understanding were "formal operational" and do not "develop" until the teen years (Elkind, 1976; Hallam, 1969). Also, Piaget's account of the young child as a "preoperational" or "concrete operational" thinker has implied that historical material cannot be very fruitfully engaged. The cumulative effect of these influences is a curriculum that leaves young children largely ignorant of history, because it is assumed that they cannot understand it on the one hand and on the other that their attention and activity should be engaged in dealing with and expanding from their everyday experience and local environments.

"Formal" concepts crucial to historical understanding, such as causality, do not "develop" out of the blue in teen years. And even if a concept of historical causality is not grasped by young children, they do clearly grasp the causal principle that moves along stories like *Hansel and Gretel, Cinderella,* or

Peter Rabbit. Moreover, if teenagers are to develop sophisticated concepts of historical causality, prerequisite causal concepts must be stimulated and developed. The "narrative causality" of *Peter Rabbit* is an obvious logical precursor of the historical causality of Thucydides. Instead of banishing history from the curriculum, we could introduce historical content structured on the kinds of concepts young children obviously do understand. Those concepts can be made accessible not only by orderly expansion from the practical, everyday activities of the child but also, and perhaps more engagingly, by use of the binary structuring we find so common in children's thinking.

One might, for example, introduce in the first grade a narrative history of the world structured on the opposition between freedom and oppression, knowledge and ignorance, or security and fear. These oppositions are clearly meaningful to young children because we see them in their favorite stories, in their own fantasy narratives, and in discussions about how they make sense of their own experience (Paley, 1981, 1984, 1990). After all, our history is the greatest story we know, full of drama, incident, vivid characters. One would, of course, have to simplify historical reality to construct such a narrative for five-year-olds, but the simplification would be only in degree different from how the most sophisticated historical writing simplifies reality. Such a narrative would be built upon concepts that are vividly a part of children's experience. Whether at home, in their neighborhood, in the classroom, or in the school yard, children already deal with matters of freedom and oppression. To use and elaborate those concepts while learning that their world has gone through great struggles and problems analogous to their own makes simple educational sense.

Note, too, that when telling the story of *Hansel and Gretel,* the narrator does not explicitly discuss and explain the concepts of opposition—in this case, security and fear. We presuppose that in some profound way children already know those concepts; the narrator is using their familiarity to make events in some distant forest at some distant time meaningful. Similarly, in a narrative history of the world we would not be explicitly teaching about oppression and freedom or even necessarily using the words; we presuppose that these underlying concepts are meaningful to children from their experience of home and school. We *use* them in our narrative structures to make historical events meaningful. Binary structuring is a tool that provides the child with a grasp on new content; we do not teach the structure.

Binary structuring is a feature of language and minds, not of the world, as Nietzsche so insistently argued. The world is not structured in binary terms, but our initial grasp on it can efficiently reduce it to binary terms. The process of learning involves elaborating the mind's terms to conform more truly with the complexity of reality. The mind's terms—language significantly—are always inadequate to the task of raiding the inarticulate, but the intolerable wrestle with words and meanings that slip, slide, perish, decay with imprecision is central to education. So the educational point is not to teach binary concepts, nor to teach that the world is structured in binary terms, but always to lead toward mediation, elaboration, and conscious recognition of the initial structuring concepts. Some initial grasp is required, however, or there is nothing secure to elaborate, and binary structures are one kind of effective grasper of new meaning. (This prosaic way of putting it nevertheless reflects a central theme of Buddhist thinking and is found in the earliest Western writings, such as Heraclitus's teaching that wisdom is not the knowledge of many things but the perception of the underlying unity of warring opposites.)

But there is still the progressivist principle that, even if we could teach world history to children, we should not start with it, and it cannot involve any kind of "active doing." Take the latter point first. This has been tied to Dewey's observation that the "[k]nowledge which comes first to persons, and that remains most deeply ingrained, is knowledge of *how to do;* how to walk, talk, read, write, skate, ride a bicycle, and so on indefinitely" (1966, p. 184). This seems simply wrong. Before we learn to walk and ride a bicycle, and after we can do neither, we grasp concepts of oppression and freedom, love and hate, good and bad, fear and security. Now this comparison is obviously peculiar because it does not involve equivalent kinds of knowledge. As our concern is education, however, these conceptual bases for sense-making may be more important than how-to-do skills.

It is a commonplace of early education that new knowledge "should be built on what the child already knows" (Jarolimek, 1982, p. 12)—I choose a textbook at random; virtually all of them express the same point as though it were beyond question. This has been a keystone of progressivist thinking, a principle that has had enormous influence.

The problem with this truism lies in how it has been interpreted. Young children are assumed to know the contents of their everyday environment, so they are taught about mailcarriers, their neighborhood, and families, but they are not assumed to know freedom and oppression, so they are not taught about Greeks and the Persian Empire, or West Africans and the slave trade, or the ancient dynasties of China, or the struggles, triumphs, and disasters of men and women and communities down the ages.

If instead we thought of what children know *also* in terms of the binary concepts they use to gain an initial grasp on the world, then we could introduce them to any content, any knowledge, that can be articulated on such concepts. Accepting that we should start with children's experience and move from the known to the unknown does not necessarily imply the kind

43

of early curriculum we have in place today. Children's early experience is of love and hate, fear and security, oppression and freedom no less than it is of a particular set of local conditions and activities. They have imaginative experience as well as basic pragmatic experience. This experience can serve as a starting point for a far richer curriculum than what we have today—an intellectually impoverished set of topics focusing on local trivia and "hands-on" activities at a point when children's imaginations are energetically alive to grasp the world.

I do not mean to suggest that binary opposites and mediation are the *only* ways in which children can learn anything. Rather, they provide just a few of an indeterminate array of procedures children commonly use in learning. I emphasize them here because their implications vividly disrupt an enormously influential and restrictive view about how children's learning proceeds. I consider them not so much dominant in children's learning as exemplifying a feature of children's learning that is largely ignored, a feature that teachers can deploy relatively easily to make curriculum content engaging and meaningful to children. Jerome Bruner has been criticized for his claim that "any subject can be taught effectively in some intellectually honest form to any child at any stage of development" (Bruner, 1960, p.31). I suppose this section of my discussion could be read as an additional argument supporting Bruner's claim.

There is something a little odd about trying to point out the prevalence of binary structuring: this has been obvious throughout most of Western cultural history, and the obvious educational response has been the use of dialectic—the logical analysis of arguments based on setting up opposing positions and supporting one against the other or mediating in the direction of a new position. Dialectic seems to have faded with the retreat of rhetoric in academic life. Peter Ramus (1515–1572), that enormously influential but largely unoriginal scholar, reflected the belief that dialectic "supported the whole fabric of the world's consciousness" (Ong, 1958, p. 3). My conclusion is somewhat more modest, but the prevalence of binary structuring deserves more attention than it has received in education.

Fantasy

A distinguishing feature of myth stories is their fantasy, their dislocation from the everyday rules of the waking world we live in. Young children, apparently universally (Brown, 1991), delight in fantasy stories full of talking, clothed rabbits, bears, or other animals, also dislocated from anything familiar in their everyday waking experience.

Some people suggest that children's delight in fantasy results simply from adults' telling them that kind of story. I think there are a number of reasons not to accept this explanation as adequate.

First, audiences are not uninfluential in the stories told to them; children's response plays a significant determining role in the stories adults tell them. If children's understanding were tied to their immediate experience, local environment, and hands-on activities, as is asserted in so many educational textbooks, parents would soon give up telling fantasy stories. In surveys of first graders' likes and dislikes in stories, Rogers and Robinson (in Favat, 1977) found that while a wide array of stories appeal to various children, they ranked first in preference fairy-tale stories that include "an animal who could talk," "a prince and a princess," and "a magic ring." They ranked last, real-world accounts of "what an astronaut does," "a person on TV," and "building a bridge."

Second, that fantasy has so much in common with myth stories from around the world suggests that something more than parental conditioning is at work.

Third, narratives constructed by very young children, in groups or alone, very commonly involve transformation of the home and local environment into fairylands, pirates' islands, or magic realms. The impulse for such fantasy seems inadequately accounted for by a few stories they have heard. Finally, the persistence of various forms of fantasy at every stage of life suggests that it is not some contingent, accidental invention of a few storytellers but is somehow tied up with profound features of our mental lives.

Arthur Applebee advances the traditional argument to explain why young children typically understand and enjoy a story such as *Peter Rabbit:* "The sort of familiarity which a child demands in a story is often a social one, a doing of things which the child expects to have done. Thus *Peter Rabbit* is a manageable story for Carol at two years eight months because of its familiar family setting" (1978, p. 75). This view is pervasive in educational textbooks, and its influence on curriculum is perhaps most clearly evident in social studies: "Thus, kindergarten and first-grade students spend a lot of social studies time studying self-awareness and families because these two topics have a sense of relevance and immediacy to young children" (Ellis, 1986, p. 9).

But if it is the familiarity and immediacy to the young child's experience that make content or stories accessible, meaningful, and manageable, one must wonder why Peter is a talking, clothed rabbit. One might wonder also about the wild wood, which is safe, and the cultivated garden, which is dangerous, and the closeness of death, and so on. Why do children so readily accept such inversion of the normal experience of safe gardens and wild woods, or so readily take the rabbit's perspective on these matters, scan-

45

dalously disregarding theorists who emphasize children's "egocentric" thinking?

That Peter is a rabbit is not incidental; he is simply one of an endless menagerie of fantasy creatures that fill children's favorite stories. So, where does the talking rabbit come from? Well, consider the binary opposites: they help the child to gain a linguistic and conceptual control over a very wide range of phenomena. After talking with the cat for a while, for example, the child learns that the animal cannot talk back, it resists wearing clothes, and it certainly doesn't use a knife and fork when eating. Animals, it becomes clear, are in some significant way different from human beings. So we have another binary set—human/animal—constructed. Similarly, children recognize an important difference between things that have been culturally transformed and things that are natural. The child will rarely *articulate* binary terms like life/death, nature/culture, human/animal, but they are basic discriminations made at a structural level in constructing a sense of the world.

What do you get when you apply to these binary structures the mediating procedure that proves so successful in elaborating conceptual control over temperature? Hot and cold yield warm, wet and dry yield damp, and life and death yield—well, ghosts, for one thing. Ghosts are to life and death as warm is to hot and cold or damp is to wet and dry. How about human and animal? Yeti, mermaids, Sasquatch. And how about nature and culture? Well, there are talking rabbits like Peter. Peter is a natural creature with the cultural characteristics of speech and clothing.

Is this the explanation, or a part of the explanation, of fantasy—the product of a technique for gaining greater linguistic and conceptual control over the world overgeneralized to inappropriate concepts? Language names things, sets up categories, conveniently organizes many continuous phenomena in binary structures, elaborates its grasp by mediating between the binary terms, and, because some basic binary oppositions are discrete and have no mediating categories in reality, spins a world of fantasy wherein the technique of conceptual elaboration can play unconfined.

If it is, relatively, so straightforward, what about those immensely elaborate psychoanalytic explanations of fantasy? If we are to wield Ockam's chainsaw, we will cut away explanations, such as those of Jung and Freud, as unnecessarily complex, and go with the simplest adequate one. But, of course, none of these explanations escapes a large amount of speculation. What is significant here is the recognition that we also find this universal tendency to fantasy and dislocation in the myths of the world. The suggestive explanation of children's fantasy as a mediating category between profound binary discriminations echoes Lévi-Strauss's suggestive explanation

for the fantasy and dislocation of myths.

One educational implication of this ready engagement with fantasy and dislocation reinforces that made in the previous section: children's learning does not always proceed in logical progression from a known to an associated unknown content. If such a procedure were dominant, we would have difficulty explaining why very young children seem to grasp wicked witches, star warriors, and talking rabbits so readily, whereas this ready engagement is very simply explained in terms of the binary structuring and mediating procedure described above. Clearly, we do learn many things by making content associations. But that we do so has been taken as an exclusive dogma by curriculum designers. If, to repeat an important point, the binary structuring and mediating procedure is recognized as another route by which children can access knowledge, then some current restrictions on the early curriculum can be safely, and beneficially, dispensed with. I am thinking particularly, again, of the "expanding environments" dogma that has, I believe, contributed significantly to the educational impoverishment of so many children.

Abstract Thinking

It is generally accepted in current educational textbooks that young children are "concrete" thinkers, and teaching practices and curricula throughout the Western world have been profoundly influenced by this belief (Roldão, 1992). *Concrete* and *abstract* are, of course, odd terms to use about the contents of the mind; it isn't a place one would look for concrete, and everything in the mind is in some sense abstract. But we use the terms to signify relative degrees of generality or particularity, and young children are represented as able to deal intellectually with the particular, with what is more immediate to the senses.

My point is that the development of language inevitably involves the use of abstractions, and that abstract thinking—in the everyday, rather vague sense of the term—is no less common in young children than is concrete thinking.

"Language creates distance between the self and the object; language generalizes, transferring a unique perception into a common one; language transmutes realities into abstractions" (Coe, 1984, p. 253). That is the sense in which language necessarily involves the mind in dealing with abstractions. More profoundly, it has been argued that abstract ideas do not grow as a result of encountering concrete objects; rather, only by the deployment of abstractions do concrete objects become recognizable:

[I]n our conscious experience, or introspectively, concrete particulars occupy a central place and the abstractions appear to be derived from them. But this subjective experience   47 appears to me to be the source of the error with which I am concerned, the appearance which prevents us from recognizing that these concrete particulars are the product of abstractions which the mind must possess in order that it should be able to experience particular sensations, perceptions, or images. (Hayek, 1970, p. 311)

A feature of young children's fairy stories, as noted above, is that they are structured on binary opposites. An evident feature of these binary opposites is that they are immensely abstract concepts. Further, children's access to particulars like Darth Vader, wicked monsters, or talking rabbits comes by means of the abstract concepts they "body forth" or give concrete form to, a point that seems to illustrate Hayek's argument.

The prevalence of the view that young children are concrete thinkers has obscured the sense in which they are *also* obviously abstract thinkers. For example, if abstractions like oppression/resentment/revolt, and their relationships, were not in place in some form by age four, the typical child would be unable to understand the story of Robin Hood and the Sheriff of Nottingham or Luke Skywalker and Darth Vader. This does not mean that the child typically articulates the words "oppression," "resentment," and "revolt" or even could define them. But such concepts have to be a part of the child's understanding of events whose meaning turns on grasping them and their relational dynamics. They need not be conscious, or even subconscious, but may be better thought of in Hayek's sense as "superconscious" "because they govern the conscious processes without appearing in them" (1970, p. 319).

Hayek suggests that what we mean by abstractions might be better thought of as "operations of the mind" rather than as concepts. Abstractions become conscious, become concepts, as a result of the mind's reflecting on itself. The formation of abstract concepts, then, is not the outcome of some conscious process but rather the discovery of something that already has guided the mind's operations. So the absence of awareness of abstractions in young children, or their lack of articulation of, or ability to manipulate, abstractions, is not a sign that abstractions are not at work in their thinking any less than in the typical adult's. The absence signifies only that they have not reflected on their thinking, or are not aware of their thinking in such a way that they consciously deal with the abstractions they use all the time. So the later appearance of abstractions in our language development is not a result of genetically following the concrete but represents discoveries of our long active mental operations by reflection on them.

If we look to the evolutionary, archeological, and historical record, we find similar conclusions. Earlier it had been believed that language must have developed and been elaborated in aboriginal cultures around practical, concrete activities, like tool-making and food preparation, and then gradu-

48

ally was found useful in more elaborate forms of social discourse, leading in relatively recent times to the complexity of myth. But as Donald has persuasively argued (1991, ch. 7), practical skills are passed on largely by apprenticeship, in which language is typically of little importance. In tribal societies, and from what we can infer from Upper Paleolithic cultures,

[the] most elevated use of language . . . is in the area of mythic invention—in the construction of conceptual "models" of the human universe. Even in the most primitive human societies, where technology has remained essentially unchanged for tens of thousands of years, there are always myths of creation and death and stories that serve to encapsulate tribally held ideas of origin and world structure. . . . These uses were not late developments, after language had proven itself in concrete, practical applications; they were among the first. (p. 213)

What Donald writes about aboriginal human cultures seems to me reflected in children's development of language today. His characterization of "mythic" peoples, and consequently all who come after them, is that they are "constantly modeling the world and storing the results" (p. 256). So, too, do children. The integrative, symbolic, mythic models that are being constantly constructed drive the development of linguistic forms to express them. The driving force in this process is not concrete particulars but a new kind of understanding, "a new, much more powerful method of thinking" (p. 216).

We still know very little about how human beings developed, and each of us individually develops, language, but neither process can sensibly be described in terms of moving from the concrete to the abstract. It seems, as Donald also notes, that it is more likely to be analogous to our perceptual processes that begin with some holistic impression within which concrete details are then located; on entering a room, for example, we do not build up an impression of it by composition of all the particulars into some whole, rather we initially form an impression of the whole and then we locate particulars within it. Whether we describe children's early conceptualisations as abstractions or the "superconscious" or "integrative myth" (p. 267) or as "Gestalts," the kind of thinking is fundamentally tied into the symbolic models of the world children constantly construct and reconstruct. Concrete particulars have meaning only within these models; that children do not express the background symbolic models does not mean that the symbolism is not there or that it is not primary in the children's understanding. Given the looseness of match between these complex conceptual processes and the crude terms we use to refer to them, it seems reasonable to keep the term "abstract" to refer to a fundamental part of children's everyday thinking.

It is useful to note in passing that "developmental researchers have been accruing impressive evidence that even toddlers can appreciate quite abstract qualities in the world (ranging from numerosity to animateness to various kinds of causality)" (Gardner, 1993, p. 182). Gardner cites Carey and Gelman's work (1990), his own study of "the unschooled mind" (1991), and Keil's (1989) study showing that very young children will sometimes override strong perceptual or concrete cues in favor of abstract properties.

A major support for the view of young children as concrete thinkers has come from Piaget's developmental theory. There are many grounds on which the validity of Piaget's position might be questioned (e.g., Brainerd, 1978; Donaldson, 1978; Egan, 1983; Gardner, 1991; Siegel and Brainerd, 1978), but regardless of how persuasive such arguments may be, a much stronger point is relevant here. Piaget's theory, and its extensions in more recent neo-Piagetian research (e.g., Case, 1985, 1991; Fischer, 1980), deals only with a limited range of children's thinking. It focuses on what has been called logico-mathematical thinking, or essentially numerical competence. Even when the object of study is dreams, play, or more recently, emotions or art, the researchers locate their central concern "in the human sensitivity to number, numbers, and numerical relations" (Gardner, 1991, p. 28). Gardner goes as far as to conclude—he admits slightly exaggeratedly—that Piaget's major achievement "was the development of a deep understanding of what it means for a creature to be numerate and . . . his view of human development centered upon the capacity of our species to achieve sophisticated knowledge about numbers—or Number" (p. 26).

The problem for education has come from the generally uncritical acceptance of Piaget's theory as a description of the totality of children's thinking. There is no good reason to believe that what may be true about the development of number competence is also true of metaphorical competence, or that what may be the case about logico-mathematical thinking is also true of the imagination. Indeed, there are good reasons to believe otherwise (Gardner, 1991, ch. 2). Sensitive attention to children's thinking makes clear that their thinking routinely includes metaphysical speculation and philosophical reflection of a highly abstract kind (Ashton, 1993; Matthews, 1980, 1984; Paley, 1990).

So, while notions of "abstractness" and "concreteness" in thinking are imprecise, the currently prevailing view that young children's thinking is restricted to the "concrete" is clearly inadequate. Children's patent deployment of powerful abstractions calls aloud for us to reconsider claims about the concreteness of children's thinking and to reconsider the influence such claims have had on teaching and curricula for young children. The belief that young children are generally concrete thinkers has meant shunning content that seems to involve abstractions, instead focusing on "active doing" and practical manipulation that has made the typical elementary classroom less intellectually rich than it should be.

Children can have ready access to all kinds of knowledge, provided it is articulated on the kinds of powerful abstractions that they clearly use, even if they do so "superconsciously." Peter Rabbit, we can see, is engaging and meaningful to young children not only because of the family setting but also because of a narrative structured on abstract binary concepts of security/ danger, wildness/cultivation, life/death, nature/culture, obedience/disobe- dience, and also on "abstract" motives, intentions, hopes, and fears familiar to children.

The emphasis on "active manipulation" is, of course, important in cer- tain areas of learning, but its current overemphasis results from, and further encourages, the underestimating of young children's ability to grasp mean- ing by other than logico-mathematical means.

Consider a simple example in mathematics, in which one might expect views derived from Piaget to be more valid. Let us draw on the observations above to teach the concept of place value or decimalization to young chil- dren. How might we go about this task if we believe that children can readily grasp new knowledge when it is structured on powerful abstract binary con- cepts?

Once upon a time a king and queen wanted to count their army. They had six counselors, five of whom were pompous and unimaginative, and one of whom was humble but ingenious. (We have, then, our binary structure: unimaginative/ingenious. These are chosen because they are familiar to chil- dren, and we want them to associate the ingenuity of mathematics with something they recognize within themselves.)

The army is milling around on a plain, as armies do, before going off to battle. Each of the unimaginative counselors recommends an ineffective method of counting the army. Eventually the royal pair turns to the inge- nious counselor. He has the king and queen order each of the unimaginative counselors to pick up ten stones. The unimaginative counselors are then re- quired to stand behind a table side by side, each with a bowl in front of him. The army then marches in line past the table. As each soldier goes by, the counselor at the end of the table puts a stone in his bowl. When ten soldiers have gone by, and all his stones are in the bowl, he picks up the ten stones, and again puts one stone back in the bowl for each soldier who goes by. The counselor next to him has only to watch the first counselor. Each time the first counselor picks up his ten stones, the second unimaginative counselor puts one stone into his bowl. When the second counselor has put all ten of his stones into the bowl, he picks them up and starts again. The third coun- selor's job is simply to watch the second counselor's bowl. Each time the second counselor picks his ten stones out of the full bowl, the third coun- selor puts one stone into his bowl. And so on. After some time, when the 51 army has gone by, the fifth counselor has one stone in his bowl, the fourth counselor has three stones in his bowl, the third counselor has seven stones in his bowl, the second counselor has eight stones, and the first counselor has two. So the ingenious counselor is able to tell the king and queen that they have exactly 13,782 soldiers in their army.

After the story, which teachers can elaborate, the children might be invited to use this method to count each other, with two "counters" and the rest as "soldiers" marching by, or to count other more numerous objects. They could then try to use this method with bases other than ten, and so on.

Having used this example in the past, I have sometimes had teachers respond that they are glad that I have the children involve themselves in using this method "hands-on," because it is that "active doing" that makes it meaningful to them and "drives home the lesson." One teacher recently elaborated the point, saying that she had studied the U.S. Civil War when at school, learned the importance of the Battle of Gettysburg, learned Lincoln's address by heart, but it wasn't until recently when she visited the battlefield that it all became meaningful to her, and the hairs on the back of her neck had tingled. It was being there, being physically involved with the place, that made all the book-learning meaningful.

I suggested that Gettysburg is a field like other fields; what made it neck-tingling for this teacher was the book-learned history she had remembered, the significance it held for her in the story of America's formation. What makes place value meaningful to the children is the story of the counselor's ingenuity with which children can associate. The practical activities later clarify, extend, and reinforce what they have gathered from the story. Each feeds the other. Current dogma asserts that the practical activity is crucial, to the point that other intellectual capacities that children have for grasping meaning are depreciated. I think the practical activity is certainly useful, but it can best support meaningful learning in a context of powerful abstractions; it is within the abstract context that the concrete content makes sense.

The story structure allows the children to associate emotionally with the ingenuity of the clever counselor's successful strategy. The mathematical skill is thus not learned as an alien algorithm; it becomes in some significant sense *theirs*. The emotional tie to the cleverness of mathematics is another crucial feature of learning, little regarded in current early educational orthodoxy.

More generally, the pervasive influence of the ideas of the young child as learning best and first "how to do," and of being a "concrete thinker," along with the considerable focus on logico-mathematical thinking, has had a peculiar and destructive effect on early education. Enormous emphasis has been placed on those intellectual skills that young children manage least well and develop only slowly—computational, logico-mathematical skills —with an equivalent neglect of what children do best—metaphoric, imaginative thinking. The result is a curriculum and teaching practices aimed at and drawing on what are taken as young children's poor intellectual abilities rather than on their early development of capacities that come with learning language. We should focus our pedagogical attention, that is, on those areas in which young humans are evolutionarily predisposed to rapid and powerful learning, where—to put it in terms of theorists I find increasingly persuasive—specific mental "modules" are operative (cf. e.g., Fodor, 1983; Pinker, 1994).

So while "concrete thinking" is what is especially evident in young children if we focus on the explicit content of their conscious articulation, this content seems meaningful to young children in the degree to which it is tied to some powerful abstractions. Without connection to some abstract underpinnings—or superconscious operations—the concrete content or practical manipulations remain contextless and more generally meaningless. This seems the common fate of so much early classroom activity: children commonly, in T. S. Eliot's line, "had the experience, but missed the meaning."

In teaching and curriculum planning, then, we might still hold to the principle that our understanding moves "from the known to the unknown," but we would do well to think of the "known" in terms of powerful abstractions and the "unknown" as anything that can be tied to them. When we begin to think of telling or teaching children something, we might sensibly begin with what set of binary abstractions it can be built on. This will likely be—especially after nearly a century of emphasizing children's intellectual incapacity, their "concreteness," and the necessity for practical manipulations—rather difficult for some.

Metaphor

Metaphor, like myth, has long been a puzzle to scholars. Those of a positivist inclination have tended to sweep it under the academic rug, deeming it a linguistic frill that can always be reduced to the kind of literal language with which they are more at home. This last sentence is, of course, awash with metaphors—inclination, sweeping under rugs, frills, reduction, literal, at home with, all involve metaphor. I could have written: "Positivists ignored metaphor because it entailed no features not reducible to literal language." That would reduce, but certainly not eliminate, the metaphoric load. Does it say the same thing? How would one reduce Yeats's reference to "the rag and bone shop of the heart"? Could one produce a literal equivalent, in which the   53 cluttered, discarded, disjointed, rubbishy features of a rag and bone shop refer to the condition of his emotional life in old age? If we could reduce such phrases to literal equivalents, why is metaphor so pervasive?

Let us begin with the claim that metaphor is a product of language development and will therefore be evident in mythic thinking and in young children. Ernst Cassirer has pointed to the relationship of myth and language, arguing that "no matter how widely the contents of myth and language may differ, yet the same form of mental conception is operative in both. It is the form which one may denote as *metaphorical thinking*" (1946, p. 84). He points out that since the time of the Roman grammarian Quintillian it has been taken for granted that all mythic thinking is permeated by metaphor. Lévi-Strauss has suggested that "metaphor . . . is not a later embellishment of language but is one of its fundamental modes—a primary form of discursive thought" (1964, p. 102).

Whatever we make of the somewhat speculative claims about metaphor's being a visible expression of a kind of root of language, the prominence of metaphor in mythic thinking is undeniable. Do we see anything similar in young children as they develop language? Consider the following scenario. A five-year-old boy has been selling juice at the front step on a hot day, along with his four-year-old sister and three-year-old brother. Their last customer, a telephone repairman, after gratefully downing his ten cent glass of orange juice, asked jokingly whether they didn't have any beer or scotch. After he left, the five-year-old went into the house and asked his mother whether he could have some beer and scotch for the stand. He emerged a minute or so later, shrugged, and told his siblings, "Mom killed that idea."

The three-year-old has no more difficulty interpreting the meaning of the sentence than the four-year-old. Both know that they cannot have beer and scotch. Whether they have heard or used the metaphor of killing an idea before, they know it now without any explanation, and they understand this kind of metaphoric usage as an entirely normal form of speech.

Such naturalistic observations do not seem to require empirical studies to support the conclusion that very young children use metaphor easily and frequently, but empirical studies can perhaps help clarify the process of metaphoric development. Winner (1988) has reported an extensive series of studies of the genesis and growth of metaphoric competence. Among the early and, to the experimenters, more unexpected findings was the prodigal production of metaphors by some very young children. Also, in comparative tests of recognizing appropriate metaphors, it was discovered that the "highest number of appropriate metaphors was secured from the pre-school children, who even exceeded college students; moreover, these three- and four-year-olds fashioned significantly more appropriate metaphors than did children aged seven or eleven" (Gardner and Winner, 1979, p. 130). Most intriguing was "the capacity of at least some children to perform this game at an astonishingly high level. Not only do such youngsters frequently contrive clever names for the very objects which have stumped our adult pilot subjects; more dramatically, some of them can nearly effortlessly come up with a whole series of appropriate and appealing metaphoric meanings" (p. 133).

Metaphor in its grossest appearance involves talking about something in terms derived from something quite different. It is a "deviant naming" or "peculiar predication" (Ricoeur, 1991, p. 8) and establishes a new relationship between heterogeneous ideas in a way that adds something to, or throws new light on, the thing talked about. Metaphors do not so much work by recognizing similarities between things; rather "it would be more illuminating . . . to say that metaphor creates the similarity than to say it formulates some similarity antecedently existing" (Black, 1962, p. 83).

It is the generative power evident in metaphor that makes it particularly interesting to this educational scheme. The ready use of metaphor gives evidence of the human generativity that is central to learning; consequently, young children's fluency in and recognition of metaphor is something educators should find centrally important. Expansion of understanding seems often to ride on the kind of generative grasp one finds exemplified in metaphor—and that, again, follows a logic quite different from the content associations so prominent in educational textbooks. As Nelson Goodman puts it, "Far from being a mere matter of ornament, [metaphor] participates fully in the progress of knowledge: in replacing some stale 'natural' kinds with novel and illuminating categories, in contriving facts, in revising theory, and in bringing us new worlds" (1979, p. 175).

In the beginning, metaphor "governs both the growth of language and our acquisition of it" (Quine, 1979, p. 160), and "[m]etaphorical use of language differs in significant ways from literal use but is no less comprehensible, no more recondite, no less practical, and no more independent of truth and falsity than is literal use" (Goodman, 1979, p. 175). We might add to this Max Black's perhaps overly neat claim that all sciences begin in metaphor and end in algebra.

So for any "maker," whether poet or scientist, it would seem that Aristotle's observation is just: "The greatest thing by far is to have a command of metaphor" (*The Poetics*, 1459a). The generative side of metaphor is crucial to recognize because "ordinary words convey only what we know already; it is from metaphor that we can best get hold of something fresh" (Aristotle, *Rhetoric,* 1410b). The social and educational importance of developing the ca-

55

pacity for metaphor relies both on the empowerment of the individual and on the notion that "the quality of any culture is in large part the quality of the metaphorists that it creates and sustains" (Booth, 1979, p. 70).

My urge to pile up authorities on the importance of metaphor is caused by the paucity of attention currently paid to it in educational research and educational writing, compared to that given to logico-mathematical forms of thinking. Perhaps metaphor is less a simple consequence of language and more a cognitive capacity implicated in language development itself. This claim, essentially Cassirer's, is somewhat speculative; what is not speculative is the pervasiveness of metaphor in all language use, its prominence in the linguistic behavior of very young children, and its centrality to the generative functions of the human mind. Especially if one holds a constructivist view of learning—a view of the child's mind as not simply copying impressions from the world but as constantly constructing and reconstructing an individual conception of the world—then metaphor becomes a key tool in aiding flexible, productive learning.

Metaphor is sometimes represented as a kind of opposite to logic, but it is perhaps worth emphasizing that the two are far from discrete in our thinking. Cassirer makes the point that metaphor is one implication of language development, but that language carries with it the further implication of logic. As we become increasingly conscious of language—and the most potent instrument for increasing awareness of language has been writing— logic becomes more prominent. We see the network of logical relationships implicit in language and can begin to make them explicit, because by understanding them we can gain more secure pragmatic control over the world that language tries to grasp.

Metaphor develops earlier and more easily than logic, both historically and in our individual experience. Metaphor and logic represent points on a continuum of language uses; in any productive, generative thinking, we are likely to find the two at their somewhat distinct, but properly cooperative, work. Lakoff and Johnson's assertion that metaphor "unites reason and imagination" and "[m]etaphor is thus *imaginative rationality*" (Lakoff and Johnson, 1980, p. 193) may be somewhat arcane; it does, however, capture the sense in which metaphor is not some logic-less rambling but a vitally productive feature of our constructive thinking. It also echoes Wordsworth's observation of nearly two centuries earlier, that imagination "is Reason in her most exalted mood" (*The Prelude,* XIV, line 192).

These observations about metaphor, along with the findings—surprising to some—that young children's production and grasp of metaphor are commonly superior to that of older children and adults, points again to a
56 neglected conclusion about young children's thinking. In the past, children's

thinking has been assumed, even presupposed, to be unqualifiedly inferior to that of adults. All the theories of intellectual development we have—and most influentially Piaget's—take current adult forms of thinking as a kind of ideal, with children's development being measured according to the degree that it approximates the adult forms. In Piaget's case, this reflected the biological metaphor undergirding his psychological theorizing; thus, the adult was taken as the completed form and the earlier immature forms were simply stages toward it. Such theories as Piaget's are "hierarchically integrative" —that is, later stages encompass the achievements of the earlier stages. They recognize only gains in cognitive competence, not losses. In particular, they do not recognize that in recapitulating the process of Western intellectual development, children might be paying an intellectual cost that we as a civilization have paid. But so long as this cost goes unrecognized, we can't ask whether it is worthwhile or necessary.

Metaphoric capacity, in some respects, declines as children become older. Synapse development peaks in humans between nine months and two years, at which point the child has 50 percent more synapses than the adult. Metabolic activity in the brain reaches adult levels by nine or ten months and soon exceeds it, peaking around age four. Massive numbers of neurons die *in utero,* and the dying continues during the early years, leveling off at about seven years. Synapses wither from the age of two through the rest of childhood and into adolescence, when the brain's metabolic rate falls back to adult levels. Pinker infers from such observations that "[l]anguage development, then, could be on a maturational timetable, like teeth" (1994, p. 289). Given the close connection between language development and metaphor, and the importance of fluent and flexible metaphoric control for nearly all forms of thinking, it would be prudent to emphasize support for metaphoric fluency in early education.

If we could devise a developmental profile of individuals' metaphoric capacities in Western societies, it would certainly not follow the triumphantly progressive pattern of current theories of psychological development. So we might wisely recognize that Western intellectual development has involved, and involves for us individually, some losses; that in some regards young children's intelligences are less constrained and are more competent than those of their typical adult teachers.

What we need to sort out, then, if we are to get a clear grasp of Mythic understanding, is those important intellectual functions in which children are typically superior to adults. Then, we must decide what on earth we are to do about them. If, for an overly crude example, some degree of metaphoric fluency and imaginative vivacity is necessarily to be sacrificed for literacy, what should be done? Well, this is too gross and dramatic an example, of course, but it brings out precisely the kind of trade-off that I think is a part of education. We will always want to preserve as much as possible and lose as little as possible, but the current bland and comfortable belief that any skill gain comes at no cost, at no potential loss, just cannot any longer be sustained. If we fail to recognize potential or actual intellectual losses, we will certainly be able to do nothing to minimize them. And this is, I think, precisely the situation we are in, losing much more than we need because we do not recognize what is at risk.

A further constituent of Mythic understanding, then, is metaphor, and the richer and more flexible the metaphoric capacity, the greater its potential contribution to early understanding. Metaphor is one of our cognitive grappling tools; it enables us to see the world in multiple perspectives and to engage with the world flexibly. Metaphor is much more profoundly a feature of human sense-making than the largely ornamental and redundant poetic trope some have taken it to be.

"Thought is metaphoric, and proceeds by comparison [seeing one thing in terms of another], and the metaphors of language derive therefrom" (Richards, 1936, p. 940). The connection between the apparently distinct topics of binary structuring and metaphor, however, tends, like any analysis, to suggest inappropriate divisions in something that is better conceived as an organic whole.

Rhythm and Narrative

In traditional oral cultures, people know only what they can remember. Once something is forgotten by a tribe, it is generally gone forever. To combat this, oral cultures have exploited language to aid memory. They discovered, for example, that ideas or lore put into a rhythmic or rhyming form were more easily remembered. Sacred stories thus were recited to the tapping of a drum or strumming of a stringed instrument. Patterning sound helped to embed the tales in the minds of the hearers.

Rhyme and rhythm have commonly been used by young children in literate Western cultures as well. Because of writing, there is no longer the social urgency to ensure memorization of the lore of our wayward tribe; yet rhyme and rhythm are constantly exploited, and enjoyed, by children today. We find them used to make abuse more telling in rhyming nicknames, in riddles, in games, and in the treasury of the lore and language of schoolchildren collected by observant scholars of childhood, such as the Opies (1959, 1969, 1985), Paley (1981, 1984, 1990), the Knapps (1976), and Sutton-Smith (1981). The prevalence of rhyme and rhythm in TV ads, on shows like *Sesame Street,* in nursery rhymes, and in children's stories testifies to their persisting appeal.

The larger trick is attaching the rhythms inherent in languages to the more general, peripatetic pattern of everyday life—hope and despair, fear and relief, oppression, resentment, and revolt, youth and age, the rising emotions of comedy and the pity and fear of tragedy, and on and on. The elaboration of linguistic rhythms to match the patterns of our lives results in those larger forms we call narratives. "Human life has a determinate form, the form of a certain kind of story. It is not just that poems and sagas narrate what happens to men and women, but that in their narrative form poems and sagas capture a form that was already present in the lives they relate" (MacIntyre, 1981, p. 117).

Another consequence of language, then, and another constituent of Mythic understanding, and another cultural universal (cf. Brown, 1991), is the ready deployment of rhythm, especially in narrative clothing, in trying to make sense of the world and of experience. This supports the conclusion that the mind is, among other things, "a narrative concern" (Sutton-Smith, 1988, p. 22). (The mind is also a logico-mathematical concern, and an aesthetic concern, and so on.) It is well to remember Barbara Hardy's celebrated observation: "We dream in narrative, daydream in narrative, remember, anticipate, hope, despair, believe, doubt, plan, revise, criticize, construct, gossip, learn, hate and live by narrative" (1968, p. 5).

Narratives—those linguistic patterns that give body to, or "body forth," emotional rhythms—can provide a powerfully engaging access to knowledge of all kinds. Narrative was in the past generally neglected in educational research, though of late it has attracted quite a lot of attention. But there has still been relatively little ingenuity expended on working out how to turn its obvious engaging power to practical educational advantage. This would seem particularly worth exploring in a situation where so many children are functionally illiterate. Narrative is accessible to the literate and illiterate alike, to the logico-mathematically sophisticated and unsophisticated. We might wisely develop "a respect for narrative as everyone's rock-bottom capacity, but also as the universal gift, to be shared with others" (Coles, 1989, p. 30).

These observations about rhythm and narrative have some significant implications for teaching and the curriculum. They would, for example, support my earlier suggestion that a rich and dramatic world history program be introduced in the early years, and they suggest additional reasons why such a program is educationally important. The rhythmic patterns of our emotional lives find analogs in history: an action "becomes intelligible by finding its place in a narrative" (MacIntyre, 1981, p. 196). Our lives have a place in larger narratives, prominent among which is human history. "The defining characteristic of narrative is that the whole gives meaning to the parts" (Hicks, 1993, pp. 131–132). Any rhythm derives its identity not from the individual elements that make it up but from the sets of relations among them. This suggests yet another reason for abandoning the currently dominant expanding horizons curriculum in early childhood. We come to know ourselves and our environment in contexts. As St. Francis of Assisi constantly reminded his followers, it is through attending to others and in forgetting ourselves that we can come to know ourselves. And as T. S. Eliot similarly reminds us, the end "of all our exploring will be to arrive where we started / And know the place for the first time" (*Little Gidding*).

These might seem like mystical extravagances as against the common sense of assuming that children's exploration of the world must start with themselves, perhaps modifying their sense of self and the meaning of their local environment as learning proceeds. More commonly, however, the schooled exploration of the self and its locality leads to local and immediate experience being impressed on the child as the norm, as the proper, as the given, as "natural," and the different and distant and the "other" as knowable or acceptable to the degree that it conforms with the first known locality and self. Such a procedure of early education is, that is to say, a recipe for provincialism, for inflexibility, for ignorance. My point is that if meaning is established in rhythm and narrative by first grasping the whole and then making sense of its parts, we would do better to begin with general accounts of the world, its place in the cosmos, the variety of forms of life, and so on, than with the routines of the local world. Those will, after all, be learned by simple everyday experience; their meaning can be exposed by placing them in larger contexts.

Images

One curious consequence of the development of language was the discovery that words can be used to evoke images in the minds of their hearers, and that these images can have as powerful an emotional effect as the real events themselves. These mental images are unlike anything else we are familiar with. Mental images are, after all, even at their closest to quasi-pictures, quite unlike what we see with our eyes. They are also enormously varied in kind, from those quasi-pictorial mental images we think of as like real images— even to the point of "scanning" with closed eyes in search of details (Shepard, 1975)—to "images" of smells or sounds which evoke nothing like a picture in the mind.

Like rhythm, images performed in traditional oral cultures the crucial social role of aiding memorization. Myths are replete with vivid, often bizarre images that give them what we might call a powerful "literary" impact. Images achieved this end by stimulating a range of psychological effects, which continue today in quite different circumstances, long outliving the social purpose for which they were developed. Similarly, language development in children leads to the capacity to evoke mental images of what is not present and to feel about them as though they are real and present.

It is hard to discuss mental images without bringing in the imagination in general, but I do want to consider images by themselves as far as that is possible. One perhaps inevitable feature of the images we construct from words is that they carry some affective component, however small (Egan, 1992). This capacity to think and feel in terms of images has important, and somewhat neglected, implications for early education.

In professional development programs, considerable time is spent on equipping teachers with techniques for organizing content and helping them to clarify concepts. Very little time is spent discussing the power of images in communicating and teaching, and there are few techniques for systematically using images in teaching. Guided Imagery is one such. This usually involves the teacher, or a cassette-taped voice, taking the students verbally to some different time and place and describing the sights, sounds, smells, and other sensations. Guided Imagery can be a powerfully effective technique in many circumstances. What I mean by the use of images here, however, is on a much smaller scale. It does not require relatively elaborate preparations or set-piece performances. Rather it requires the teacher to be more consistently conscious of the vivid images that are a part of every topic and to draw on them consistently in vivifying knowledge and concepts.

When teaching about the earthworm, for example, the instructor can augment the facts about its senses and structure by evoking for students images of what it would be like to slither and push through the soil, hesitantly exploring in one direction then another, looking for easier passages, contracting and expanding our sequence of muscles segment by segment, and sensing moisture, scents, grubs, or whatever. As we learn about the anatomy of earthworms we can also feel something of their existence by means of images that evoke analogs of their senses; it is not so much a matter of seeing the earthworm in terms of our senses as performing the imaginative act of recognizing earthwormness in ourselves. The task is imaginatively to incorporate the world rather than simply learn facts about something "out there." Similarly, when teaching about flowers, one could imagine emerging from the cold ground, pushing toward the light, bursting with a kind of ecstasy in the warmer air, turning with passion toward the sun, feeling the rush of sap, 61 then experiencing the horror of the returning cold, and shriveling back underground. Constantly bringing to mind affective images helps to make the content memorable and, relatedly, meaningful in terms with which children are familiar.

Images allow us in a limited but very real sense to extend our grasp on the world. Affective images do not need to reduce the content being taught; rather, they provide a means for the child to "incorporate" it. This helps them to see that mathematics, history, and science are not made up of alien knowledge, something out there apart from them. By imaginatively grasping knowledge, children make it, *reciprocally*, become a part of them. So children discover that they are mathematical, historical, and scientific beings.

Mythic understanding, then, is significantly more imagistic than is common for forms of understanding built on literacy. Because of the affective charge associated with images, they are in some ways more vivid and more closely tied in with emotions. When teaching young children, we should bear in mind their potentially rich imagistic and emotional mental activity, and we should design programs that will support and develop those capacities.

Stories and Their Meaning

The discovery that certain kinds of narratives could generate quite precise emotional states in their hearers was one of the most momentous in the development of human cultures. They had two crucial powers. First, they were the most effective aid to memorization; important lore coded within a story structure thus became much easier to preserve. Second, they could orient hearers' emotions to their contents. If the contents specified appropriate social status for various groups of people, for various families, and specified proper status, economic relationships, and behavior within and among kinship groups, they could serve as a social charter for the tribe. (Malinowski [1954] has emphasized this "social charter" function of myths, somewhat at the expense of other features.)

While the memorization function of stories is much less significant in modern literate cultures, and their "social charter" role is similarly diminished, the psychological effects of stories ensure that they continue to play a prominent role in our lives. Perhaps it is better to say that the memorization and charter functions have been transformed and added to rather than diminished. We continue to tell children "cautionary tales" in order to shape their behavior; TV and movie stories often combine the attempt to entertain with messages of self-improvement or social tolerance, or the opposites.

Family stories we shape and retell serve to establish and reinforce a sense of identity (Rosenbluth, 1990).

So, again, the development of language in traditional oral cultures and in the intellectual lives of young children leads to the discovery of the varied uses and delights of the story form. Like the sentence writ large, the story is a particular linguistic unit that conveys a particular kind of meaning (Egan, 1978b). What kind? And what is a story, anyway?

If you are told that Dick shot Tom, you will have no particular or precise emotional response (unless, perhaps, your name is Tom). You might feel regret that anyone would shoot anyone else, but if you know this is an event in a story you do not, crucially, know whether to feel glad or sorry that Dick shot Tom. If further events and characters are added such that you learn that Dick was a handsome, well-groomed young man who loved his grandmother, and that Tom was generally scruffy, picked his nose in public, and used foul language in front of children, you may begin to feel glad that Dick shot Tom—given the conventions of fiction today. But if the story is elaborated further, telling you that Dick and his grandmother were leaders of a drug-pushing operation who specialized in selling to children outside schools, and that his love for his grandmother was clearly of a kind that indicates an unspeakable relationship, and that, despite his unprepossessing exterior, Tom has a heart of gold and is taking terrible risks to stop the grandmother's and her grandson's nefarious operation . . . well, you will properly begin to feel sorry that Dick shot Tom.

The good storyteller plays with our affective responses to events, and we often take a peculiar delight in the unexpected twists and turns of the plot. We know we have reached the end of a story, however, when we know how to feel about the events that make it up. (Sometimes, through incompetence or experiment, a story ends in such a way that we are left uncertain how to feel, and our typical response is one of disappointment and dissatisfaction.) There are no neat logical formulas for determining how to construct a story; no program exists that would allow a computer to distinguish between a successful story and another kind of narrative made up of characters and events. The refined instrument we have is our emotional response and the recognition of that peculiar satisfaction that tells us a story has ended, whether as comedy or tragedy. We may feel glad or sorry, elated or distressed, but we know when the story has ended.

The crucial feature of stories is that they end (Kermode, 1966). Life and history are inconvenient in this regard. Because we are "in the middest" of them we cannot ascribe determinate meaning to them. If we knew that the world would end tomorrow and that we would all die in a catastrophic environmental disaster about which we had had many warnings, our concept of human history to date would be significantly different from what it would be if we knew that human life and civilizations would go on for billions of years of moral and social improvement and benign technological developments that would greatly lengthen and increase the enjoyment of human life. We constantly revise our conception of the significance of events in our own lives in light of new events. These different conceptions of our lives and history are not simply logical calculations; they are perhaps better seen as affective evaluations that ascribe affective meaning to events.

Mythic understanding, then, finds a prominent place for the story. Nor is the structure of the story confined to fictional events and characters. Once we grasp the conventions of the story and the kind of affective meaning it can confer on events, we seem to become prodigal in applying it to events in the world, in history, and in our own lives. We try to give to our lives, and to history, the kind of determinate meaning stories provide, in order to make more secure sense of them, if only provisionally. We "storify" events, whether fictional, real, or mixed as in daydreams, in order to understand them in a particular way. Mythic understanding involves considerable story-shaping of experience so that events, facts, ideas, and people may be made affectively meaningful.

We tend to see the curriculum as a body of knowledge—knowledge about science, history, mathematics, geography, and so on—and we tend to see teaching as the skilled communication of this knowledge to children. If we begin instead to think of young children deploying Mythic understanding flexibly in getting an initial grasp on the world and on experience, and we recognize story-structuring as a prominent feature of Mythic understanding, then we are led to reconceive the curriculum as the set of great stories we have to tell children, and reconceive (recognize?) elementary school teachers as the storytellers of our culture (a recognition already in place in Waldorf schools).

This move need in no way diminish the content of the curriculum, but it allows us to see it somewhat differently. Instead of seeing math and science, for example, in terms of particular skills, knowledge, and manipulations, we would see them as among the greatest of human adventures, full of drama, hopes and disappointments, discoveries and inventions, and of people in whose lives mathematics and science played important roles. By seeing math and science not as disembodied pieces of knowledge or skill but as the inventions and discoveries of particular people, as products of their hopes and disappointments, their struggles and problems, we can begin to re-embed those subjects again in their proper human contexts, in which they initially had affective, as well as purely cognitive, meaning. And that affective meaning can be the route to the more purely cognitive meaning that tends to be the main concern in most classrooms today.

One kind of story not much mentioned in education is the joke. No doubt humor has a Somatic genesis, but language alone allows one creature to tell another a joke. Jokes are culturally universal, and laughing at jokes is a behavior specific to the human species. There is, to some minds anyway, something vaguely funny about language at the most basic level; the act of interpreting another's meaning from his or her words allows the liberty always to misinterpret them consciously or unconsciously. Pinker observes that "[m]etaphor and humor are useful ways to summarize the two mental performances that go into understanding a sentence" (1994, p. 230).

The terrible danger in writing about humor is to go drearily on and on about it. Here I want only to observe that humor is a universal consequence of language development and that its development seems crucial for adequate understanding. In this theory of education it will have an important role, developing with each kind of understanding and taking a complex, central role in Ironic understanding.

CONCLUSION

Clearly the development of language led, and leads, to forms of oral discourse that have characteristics other than the set I have outlined here. Whether living in traditional oral cultures or modern cities, we develop repertoires of discourse forms that are shaped by the particular actions and settings of the communities to which we belong. We learn appropriate forms of discourse for greetings and farewells, for formal meals, for talking with parents, for chatting with friends on the way to a monkey hunt or a squash game, for gossiping during routine work, for sharing intimacies with close friends, for speaking in public, and so on: "Our repertoire of oral . . . speech genres is rich" (Bakhtin, 1986, p. 78). Many of these genres do not involve much in the way of binary opposites or story-structuring.

Children learn to adapt their uses of language to the demands of particular settings and social activities. Because their language environments and activities—especially in middle-class families—are often profoundly and pervasively influenced by literacy and its intellectual consequences, the discourse forms children pick up and use to think with are also influenced by literacy. So the neatness of a scheme that claims that children today recapitulate forms of oral-language use common in traditional oral cultures is, at best, somewhat muddied. The cultural and institutional settings in which children learn language today are profoundly different from those in which language was initially developed in our species.

I mention these potential objections to some of my general claims to indicate at least that I am aware of them. I need to show that my scheme is not at odds with the findings of, say, Basil Bernstein (1975) nor, perhaps more pertinently, with those of Shirley Brice Heath (1983). I will discuss these complex objections later, but should at least hint here at the direction of my responses. First I selected the particular set of characteristics, or genres, above for the same reasons that those characteristics are universally selected—privileged—in oral cultures around the world and throughout history: for purposes of initiation of the young into the forms of understanding that define membership of the social group. They are the best tools that have been discovered for the job. For the tasks of education, all forms of discourse are not equal.

The second objection is more problematic, and I find it hard even to hint at my twofold response without raising a troubled host of issues. The objection is that children today grow into and absorb discourse forms that are influenced by literacy, so they cannot simply recapitulate "orality."

This objection is likely to occur most keenly to those who are critical of psychological research that has focused on individuals' development, thinking skills, or cognitive processes largely in isolation from cultural contexts. Such critics recognize that one cannot build an image of the human mind from the products of this kind of research because the human mind is not an isolated phenomenon; it is not sharply divided from its cultural context the way the physical brain is divided from the outside world by the skull. The nature of individuals' minds is shaped by and coalesces with its cultural contexts, and so it can be adequately explored only by forms of research that incorporate cultural context in what is being studied.

These insights, which seem to me undeniable, have been expressed most emphatically by critics whose ideological commitments sharpened their sensitivity to the shaping role of society in the formation of individuals' minds. Their corrective to an excessive focus on the individual apart from cultural contexts is potentially fruitful, especially for psychology—as Wertsch (1991) argues. I consider this ideological dimension relevant because it could lead us to replace one excess with another. It would be a pity to replace the isolating focus on individuals with its binary opposite, ascribing total responsibility for the formation of the mind to cultural context. We might be better with an interactionist mediation.

I can now indicate the two responses I will make to this second objection. First, the development of language is not to be understood simply in terms of the discourse of the community. The mind is also an active organ; it selects from the environment those elements that can best serve, to use Piaget's term, as "aliments" to its development. A three-year-old in a highly academic environment, in which finely nuanced irony in sophisticated grammatical structures is the normal form of discourse, will not simply adopt this discourse form. Of course the child's linguistic development will be influenced in particular ways, but the child will not be shaped into a grammatically sophisticated speaker employing subtle irony. There are constraints on the shaping role of the culture, constraints determined by the program governing our acquisition of language. That program selects certain features of the linguistic environment preferentially, attending intently to some features but remaining largely uninfluenced by others. The fact that the child's linguistic environment is heavily influenced by literate forms of discourse does not mean that these will have an equal impact on the child, or be selected equally by the child, as those "oral" features I have "privileged" above.

The second response concerns the pervasiveness of "literate" discourse forms. Such forms tend to be tied to particular activities in particular circumstances; when those conditions do not hold, literate discourse forms relax their hold on the mind, too. Even while you drive your enormously sophisticated automobile through a modern city, your thinking about your life, your daydreaming while sitting at traffic lights, is imagistic, story-shaped, and shifts along metaphoric connections. People live in highly literate environments, and children engage media that are permeated by literate forms of discourse, but that does not mean they wholly pick up literate forms of discourse.

Ours is, for much of the time, a peculiar *languaged* understanding of the world. "A defining property of higher mental functioning, one which is unique to humans, is the fact that it is mediated by tools and by sign systems such as a natural language" (Wertsch, 1991, p. 21). While we are, willy nilly, committed to languaged understanding, it seems to involve some loss of the instinctive, vivid, intimately participatory involvement with the natural world that characterizes our fellow mammals' understanding. The educational task is to make languaged understanding as rich as possible while losing as little as possible of the "oneness with nature" that is our birthright as animals.

Each of us is born with a unique consciousness, with a unique "take" on reality. Language is a conventional, shared, limiting shaper of our consciousness. The first educational task, then, is to ensure that children learn fluid and flexible language use so that it can become a means of expressing their unique perceptions and consciousness. The associated first educational danger is that the conventionalizing influence of language can become predominant, restricting and suppressing the uniqueness of perceptions and consciousness. The repertoire of discourse forms available to the child is always both enabling and constraining at the same time.

The second educational task is to ensure not only that language serve as a tool for expressing one's perceptions and consciousness, or for communicating them, or for reflecting reality, but that the child recognize that language has a distinct, dynamic life of its own. It is not only a medium into which or through which our experience can be expressed, but is itself an extension and enlargement of our experience. It may have begun as a utilitarian tool, but it has far-reaching potential for enlarging our understanding and aesthetic delight.

The third educational task is to teach children the varied conventions for using language successfully as a means of communication with other isolated, unique consciousnesses similar to but not the same as their own. Learning language, like literacy, rests on a fine educational balance, in which the discipline required to learn the conventions of language needs to be weighed against the freedom to play with and explore the limits of these conventions. The sensitive teacher recognizes that children can learn the conventions and rules best if they are encouraged to play with them and recognize their contingency.

"The earliest education is most important," Rousseau argued (1911, p. 5), echoing Plato's conclusion that "The beginning, as you know, is always the most important part" (Cornford, 1941, p. 68). Every major educational thinker has emphasized the crucial importance of the early years of education. And yet, if we consider our schools today, it is hard to believe that the predominantly provincial trivia of the curriculum and the worksheet-oriented or "hands-on" activities of common teaching practice are adequate responses to the importance of the task.

My scheme of introductory education offers as an alternative a recapitulation of the human construction of language and the kind of understanding of the world and experience that stimulation and development of language capacities entail. Some level of language development occurs "naturally" by children being brought up in a language-using environment, but fuller development of language and its associated intellectual capacities requires deliberate teaching. The most important, dramatic, and vivid stories of our world and of human experience can provide an appropriate curriculum for the earliest years.

The first educational implication of Mythic understanding, then, is that young children be encouraged to become fluent and effective users of varied language; this is accomplished through evoking, stimulating, and developing the capacities for forming binary oppositions and mediating them, for abstract thinking, metaphor, rhythm and narrative, images, stories and affective meaning, humor, and no doubt a number of other capacities language development implies. This is not to deny that young children also can attain some grasp on the world aesthetically, by quantification, logically, concretely, by hands-on experience, and so on.

These capacities might be seen as organs of the imagination. The relationship between the imaginative worlds we spin out of the possibilities created by language and reality is, of course, endlessly complex. Huizinga has called our capacity to imagine in childhood as creating "a second, poetic world alongside the world of nature" (1949, p. 23). This poetic world— emotional, imaginative, metaphoric—is the foundation of our cultural life, as a species and individually. Logico-mathematical forms of thinking, or rationality, do not properly displace the poetic world, but rather grow out of and develop along with it; *they* are among *its* implications. The language and lore, fantasy narratives, metaphoric play, and games of young children constitute an oral culture that persists from generation to generation, sustained by the techniques of the poetic imagination and the psychological capacities evoked, stimulated, and developed initially by the need to remember and increasingly by the satisfaction the enlargement of our power over language gives us.

The characteristics of Mythic understanding describe some of the major tools of the poet. It seems to me not fanciful to observe that young children's main tools for grasping the world and expressing their sense of it are poetic. This conclusion echoes Vico's conclusion of his study of myths: the main insight on which he based *The New Science* (1744) was the realization that myth was a product not of some intellectual incapacity, rational confusion, or disease of language but of the mind working in its poetic mode. Myth makers, he declared, were "poets who spoke in poetic characters. This discovery . . . has cost us the persistent research of almost all our literary life because with our civilized natures we cannot at all imagine and can understand only by great toil the poetic nature of these first [people]" (Vico, 1970, p. 5). Much the same, I think, might be said about our own childhood understanding; its poetic nature has made it difficult to understand by those who approach it looking only for the origins of rational or logico-mathematical thinking.

There are, of course, dangers of misunderstanding what we mean when we call young children's thinking "poetic." The word conjures up too general and, therefore, absurd comparisons with the more celebrated modern poets, and it furthers for some a tendency to sentimentalize childhood. If we restrict what is meant by "poet" here to those capacities discussed above, we   69 can avoid the overgeneralization and recognize the sense in which the term is appropriate.

The sentimentalizing is another matter. The notion of the child as poetic clearly suggests to some that their expressions should therefore be valued as we value those of adult poets, painters, and musicians. It connects, too, with the sentimental notion of the child as innocent, unsullied. I recall from my distant Catholic past the first Holy Communion ceremony of my school class. Ancient Father O'Brien, perhaps forty-five I now calculate, talked over the heads of us children to the adults behind us in the church. He spoke very movingly, as I recall, of the innocence of childhood. I remember very clearly thinking then that Father O'Brien was so ancient that he had clearly forgotten what it was like to be a child. Though, I reflected, perhaps, having ended up a priest, he actually had been an innocent child, of a kind entirely unlike me and my angelic-looking friends seated in the pews. It seemed obvious then that Father O'Brien was much more innocent than we, and that our varying degrees of villainy and deviousness changed over the years only in the outlets through which they were expressed.

chapter 3

Romantic Understanding

INTRODUCTION

If you tell a typical five-year-old the story of Cinderella, you are not likely to be asked "What means of locomotion does the Fairy Godmother use?" nor to be quizzed about where she is and what she does when she isn't active in the story. But if you tell a typical ten-year-old the equally fantastic story of Superman, you will need to explain his supernatural powers by reference to his birth on the planet Krypton and to the different molecular structure of our sun from that of his home star, and so on. (Alas, I've forgotten the details, and, lamentably, none of the reference books I have at hand is able to help.) For the younger audience, magic is entirely unobjectionable so long as it moves the story along. Peter Rabbit's world does not make the kind of accommodations with reality that are necessary for the rabbits Hazel and Bigwig in the world of Richard Adams's *Watership Down;* Hazel could not bring Bigwig a nice cup of chamomile tea, for instance—his paws wouldn't be able to hold it.

What happens between age five and ten that causes this difference? Common sense suggests simply that accumulated experience informs the child's understanding of which regularities tend to be more reliable. It takes some time to grasp the conditions of reality that exclude Jack Frost and the Tooth Fairy but include computer programmers and monks, that exclude magic but include its anxious relation, fiction. Children typically cease to believe in Santa Claus, ghosts, and other denizens of magicland during these years; they begin the trek out of Eden to adults' more prosaic world. This gradual accommodation with prosaic reality cannot be a sufficient explanation, because the accommodation itself needs to be explained. In some cultures this transition from a world in which fantasy and magic perform explanatory work does not take place in anything like the form that is common in the West. And one can easily overestimate how common this transition is in the West. A cursory glance over the widely selling tabloids available at supermarket checkouts suggests caution in making strong claims about how participants in literate Western societies make some marked transition from the ready acceptance of fantasy and magic in understanding the world.

Another thing that commonly happens during these years in school, that may help explain the change in stories, is that we teach children to move from perceptually based discriminations like "hot" and "cold" to abstract means of referring to the world. In the case of temperature, we teach them to connect it with the arbitrary numbers of the thermometer. Once students understand thermometric terms, they can deal easily with temperatures beyond their direct experience. So they will understand that one million degrees celsius is different from one million and twenty degrees as ten degrees celsius is different from thirty degrees. But they will still, in everyday life, refer to ten degrees as "cool" or "cold" and thirty degrees as "warm" or "hot." It is fairly useless to describe the center of the sun as "hot," but "hot" can be a useful term to shout upstairs to one's son or daughter about the temperature of the bath.

So learning the abstract, "objective" ways of referring to the world does not *displace* the perception-based ways. One could shout upstairs that the bath is "about seventy-four degrees Celsius" or that it is "hot." The two live on in our minds together. The trick is to learn both systems fluently and be able to apply the appropriate one in the relevant context. Easier said than done, and easier with temperature than with morality.

Learning abstract systems of reference to things like temperature, space, and movement, relies largely on grasping numbers and their relationships. The related symbol system for abstracting language from the body is writing. Oral-language use is a bodily activity, involving "the whole person"; writing is language transported outside the body, involving the eye and mind.

Schools' failures to inculcate fluent ease in dealing with these "disembodied," "decontextualized," "literate" techniques is a source of much noisy dissatisfaction. To the schools' paymasters, an unacceptably small proportion of students develops adequate literacy skills. To educational thinkers, an even greater frustration is the fact that even those students who "test out" as successes commonly exemplify only the most superficial mastery of the techniques of literacy.

Touted as the transformer of thought, the golden road to the accumulated treasure store of indirect experience, the great enhancer of understanding of ourselves and of our world, the privileged access to reality, literacy seems to do little for most people beyond the pragmatic functions for which it is required in their jobs or for reading instructions or the newspaper. Such, anyway, is the representation of many frustrated educators. Providing the means isn't even half the battle, they say; most people apparently need to be goaded, cajoled, pushed, seduced, compelled toward their culture's intellectual delights. Plato's grim solution was that fifty-year curriculum designed to compel literate minds to develop their full potential as thinkers, as he saw it. Rousseau admonished dull pedagogues who measured educational success in terms of crude skill mastery: "The apparent ease with which children learn is their ruin. You fail to see that this very facility proves that they are not learning. Their shining, polished brain reflects, as in a mirror, the things you show them, but nothing sinks in" (Rousseau, 1911, p. 71). More recently, research with honors students in college-level physics courses has shown that they are commonly unable to solve the most basic physics problems if posed in a context even slightly different from the ones in which they were formally instructed. Typically, they display exactly the same confusions and misconceptions that one encounters in primary school children (Gardner, 1991, ch. 1). Such students are very successful at learning particular skills and knowledge, but skills and knowledge fail to transform their understanding of physics. Gardner shows that similar misconceptions, confusions, and stereotypes, formed early in life, remain in most students stubbornly resistant to education. "Successful" students, as measured by standardized tests, when moved even slightly from the supporting formal contexts of their studies, respond to problems with no greater understanding than is shown by "the unschooled mind" of the young child.

Education, I am proposing, can best be understood as a process in which the individual recapitulates the kinds of understanding developed in the culture's history. Such a view implies that we can learn something of practical value for education by studying how this transition was made historically, and we might also understand why the transition is so problematic for many and only superficially attained by many more. If we find that in our cultural history the transition from "prescholastic" to "scholastic" ways of knowing (to use Gardner's terms) has been problematic, we may be less surprised at students' difficulties, and by analyzing how the historical process of development occurred we may be able to devise a curriculum and methods

73

of teaching better suited than current forms to supporting that development in students today.

The development of understanding we want to encourage in students has to do with . . . well, look at the words for it in this brief introduction—"schooled," "theoretic," "disembodied," "decontextualized," "abstract," "formal," "disciplined," "objective" thinking. The shift from learning the first symbol system of oral language to the second symbol systems of written numbers and the alphabet occurred gradually and in distinguishable stages in our cultural history, and it can best be recapitulated in similar distinct stages in education today. The first major step leads to what I call Romantic understanding.

REASON, REALITY, AND WRITING

If you, noble reader of this text, were faced by what is now a celebrated problem once posed by A. R. Luria to illiterate villagers in central Asia, you would have no difficulty giving the right answer: "In the far north, where there is snow, all bears are white. Novaya Zemlya is in the far north. What color are the bears there?" If you learn that due to a curiosity of evolution on the seventh planet orbiting Sirius, all the flowers are blue and, further, that one of the planets' more spectacular flowers, called by its Irish discoverer the Flowering Shamrock, grows more than fifty feet in height, and should you also be asked what color the Flowering Shamrock is, you will have no difficulty answering correctly that it is blue. If you are told that all the cats in a room are black, and that one of the cats is called Snowy, and you are asked what color Snowy is, you will be easily able to deduce that Snowy is black, and deduce also that its namer probably has a quirky sense of humor.

If, being patient of endless daft questions, you are further asked what smaller word can be abstracted from the word "window," you would easily answer "win." If you were asked to say what word is formed when you delete the hard "c" sound from "cat," or when the "l" is removed from "flat," you would have no difficulty giving the correct answers. You could also easily identify the two smaller words that can be derived from such compound words as "stopwatch" or "lighthouse" or "daytime."

You may be fairly unimpressed by your prowess in dealing successfully with these problems. But answering such questions prove difficult if not impossible for illiterate people in traditional oral cultures. The syllogisms in the first paragraph can be successfully answered if one attends to their internal logic. They are examples of a language/logic game at which we Western

74

high-literates become very efficient. The villagers to whom Luria posed the first problem were no doubt no less intelligent than you or I, but their responses suggested a total unfamiliarity with this conditional, "decontextualized" use of language. They would, to be polite, answer that they had never been to Novaya Zemlya, and that if Luria wanted to know about bears there, he should either go himself or ask people who had been there. The second problem is easy if one ignores all the elaboration and invention about Flowering Shamrocks and concentrates on the logic of the syllogism. We high literates are unlikely to be thrown by the black cat's name being Snowy because we follow the logic of the syllogism rather than refer outside the text to our experience and pragmatic expectations (cf. Cole and Scribner, 1974; Luria, 1976, 1979; Tulviste, 1979).

These tasks cannot be managed easily or at all by people who cannot read alphabetic script; this includes young English-speaking prereaders, people who can read but whose orthography is not alphabetic, and adult illiterates (Bertelson and DeGelder, 1988; Scholes and Willis, 1991). As Olson has convincingly argued, "Writing systems create the categories in terms of which we become conscious of speech" (1993, p. 15). That is, the particular graphic script people use serves as a model for how they think about language. The Greek alphabet, from which all alphabetic systems are derived, has particular characteristics for making us conscious of our language, or, rather, for determining the kind of consciousness of language that we develop. The alphabet, for example, ensures that we hear our speech as made up of elements that can be broken into phonemic segments. So we can perform the tasks I have outlined easily. Chinese readers of traditional characters do not detect such phonemic segments, but Chinese readers of the alphabetic Pinyin script do (Read et al., 1986).

Eric Havelock writes about "the superior technology of the Greek alphabet," which remains the "sole instrument of full literacy to the present day" (1991, pp. 24 and 26). That technology was superior to other scripts and to oral modes of communication, in Havelock's account, because it led to a conceptual revolution in ancient Greece in which "a reflexive syntax of definition, description, and analysis" was exploited by Plato, Aristotle, and other ancient Greeks and all their alphabetic successors. They generated the philosophic, scientific, historical, descriptive, legal, and moral forms of discourse that make up what we call the modern mind.

As my interest is the transition to "the modern mind" and the kinds of understanding that constitute it, and as literacy seems so tangled up in that transition, whether as cause, catalyst, or result, then some attention to the recent research on literacy is appropriate. In particular I am interested, as a result of the clue that the changing character of children's stories seems to give, in the development of a conception of reality, access to which seems to become problematic for literates.

Within a relatively short time in ancient Greece, the peculiar cultural development that seems tied up with what we mean by education was given a decisive kick forward. At the end of the archaic period, the Greek city-states enjoyed and suffered a cultural and social life not markedly dissimilar from that of their neighbors. Their material culture was not obviously different, their heroic ballads of war were of a common genre, and their myths' vividness and power did not clearly mark theirs from others'. (Perhaps I should not be so cavalier with such assertions, as much scholarly activity has been spent on detecting the seeds of the developments to come in distinctive features of archaic Greek life, and particularly in their political and social institutions [Lloyd, 1988, 1990; Vernant, 1982].) But accelerating during the sixth century and roaring through the fifth comes something culturally dramatic that now, for good and ill, influences nearly all human experience.

Much ingenious attention has focused on the causal or catalytic role of alphabetic literacy. While many of their neighbors were using writing systems to mark pots of grain, wine, and olives, list kings and priests, and celebrate in stylized form victories over traditional enemies, the Greeks began to exploit their writing system in ways none of its inventors could have imagined. Writing, after all, was simply a device for helping the memory with quantities or with activities that were becoming too numerous or too complicated. Many tools not only permit us to perform more efficiently the task for which they were designed but also open up new possibilities. In this regard there has been no tool within the historical period like alphabetic writing. Among much else, it opened up what we call the historical period. Fluent literacy is not simply a matter of thinking and then writing the product of one's thoughts; the writing, rather, becomes a part of the process of thinking. Extended discursive writing is not an external copy of a kind of thinking that goes on in the head; it represents a distinctive kind of literate thinking.

Over the past thirty years, a number of scholars have argued with significant success that the fifth-century developments that had in the earlier part of this century been romantically referred to as the "Greek miracle"—giving birth to democracy, logic, philosophy, history, drama, reflective introspection, and so on so suddenly—were explainable in large part as an implication of the development and spread of alphabetic literacy (Havelock, 1963, 1982, 1986; Goody, 1977, 1987; Goody and Watt, 1963; Olson, 1977; Ong, 1977, 1982). Plausible accounts of how the generation, elaboration, accumulation, and interpretation of texts led to these intellectual developments have been given by the scholars mentioned above, and by others, during the 1980s and 1990s (see Olson and Torrance, 1991 for an excellent description of this energetic and engaging area of study). The developments were not simply in the new kinds of texts being produced in ancient Greece, such as Herodotus's *Histories,* but were somehow in the kind of thinking that went into writing and reading such texts, or listening to such texts being read or performed.

If the development of alphabetic literacy in ancient Greece caused these new kinds of thinking, then perhaps simply being schooled into literacy to-day causes the kind of thinking we call "modern." In one important regard, this looked like a liberating conclusion. What had been taken as the greater practical efficiency of modern Western thinking over that of traditional oral cultures could now be seen as the result not of some assumed genetic superiority in Europeans' brains but of the technological advantage accruing from the trick of alphabetic literacy. Scholars thus could study differences between "modern" and "traditional" thinking without becoming entangled in racist or ethnocentric assumptions or conclusions.

There are two problems with this. First, past ethnocentricity, which was framed in terms of Caucasian genetic superiority, is now disguised in the seemingly neutral and contingent technological trick of literacy. However scholars try to suggest that orality and literacy involve alternative technologies, each with its distinct advantages and disadvantages, invariably the superiority of literacy is asserted by associating illiteracy with "poverty, malnutrition, lack of education and health care" (Pattanayak, 1991, p. 105). These "oppressive theorizations" are much harder to combat and dislodge than the simple racism of the past because superiority/inferiority associated with literacy seems so obvious and becomes a "problem" amenable to solution by programs of universal literacy. Thus, in order to make their lives and forms of thinking more satisfactory, the world's 800 million illiterates are seen to be in need of the Greek cure.

The second problem is that inducing literacy does not always stimulate the cognitive changes or social transformations that have been linked to its development in ancient Greece and in medieval Europe (Stock, 1983). Scribner and Cole's report of their studies among the Vai people of Liberia suggested that they could detect no "general cognitive consequences of literacy among the Vai" (1981, p. 158; but see their co-authored chapter and the discussion in Goody, 1987, chs. 9 and 10). Further, the remarkable story of the rapid spread of a syllabic script invented by a Methodist minister, James Evans, for the Cree language in Canada in or around 1840, is suggestive of the limited effects literacy can have. The script spread far and fast among the Cree, quickly outpacing missionaries' activities, and virtually universal literacy was achieved within a decade, despite the Cree's lack of paper, pens, and formal schooling. The Cree seem to have used the script almost exclusively for writing notes and letters, keeping journals and records, and other "private" activities. The script seems to have served as a social convenience and gives no evidence of having stimulated any of the dramatic cultural changes or cognitive effects associated with the Greek alphabet. Similarly, Narasimhan has pointed out that in India, "in spite of the availability of a textual tradition involved in active textual literacy practices, the kinds of scientific and technological developments at the social level, and cognitive developments at the individual level, that a textual tradition is supposed to result in did not materialize" (1991, p. 179). Despite India's long literate tradition, a systematic distinction between myth and history or between supernatural explanations and rational ones was not developed. Being literate clearly does not compel the mind to such distinctions. Muddying further the implications of earlier claims about the causal relationship between literacy and cognitive activity, Feldman has argued that certain forms of thinking considered distinctively modern, Western, and a product of literacy can be found in a number of traditional oral societies. She shows that particular artful uses of language, distinct from everyday discourse, in Ilongot oratory, Wana Kiyori, and Indian mythic poems invite reflection and interpretation. She argues that "it is genre rather than writing that permits the separation of text and interpretation, and the development of reflectivity" (1988, p. 210).

These and other inconveniences compel one to observe that "what is cognitively innovative about literacy is not universally exploited by all cultures with writing" (Kittay, 1991, p. 169). Educators make a related observation, of course: what is cognitively innovative about literacy is not universally exploited by all children who pass as literate in our schools. They will generally manage the syllogisms and phoneme deletion tasks above, but disciplined thinking of the kind some ancient Greeks took to such a refined pitch seems much less commonly recapitulated.

We might divide the debate about the cultural and cognitive consequences of literacy into two parts: what *must* happen as a result of developing literacy and what *can* happen. It seems that nothing much *must* happen either culturally or cognitively, though there remain doughty arguments that *some* cognitive consequences follow from externalizing a part of one's bodily activity—language—and making it visible in graphic form. But at a social level, literacy seems to be absorbable into a variety of patterns of living and thinking, playing a minor role of casual utility (Heath, 1983; Street, 1984). What *can* happen is all that "Greek miracle" stuff—providing fluent access to the treasure house of stored experience, ideas, and dreams and fulfilling the promise of making our lives more abundant. We must recognize, however, that with this potential abundance comes a twofold cost: first, the time and discipline—moral as well as intellectual—required properly to access and benefit from the experience stored in writing; second, the losses in forms of thinking that consequently become less clear, less accessible, less life-enhancing.

How can we optimize the gifts reserved for the literate while minimizing the losses? What is the first big step into a new kind of understanding (which I call Romantic) that literacy can help us to take? One of the key features of this understanding is the generation of a new consciousness of something we call reality, access to which becomes problematic but can be achieved by developing what we call reason. These terms and our sense of them owe much to Plato and Aristotle, but we can trace steps in the development of this understanding during the centuries preceding their systematizing of it. It is possible to see a clear recapitulation of the process as children develop literacy today. As Bruner puts it, "literacy comes into its full powers as a goad to the redefinition of reality" (1988, p. 205).

Early prose-writing Greeks such as Thales, Anaximander, and Anaximines, all of whom lived in Miletus, began to treat the natural world as an object for detached, systematic investigation (*historia*) and aimed to provide a comprehensive, accurate view of how things really are (*theoria*). Our notion of "myth" as something false is inherited from these early literate Greeks who dismissed the sacred stories of their predecessors as useless: "the stories of the Greeks are many and in my opinion ridiculous" wrote Hecataeus, another Miletan. The recent scholars of Greek alphabetic literacy, cited earlier, have given plausible models of how the ability to gather and inspect texts invited and supported, if not compelled, this new kind of inquiry that aimed to uncover what is real and true. The nature of things, which had been largely unproblematic to minds governed by mythic thinking, became an object of wonder, exploration and of inquiries that now seem ceaseless. Near its literate beginning was the discovery that "reality is no longer something that is simply given. The meaningful no longer impresses itself as incontrovertible fact, and appearances have ceased to reveal their significance directly to man. All this really means that myth has come to an end" (Snell, 1960, p. 111).

Well, perhaps Snell overstates things. Thales, at the fountainhead of this new rational tradition, concluded that everything was made of water. Why would anyone reach such an odd conclusion? Indeed, why would anyone conclude that everything is made of some ultimate material in the first place? We can give fairly clear answers to these two questions, thanks to F. M. Cornford. He showed that to understand the odd claims of Thales, and of Anaximander and Anaximines, we have to be familiar with the *a priori* forms of thought, the "scheme of unchallenged and unsuspecting presuppositions" 79

(1907, p. viii) that those Miletans worked with. Cornford (1912) shows that the kind of questions that guided their rational inquiries were questions about the nature of things that had shaped the earlier answers given in myths. That is, what we see in these early Greek inquirers is a rational form of inquiry, but one still profoundly influenced by mythic elements.

The sharpness of the break from mythic to rational inquiries in ancient Greece is somewhat illusory, then, as Cornford showed earlier in this century and others have elaborated since (e.g., Dodds, 1951; Lloyd, 1990). What was dramatic was the eradication of magic and gods as explanatory devices and the new focus on an autonomous reality; what has tended to receive much less attention is the persistence of myth at a "subterranean," or, at what we might today call a structural, level. So, for example, the authors of the Hippocratic canon concluded that health was crucially bound up with achieving a balance between the four humors. Why? Because this represented a "rational," real-world theory reflecting nevertheless the Greeks' cosmogonic myth, in which the world was divided between Zeus, Hades, and Neptune while the earth was common to all (Iliad, XV, 187ff.); this view yielded or reflected the divisions among sky, underworld, sea, and earth that had to be preserved in balance for harmony to prevail (Cochrane, 1929; Cornford, 1912). The precise observations of the Hippocratics, that is, still carried a considerable burden from the proto-speculation of myth. Even the austere historical writing of Thucydides can be seen to rest on "unsuspected presuppositions" derived from myths (Cornford, 1907; Egan, 1978a).

Whatever may remain debatable about Thomas Kuhn's theory of scientific revolutions (1962), he has shown convincingly how each "paradigm generation" tends to rewrite and reinterpret the conclusions of its predecessors as though their concerns, questions, methods, and viewpoints were similar. Rational scholars have tended to emphasize the rational elements in ancient Greek inquiries at the expense of the persisting mythic elements. Sophisticated rationality did not emerge full grown, like Athena from the head of Zeus. It developed bit by bit, carrying its mythic origins well into the modern period. Romantic understanding represents crucial elements of rationality developing along with persisting features of myth—in both cultural history and in education today.

Recapitulation of the move from myth and magic to rationality and reality can be seen at many levels. David Olson (1994) describes some of the developments of writing in the ancient Near East. He notes, for example, the significant move from signs representing things to signs representing words for things. In the earliest scripts, four sheep might be represented by the sign for "sheep" made four times. It is a significant development to represent four sheep by two signs, one representing sheep and the other the number. Such a move allows economy and encourages generativity in the writing system (Harris, 1986). It also represents a new kind of abstraction. As this development of signs for words rather than for things becomes increasingly sophisticated, it in turn generates new ways of thinking about the language it represents: "a new understanding of language as consisting of words also has conceptual implications. It spells the death of word magic. . . . When the word is thought of as representing a thing rather than an intrinsic property of the thing, word magic loses its power. An action on the name, as in a *hex*, does not affect the named because the word, unlike the name, is not a part of the thing; it is just a word" (Olson, 1993, p. 7).

In passing, Olson writes:

It is interesting to note that in learning to read and write children go through just such a shift in understanding. If non-reading pre-school children are given a pencil and asked to write "cat" they may write a short string of letter-like forms. If then asked to write " three cats" they repeat the same initial string three times. Conversely, if such pre-reading children are shown a text which reads: "Three little pigs" and the text is then read to them while the words are pointed out they tend to take each word as a representation, an emblem, of a pig. Consequently, if the final word is erased and children are asked, "Now what does it say?" they may reply "Two little pigs." Alternatively, if each of the three words is pointed to in turn and the child is asked what each says, they reply, "One little pig; another little pig; and another little pig." (Olson, 1993, p. 8)

He notes a number of precise recapitulations of this kind between the development of writing systems and children's development of literacy today. What I want to go on to now are more general recapitulations—of a complex kind of understanding that is influenced partly by detailed recapitulations of alphabetic literacy within institutions trying to encourage literacy development so as to exploit its potential for abstract, decontextualized thinking. What I will try to be sensitive to, and what is usually ignored, is the persistence of mythic elements in this initial foray into rationality. The mixture of the mythic with the rational constitutes the central defining feature of Romantic understanding.

SOME CHARACTERISTICS OF ROMANTIC UNDERSTANDING

An early and quite clear expression of Romantic understanding is found in *The Histories* of Herodotus, written when literacy was becoming integrated into ancient Greek social life. It is also a work that enjoyed a wide and enthusiastic audience in ancient Greece, and has remained one of the most engaging texts still enjoyed from the ancient world. I will try to show surprising   81 parallels between *The Histories* of Herodotus and forms of thinking commonly evident in students today during the years when literacy becomes integrated into their daily activities and when they are learning the "abstracting," "decontextualizing" skills that go with rationality.

Herodotus, "the father of history," was born in Halicarnassus, on the coast of Asia Minor, south of Miletus, sometime between 490 and 480 B.C.E. *The Histories* describe the Persian Empire, its neighbors, and its great war against the Greek states. The rational prose writers who had turned their attention to the past before him (including Hecataeus, who began his *Genealogies* with the personal judgment that the Greeks' stories were ridiculous), seem to have compiled inscriptions, local records, family histories, traditional accounts, and whatever else they could find that seemed to give some more reliable information than the myths (Pearson, 1939; Fornara, 1983). *The Histories* had in common with them the mixing of ethnographic material, anecdotes, and geographical information, as well as what we tend to think of as more straightforward history. But nothing written previously could compare with the scope of Herodotus's work or with his organization of material into a coherent epic account. Much of it dealt with relatively long-past and long-distant events. Among Greeks who closely associated "knowing" and "seeing" (Snell, 1960, ch. 7), Herodotus's method of describing what he could not have witnessed or reliably known earned him also the title "father of lies" (Momigliano, 1966).

The Histories remains a fascinating read, full of the exotic, strange, and wonderful, of stirring events and an epic conflict between the awesome Persian Empire and the tiny, quarreling Greek states. It would be no wonder if Herodotus had been paid in Athens to read parts of it aloud to appreciative audiences, as was later claimed. He would have been an odd kind of latter-day bard—reading prose rather than reciting poetry. Open up the first four books at random, as I do now, and learn about the black pygmies who attacked and carried off a group of Lybian explorers; about why Egyptians were reluctant to let the embalmers have the bodies of beautiful or prominent women until three or four days after death; about the twenty-two tons of gold used in building the figure of Bel (the Biblical Baal) in Babylon; about how the Egyptian women attended market and did business while the men stayed home and wove *and* how the women stood up to urinate whereas the men squatted down; about how to catch crocodiles; about how Amazon women came to settle with a detachment of Scythian young men but preserved such customs as not marrying until after killing an enemy in battle; about how the Persian king built a dam on the Aces river and the problems it caused the tribes who had relied on the lower branches of the river; and about the endless stories of outstanding cunning, daring, cruelty, revenge, murder, thieving, and sexual misbehavior. Much of the text bears more than a passing resemblance to those papers at the supermarket check-out.

The remaining five books are more focused on the Persian attacks on the Greeks, detailing the amazing size of the Persian armies and navies. The small, independent Greek states, and particularly freedom-loving Athens, despite terrible setbacks, constant bickering, impossible odds, and cliff-hanging decisions, nevertheless finally managed to defeat the tyrannical Eastern empire.

The Histories reads like an ancient *Guinness Book of Records,* crammed with stories about the brave and noble, descriptions of the exotic and bizarre, and expressions of wonder at amazing achievements and huge and strange buildings. The kind of understanding it displays is not easily sustained without writing. We may see it recur, sometimes more energetically than others—as during the Romantic period in modern Europe, to which I will also make occasional reference.

The Limits of Reality, the Extremes of Experience, the Context of Our Lives

Herodotus begins his narrative by telling us that what he "has learnt by inquiry [*historie*] is here set forth: in order that the memory of the past may not be blotted out from among men by time, and that great and marvellous things done [*erga*] by the Greeks and Barbarians and especially the reason why they warred against each other may not cease to be recounted." The emphasis throughout the work is on the *mega ergon,* the great achievement. The odd shape of the work is partly the product of Herodotus's desire to record whatever great *erga* he has learned about: "I am about to lengthen my *logos* on Egypt because Egypt has the largest numbers of wonders, more than all the rest of the world. And of all the countries of the world, it is Egypt which contains *erga* which actually surpass their reputation" (*The Histories,* II, 35).

It is perhaps hard for us to imagine the dramatic impact in ancient Greece of this narrative born of inquiry. Herodotus's invention created a way of making the reader or hearer a kind of witness, vicariously present at the great events described. The technique drew something from drama and from epic poetry but it dealt with reality, with real people and real events as they really happened—or so it represented itself as doing. You are there, a witness to Croesus's conversations, to Xerxes' planning, to the great battles themselves. It has also all the delights of gossip with the justification of high seriousness.   83

THREE

Herodotus was accused of creating a disproportionate work because of his seeming inability to leave out a vivid story or odd custom, however slender its relevance to his narrative thread. But the thread is not lost; rather, what we read is a typically romantic description of the world. Such an approach obviously does not provide a full understanding of events, but it provides a kind of understanding—indeed, a romantic kind of understanding. And while Herodotus is my chosen example here, it is clear that these characteristics are prominent in, and in part definitive of, all appearances of romance in Western history. European Romanticism is notoriously the object of rather disparate descriptions, but no one can omit its "preoccupation with otherness, with what is different, remote, mysterious, inaccessible, exotic, even bizarre" (Ong, 1971, p. 255).

The preservation of great events, of the memory of the outstanding, has been central to romantic history writing from Herodotus's time to our own. A medieval historical text puts the sentiment ideally, echoing Herodotus:

The stream of Time, irresistible, ever moving, carries off and bears away all things that come to birth and plunges them into utter darkness, both deeds of no account and deeds which are mighty and worthy of commemoration. . . . Nevertheless, the science of History is a great bulwark against this stream of Time; in a way it checks this irresistible flood, it holds in a tight grasp whatever it can seize floating on the surface and will not allow it to slip away into the depths of oblivion. (Comnena, 1969, p. 17)

Referring to Herodotus's work as *The Guinness Book of Ancient World Records* is a joke whose point turns on the very real similarity between the two works. The modern work strives, with a slightly comic earnestness, to apply rational modes of inquiry to discovering precisely who really was the biggest, the smallest, the fastest, the slowest, the hairiest, the oldest, and so on. It seeks to sweep away myths and wild claims and to establish the limits of reality and the extremes of experience. Herodotus's text is similarly crammed with details whose only justification is that they represent a record. We learn, for example, that King Psammetichus of Egypt was engaged in a siege around Azotus in Syria for twenty-nine years. There are no strategic implications of this; the siege is mentioned only because "it was the longest of any in history" (*The Histories, II,* p. 157). (I am delighted to discover that this is also included in *The Guinness Book of Records,* 1992, p. 241.)

Why are the contents of *The Guinness Book of Records* so much more engaging than the typical math or geography textbook to the average ten-year-old? Why is the average ten-year-old so interested in who was the tallest person who ever lived? (The average ten-year-old male slightly, but only slightly, more interested than the average ten-year-old female, according to my informal surveys.) One answer is that such facts are more romantic; they tell about the wonders of the world, the most extreme experiences, the limits of reality, the greatest achievements, the most exotic forms of life, the most amazing events. *The Guinness Book of Records* is one of the most accessible collections of *erga* for children. For the literate student faced with a seemingly infinite autonomous reality, the records provide a very neat summary of the range and extent of reality, with the associated security that reality isn't infinite in all regards.

If this autonomous reality were infinitely extensive, we would be infinitely insignificant. By discovering the real limits of the world and of human experience, we form a context that enables us to establish some security and to establish proportionate meaning within it. Knowing about the biggest and smallest people allows us, on the one hand, to wonder at their extreme sizes, but, on the other, to be reassured about our own scale. Once we have some sense of context, we can begin to develop some sense of the proportionate meaning of things.

It is a little odd that the eight- to fifteen-year-olds' enjoyment of books, TV shows, and films that deal with the exotic and the extreme has had so little impact on learning theories and curriculum planning. To pick up a thread from the previous chapter: still by far the most common learning principle urged on teachers is that children's learning moves "from the known to the unknown," and that, to engage their interest and make new knowledge meaningful, one must begin with something relevant to their everyday experience and connect the new knowledge to that. If this indeed is how children learn most effectively, one must wonder what does the fattest person who ever lived have to do with their everyday experience, or the most expensive postage stamp, or the longest beard?

While I will take up implications for teaching later, it is worth pausing briefly to consider how this first characteristic of Romantic understanding leads us to think rather differently about children's learning during these years. The "romantic" principle inclines us to an alternative observation about the logic of human intellectual exploration and discovery—of learning new knowledge—from that currently dominant in education. Suppose you were placed in a hill town somewhere and invited to explore it. You would be foolish to begin by concentrating in detail on the familiar features of the hotel room around you and gradually working out from there, constantly connecting what you were discovering with your familiar material culture and experience. More sensibly, you would begin by trying to find out how extensive the town is, where its walls or limits are, what the major buildings and open spaces are, what kind of activities people engage in, and so on. That is, you would get some sense of the context, the limits, the major *erga*, the exotic features, and so on. This would be very much an Herodotean approach, in which one makes sense of the different, the strange, by establishing the context within which it exists, not by some gradual extension from what is already familiar.

Now, clearly *both* strategies are available to us (and so is an indeterminate number of others). My concern is that the currently dominant attempt to build understanding by gradual extension from the familiar is only part of the story; it is not particularly effective in developing Romantic understanding and, indeed, by itself it is ineffective. The traditional conception represents learning as building understanding by composing it bit by bit, rather the way a jigsaw puts together a picture of something. The "romantic" alternative conception represents learning as building understanding by gradually clarifying a picture the way the pieces of a holographic plate work. If one takes a piece of a smashed holographic plate and shines a laser through it, one will generate a blurred image of the whole picture. As further pieces of the plate are added, the image becomes clearer.

Of course, we use both the holograph and jigsaw procedures in constructing understanding: we learn by making associations between the familiar and new knowledge *and* by fitting new knowledge into overall, vaguely grasped contexts that the new knowledge in turn helps to clarify. The holograph procedure seems particularly important for establishing meaning, by building the new knowledge into sets of relationships stretched across the contexts we more or less tentatively hold in place. The principle of learning implied by the holograph metaphor, however, has received very little attention in education even though it coheres with much of our experience.

With their literacy-supported discovery of autonomous reality, students begin to lose their ready engagement with giants who were a mile high and midgets no bigger than your thumbnail. They turn intellectually to discover who was really the biggest and smallest person who ever lived. Myth gives way to reality while also persisting in providing a template for the questions and interests that drive our inquiries. The simple binary structures of mythic understanding begin to fall away as we grasp an increasingly complex reality: "Such [binary] relationships are good for thinking, but reality does not always follow suit; a certain stubbornness of the facts remains" (Burkert, 1985, p. 217). We see in the move from giants to the tallest person *really,* the gradual accommodation between the mind and reality. The stubborn facts are the objects to which we try to make our ideas conform; theories are mental constructs that try to represent stubborn reality. But between the myths that shape the world to the requirements of mental structures and theories that try to conform with the actual structure of the world, we have romance. Romance deals with reality, but it does so with persisting mythic interests. It is a compromise with, rather than a capitulation to, reality.

I have mentioned only *The Guinness Book of Records* as an example of students' sharing with Herodotus a ready engagement with the extreme and the exotic. It would be easy to elaborate examples at length, but I assume that the interest in these features of reality is so obvious during these years, and thereafter, that elaboration is not necessary. Engagement by the wonderful and different is so taken for granted that it seems not to invite inquiry.

One other distinctive characteristic of students' intellectual activity during these years is the obsession with hobbies or with collecting. I discuss these at greater length elsewhere (Egan, 1990), but here we might note the often passionate drive to complete a set or to enlarge and organize, or constantly reorganize, a collection. The collection may be of stones, shells, stamps, dolls' outfits, comics—almost anything. The hobbies may be equally varied. This drive in Western culture typically begins with literacy, peaks at about age eleven, and fades away by about fifteen.

What is going on here? Well, we can recognize collecting and hobbies as an engagement with reality that is in one regard like the pursuit of the exotic and extreme. By collecting the set, or by mastering in great detail some area of the world, one gains the assurance that reality is not limitless, that one can grasp it. By learning about *something* exhaustively, one gains the security that the world is in principle knowable. So one reduces the threat that one is insignificant or at the mercy of an unknowably vast reality. Of course, many people do not gain this security, but it is one of the important contributions of a developed Romantic understanding.

All this talk of the exotic and the bizarre will no doubt raise warning signals for many. It smacks of entertainment and trivia rather than the important skills required by the practical world the student has to inhabit. It suggests a curriculum focused on the extremes of reality and the limits of experience rather than on the students' own environments. Those are all reasonable inferences, but I should make a few quick qualifiers. First, the focus on the exotic and the bizarre is not the only characteristic of Romantic understanding, and each of the others will have its implications, so we will not expect students' time to be spent entirely on the exotic and bizarre. Second, by learning about the limits of reality and the extremes of experience, students *are also* learning something profound about the everyday world around them; such limits help to set the everyday in context and hence establish its meaning. Third, anything in the world may be made an object of romantic engagement if only we see it in the appropriate way. The fattest and hairiest person who ever lived may have an easy dramatic appeal, but by showing students the romantic aspect of an old Styrofoam cup or a building lot or the desks they sit in or the air they breathe one can engage and enlarge

87

students' Romantic understanding. Fourth, while education and entertainment are concepts with some important distinguishing characteristics, the need to acknowledge the distinctions should not make us exaggerate them. Learning *can* be fun, and during these years in particular romantic engagement is an enemy of dullness and pervasive boredom.

Put simplistically, literacy generates conceptions of reality, and the mind explores reality by trying to grasp its limits and extremes; we see the same process at work in cultural history and in students today. By grasping at the limits and extremes, we set in place a context that establishes more ample, clear, and "realistic" meaning to the details and experiences of our everyday world.

Transcendence within Reality

The archetypical romantic figure is the hero. The hero lives, like the rest of us, within the constraints of the everyday world but, unlike the rest of us, manages somehow to transcend the constraints that hem us in. The mythic gods who transcended the constraints of nature at will were swept away by the rational drive to represent the world accurately. (Such a romantic image! "Rationality sweeps away the old gods." It could be a theme—it probably was—for one of those romantic allegorical paintings of the nineteenth century.) But while the gods might have disappeared from early rational narratives, they left a template that gives form to early rational attempts to make sense of events. In the place of the gods and their will, we find heroic figures and their will.

The trick of rationally representing the world, as one of the great proponents of the method put it, is to keep "the eye steadily fixed upon the facts of nature and so [receive] their images simply as they are" (Bacon, 1965, p. 323). Well, it hasn't proven quite as simple as Bacon suggests; we seem to find it very difficult not to contribute something to the facts of nature as we receive them.

If we look at how Herodotus represented causality in his histories, for example, we see events as the result of the emotions and consequent actions of important individuals. In sophisticated modern historical texts, we see causality in social and economic conditions, in complexes of prior social and psychological influences. Herodotus's text, however, is full of heroic characters who are extraordinarily clever or daring or cunning. Their heroic actions are represented as the causes of events. In modern historical texts, establishing causal conditions will involve an analysis; in Herodotus's text it involves a story, or many stories.

88   What caused the great war between the Persian Empire and the Greek

states? Herodotus sweeps aside earlier stories and locates the initiating cause in Croesus's greed and his desire for vengeance against Cyrus. Essential to the story is the background explaining how Croesus came to lead so great an empire. Lydia, for example, passed into Croesus's family because its previous ruler, Candaules, thought his wife the most excitingly beautiful of women and he half-persuaded, half-compelled one of his favorite bodyguards, Gyges, to watch at their bedroom door to see her undress so that he might confirm Candaules's estimate. The naked, and unnamed, queen saw Gyges as he slipped away. The next morning she gave Gyges a simple choice: be killed immediately, or kill Candaules and rule in his place. Poor Gyges chose the latter, and his great-grandson Croesus thus later inherited the throne. (Herodotus tells us that, as king, Gyges attacked the Greek Ionian town of Miletus: "That, however, being his only act of importance during a reign of thirty-eight years, I will pass on without further comment" [*The Histories,* I, 13]).

Clearly the criteria that rational Herodotus uses in selecting what to include in his narrative are somewhat different from those that shape typical modern historical texts. The form of causality Herodotus uses is readily comprehensible to us, and remains popular in modern films, novels, soap operas, and journalism. His text is full of individuals whose emotions cause the events that make up his narrative. Those emotions are much the same set that stimulated the old gods to interfere in human affairs—greed, revenge, lust, the will to power, compassion, love (perhaps not in that order). Herodotus's text is full of characters who can no longer transcend reality the way the magical gods used to, but they share with those gods some qualities that are only vestigial in the mundane world. The heroic transcends not just the bounds of reality or the laws of nature but inner constraints, too, and the everyday constraints of conventional institutions, behaviors, physical attainments, and so on.

Two observations seem appropriate here. First, heroes engage our interest because they "body forth" in unusual degree a human virtue that enables them to transcend conventional constraints. Our engagement with heroes and their achievements comes through our association with their transcendent human qualities; we all share those qualities, though, alas, in more limited degrees.

Second, the archetypical hero in the Western tradition has been a male power-oriented doer of usually violent deeds. There is, however, a wide range of qualities that we associate with in any hero—sanctity, compassion, selflessness, elegance, wit, ingenuity, patience, or whatever, equally as well as testosteronic violence. So we can see a saint, a nurse, a scientist as heroic, no less than the debased successors of Ulysses and Sir Galahad.

When we are ten, facing that more or less and increasingly autonomous reality, we need to establish some kind of intellectual and psychological security. The past security of Mythic understanding—which did not have to deal with an autonomous and alien world but which involved an unreflective, Eden-like acceptance of it—is no longer available. Romantic association offers one prominent technique for forging a new security in the face of this threatening reality; both Herodotus and the modern newly literate explorer associate with those features of reality that seem best able to transcend the threats of the everyday world. By associating with whomever or whatever in the world seems best able to transcend those threats, we too feel some security against such threats, some confidence that we might transcend them.

When we are ten, we are very much at the mercy of the world around us. We are typically subject to endless rules and regulations—parental, societal, and, not least, natural. The person, institution, or team that the child associates with usually gives clear clues to the constraints found most problematic. The immensely rich, decadent, dirty rock star offers one kind of hero, the skillful soccer player another, and likewise the successful writer, the outrageous singer or actor, the powerful hockey or football team. The tension characteristic of romance comes from the desire to transcend a threatening reality while seeking to secure one's identity within it.

A characteristic of Romantic understanding, then, is its ready association with transcendent human qualities, or human qualities exercised to transcendent degree. This observation is important for the education of children from about eight to fifteen because almost any curriculum material can be made understandable if students can associate "romantically" with such qualities within it. This is, I might note in passing, not a matter of manipulating students to learn the knowledge we "privilege," but rather a matter of having the courtesy to attend to how they can best make sense of any knowledge.

So we can come to understand important features of, for example, the Industrial Revolution by associating with the energy and ingenuity of its heroes, such as Isambard Kingdom Brunel or James Watt. Though that does not put it quite right. The trick is to show the Industrial Revolution—the inventions, the statistics of population growth, farm production, and so on—as an expression of an energy and ingenuity the students can associate with; or to show it as an attempt to subjugate nature so transcendingly arrogant and impious that it threatens now to destroy all life on earth.

Similarly we can understand the movement to emancipate slaves by associating with the courage, compassion, and persistence of those who struggled and suffered, and struggle and suffer still, in this cause. Or we can understand the life cycle of eels by associating with the patient ingenuity of Johannes Schmidt, who spent twenty years pursuing eel larvae, gradually uncovering detail after detail about their lives and astounding migrations. Or we can understand rock formations, Latin conjugations, chemical processes, grammatical structures, and *anything* else, by locating within it a human quality in transcendent degree with which students can associate. Anything can be made the object of a romantic association if we see it in the appropriate light, and doing so is the key to successful teaching and learning during this period.

The kind of understanding these romantic associations allow is clearly limited. But so is all understanding. Understanding is not an on/off condition; it is, as the holograph metaphor suggests, amenable to ever-increasing clarity. It may reasonably be called an immature form of understanding, but immaturity is not something to complain about in the immature. While nineteenth- and early twentieth- century critics analyzed Herodotus's conception of historical causality, and his very conception of history, as inadequate and immature compared with more modern conceptions, theirs is a limited criticism. In part it derives from seeing his work exclusively in terms of their own, and judging his as a failure to conform with their criteria of proper historical writing. This is a reasonable judgment only if the critic also shows sensitivity to the criteria by which Herodotus worked and by which his history remains a triumphant success.

A. N. Whitehead characterizes romance as an "excitement" following on the "vividness of novelty" and the "unexplored connections with possibilities half-disclosed by glimpses and half-concealed by the wealth of material. . . . Romantic emotion is essentially the excitement consequent on the transition from the bare facts to the first realisations of the import of their unexplored relationships" (1967, pp. 17–18). He adds that this "great romance is the flood which bears on the child towards the life of the spirit" (p. 22). While my interest is purely secular, one cannot talk casually about transcendence without acknowledging the spiritual role that the idea has played in the Western tradition. Romantic transcendence, even if we wish to avoid its mystical associations, does have an affective component. In addition, successfully associating with transcendent expressions or embodiments of such qualities as compassion, courage, pity, and so on, involves a recognition within others of the autonomy one recognizes in oneself. This ability to associate with transcendence in others leads at a simple level to recognizing virtue in one's enemy, as does Herodotus. Early in the Western literate tradition, this ability was reckoned rare and strange. Saxo Grammaticus wrote in his *Gesta Danorum:* "The men of Thule [Iceland] are very fond of learning and of recording the history of all peoples and they are   91 equally pleased to reveal the excellences of others or of themselves" (Borges, 1968, p. 170). One is not far, at this point, from deconstructing the concept of "enemy" and reaching the insight of the literate Jesus of Nazareth that one should love one's enemies and indeed see in them a transcendence we can all share.

Well, I think it is reasonable to see the ability to form "romantic" associations with human qualities in transcendent degree as one aspect of what has traditionally been called "spiritual development." One may prefer to avoid such terms, but even so one may recognize in them an expansion of one's range of human sympathies. Inevitably we are associating with the external world by means of qualities we recognize in ourselves, and we properly elaborate them in ourselves by continually associating with varied features of the world. In turn, we begin to conform our understanding to the features of the real world, and this requires courage; it requires that mystical ability to forget the self and acknowledge difference and autonomy in the other. The journey out of Eden is also a freedom from the all-encompassing ego, to use Freud's metaphor.

Humanized Knowledge

The author of an earlier and more troublingly potent Superman than Clarke Kent's *alter ego* insisted that we must ever love and honor great individual human beings, and that the task of scholarly study of the past was to bring such people constantly to the forefront of our minds (Nietzsche, 1962, preface). Herodotus's history certainly exemplifies this principle. Each *mega ergon* is shown as the product of some person's or some people's actions. The frequent accounts of battles focus on the few outstanding fighters and, commonly, their motives for distinguishing themselves. Worthy of record after the description of each battle are the names of those soldiers who acquitted themselves best. So the name of the Spartan Philocyon will be remembered forever because he was brave in transcendent degree. As your eye passes over the name, you might wonder what kind of reward this is.

This focus on individuals, and the emotions that stimulate them to act, is characteristic of the romantic way of understanding the world. One can give an account of the world as an accumulation of the products of individuals' acts, made further comprehensible in terms of the emotions that generated them—emotions that we all share. All knowledge, after all, is human knowledge. Everything we know is knowable through the lives of its inventors, discoverers, or users, and we can have access to that knowledge through the hopes, fears, or intentions that drove them. Access to Pythagoras's theorem, for example, can come most easily during this period if the student sees the theorem in the context of Pythagoras's life and as a product of Pythagoras's hopes and fears (see Egan, 1990, pp. 267–70).

Another way of making this point is to draw on R. G. Collingwood's (1946) argument that all history is the history of thought. That is, the understanding we can construct from any historical event, document, ruin, or artifact is constrained by the degree to which we can infer the human thoughts that brought it about or were involved with it. Romantic understanding in particular is constructed by seeing the object of study in the context of someone's or some people's thoughts, intentions, hopes, or fears. Where Collingwood writes of "thought," we might, in the case of Romantic understanding, interpret that in the sense that would clearly include emotions. What Collingwood argues about historical understanding may be thus extended to Romantic understanding of any knowledge of the world. It is not, of course, impossible to construct some understanding of earthquakes or algebra or Milton's *Paradise Lost* by means other than the emotions of the people involved; during the early adolescent years in our culture, however, the most ready and engaging access to understanding is achieved through the emotions and thoughts most intimately tied in with the phenomena to be studied.

Journalists and teachers recognize that knowledge can be effectively communicated if it is put into an engaging context for readers or students. Journalists commonly refer to finding "a human interest angle." Teachers know that an illustrative anecdote, particularly if it is rich in emotional motivation, can have a remarkable effect on engaging interest. The usual problem in teaching is that such anecdotes are thought of as "hooks" to attract students' interest as a prelude to the real work of the lesson or unit. The trick is to expand through the lesson or unit the principle that makes the hook work.

As discussed earlier, one of the incidental products of literacy has been the compilation of dictionaries, encyclopedias, and textbooks for storing knowledge. "Storing knowledge" is how we rather innocently put it, forgetting the metaphorical sense of "knowledge" in such a phrase. When we test students' educational achievement in terms of what they remember of the knowledge taught them—which remains by far the commonest form of evaluation—we reinforce the image of the textbook, encyclopedia, or dictionary as the paradigm of the successful knower (de Castell, Luke, and Luke, 1989). It becomes important in such a climate of opinion to emphasize that books do not store knowledge. They contain symbolic codes that can serve us as external mnemonics for knowledge. Knowledge can exist only in living human minds.

No sensible aim of education can include making human minds mimic   93 textbooks, yet we see constant examples of just this. The alternative educational task is to teach students how to revivify the symbolic codes by transmuting them into human understanding, reconstituting the inert codes as living human knowledge. We can encourage such reconstitution by showing the knowledge within the life of its inventor, discoverer, user, sufferer, or author, and this can be made readily comprehensible if we connect such knowledge with the students' emotions.

If, for example, we wish to teach the geography of the Americas, we might introduce it in the context of the emotions of the first discoverers and settlers. It is not just that we will see the landscape and climate, the flora and fauna, through the eyes of those who first came across the Bering Strait land-bridge, but we will *feel* those features through their emotional responses (as we can reasonably infer them). We can learn about mountains and rivers through the expectations, hopes, and fears of people as they traveled east and south. The landscape becomes humanized in terms of the challenges it presented, the food sources it provided, and the material culture it supported. With more detailed authenticity we can feel the "new" world through the written words —the diaries, letters, official documents, poetry—of those Europeans who spread through the Americas.

Everything we know was discovered or invented or authored by somebody. We have taken some pride in abstracting the hard-won fragments of knowledge from the lives of its makers and laying them out in textbooks, encyclopedias, atlases, and dictionaries. These are wonderfully convenient devices for retrieval purposes. But for first access to knowledge during this layer of educational development, we would do better to re-embed it in the lives of its makers. That way students can also *feel* why someone might care about the structure of the universe, the behavior of insects, the interactions of chemicals, and so on.

Romantic Rationality

These emphases on the exotic, transcendence, and human emotion will no doubt continue to set off warning signals in many minds. Are we to turn over the intermediate years of schooling to sensationalist material and activities? Stimulating students' imaginations may be all very well, but there is also the serious business of kitting them out with the practical knowledge and skills they are going to need in order to deal with the social, political, and economic worlds out there. My general argument is that attending to the characteristics of Romantic understanding will provide the most effective means of ensuring that students master whatever knowledge and skills they need in order to deal successfully with the world.

Our cultural development and that of students today does not involve moving from mythic thinking to a more or less discrete, better, and more practically efficacious kind of thinking we call rational. Rather, these two kinds of thinking share a great deal more than what distinguishes them, and the dramatic difference between them masks a significant continuity underneath. It seems useful at this point to indicate in what sense the earlier form of rationality that characterizes Romantic understanding is distinctively rational and distinctively nonmythic—apart from its lack of magic.

Let us return to the example of Herodotus, father of a distinctive form of rational inquiry. Unlike his successor, Thucydides, Herodotus does not formulate a theory of history; he is too intent on describing remarkable *erga* and constructing an engaging narrative. But neither does he simply tell a story like the earlier writers of myths or the poets. Homer told the story of an earlier war, and used factual material in the telling (Gomme, 1954; Wood, 1985), but Homer's account is primarily loyal to *poetic* criteria rather than to describing precisely what happened: the vividness and emotional impact of his story are paramount; its need to convey universal truths about human life in general is uppermost. While Herodotus also shapes his account into a narrative, his determination to represent what really happened and what really is the case generated a new form of expression.

We have become very sensitive to the ways in which the shapes of narratives tell more than the simple facts they purport to represent. Herodotus's narrative is shaped by his desire not only to represent reality but also to tell a good story and to affect his audience's emotions. His selection of the great conflict with the Persians, and of events to "body forth" this conflict, is not innocent of the storyteller's art. Even so, we recognize that he is constrained, unlike the fictional storyteller and Homer, by what really happened. He might select the most interesting war and events to narrate, but he does not make up wars or events in order to create a particular emotional response in his readers or audience.

Herodotus generated a new kind of narrative—a compromise between the poet's desire to evoke an emotional response and the rational desire to describe the world as it really is. We can describe it as a compromise because we know about the scientific method that is yet to come. Herodotus's rational inquiry mixes elements of poetry or myth and elements of science; it is post-oral but prescientific or pretheoretic. Now this description results from our fitting his work into one of our narratives of historical development. His work is a distinctive and autonomous form of inquiry by itself; it yields a particular kind of understanding and prefigures endless forms that have developed since. Most journalists today, for example, aim to tell a dramatic story while adhering, more or less, to what really is the case, but they are selective in the stories they choose to tell and the incidents they think will be interesting. The Romantic movement shares the commitment to the extremes of reality, the limits of experience, the fascination with the mysterious and the *mega ergon*. We may recognize this form of understanding in ourselves.

"We all know by now that many scientific and mathematical hypotheses start their lives as little stories or metaphors, but they reach their scientific maturity by a process of conversion into verifiability, formal and empirical, and their power at maturity does not rest on their dramatic origins" (Bruner, 1986, p. 12). This distinction between stories and theories, what Bruner settles for calling "narrative" and "paradigmatic" forms of thought, marks off starting and ending points of some developmental process but attends little to their distinctive forms of thought. During middle school years we are dealing with forms of thought that are not shaped by stories in the sense that Mythic understanding tends to be, nor have they yet reached "maturity." They are nevertheless typically rational in their attempts to conform with reality, exclude magic, recognize the importance of noncontradiction, and handle the kinds of syllogisms with which this chapter began.

The vulgar notion of romance tends to highlight the exotic and wonderful, and not recognize that these as the margins of *reality* are crucially distinctive of a romantic view. It is well to remember that reality was the main discovery of Romanticism in European cultural history, as far as its participants were concerned. They saw their great achievement as a sweeping away of the clutter of artificiality that prevented people from engaging directly with nature in all its uniqueness and particularity. The excitement of Romanticism was not simply a product of the sense of the imagination being free, but of being free to explore afresh the reality of human experience and the natural world. Blake expressed this engagement with reality in terms of cleansing the gates of perception, Shelley as the lifting of a veil from the hidden beauty of the world. The romantic perception is focused on the details of the world: "Romantic art, then, is not 'romantic' in the vulgar sense, but 'realistic' in the sense of concrete, full of particulars" (Barzun, 1961, p. 26).

This is very much the world Herodotus and his near-contemporary *logographoi,* philosophers, and proto-scientists present to us. Once one can write, one can try to describe in various extensive forms the concrete particularity of the world. Subsequent inquirers can observe the world and previous descriptions of the world and then match their observations against those descriptions. They can then construct their descriptions to match more closely their sense of reality (Gombrich, 1960). The making/matching process can lead to increasingly precise representations of reality, in pictures, maps, and written descriptions. It is a rational process that can be quite untheoretic or nonscientific. It is a form of "romantic" rational activity that is common, focused on the particular, and also prerequisite to theoretic scientific thinking. When Darwin wondered at the diversity of species of finch on the Galapagos Islands he exhibited a romantic engagement and romantic rational inquiry without which his reflective theoretical inquiry could not have successfully gone to work. Without the initial wonder, it is hard to see how more systematic theoretical inquiry can get fruitfully under way.

Thus we might want to see whether certain forms of rational inquiry can be devised for the middle school years that stimulate and develop Romantic understanding and do not prematurely try to exercise a kind of theoretic thinking for which the prerequisites are not developed. Much of our failure in encouraging mathematical and scientific understanding in schools may stem from the general failure to distinguish Romantic understanding and its distinctive ways of engaging and making rational sense of the world as prerequisite to theoretic thinking.

What Is in Danger of Being Lost

I believe it is a serious mistake to view education as an inevitably progressive process, as an enterprise in which we succeed to the degree that children learn more, become more skilled in literacy and numeracy, give evidence of higher stages of psychological development, and so on, while ignoring or neglecting the losses associated with each gain. To beleaguered schools and teachers, I recognize that this may seem a somewhat exotic new complaint. And while so many students seem to acquire so marginal a degree of basic literacy and numeracy, the idea that even these meager successes might be snatched away can be very depressing. Depressing or not, it needs to be faced. I think the result of facing it can, in the context of the discussion of Romantic understanding, be liberating rather than the opposite because then we can see better how education might go forward during these years.

Literacy, for example, not only stimulates and supports Romantic understanding but at the same time supports an alienation from characteristics of Mythic understanding. At a cultural level we can see this in the incomprehension literacy created about nonliterate societies. The literate Hecataeus's dismissal of his predecessors' myths as ridiculous strikes a chord that echoes again and again through Western cultural history. "The primitive mind" is made mysterious, even though it is our inheritance; Mythic understanding becomes alien and unrecapturable after the "paradigm shift" to literate rationality. An insistent theme of Western consciousness is that one cannot go home again, one cannot return to Eden or comprehend the heart

97

of darkness. These images are so potent because they capture, however imprecisely, the sense of loss that is a part of literate rationality's heritage. "More than any other factor in human experience, it is the use of rational language which destroys the child's 'inituitive' relationship with the world" (Coe, 1984, p. 253). In developing more realistic and practically efficacious intellectual tools we run the danger, in Wordsworth's terms, of giving "our hearts away." The sense of alienation that comes with the recognition of an autonomous reality is largely an alienation from the earlier sense of participating in nature. After that break, "little we see in Nature that is ours," as Wordsworth put it. This sense of being cut off from the natural world by the tools of rationality has, of course, been a matter of indifference to many people in Western cultural history, whose delight rather has been in the practical control over nature that these tools have given. For others, like Wordsworth, it has created a sense of being "forlorn" (Sonnet, XXXIII).

Plato had long ago expressed his concerns about the potential losses that came along with literacy. He puts his caution, significantly, in a story. Socrates tells his young friend Phaedrus the old Egyptian legend about Thoth, the god-king of ancient Naucratis. Thoth was the inventor of draughts, dice, arithmetic, astronomy, and much else, including writing. Then Thoth took his inventions to Thamus, the god-king of all Egypt—perhaps looking for venture capital to get astronomy off the ground and the dice rolling. Thamus was impressed with many of them, but he had no time for what Thoth considered his greatest invention, writing. He expressed his objection thus:

> The discovery of the alphabet will create forgetfulness in the learner's souls, because they will not use their memories; they will trust to the external written characters and not remember of themselves. Your invention is not an aid to memory. . . . You give your disciples not truth, but only the semblance of truth; they will be hearers of many things and will have learned nothing. (Plato, *Phaedrus*)

Thoth might reasonably have complained that the point of writing was to release a burden from memory and free the mind for other kinds of more productive activity. But Thamus had a deeper insight: by replacing the imagistic, story-shaped, and story-shaping world of mythic consciousness, one did not simply gain a release from a burden. Literacy has not been a pure gain. One also lost the intensity of participatory experience in an immediate life-world, in which one's store of knowledge and lore was profoundly and vitally meaningful. As the eye, which derived knowledge efficiently from writing, replaced the ear as prominent in accessing information, so the participatory, emotion-laden message of the speaker no longer enveloped and produced a direct effect on the body of the learner (Havelock, 1963, 1986; Ong, 1982). The message was increasingly coded in written symbols, access to which was a more indirect, intellectual matter.

At an individual level we can see common losses of mythic capacities as children are taught literacy and rational skills in modern schools. To take the example of metaphoric fluency, which seems crucial to enriching and enlarging our language-use and to our imaginative exploration of the world, we see it become constricted in the process of literacy instruction. Winner's research, referred to in chapter 2, concludes that "[c]hildren around the ages of eight, nine, and ten often reject metaphors addressed to them, insisting, for instance, that colors cannot be loud, and people cannot be icy," and that "[t]he incidence of spontaneous metaphoric speech appears to decline rather dramatically during the early school years" (1988, p. 103). Consider some of Winner's observations about the importance of metaphors: they "are economical, vivid, and memorable, and sometimes they are the only way we have to say what we want to say. . . . The effect of a metaphor is to clarify, to explain, to reveal—to alter the listener's understanding of the topic. Metaphor helps us to acquire knowledge about new domains, and also has the effect of restructuring our organization of knowledge" (p. 116).

Now, it would obviously be improper to see a simple causal connection between literacy instruction and the decline of metaphoric fluency. We have a correlation, but we would need to know whether metaphoric fluency did not also decline about this age with children in oral cultures just to enhance the correlation, and then we would need to know much more about the processes by which our typical modes of literacy instruction affect metaphor use. The earlier observations about the possible declining influence of a genetic "language module" might better explain the reduction in metaphoric fluency, of course. But, even so, we can informally observe that this reduction may be more or less acute depending on whether literacy instruction encourages and stimulates metaphor production or discourages and suppresses it.

Eric Havelock also recognized the importance of building literacy instruction on the capacities developed earlier in life and in cultural history:

The mechanisms of modern education place primary emphasis on the speedy mastery of reading and writing as a preparation for the curriculum of secondary schools and adult life. Should we not be prepared to consider the possible conditions imposed upon the management of our educational systems by our oral inheritance? . . . The proposition I would offer is that the developing child should be expected in some sense to relive the conditions of this inheritance—that the teaching of literacy be conducted on the supposition that it is to be preceded by a curriculum of say, dance, and recitation and that it be accompanied by continual instruction in these oral arts. (1991, p. 21)

The idea that we can lose *more* than we gain in the process of education is, I realize, an odd notion in a culture that takes even the most superficial trappings of rationality as constituting vast superiority over traditional mythic forms of thinking. The "binary opposite" perception that superficial rationality and literacy provide only a marginal utility at the enormous expense of a wisdom and harmony of mythic consciousness has become a fashionable position. The fashionable alternative also tends to value traditional oral cultural forms of thinking as superior to even the most sophisticated Western forms, inescapably enmeshed as they are supposed to be in patriarchal, racist, or sexist epistemologies. The fashionable alternative does, however, help to point out that a literate intellectual life bounded by sensationalist papers, TV sports, tourism, Hollywood movies, and joyless material consumerism is not an obvious advance in understanding the world and experience over what is provided in many traditional oral cultures.

The conclusion I want to draw here is that literate rationality can support a kind of understanding that can enhance our lives and make them more abundant. Induction into literate rationality supports Romantic understanding, and that induction can be managed better or worse. Better involves preserving, perhaps in a somewhat transformed way, the characteristics of the prior kind of understanding; worse involves the suppression of characteristics of Mythic understanding. Worse, I fear, is the more common.

CONCLUSION

Romantic understanding, then, is a somewhat distinctive kind of understanding supported by an alphabetic literacy bent to the development of rationality. Central to Romantic understanding is a sense of an autonomous self and a relatedly autonomous reality. This is, of course, an imprecise and unsatisfactory way of putting it. Clearly, younger children live and deal with reality and with an autonomous, external world. But, equally clearly, there is commonly a shift in children's understanding of that reality around the period when literacy becomes internalized. Sandor Ferenczi writes of the slow growth in children's development of a sense of reality and of the development of a notion of objectivity and autonomy resulting from separating the sense of self from the external world. Freud, too, with an equally unsure use of metaphors, writes of the ego originally including everything and only gradually detaching itself from the external world. This very complex change in the way the mind stands in relation to "external" reality is difficult to grasp and represent, and I have chosen the metaphors of "mythic" and "romantic" understanding as the best I can find to point to some important and somewhat neglected features of the change.

I have drawn largely on an ancient Greek example to represent a cultural-historical expression of Romantic understanding. This may seem a bit perverse when a whole movement in more recent cultural history has been named "romantic." I have explored connections between Romanticism and romantic understanding elsewhere (Egan, 1990), but might usefully draw here on the foremost Romantic poet in English to summarize some distinctions between Mythic and Romantic understanding.

Wordsworth wrote extensively and insightfully about education, but in verse, so one doesn't see him much referred to in the professional literature in education. He characterizes childhood perception and understanding as vivid, bright, and rich—using terms similar to those used by nearly all who have written extensive autobiographies of childhood, and who try to recapture in words a sense of intimate participation in a vividly sensed world (Coe, 1984). That early childhood perception is then disturbed, and the vividness fades "into the light of common day." He talks of shades of the prisonhouse closing on the growing child: "Wordsworth is talking about something common to us all, the development of the sense of reality" (Trilling, 1950, p. 148).

In *Intimations of Immortality* Wordsworth makes two responses to this development of a sense of reality. On the one hand, there is a profound and irredeemable sense of loss: "But yet I know, where'er I go, / That there hath passed away a glory from the earth." On the other hand, he recognizes that something survives after all, something of the early splendor that is "a master-light of all our seeing" and that can continue to vivify the "years that bring the philosophic mind." Wordsworth resisted the easy contrast of the romantic imagination with dull rationality, a theme common among other romantic writers such as Coleridge. The philosophic mind, in Wordsworth's developmental theory (and in mine that borrows from him), comprises as far as possible the freshness of early understanding along with imagination and rationality. Imagination is crucial to preserving the capacities of Mythic understanding, but imagination is not in any sense in conflict with developing rationality and its view of reality, seen in the light of common day. Rather, "Imagination is . . . Reason in her most exalted mood" (*The Prelude*, bk. XIV, line 192). One of the weaker and more mischievous inheritances of Romanticism for twentieth-century thinking has been the easy opposition of reason and imagination, following John Stuart Mill's observation of how easily distinctions slide into oppositions. But we need not accept this unfruitful binary structuring.

Central to Romantic understanding is the growing sense of an autonomous reality. The sense of reality seems tied in with schooling in literacy and in the decontextualized thinking techniques that have proven effective in describing and controlling reality. But while schooling seems commonly successful at disturbing features of Mythic understanding and stimulating a sense of an autonomous reality, it seems less successful at engaging students imaginatively with the aspects of reality that are laid out in the curriculum. ·

This is the danger of schooling during the intermediate years: decontextualizing literacy, numeracy, and rationality undermine Mythic understanding but are so inadequately introduced that Romantic understanding does not develop to the point where it provides a coherence, security, and meaningfulness equal to what has been displaced. Herein lie the roots of alienation. The better path is to recognize Romantic understanding as a somewhat distinctive kind of understanding and to shape teaching and the curriculum during the middle school years in order to stimulate and develop it. Because this widely recognized transition in our early lives has been posed simplistically as moving from the irrational to the rational, from concrete to abstract thinking, from prescholastic to disciplinary, the distinctive first layer of rational understanding has been largely neglected; it is properly a mediator between those common binary oppositions.

Romantic understanding represents a gradual transition. Students' forms of thinking gradually accommodate to the shapes of autonomous reality, but they first make sense of reality in "romantic" terms.

Romantic understanding is lively, energetic, less concerned with systematic structures than with unexpected connections and the delight they can bring. (For example, what state in the United States is named for Julius Caesar? When invading Britain, Caesar quartered his armies on islands off the coast of Gaul. They become known as Insulae Caesareae. Over the centuries "Caesareae" degenerated into "Jersey." They are now called the Jersey Islands, and New Jersey might more properly be called New Caesar.) Readers who did not already know this might like to explore the small fillip of pleasure such an unexpected connection between disparate pieces of knowledge can bring. One could learn a great deal of geography (and history and all kinds of other things) through such little anecdotes. It would not necessarily be systematic, theoretic geographical knowledge, but it would be knowledge of a kind that I consider prerequisite to making subsequent theoretic knowledge more meaningful.

I have touched on just a few characteristics of Romantic understanding, ignoring the revolt and idealism, the distinctive boredom and the sensibilities that are features of a romantic sense of the world. I have even neglected the sense of the self that develops as a kind of side effect of the discovery of autonomous reality; we come to recognize that it is from our "self" that reality is autonomous. But I hope this brief characterization is enough to establish the Romantic as a somewhat distinctive kind of under-standing. Like the Mythic, it is not something that is properly superceded as we develop further kinds of understanding. It will in some degree coalesce with those. Its characteristics should, then, be readily recognizable in our general understanding of the world.

chapter 4

Philosophic Understanding

INTRODUCTION

These kinds of understanding are not neat, discrete categories, each in its distinctive primary color, each marked off definitively from the others. They do not represent irreconcilable features in the minds of their users; they do not represent incommensurable *mentalités*. In daily life we think, talk, and communicate using one kind or another, slipping more or less easily from one to another, combining or coalescing one with another. I have referred to them as "somewhat distinctive"; more like different perspectives than different *mentalités*, by means of which particular features of the world and experience are brought into focus and prominence and combination.

Working with the "tools" of oral language leads to the set of characteristics—the perspective on the world and experience, the style of sensemaking, the kind of understanding—I am calling Mythic. Oral-language use is by far the most prominent influence on, or shaper of, that kind of understanding. The Romantic layer is a little more complicated; I have identified it not simply with the "tool" of alphabetic literacy but with a cluster of further, related social and cultural developments in ancient Greece. This Philosophic layer is shaped by an even more diffuse "tool," or "mediational means"; it requires not only a sophisticated language and literacy but also a particular kind of communication that in turn requires particular kinds of communities or institutions to support and sustain it. The central feature of Philosophic understanding is systematic theoretic thinking and an insistent belief that Truth can only be expressed in its terms.

I call this kind of understanding Philosophic primarily because it was developed in the program that Plato and Aristotle refined and bequeathed to the world with such an intimidating weight of intellectual authority. They were magisterial combatants on behalf of "philosophy, or rather a particular style of philosophizing, as the sole repository of the truth in opposition to all comers" (Lloyd, 1990, p. 128). This style reached a further distinctive pitch after ancient Greek texts became again accessible and influential through the European Renaissance; these texts in turn stimulated ramifying intellectual developments, leading to what was unself-consciously called the Enlightenment and giving birth to what we call the modern world on July 15, 1662. On that day the Royal Society of London was founded (or, rather, on that day it received a charter from King Charles II), and 1662 makes as useful a marker as any for the transition to a clear acknowledgment of science as a central distinguishing element of European civilization.

In the Western rational metanarrative, the kind of thinking promoted by Plato and Aristotle, and many others, is seen as an inevitable progress from its predecessors, but we would do well to be wary of the easy patterns of hindsight. Instead we might focus on the ancient polemical battles in which that particular form of abstract, generalized, theoretic thinking with its universal ambitions enjoyed a remarkable victory. It produced a kind of understanding that has proven to have its uses, some of them spectacular, and in educating today we will want to make best use of these. But, like each kind of understanding, it also has its limitations; it occludes significant features of other kinds of understanding, and in educating today we will want to be aware of these, too.

Philosophic understanding is one of an indeterminate set of possible implications of language and literacy development. It is a kind of thinking that did not gain in other ancient civilizations the dominance it won in Greece. That is to say, there is no "natural progression" in this direction; the reasons for its development have to be sought in the particularities of ancient Greek society and in the aggressive program of a particular group of intellectually talented people. Certain individual imaginations grasped in this direction with tools that gained a hold on something, and they worked energetically to elaborate both the tools and the understanding of the world those tools generated.

With hindsight we can see some of these preliminary tools developing within the Greek language. Bruno Snell has tried to trace what he calls *The Discovery of the Mind* (1960) in the changes in language from Homer to the time of Plato and Aristotle, and tries to expose in chapter 10 of that book "[t]he origin of scientific thought." One tool important in the earliest appearance of scientific thinking, he argues, is the development of the definite article in Greek. In the oral past, one might refer to a good goat or a good rope or a good bowl. Literacy made the sounds of language into visible marks which could be manipulated, juxtaposed, and observed in ways that were less easy in an oral/aural world. One might, for example, attach the definite article to an adjective and create a new abstract noun such as "the good." What, one might then ask, do a goat, rope, and bowl have in common by sharing "goodness"? What is the nature of "the good"? Referring to Heraclitus, Snell argues that "the waxing power of the article is a prerequisite of his abstractions" (p. 229). Such linguistic developments helped the formation of what we now, as a result, call philosophical problems.

This theoretic thinking is not easy, nor is it obvious how such an abstracted use of language can be an effective route to dealing with practical problems. One does see examples of this kind of thinking in other ancient civilizations and in oral cultures, but unique to ancient Greece are the systematic cultivation of this level of discourse and the assertion that it is the *only* form of language that can capture what is real and true about the world and experience.

The difficulty of learning and sustaining this theoretic discourse was in part overcome by communities dedicated to it. Among the earliest was the Pythagorean community at Crotona in southern Italy. It had political and religious aims as well as philosophic and proto-scientific interests, a combination that would have been recognized without any sense of anomaly by the founders of the Royal Society (though the dietary and hygiene rules might have seemed a tad alien in seventeenth century Britain, as might such Pythagorean injunctions as "Touch the earth when it thunders" or "Abstain from beans").

The diffuse community of Hippocratic practitioners and writers, trying to forge a rational, proto-scientific approach to medicine, also were prominent in developing theoretic thinking, as were the argumentative law courts of the Ionian cities and of Athens. In these courts people developed procedures for publicly establishing and verifying the truth about cases; this discourse was carried to and fro between law courts and the disputatious democratic assemblies, where the work of developing knockdown arguments against opposing positions was carried on with urgency (Lloyd, 1990; Vernant, 1982).

This new kind of thinking tended to undermine the authority of tradition and to encourage a rational reassessment of affairs, enlarging the initiative of merchants no less than of politicians and scholars. "When Tom, Dick, and Harry began to call themselves Society and The State and start meddling with the moral deportment of individuals" (Shaw, 1965, p. 257), the authority of the gods or sacred ancestors and tradition lost ground to individuals analyzing their activities in terms of rational considerations of their interests. Thus Max Weber (1864–1920) sees sophisticated rationality developed as a tool for analyzing the successors of these early developments in capitalist economic activity, bourgeois law, and bureaucratic authority; this rationality "is capable of being expressed in numerical, calculable terms" (Weber, 1975, p. 85). Eric Havelock notes as central to the new "conceptual" language developed in ancient Greece that it is "a counting, calculative use of language akin to arranging units of speech in some new and unrhythmic order, a rationalized language" (1982, p. 77).

Plato's archetypical academic community required its students to be familiar with geometry, an abstract, calculative form of knowledge that established unequivocal truths that were subject to no knockdown response. Communities and institutions in the postclassical world have continued to nurture and develop this kind of theoretical thinking and the philosophic understanding it produces.

Communities are important to this kind of understanding because it is carried only in part by philosophic texts; it is "oral discourse about written texts that provides such fertile ground for modern, skeptical, interpretive thought" (Olson and Torrance, 1991, p. 1). Talking about such texts helps to make the abstract language a part of one's everyday thinking, or makes it fluently available when one is confronted by problems or circumstances with which it can effectively deal. The isolated scholar, the antodidact, will often engage this level of discourse energetically but is more likely to become lost or eccentric as a result of manipulating its abstractions than is the scholar in a community—not that becoming lost or eccentric is so rare among the most clubbable navigators of the philosophic realm. Something about throwing the first stone comes to mind.

ANCIENT GREEK AND MODERN EUROPEAN THEORETIC THINKING

Let us return to the new form of historical narrative Herodotus invented and see what happened to it, because the developments in history writing exemplify a more general development of theoretic thinking. For present purposes, two distinct developments can be charted. First is a continuing tradition of "romantic" histories like Herodotus's. From his time to today, histories of this kind have been most popular. They involve a focus on dramatic events, preserving the memory of great deeds and outstanding people from sliding unjustly into the river of forgetfulness and being carried away, as   107

Anna Comnena put it. From Xenophon's description of his desperate "march up-country," through Arian's account of Alexander's life and conquests, up to modern semi-journalistic books on self-immolating cults or serial killers and their trails of mayhem, or hagiography-tinged memorials of outstanding figures or popsingers, the note of "romantic" history writing persists. Such narratives can be precisely accurate, intricately detailed, and sophisticated in expression; their expression of, and appeal to, Romantic understanding is evident in their interest in the *mega ergon* and their embodiment of various of the characteristics sketched in the previous chapter.

The second development was to a significantly different kind of history, such as that written by Thucydides. He wrote about the Peloponnesian War between Athens and Sparta, but, unlike in "romantic" histories, he focused on establishing a more general truth beyond the particulars; he articulated a theory of history as well as a narrative of particular events.

Thucydides' ambition to capture some general truth about the historical process, though he may have started with the idea of writing a handbook on strategy, led to one of the stranger books that has survived from the ancient world. It is a carefully researched, massively detailed, dispassionate record of a terrible, passionate war. Thucydides, himself an Athenian general, describes briefly his part in the loss of the city of Amphipolis. He tells us only that he set out as fast as possible with his seven ships, that it was winter, and that he arrived just too late to prevent the surrender of the city. Later he notes in passing (to explain how he was able to spend so much time researching details of the war) that for his part in this action he was banished for twenty years from his native Athens. There is no exculpation, no apology, no detail relevant to his case beyond what the narrative of the war calls for. This is not what we have come to expect from generals' memoirs of their wars. Thucydides suppresses personal interest in favor of a greater ambition.

He begins his history by telling us that we should expect a difficult read; he is not in the business of providing entertainment, like Herodotus, nor something of simply local and immediate relevance, but rather he is writing a book whose value will "last for ever" (I, 23). He shows us Athens in her glory, under the steady hand of far-sighted Pericles, and then describes her growing confidence in the certainty of success in the war and her increasing conviction that she was immune to fortune and chance. Influence over the conduct of the war later passes to the unstable Cleon, "the most violent of citizens," and to the deluded lion, Alcibiades. Thus we follow the city's psychological condition from the richness and confidence of the early years to the unbearable end, prefigured in the greatest and most daring action that culminates in the destruction of Athens' hopes and the flower of her army in a stone quarry in Syracuse. Full of pathos and drama, the war is given the narrative shape of a tragedy (Cornford, 1907; Egan, 1978a).

Thucydides' aim was not to record the great and wonderful deeds that should be remembered, except insofar as this was incidental to preventing the whole war from "sliding over into myth" as the Trojan war had, left to Homer, or into a romantic, audience-gratifying entertainment, as the Persian wars had at the hands of Herodotus. Both historians had failed to recognize the proper aim of history, which was to establish the truth, not just about a particular war, but about war in general. Thucydides seemed to believe that war was like a disease, and as we can trace the symptoms and course of a disease, like the Hippocratic writers on medicine, so we can establish how war occurs in human affairs. He uses an odd phrase, to modern ears, claiming that he is going to describe this war in detail so that "when similar events recur, as they will, human nature being what it is, people will be able to recognize them" (I, 23). That is, it is as though the Peloponnesian War is serving as a paradigm of wars, the underlying structure of which his investigation exposed. Like Hippocratic medical researchers, Thucydides clearly has a nascent scientific ambition—the discovery of a "general law" determining the course of human affairs.

Thucydides seems to have seen history not as a set of diverse particular events but rather as a single complex process whose underlying order, rules, or laws could be exposed by careful, dispassionate inquiry. His ambition has been shared by many since. We call them "metahistorians," or "philosophers of history" in the nineteenth-century sense of those who focus on exposing some general truth about the historical process as a whole; that it is a tragic process, or an ameliorating process, or one involving the organic birth, maturity, and death of civilizations.

A more familiar source of theoretic thinking is medicine. The Hippocratic writings certainly aimed to establish general truths about their phenomena of interest, even though some of their prescriptions seem no more likely to effect cures than those dispensed in the temples by priests according to gods' diagnoses. The Hippocratic prescription for moving a misplaced womb, for example, involved the patient crouching alternately over sweet and foul odors to encourage movement in one direction or another. Lloyd describes the canon of writings as involving "dogmatism, arbitrariness, and wild speculation" (1990, p. 32), often indistinguishable from the folk-medicine they were attempting to displace. But their approach exhibits a sputtering commitment to something we cannot but recognize as the beginnings of rational, scientific medicine. There is, particularly, the appeal to what we would call empirical principles—as the author of *On Ancient Medicine* put it:

> Hence I claim that it has no need of empty postulates such as are inevitable in dealing
> with insoluble problems beyond the reach of observation, for example, what goes on in
> the sky or beneath the earth. If a man pronounces some opinion he has formed on how
> these things are, it cannot be clear either to himself or to his hearers whether what he says
> is true or not; for there is no test that can be applied so as to yield certain knowledge.
> (Cornford, 1952)

Certainly the Greeks did not invent medicine, as they did not invent geometry, or astronomy, but they were, "as far as we know, the first to engage in self-conscious analysis of the status, methods and foundations of those inquiries, the first to raise, precisely, the second-order questions" (Lloyd, 1990, p. 58), and they were the first to organize institutions to support and further this straining, complicated kind of inquiry. No doubt many folk remedies, or contemporary pharmacopoeia, might contain as good or better practical help for the sick; what they did not seek to develop, which the Hippocratics did, was a body of theory.

Another feature of this new method was that it encouraged a disengaged perspective. More radically than the rationality of Romantic understanding, this philosophic method encouraged its communities of users to grasp things not as they impinge on their interests but as they are in reality. We have become very knowing about the difficulties in achieving such a grasp on reality, of course, but pursuing it, trying to attain it, has led to a rather odd program of inquiry, with surprising results, in which people began to inquire into all kinds of things that have no pragmatic interest or value, or serve no one's apparent social purposes. Inquiry was constrained only by what the available methods of inquiry did not allow. So the swing of the Pleiades or the behavior of ants became as interesting, or more interesting, to these calculating theory-makers than one's daily cares. An epistemologically omnivorous form of inquiry resulted, one which—its proponents polemically proclaimed—could deliver the truth about the world.

Plato and, more comprehensively, Aristotle spelled out the conditions for attaining this new kind of Philosophic understanding. Crucial was the elimination of "the poetic" from inquiry; the arts only introduced vagueness and turned the focus to matters that the new calculative methods could not grasp. Metaphor, intuition, images, and speculation untied from calculation and precise observation were declared out of bounds.

Aristotle, like Plato too to some extent before him, was engaged in establishing and validating a new style of inquiry. They were both concerned to recommend the pursuit of philosophy, as they each construed it, and in Aristotle's case that would include also his conception of natural science. But this inquiry into nature had, he believed, to be given a firm foundation. It is for that purpose, especially, that he insists that, at least from the point of view of his ideal, there can be no room for the metaphorical. Yet this new style of inquiry not only set itself high standards—impossibly high ones, we might think—but it also negatively and destructively *ruled out* much of the competition as failing in precision, in clarity, in the direct, the literal. (Lloyd, 1990, pp. 22–23)

Indeed, Aristotle's rigor was to rule out significant features of Plato's work, including the whole theory of Forms. But, even so, their polemical victory on behalf of philosophy against forms of thinking common in the arts, in oral cultures, and among competing sophists—all dismissed as "mythic"— generated a new faith "that was and remains the basis of scientific thought . . . that the visible world conceals a rational and intelligible order" (Guthrie, 1962, p. 29). This victory identified and established the method of discovering that order and the language in which it could be expressed.

What we see through Plato's and Aristotle's promotion of philosophic thinking is its intense and systematic development and its claim to provide a privileged view of reality and an exclusive path to truth. Let me leap over other ancient civilizations, then, including the Roman Empire, pausing at the renaissance of the twelfth and thirteenth centuries only to note the influence of the rediscovery of Aristotle's writings, and rumination and commentaries on them by Arabic and Jewish scholars. Within the Christian West, the parables of Christ that conveyed the essence of his teaching were reformulated into the abstract, theoretic theology of the medieval schools and universities. From the illiterate kingdoms of Europe it is possible to trace, as Vico (1970) argues, a *ricorso* of the Greek experience, whereby the oral and mythic gave way to "*ratio scientiam quaerens,* reason seeking out knowledge" (Stock, 1972, p. 23; Stock, 1983).

The next definitive clarification and refinement of Philosophic understanding is most easily seen in the seventeenth through nineteenth centuries in Europe. The early and commonly recognized avatars of this development include René Descartes (1596–1650) and the odd Englishman, Francis Bacon (1561–1626). Bacon's upbringing by an earnestly Puritan mother and a father intent on making him every inch a worldly courtier perhaps encouraged his enormously flexible and powerful intellect, and perhaps even prepared him for his remarkable rollercoaster career in the treacherous years of Elizabethan and Jacobean politics. (When compelled to resign the chancellorship in 1621 for accepting bribes, Bacon rather engagingly argued in his defence that he never let the bribes affect his judgment of cases.) While only a part-time practical scientist himself, Bacon set out in powerful terms the program that a new science had to pursue. He used his periods in power to propose (without much practical success) that scientific research needed to be organized on a large scale and be lavishly financed.

Underneath the theorizing of Bacon and Descartes was the continuing development of the printing press. The print shops, as Elizabeth Eisenstein (1979, 1983) has shown, from the earliest days began to accumulate around them communities of scholars and stimulated through their subscription lists a wider "virtual" community around Europe. This "virtual" community was made up of varied smaller communities, some attached to universities, some to metropolitan centers and, later, to their coffeehouses, *salons,* or wine shops, and some encouraged by monarchs. Few monarchs, though, had quite the enthusiasm for the new learning as Queen Christina of Sweden. Her insistent invitations to Descartes, and then the rigorous schedule she kept him to in the rough Stockholm climate, managed to kill him. In England, the most famous of these scholarly groups was given a charter, but no cash, by Charles II in 1662, and became the Royal Society of London. (The lack of government cash did mean that the members retained their political independence. Joseph Addison took some delight in passing on the suggestion that Richelieu had founded the French Academy, in 1634, "to divert the Men of Genius from meddling with Politicks" [cf. Rawson, 1988, p. 1336].) The Czech scholar Comenius dedicated his 1668 treatise *Via Lucis* "to the torch bearers of this enlightened age, members of the Royal Society of London, now bringing real philosophy to a happy birth."

Bishop Thomas Sprat, an early member of the society and its first historian, noted that its aims were not only the advancement of science but also the improvement of "the English tongue, particularly for philosophic purposes." What was needed for "real philosophy" to advance was a pure, unpoetic, simple, unambiguous prose, something close to a mathematical plainness that would reflect the natural world like a mirror. The society's overall aim, though many of the early members were clerics, was to achieve a more general truth than religious controversy allowed: "For they openly profess, not to lay the Foundation of an *English, Scotch, Irish, Popish,* or *Protestant* Philosophy; but a Philosophy of *Mankind*" (Sprat, 1958, p. 63). Sprat also emphasizes the importance of communal activity:

Nor is it the least commendation the *Royal Society* deserves, that designing a union of men's *Hands* and *Reasons,* it has proceeded so far in uniting their *Affections:* For there we behold an unusual sight to the *English Nation,* that men of disagreeing parties, and ways of life, have forgotten to hate, and have met in the unanimous advancement of the same *Works.* There the *Soldier,* the *Tradesman,* the *Merchant,* the *Scholar,* the *Gentleman,* the *Courtier,* the *Divine,* the *Presbyterian,* the *Papist,* the *Independent,* and those of *Orthodox Judgment,* have laid aside their names of distinction, and calmly conspir'd in a mutual agreement of *labors* and *desires:* . . . For here they do not only endure each others presence without violence or fear; but they *work* and *think* in company, and confer their help to each other's *Inventions.* (1958, p. 427; emphasis in original)

While the kind of thinking Plato and Aristotle bequeathed to modern Europe assumed a somewhat distinctive form in "the real philosophy" of empirical science, the same impulses to establish the truth about reality with rigorous theoretic clarity were evident in the humanities generally, and also in reflection on everyday affairs. Dictionaries—Dr. Johnson's was published in 1755—and encyclopedias—Ephraim Chambers's appeared in 1728, influencing the indomitable Denis Diderot and the great French *Encyclopédie,* whose *philosophes* contributors aimed to change the way people thought— supported the process of clarification, precision, ordering, and accessibility of knowledge. (The entry under *philosophe* in the *Encyclopédie* notes, "Reason is to the *philosophe* what grace is to the Christian.")

During the eighteenth century, a growing community wanted to discuss topical issues, literature, art, economics, history, and politics in a manner that more nearly matched the seriousness, precision, and authority of the scientists. Examples of this theoretic philosophic discourse, addressed to a wide "virtual community" in a style, like Thucydides', written with an eye to a permanence beyond coffeehouse opinion, found a home in the great reviews of the late eighteenth and early nineteenth centuries. The *Analytical Review,* founded by a radical young Scotsman, Thomas Christie, and by Joseph Johnson, a book dealer ("the father of the booktrade") and publisher, ran from 1788 to 1799. *The Edinburgh Review* was founded on a stormy night in March 1802 on the third floor of 18, Buccleuch Place, Edinburgh, and the *Quarterly Review* followed in 1809. The contributors of the last two in particular did not succeed in calmly conspiring in a mutual agreement like the scientists, as the two reviews reflected Whig and Tory party interests, respectively. But by 1812 they had an estimated joint readership of around one hundred thousand, each selling more than twelve thousand copies per issue. "To be an Edinburgh Reviewer is, I suspect, the highest rank in modern literary society," wrote Hazlitt (McClure, 1989–90, p. 1436; see also Shattock, 1989). And around the reviews were communities of talkers, whose conversations were encouraged to use the 'philosophic' discourse exemplified by the reviewers. Perhaps the most brilliant was Sydney Smith, another cleric and a prime mover of the *Edinburgh Review,* who moaned loudly when dragged back to his parishes from the magic square mile around Holland House, and whose startlingly lively wit was such that people rushed home after conversing with him to write down what he had said—fortunately for us (Pearson, 1948). Smith's clean, sharp, abrupt style seems entirely modern; as do many of his sentiments. How can we think of as anything other than a contemporary a person who said, "I am not fond of expecting catastrophes, but there are cracks in the world" (Pearson, 1948, p. 308).

113

The philosophic note can be found in all areas of inquiry. Edward Gibbon published the first volume of his *Decline and Fall of the Roman Empire* in 1776, to near-universal acclaim (the clergy, notably,were reluctant to see Christianity treated as a villain of the piece). Gibbon had been influenced by the *philosophes*, particularly Montesquieu. Quoting David Womersley's 1989 book on the writing of *The Decline and Fall,* John Kenyon notes: "The philosophic historian 'hopes to dissolve the surface of historical change and thereby reveal the unchanging principles governing human society and action'" (1989, p. 1380). This philosophic ambition gathers force in the history writing of the nineteenth century. The great figure of Leopold von Ranke (1795–1886) reformed historical research, claiming that it was only by meticulous care in uncovering the particulars of past events (*Wie es Eigentlich gewesen)* "for their own sake" that "the development of the world in general will become apparent" (Ranke, 1956, p. 57). If Thucydides' conception of history was tragic, Ranke's is comic; he presents a general image of the historical process as a God-guaranteed progress of the nation-states toward unity and harmony.

For the pure Philosophic inquirer of the Enlightenment, all general questions have a single true answer, these answers are in principle discoverable and knowable, and each answer will be compatible with all other answers composing a single, correct, coherent view of the cosmos, which we will share with God.

Through the nineteenth century, communities and institutions supporting philosophic discourse increased: "Not since the genius of the seventeenth-century virtuosi stirred learned imaginations had so many eloquent voices praised the cause of science" (Turner, 1974, p. 9). As Hayden White observes, "[n]ineteenth century European culture displayed everywhere a rage for a realistic apprehension of the world" (1973, p. 45) that its "philosophic" forms of inquiry were intent on supplying. So John Stuart Mill could write:

The supremely important fact [of our era], the gradual reduction of all phenomena within the sphere of established law, which carries as a consequence the rejection of the miraculous, has its determining current in the development of physical science. The great conception of universal regular sequence . . . could only grow out of the patient watching of external fact, and the silencing of preconceived notions, which are urged upon the mind by the problem of physical science. (Dale, 1989, p. 3)

Mill was influenced by, and repaid by financially supporting, Auguste Comte (1798–1857), the French philosopher and social theorist who invented the term "sociology" and described the process whereby it was to be made scientific. Comte also gave an elaborate, programmatic outline of "positivism" in his six-volume *Cours de Philosophie Positive* (1830–42). He argued that the human mind in cultural history has passed through three inevitable, irreversible stages: theological, metaphysical, and positive. Positivism is marked by the final recognition that science provides the only valid form of knowledge and that facts are the only possible objects of knowledge; philosophy is thus recognized as essentially no different from science except that its task is to seek more generally for principles common to all sciences and use these principles to guide human conduct and the organization of society. Ethics, politics, social interactions, and all other forms of human life about which knowledge was possible would eventually be drawn into the orbit of science, become thereby properly ordered, and so lead to universal human betterment. Though Comte at age fourteen had announced to his ardently Catholic family that he had "naturally ceased to believe in God," his image of the world and the new humanity to be created by the application of positive science had a considerable romantic and religious tinge and was described by Thomas Huxley as Catholicism without Christianity.

Nineteenth-century positivism was one direction taken by Philosophic understanding. The positivists' program for mapping the inexorable and immutable laws of matter and society seemed to allow no greater role for the contribution of poets than had Plato. The poets, however, had a counter-claim to make. During the early part of the century they had asserted powerfully that access to truth and knowledge were far from exclusively achieved by reason and science. Perhaps the most cogent and comprehensive statement of poetry's claims on truth is Shelley's *Defence of Poetry* (written in 1821, and first published in 1840), in which he argues: "Poetry . . . is at once the centre and circumference of knowledge; it is that which comprehends all science, and that to which all science must be referred" (Brett-Smith, 1921, p. 53). He concludes that poets are the unacknowledged legislators of the world. These claims, however, are stated in abstract theoretic terms, no less philosophic than the more prolix claims of Comte, Mill, and Herbert Spencer. That is, distinctions among Enlightenment, Romanticism, and post-Romanticism, which have played a large part in categorizing cultural history, are not very significant from the perspective of these kinds of understanding. Certainly we find clear cases of Romantic understanding in Romanticism, but we will also find that the leading Romantic writers routinely used features of Philosophic understanding, particularly when arguing on behalf of the propriety of their poetic program of exploration. We will find, that is to say, all five kinds of understanding interleaved in complex historical movements, sometimes one kind showing more prominently, sometimes another.

What Plato represented as the quarrel between philosophy and poetry is resuscitated in the "two cultures" quarrel of more recent times between the   115 humanities and the sciences. Both sides have conducted their quarrel in "philosophic" terms, both building their arguments rationally and constructing theoretic positions. The polemical beginnings of the quarrel were tied to claims about what kind of education best formed the mind. (After all, for much of their lives Plato and Aristotle were professional educators.) The "two cultures" quarrel of recent years continues a debate that has long had as one of its important implications the appropriate structure of the school and university curriculum. What deserves greater attention, the sciences or the humanities? Which is more important for the development of the mind? As with most educational questions, these have run into a general *impasse;* "solutions" are compromises that seem to do justice to neither side of the quarrel and to satisfy no one. This state of affairs is a result, I think, of our current incoherent conception of education, which allows no adequate handle on the quarrel.

The quarrel is seen as a battle for the human soul, or, which is much the same thing, a battle over how we should educate the young. The scientists' side of the argument is commonly pressed in a regrettable tone that contains a regrettable truth, as in this recent example: "Science involves an unnatural mode of thought which alienates and humiliates those who are ignorant of it" (Wolpert, 1993, p. 4). It follows that those who are ignorant of science can have nothing of value to contribute. This dismissiveness can easily be read as a "know-all, imagine-nothing style" (Osborne, 1992, p. 31), and the claims of imagination and the "shadowy things" inaccessible to the methods of inquiry available to scientists are reasserted as central to a full human life and education.

But it is inappropriate to call Philosophic understanding "unnatural"— as Wolpert describes the empirical science form of it, echoed in the title of his 1992 book, *The Unnatural Nature of Science*—any more than it would be to call Mythic or Romantic or Ironic understanding unnatural. Rather, one might better say, it is not a kind of thinking or understanding that is usually developed in any systematic way apart from communities or institutions dedicated to encouraging it. Like the other kinds of understanding, it is relatively easy to acquire if one is in an environment that insistently uses it; it requires the "mediational means" of a consistent and persistent theoretic discourse.

Some Characteristics of Philosophic Understanding

My general argument is that a proper education today requires that individuals accumulate and recapitulate the intellectual capacities represented by each of these kinds of understanding, and deploy them together—"to-gether" in some manner yet to be made clear. Philosophic and Romantic understanding, and no doubt the Mythic kind, too, trumpeted their historical development by setting themselves up in opposition to their predecessor; or, at least, that is how some of their more polemical proponents represented them. I used Hecataeus's dismissal of the stories of his ancestors as emblematic of the early rational contempt for Mythic thinking, and Thucydides, the Hippocratics, Aristotle, Bacon, Descartes, and so on, as decriers of earlier and contemporary "Romantic" inquiries. This common feature of Western cultural history is unfortunate for many reasons, not least because it seems to take most people a long time to recognize that the preceding kind of understanding is not simply the pit of villainous confusion represented by its successors but in fact forms a foundation to their own preferred kind.

In cases where people have deliberately struggled to extirpate all vestiges of prior kinds of understanding, the result seems to be sterility, desiccation, and a danger of inhumanity in the development of the new kind. It seems fair to describe positivism and behaviorism as examples of this. As Charles Taylor puts it:

Once one has broken out from the world view of a very narrow form of naturalism, it seems almost unbelievable that anyone could ever have taken a theory like behaviorism seriously. It takes a very powerful metaphysical set of preconceptions for one to ignore or over-ride so much that is so intuitively obvious about human life, for no valid scientific or explanatory reason. (1985, p. 5)

The polemical accompaniment to the development of Philosophic understanding represents the new form as sweeping away the insubstantial folk knowledge, the emotionalism, the metaphor-induced confusion, the glittering superficiality of its predecessors, and replacing these with cold, hard factuality and sharp-edged theoretical truth. This is the stance of the self-consciously tough-minded.

But cultural development has come, in Ong's phrase, "not in the hollow of men's minds but in the density of history" (1971, p. 7). The gender reference in the quotation is notable in that the communities that have supported Philosophic understanding in the density of history were, until the twentieth century, almost exclusively male. All the developers of Philosophic understanding mentioned in the previous section were men. Does this mean that Philosophic understanding, engendered by a gaggle of patriarchs, is a masculine form of thinking? Is my scheme, which will recommend Philosophic understanding as a necessary acquisition in the process of becoming educated, simply another of those sexist developmental theories that prescribes male intellectual norms into which women are simply supposed to fit? If a third layer of understanding had been developed in the matrix of women's minds and the density of a female-dominated history, would we have seen something different from the Philosophic kind being characterized here? That is, is Philosophic understanding only contingently gender-biased or is it necessarily a male-oriented kind of thinking?

I doubt that any conclusive answer can yet be given, though I suspect that any gender association of Philosophic understanding will prove to be almost entirely contingent, to a point of vanishing significance for educational purposes. Any evident difference in access to and ease in using Philosophic thinking between males and females must be largely a product of women's lack of access to the communities that formed and supported such thinking. Their absence from these discussions continues to have profound and pervasive residual effects on the ways they are treated in such communities today, on the expectations held of them by males, and on their own expectations of themselves.

That the slant and tone of, and styles of initiation into, the most prominent traditions of Philosophic thinking give evidence of male bias, particularly in the sciences and mathematics, seems to me a product of the polemics that have accompanied their development in male-dominated communities, not something essential to Philosophic thinking itself. A feature of these polemics, as I suggested above, is that they depreciate kinds of understanding that are properly foundational to the Philosophic. My argument is that adequate Philosophic understanding must incorporate the capacities acquired while developing Mythic and Romantic understanding. When we see Philosophic understanding enriched by imagination, metaphoric thinking, romantic associations, and so on, it will, I trust, be less vulnerable to claims of gender bias.

Philosophic understanding begins to become prominent today at roughly age fifteen. Why this should be the case I will address below. But, I want to emphasize that this is not something that happens *routinely* as a result of maturation. Systematic development of Philosophic understanding seems at present normal for only a smallish proportion of the population—those who enter and interact with communities that support this kind of thinking, such as some academic streams in senior high schools and in colleges and universities, and who also have adequately accumulated Mythic and Romantic capacities.

The Craving for Generality

Earlier we saw Snell's argument that developments in the Greek language were prerequisite to abstract, theoretic thinking. So, too, in early modern Europe we find significant shifts in language preceding and accompanying the period when the *philosophes'* and scientists' programs were getting underway. Lucien Febvre (1878–1956), co-founder of the French *Annales* school of historians, pointed out that the sixteenth-century French language lacked words for "absolute," "relative," "abstract," "concrete," "intentional," "inherent," "transcendental," "causality," "regularity," "concept," "criterion," "analysis," "synthesis," "deduction," "induction," "coordination," "classification," "system," and a range of terms that the Philosophic programs of the next century would use prominently. According to the data banks of the American Research on the Treasury of the French Language, the word "société" was used 620 times in the century before 1700 and 7,168 times in the following two (cf. Gordon, 1994). Latin, of course, was still important for scholarly discourse and was not as impoverished as the vernaculars in this regard. But beginning in the sixteenth century, and becoming a flood in the seventeenth, words flowed into the vernaculars; in the process, many of them seemed to gain a metaphoric extension from a restricted, relatively concrete meaning in Latin to a more free, flexible, abstracted use in the vernaculars.

Take, for example, the word "hierarchy." It comes from the Greek *hieros,* meaning "sacred" or "holy," and *arkhēs,* meaning "ruling." It was used to designate a state ruled by priests. The word later became Latinized and Christianized to refer to the ninefold rank of angels—the *hierarchia* of cherubs, seraphs, and other sadly neglected creatures (oh, very well, if you insist: seraphim, cherubim, thrones, dominions, virtues, powers, principalities, angels, and archangels). It arrived in Middle English as *ierarchie* with its Latin meaning. It commonly occurred with more or less its modern spelling, and medieval meaning, in the sixteenth century. In the seventeenth century, the word was extended to apply not only to angels but to the ranks of the clergy, a somewhat different group, and very soon thereafter we find its metaphoric extension to mean any graded system, much as we use the term today. Words like "evolution," "concept," "deduction," "causality," and many of those listed by Febvre follow a roughly similar trail, the Oxford English Dictionary indicating significantly new and more flexible meanings adopted through the seventeenth century. The result was an enriched conceptual vocabulary for dealing with the enlarging realm of theory.

Walter Ong relates this development in modern Europe to an effect of the printing press and the massive accumulation of detailed documented knowledge. The security and accessibility of constantly enlarging bodies of knowledge allowed people to generate what he calls "portmanteau" concepts like culture, civilization, and evolution. Clearly the Greeks managed to develop related concepts without the printing press, but perhaps the peculiar modern European shape of Philosophic understanding owes much, as Ong

(1971) and McLuhan (1962) suggest, to the constantly replicating thump of the press.

The vocabulary of late adolescents engaged in academic work commonly begins to sprout "portmanteau" concepts, including many of those mentioned above. Ong emphasizes that such terms cannot be generated, however, without a significant accumulation of detailed knowledge (1978). Sometimes we find words students had long known and could have defined, such as "society," quite suddenly emerge into their everyday serious discourse with energy and prominence. Clearly the word has taken on a new and more precise meaning; some referent of the word has come into focus. "Society" is no longer a vague term used by adults to refer to an amorphous, indistinct concatenation of houses and services and politicians but becomes the name for the general *entity* that encompasses all those bits and pieces. It is as though an *object* has been discovered—a very complex one, but one that can be grasped by means of the portmanteau term. We can commonly note words like "nature," "culture," "the environment," "system," and "process" being used to refer to a theoretic world whose abstract inhabitants begin to emerge as clear, definite, real things. "Society" might be an enormous generalization but, to the Philosophic mind, it refers to something real; not just something made up of the sum of its parts but something having a reality more intellectually apprehensible than the sum of its parts. Indeed, the parts begin to take on meaning in terms of their place in the greater whole.

In the development of the theoretic realm, the new objects that come into focus are significantly different from those illuminated by the perspective of Romantic understanding. (The slight disjunction of metaphors in the last sentence is deliberate; "bringing into focus," "illuminating," and "perspective" are somewhat at odds with each other, preventing a simple image from developing. The visual metaphors we commonly deploy to discuss ideas can easily displace the slippier realm of concepts with the solid realm of physical objects. The point of this perhaps overly cute observation is that Philosophic understanding, particularly when we initially engage it, seems prone to this displacement, taking the very general concepts as though they refer to something tangible. But they will appear so only to those whose thinking is excessively "Philosophical." As former British Prime Minister Margaret Thatcher notoriously claimed: "There is no such thing as 'society'!")

The romantic perspective on history or on the social or natural worlds focused the younger student's mind on the extremes, on the more fascinating facts, on vivid true stories, dramatic events, heroes, and so on. The Romantic student recognizes, of course, that all these bright bits and pieces are parts of the one real world, but the connections among them are not particularly interesting. The new theoretic language helps to generate, or is a symptom of, a significantly different perspective in which the bright bits and pieces are seen increasingly as parts of general wholes, systems, and processes. History, for example, is no longer perceived primarily as a set of vivid events, styles of living, and heroic characters but rather as a single complex process, a continuum of styles, examples of the possible range of human behavior and human nature. The connections among things come increasingly into prominence, and the Philosophic students' connection with things comes increasingly from the realization that they themselves are parts of the complex processes and systems that make up the world.

This perception gives rise to new questions about the nature of the historical process. Is it an ameliorative one, in which the nasty, brutal, and short life of our savage ancestors gradually became a harmonious, healthy, intellectually enriched experience? Or perhaps it is a tragedy, in which things began to fall apart for humans with the invention of agriculture, which led to private property, population explosions and social disruption, surpluses and hierarchies—as Rousseau and St.-Simon viewed it. Or perhaps the agricultural utopia was destroyed by the discoveries of metallurgy, which led to hierarchies, hereditary secrets, a primitive bourgeoisie, greed, and war—as V. Gordon Childe presents it. Or perhaps the invention of writing was the cause of all our woes. What are the laws that determine the natural world? What is the truth about society? What is natural human behavior? What— the unsophisticated philosophic mind accepts as a meaningful question—is the meaning of life?

The Philosophic mind focuses on the connections among things, constructing theories, laws, ideologies, and metaphysical schemes to tie together the facts available to the student. The student then begins to acquire the knowledge necessary for rounding out the scheme. Take, for example, a discussion stimulated by local political candidates' lawn and window signs during a current election campaign. The Romantic child asks whose side "we" are on, why the different parties use the colors they do, and so on. The Philosophic fifteen-year-old wants to know details of the process that accounts for the electioneering signs' presence on lawns or in windows. Do the parties or candidates pay to rent space on the lawns, like advertising, or do people pay the party to get the signs? Do they have to pay more for a big one than for a small one? How many people are swayed by such signs? What kinds of people? Wouldn't the money be better spent on TV ads? Bit by bit, the fifteen-year-old composes the information required to flesh out an understanding of the election *process*.

What I have described here is a development that many people—some of whom I quote below—have observed and referred to. It is a development based on empirical observations of students in contact with Philosophic communities around this age and on a study of the reading, films, TV shows, writing, games, and stories that such students identify as most interesting and important to them. But I will not be citing supporting empirical research, for two related reasons. First, I am not aware of any; current research methods in psychology and education would have difficulty grasping, for example, changes in vocabularies and changes in the use and meaning of terms over a period of many months to a few years. Second, we have not hitherto had a sufficiently clear theory of this development to guide researchers to devise empirical tests. The one theory that makes some overlapping observations is Piaget's. His notion of "formal operations," while problematic and the subject of much controversy (see for example, Modgil and Modgil, 1982; Siegel and Brainerd, 1978), does reflect a common recognition of the construction of a theoretic realm in academic students in later adolescence. Piaget focused on a set of internal, spontaneously developing, logico-mathematical structures that are paradigmatic Philosophic entities: immensely abstract, largely inaccessible, and containing *the truth* about the process of development. What I describe in general terms as a characteristic of Philosophic understanding—that students increasingly identify the truth as belonging in this theoretic realm—Inhelder and Piaget described as follows:

[I]n formal thought there is a reversal in the direction of thinking between *reality* and *possibility* in the Subjects' method of approach. Possibility no longer appears merely as an extension of an empirical situation or of actions actually performed. Instead it is *reality* that is now secondary to *possibility*. . . . The most distinctive property of formal thought is this reversal of direction between *reality* and *possibility;* instead of deriving a rudimentary theory from the empirical data as is done in concrete inferences, formal thought begins with a theoretical synthesis implying that certain relations are necessary and thus proceeds in the opposite direction. (1958, p. 251)

This openness to "possibility," which is one feature of what I call general schemes, can leave students vulnerable. It has long been evident to those attempting to attract adolescents to some ideological position that intense commitment can be generated by convincing them of *the truth* of the view of the world it represents. Consider the way typical nation states enlist the commitment of the young by the presentation of their national story; in liberal and pluralist states the result is typically a commitment to liberal pluralism, in more determinedly indoctrinating states, such as Nazi Germany, the result can be a passionate dedication, evident in the fervor of young eyes and behavior. A few decades ago, it was not uncommon in Western universities for bright students' minds to be captured by Marxism. "Capturing the mind" is perhaps a slightly dramatic metaphor, but Marxism's appeal lay in its enormous generality and its promise to tell the general truth about all the facts, events, institutions, emotions, consciousness—past, present, and future —in the interplay of three ideas: the Hegelian thesis, antithesis, and synthesis, each of which takes different forms in different times and circumstances but rolls inexorably on. All the disorganized information learned earlier— about medieval villages, knights and their ladies, monasteries, and wool production—slide neatly into their *true* places as part of the overarching process of conflict between feudalism and a rising bourgeoisie, which would spawn its own antithetical proletariat, and so on, to the ideal classless society. Such a general scheme has the added virtues of informing the student of his or her own place in the overall process, thereby defining a social role and re-establishing a secure identity.

Some general schemes act like a powerful magnet, organizing virtually everything in the student's mind; others are weaker, bringing about a more diffuse order. Some are very simple, dividing the world for the student into two, good and bad, black and white, right and wrong; others may be much more sophisticated, generating complex and subtle patterns. Once they emerge in the clutter of the Romantic mind, such schemes seem to reach definition quite quickly and to assert their magnetic influence over the clutter: "When we begin to believe anything, what we believe is not a single proposition, it is a whole system of propositions" (Wittgenstein, 1969, p. 145).

Initial symptoms of Philosophic understanding begin to emerge in Romantic thinking. Mary Warnock notes how "Imagination can stretch out towards what imagination cannot comprehend" (1976, p. 58). One of the things it "stretches out towards" is what used to be called, during the Romantic period, the Sublime. The mind was filled with somewhat inchoate but enticing images of infinite space, endless numbers, and eternal duration. As Kant argues, this use of imagination leads us beyond what is accessible to the senses, but also toward the realization that there is *something signified* by these concepts that we can express but somehow cannot grasp, though we can grasp *toward* them. Romantics' sublime ideas are not so far removed from the "Enlightenment's tendency to produce vast schema for society on a universal and historical scale" (Butler, 1981, p. 126). The student today who becomes engaged by the Gaia hypothesis, or who sees history in Marxist terms, is recapitulating an intellectual process we can chart in our cultural history. The move from Romantic to Philosophic understanding follows the stretch of the imagination and the subsequent construction of the linguistic and conceptual tools required to secure the mind's hold on what the imagination grasped toward.

Recall my earlier representation of the Romantic exploration of a hill town as in the fashion of a tourist, first seeking out the main square, the 123 walls, and the most dramatic features. The Philosophic exploration might be represented as that of a map maker, for whom all the features are significant in the creation of an accurate representation of the whole town.

From Transcendent Players to Social Agents

One constant of cultural history is the changing sense of self. The major theoretical achievements of the modern world, from Copernicus's new model of our place in the universe to Darwin's new model of our place in the natural world, had major impacts on people's sense of their selves. Aristotle's observation that humans are social animals achieved a new gloss in the growing cities of the sixteenth and seventeenth centuries. No one is an island; our sociability and interdependence were increasingly recognized as due not simply to our all being related as "children of God" but to something in our animal nature. During this period, people become increasingly *historical* animals: we may have a nature, but it is an historical one—a cultural nature. The general cosmological and evolutionary schemes (the latter had been broached long before Darwin came up with a mechanism that would explain the sequence of changes in the fossil records) provided new and not always welcome ways of determining one's sense of self.

As modern students recapitulate such schemes, their sense of self changes as well. The "romantic" self, sustained by associations with chosen embodiments of transcendent human qualities (the pop singer, sports player, social activist, self-sacrificing helper), begins to fade into the background. Students begin to see that they are connected to the world not via transcendent associations but by complex causal chains and networks. They come to realize that they are "born with a past" (MacIntyre, 1981, p. 205) and that that past not only constitutes the present self but begins to shape the future.

On the one hand this may seem a terrible loss of freedom—a later departure from another Eden—but on the other hand it yields a more adequate grasp on what is real and true about the world. Students begin to grasp that what we are does not result from romantic choices and associations but from laws of nature, human psychology, social interactions, history, and so on, which apply to our selves as to everyone else. The fading of the importance of romantic associations, then, can appear more a matter of putting aside childish things; having seen as through a glass darkly, students can attain a fuller, theoretic, consciousness of their place in the world.

The sense of enlarging consciousness comes to many students as liberating and energizing. In his autobiography, W. H. Hudson describes such a change at age fifteen in these terms: "It was as though I had only just become conscious; I doubt that I had ever been fully-conscious before" (1918, p. 292). This is something that nearly all educated people I have surveyed recognize, though some recall it as having more dramatic impact than others. We do not commonly fall off a horse with the impact of the flash of an idea capturing our minds, but it is common for people to use a visual metaphor to characterize what I am calling the relatively sudden access to Philosophic understanding.

If students perceive themselves to be parts of natural, social, historical, and other processes, their understanding of themselves and their roles in the world depends on their knowledge of how these processes work. During the years from about fifteen to the early twenties, then, students will characteristically search for or attempt to sustain a conception of the truth about human psychology, the laws of historical development, and the truth of how societies function.

Let us return to Marxism as an example. Here the student is directed to search out knowledge and perform actions that will point to the contradictions of capitalism, hinder the aims of reactionary bourgeois ideas and activities, and further the cause of the proletariat. (How old-fashioned this language has rapidly become.) The general scheme, that is, points the mind precisely toward particular knowledge that can support or challenge it, and toward behavior that brings it more evidently into reality.

Establishing the truth about history, society, and the cosmos is serious business. When Philosophic understanding dominates the mind, it can work with powerful intensity. The seriousness of Philosophic concerns, and the focus on knowledge that supports or challenges any one general scheme, tends to reduce interest in the extremes and in the dramatic. Romantic knowledge thus is often dismissed as irrelevant, pointless, a trivial pursuit; Romantic hobbies and collections lose their interest. The comic collection is sold, given to the Salvation Army, or stored in the attic to demolish the mortgage some decades on. The doll collection gathers dust for awhile before diving into the plastic bag and heading off to the attic or to the infant niece who cannot believe her luck. A note of earnestness common in modern Philosophic students echoes Victorian high seriousness. Both are engaged in a serious enterprise, after all, and surrounded by so many people unable to see the truth of their general scheme. The Victorians had missionaries, legislation, and the Gatling gun to carry their truth to the world; today's Philosophic students have social and political action groups, computer modems, and the Internet.

That the "expanding horizons" general scheme has had so much influence on teaching and the curriculum, especially in North America and Australia, implies that in the last years of high school the student is able to deal with content distant from "the self," knowledge of the self being the educational starting point of that scheme. (Note the peculiarity of this expectation about education for students whose private lives in late high school years are haunted by self-consciousness.) But there is a sense in which Philosophic understanding represents a new and closer apprehension of the self. Educational development, I am suggesting, is a process whose focus of interest and intellectual engagement begins with a myth-like construction of the world, then "romantically" establishes the boundaries and extent of reality, and then "philosophically" maps the major features of the world with organizing grids. In this "philosophic" activity, students recognize themselves as parts of complex processes; they set about establishing the truth concerning them with some psychological urgency because in doing so they will discover the truth about themselves.

This form of intellectual activity can easily slip into narcissism; students' interest in the world is not so much for its own sake as for what the discoveries will reveal about themselves. Students become attracted to academic subjects such as anthropology, psychology, and sociology that seem to promise direct knowledge about themselves. To the despair of anthropology teachers, many students' interest in other cultures seems directed largely by their desire to know what about themselves is determined by culture and what is their basic human genetic endowment rather than a desire to study the uniqueness of the people being discussed. The general scheme—the nature of human nature—is what they attend to; particular information is of interest only to the degree that it enlightens the scheme. If the teaching of these subjects, and of history, too, treats the search for general laws and huge explanatory schemes as misguided, Philosophic students tend to become disenchanted and switch off, turning perhaps to such magazines as *Psychology Today,* which deal with the subject in a largely Romantic and occasionally Philosophic manner.

"The story of my life is always embedded in the story of those communities from which I derive my identity" (MacIntyre, 1981, p. 205). To the degree that this is so, education seems largely a matter of "having an adequate sense of the traditions to which one belongs or which confront one," and having "an adequate sense of tradition manifests itself in a grasp of those future possibilities which the past has made available to the present" (p. 207). This need for "an adequate sense" forms one plank of a platform to be built in this book about the educational necessity of simply knowing a lot. General schemes, to be at all adequate, need to construct their patterns from a wide array of particular knowledge. The more diverse and intricate the factual base for a scheme, the more likely it is to reflect the world reliably. Build-

126

ing reliable general schemes is necessary for the individual student to become a realistic and sensible agent in the world.

The Lure of Certainty

We have inherited from the Classical period and from the Enlightenment the belief that Truth—some ultimate, fundamental truth about the world and our place and purpose in it—is attainable. This belief has mythic and religious roots. The truths that had earlier been accepted as coming appropriately from divine revelation were increasingly accepted as coming from disciplined inquiry. We can see how, during the seventeenth century, early scientists like "the incomparable Mr. Newton" saw no sharp division between divine revelation and disciplined inquiry. God has made Truth accessible to the person who studied the divine Word of the Bible or the divine Work of the physical world. These scientists seemed to believe that God had made the world and sprinkled it with puzzles, so that solving the puzzles brought greater understanding of God. To the artist and scholar of the humanities, the capacities earlier associate with the soul were increasingly associated with the more secular imagination (McFarland, 1985).

A common feature of Philosophic understanding is a tendency to assume that the patterns, theories, and general schemes used to order the world are true to the extent that, and in the way that, the particulars from which they are composed are true. That is, it is assumed that the truth of a general scheme is a function of the truth of the facts and events themselves and that the selection and organization of facts and events can be neutral or "objective" if appropriate care is taken. Failure to recognize that a general scheme involves reducing the diversity of the world can lead to a common overestimation of the security of one's general scheme and the nature of the truth that such schemes can claim.

This tendency to overconfidence in one's own theories has long been noted. The air of authority cultivated by Edinburgh reviewers, for example, readily escalated into arrogance. Sydney Smith satirized this excess, suggesting how the typical reviewer might discuss the achievement of constructing the solar system: "bad light—planets too distant—pestered with comets—feeble contrivance—could make a better with great ease" (Butler, 1981, p. 71). Mary Shelley warned against overconfidence in improving the feeble contrivance of the human being in Frankenstein (1818). Alfred Weber (1868–1958), Max's younger brother, wrote about the "dogmatic progressivism" and "dangerous sort of optimism" (1946, p. 49) arising from the Enlightenment's ideology of science and scholarship and its belief that it could secure certainty about the issues they address. To use Freudian terms, one could say that the assertiveness often shown by proponents of philosophic schemes is due to the suppression of their own hidden doubts.

The inappropriate sense of certainty that can come with Philosophic understanding in individuals' education is observed with disapproval from the classical period to the present. Plato recognized it as a danger point in his educational program: "You must have seen how youngsters [late teens], when they get their first taste of [dialectic and the *dianoia* curriculum], treat argument as a form of sport solely for purposes of contradiction . . . delighting like puppies in tugging and teasing anyone who comes near them" (*Republic*, VII, 539). The distress of overconfident youths is loud through the Enlightenment: "It is a frequent and growing Folly of our Age, that pert young Disciples soon fancy themselves wiser than those who teach them" (Watts, 1741, pp. 102–103); "Young people never show their folly and ignorance more conspicuously, than by this over-confidence in their own judgement, and this haughty disdain of the opinion of those who have known more days" (More, 1777, pp. 92–93). In a more psychologically alert age, like our own, the observation is put into this form: "The tentativeness implicit in the adolescent condition makes youth vulnerable to ideological certainty" (Spacks, 1981, p. 262). In part this excessive certainty arises because students are attracted to the power of theoretic ordering concepts without questioning the security of hold (or lack thereof) theories give over the phenomena to which they are applied. And so the "chief source of human error is to be found in general and abstract ideas," was Rousseau's related conclusion (1911, p. 236).

Earlier we looked at "hierarchy" as an example of a term typical of the set that supported Philosophic thinking. If we consider how hierarchization is put to work early in students' experience with Philosophic thinking we can see how the lure of certainty can draw the student toward inappropriate uses. In their later teens, some students begin to appreciate "classical" music, for example. Pushed by the Philosophic impulse, they will try to impose order; they will often argue about who is *the best* composer, and who is the second best, and so on. In so doing, they tend to search for the most fundamental criterion that will allow them to organize all composers (or football players, saints, actors, automobiles, writers, beers, whatever) by slotting them into place on some hierarchy. Not uncommonly this leads them to reduce the complexity by imposing an inappropriate single criterion.

Of course, it makes little sense to ask who is the *best* composer, as composers do different things more or less well. But sorting out what one means by that leads to increasingly sophisticated distinctions—and to the related question, "best for whom?" The notion of best, in terms of a single-criterion hierarchy, becomes meaningless. It does, however, make sense to ask who is one's *favorite* composer. It is common in the early stages of Philosophic understanding to confuse one's hierarchical scheme with an objective criterion of truth; once one has identified the *right* criterion for ranking composers (or football players, saints, writers, beers), and once one has found the ideology that shows *the truth* about the historical process, one can feel confident in dealing with particular composers, beers, writers, historical events, or whatever; understanding then becomes a task of slotting them into place in the scheme or on the hierarchy.

The observation that some students are overconfident follows from their seeming to think that they know the meaning of everything. This is an accurate description of many students moving into Philosophic thinking. They think they do know the true meaning of everything, even of things they have not yet learned. That is, with an established general scheme, an ideology, an overarching theory, they think that they understand the general principles from which the meaning of particulars is derived. Since they know the truth in general, they consider further learning and organizing the particulars within it as an essentially trivial task, even an unnecessary waste of time. Why bother with details when one already grasps the general truth?

General Schemes and Anomalies

One reason for bothering with details is that their support of general schemes is not always reliable. If intellectual security and even one's sense of identity is tied in with the general schemes one uses to make sense of the world and of experience, then one has a vital stake in ensuring the adequacy, validity, and truth of one's schemes. The problem is that, however sophisticated one's general scheme, there always seem to be facts around that do not fit it well at best, and, at worst, challenge it.

Leopold von Ranke composed a general scheme about the development of modern European history, as did Thucydides about Greek history and, by implication, all history. Each considered the truth of his general schemes to be established by his meticulous accumulation of reliable details, organized and expressed *sine ira et studio,* without anger or partiality, as Tacitus admonished. The truth of their general schemes emerged from the details, as might a mosaic from the precise placement of its component pieces. That the overall picture looks nothing like the individual pieces that make it up is simply a feature of how mosaics are composed; that the kind of knowledge claimed by a general scheme is not like that claimed by an exhaustively researched 129 historical fact is, to the Philosophic inquirer, just an uncontentious feature of how knowledge is built. (As I will explore in chapter 5, a more ironic view tends toward suspicion about patterns "emerging" from accumulated facts; the ironic eye tends to look for what Cornford called "some scheme of unsuspected presuppositions" that determines the selection of facts to compose a particular image.)

What happens, though, when one turns up facts that do not fit the general scheme, or when supporters of some competing general scheme thrust out such facts? How does a Marxist scheme accommodate the collapse of Eastern European and Russian economic and political systems and their adoption of capitalist and Western democratic practices? After all, it was the capitalist states that were supposed to collapse. Admittedly this is an extreme case of facts and events that are anomalous to a general scheme, but the daily life of the Philosophic mind is made up of the constant calibration of general schemes to facts. The movement of scientific research seems to follow a formally similar process, as theories evolve and are reconstructed in the face of further facts. Again, the use of somewhat discordant metaphors—calibration, evolution, construction—is intentional, suggesting that the workings of the mind have no precise analogs in the world outside them.

The constant interaction between general schemes and particular knowledge fuels students' development through Philosophic understanding. The general scheme constantly requires further knowledge to support it; the further knowledge will commonly be somewhat anomalous and require refinements or revisions of the general scheme, which in turn will require further knowledge more adequately to support the newly refined or revised scheme. In the inescapable and irresolvable difference between reality and our ideas about it lies the fuel of Philosophic inquiry.

A mass of diverse knowledge is necessary to drive the dialectical process between general scheme and particular knowledge, and a good deal more knowledge is required to keep it going. When students accumulate only a relatively small amount of knowledge, or too specialized a knowledge, by the time they enter communities that stimulate and support Philosophic thinking, they are able to generate only rather crude and simple general schemes. The problem is not that a crude, simple scheme does not organize enough knowledge but that it can comfortably organize *anything*. Simple forms of fundamentalist religious beliefs are a common example. If it is crude enough, everything becomes evidence to support it, and nothing challenges it.

Contact with other cultures, on the other hand, tends to compel adjustment of general schemes, or, as Peter Winch observed, "seriously to study

130

another way of life is necessarily to extend our own" (1970, p. 99). European explorations of discovery during the Renaissance generated bundles of anomalies for the general scheme of Christian cosmology. Why had the Christian God created these other races who could have no knowledge of Him until the missionaries arrived? And what were European Christians to make of the strange gods of the "savages"? One could, in the circumstances, forgive a sigh of relief in the Vatican when the first Martian landers discovered no clear signs of life on the planet. Flexible minds can adjust general schemes to accommodate such anomalies, and, of course, C.S. Lewis has already had a go at the theological problems presented by intelligent life elsewhere in the galaxy in *Out of the Silent Planet* (1938) and *Perelandra* (1943).

What we have here, incidentally, is a further argument for learning a lot. Everyone holds that ignorance is incompatible with education, but conventional, traditionalist arguments for mastering certain forms of knowledge have an arbitrary note to them. They have tried to tie *the* meaning of education to a liberal tradition of learning a basic amount of a range of disciplines. The progressivist position, in contrast, seems hard put to justify any particular curriculum and the learning of any particular knowledge; erudition has always taken its place behind other more important progressivist objectives for educational institutions. If the scheme I am composing appears to lean more to the traditionalist, academic, content-rich curriculum, I should emphasize that it also implies significant differences from the canonical content of the traditionalist curriculum.

To be a teacher of "Philosophic" students requires flexibility, sensitivity, and tolerance in abundance. The teacher needs to support the students' developing general schemes, even when those schemes seem simplistic or, perhaps, offensive. The teacher needs to be sympathetic with students' occasional overconfidence and must be ready to support them at those moments of fearful insecurity when the inadequacy of a general scheme threatens. The teacher must introduce anomalies and dissonance gradually, to encourage greater sophistication in students' general schemes. (Of course, one has to wonder what educational institution can afford such a paragon?)

Anyone who has dealings with intellectually energetic students will readily be able to translate my abstract talk of disturbances to general schemes into the very real emotional crises and difficulties they encounter; angst, tears, depression, suicide, pills are among the real world correlates of the process. It is a lucky student who makes this intellectual journey buoyed constantly by the excitement of discovery and not dragged down by the distresses and emotional turmoil attending the recognition of inadequacy in the schemes used to make sense of the world.

The Flexibility of Theory

The reader might very well conclude that Philosophic understanding represents a regression rather than a development. Thucydides' narrowly focused inquiry, driven by his desire to lay a plot on the diversity of historical events, may seem a step backward in some ways from Herodotus's open-minded exploration of difference and diversity. If this is supposed to be an improving process of cultural development, we might choose not to recapitulate it. We might come to agree with Callicles's wary observation that "too much philosophy is the ruin of human life" (*Gorgias, 484*).

I did promise a conception of education that involved losses as well as gains. The losses may be only too evident so far. We are all familiar with Philosophic thinkers in thrall to general schemes; earnest ideologues, for example, who know that history, God, the environment and its natural processes, or some other scheme is on their side. Philosophic thinking has given us those fashionable villains "technical rationality," positivism, behaviorism, the bomb, genetic engineering, with their ardent promoters reeking of *hubris*.

Let me give two examples of Philosophic thinking, chosen serendipitously; one I was reading about a few days before writing the first draft of this section, for some reason I can't recall now, and the second arrived in the mail this morning as I was revising. First, I will briefly mention the career of some of the ideas of Ptolemy, the Egyptian astronomer and geographer (not the example that came through the mail today), whose major work was done between about 127 and 148 C.E. While not the originator of some of the ideas associated with his name, he was an energetic synthesizer, and his are the works that have survived. His astronomical writings, now best known under the title Arabic scholars gave it, *The Almagest,* dominated astronomical theory until the sixteenth or, for most people, the seventeenth, century. In Ptolemy's scheme, the earth is the center of the universe; the sun and stars circle it, and the planets spin eccentrically around it. His geographical works also dominated people's sense of the globe for nearly a millennium and a half. Unfortunately, he accepted Posidonius's underestimation of the earth's circumference, at 180,000 stades, rather than the remarkably accurate measurement of Eratosthenes, at 250,000 stades. One result of this was a serious underestimation of the distance between longitudinal lines. He also hypothesized the existence of a southern continent, Terra Australis, but he imagined it connecting the east coast of Africa with China. The reduced size of the globe would have been less of a problem if America did not exist. To use the old adage, travel broadens the mind (that is, it tends to undermine and reform one's general schemes), and the confusion of the early European explorers sailing westward with their Ptolemaic general scheme was quite understandable. They assumed they must have hit Asia somewhat sooner than expected, but after getting a sense of America's scale and then seeing the Pacific beyond, they quite reasonably experienced dumb surmise—the sound of a general scheme crumbling against a major anomaly. Similarly the observations and calculations of Copernicus (1473–1543), Kepler (1571–1630), and Galileo (1564–1642) pointed up anomalies in Ptolemy's scheme of the cosmos, leading to the radical revision that displaced the earth from its center.

The second example of Philosophic thinking—the one that arrived in the mail today—comes from a "Collaborative Newsletter" coordinated by a remarkable teacher, Miranda Armstrong, at Eltham College, a K—12 private school north of Melbourne in Australia. She begins with a discussion she had with her son, Christopher, over breakfast, in which he suggested that trees are aliens.

"What do you mean, son, that a tree is an alien being?"

"Not an alien necessarily, but it might not be what we think it is. Take a spider for instance, an inferior being by comparison to us. When they observe a house, they think of it as a natural phenomenon. A given. It 'is' and therefore it is 'real.' Right?"

"I suppose. So what?"

"So it isn't, is it? It is man made. They believe it to be natural when in fact it is something quite different. And take mountains."

"Pardon?"

"Humans think of mountains as natural—but what if they were actually alien artifacts? Everything we perceive is defined by what we know, or think we know."

"I know you are going to be late for your train."

"Why do you always do that? Why, when things are just starting to get interesting, do you tell me my train is coming or my room needs tidying? How can I be late for my train after all when time is a figment of the human imagination? An invention of the mind."

The theories and hypotheses generated by Ptolemy and Christopher Armstrong are odd entities. They are not facts, nor are they generalizations from facts; they are guesses, suggestions, or assertions about the nature of things, about some whole or essence, that are *based on* facts and generalizations. The data on which they are based may be few or many, but the resulting schemes go beyond the sum of supporting data. Between the idea and the reality, as T. S. Eliot observed, falls the shadow. We can happily leave the shadow to philosophers, except that we need to remember it is there. Between secured knowledge and general schemes there is an act of mind, of imagination, of faith, that generates a conception of things that is different in kind from the things themselves. In other words, the realm of theoretic thinking is distinctive not only from things but from our more common ways of thinking about them.

Philosophic thinking exercises and develops the capacity to see patterns, search for the recurrent, perceive processes, look for essences, and make ordering principles and theories. It would perhaps be more accurate to say that Philosophic thinking *generates* the patterns, recurrence, processes, essences, ordinary principles, and theories. They are in shadowy part what the mind contributes to our knowledge of the world in the process of making sense of it. This is clotted stuff, of no particular interest here except to help make clear that Philosophic thinking has given us historically, and can give us individually, increased pragmatic control over the world. The general schemes of philosophy do not so much reduce the world as set up an additional "mimic" world made of ideas, concepts, knowledge—mind stuff.

We make reduced representations of reality in mind stuff, in concepts, but these reduced representations are precisely what we can deal with effectively. If we learn to make them well, we can remove all the irrelevant and confusing contingencies of reality and focus on a neat representation of the essence of something, or an underlying process, or a pattern of occurrences. The person who is skilled at Philosophic thinking often seems the most effective at getting to the heart of the matter, at being able to think about an issue clearly and then act on it decisively. Such clarity and decisiveness result from what is invariably a reduction. And if the reduction ignores some relevant feature of reality, the decisive action that follows can be disastrous. But the more sophisticated Philosophic thinker generates schemes that are attentive to anomalies and that become increasingly able to reflect relevant features of reality for particular purposes. Flexible revision of general schemes is the appropriate result of education at this point.

In the development of Philosophic understanding, implicit features of Mythic and Romantic understanding become explicit, bubbling, as it were, to the surface of consciousness. Indeed, the *recognition* of general schemes is a central feature of Philosophic understanding; they are there all along, now clearly recognized for what they are (like Hayek's "operations of thought"). What had undergirded Mythic and Romantic thinking but had been a focus of mental attention only fitfully and vaguely, as through that glass darkly, now becomes the primary focus of mental activity.

The ability to generate schematic conceptions of reality can liberate us from the constraints of the conventional ideas, beliefs, general schemes into which we grow up. Such conventions appear no longer as the unquestionable frame of conventionally perceived reality but, rather, as general schemes that, like others, are vulnerable to anomalies and revisable. Once students begin to generate and refine general schemes, they can also recognize and similarly deal with those undergirding the conventions they inherit. Both Ptolemy's revisers and Christopher Armstrong exemplify different ways in which inherited general schemes come up for revision—under the compulsion of irresistible anomalies or in the play of the exploratory imagination.

The conservative political ideology of parents, which children at first tend to accept without question, comes to be seen as just one of a number of schemes that can organize the facts and events of social and political life. For students who feel irked and constrained by their parents' world view, alternatives such as radical Marxism, feminism, environmentalism, or even stricter conservatism can be proffered against them as a "truer" account of reality.

It may not seem much of a liberation to be taken over by one's own general schemes rather than continuing to accept those one inherits. The inherited schemes usually have, after all, the warrant of tradition and wide acceptance. One's individually formed schemes may be eccentric; Christopher Armstrong's may seem so. But the generation of schemes is only the beginning of the process. If the student's Philosophic community is effective and intellectually energetic, the schemes will quickly begin to be bitten by anomalies, and will change in response, seeking further support and turning up further anomalies. Schemes such as those of Christopher Armstrong will tend to be abandoned because they cannot generate anomalies; no data can be brought to bear on them, for or against. (Though many a lifelong ideological foot soldier lives with this condition without abandoning the general scheme.) But even eccentric schemes are a symptom of an energetic imagination probing around in the early stages of Philosophic thinking. Liberation and flexibility come from recognizing as a function of the mind what had been taken as a part of the structure of the world.

CONCLUSION

A plethora of critiques currently focuses on what has been lost in, or sacrificed to the gains of, Philosophic thinking. The past few decades have been noisy with complaints about the damage done by "the scientific world view," "technical rationality," and so on. The main loss stems from the Philosophic tendency to embrace a narrow, disembodied rationality, which links itself with the cognitive but distances itself from the affective. It encourages a division between the cognitive and the affective, and the mind and the body, in which rationality is connected with the former. The imagination is conceived as playing no significant role in cognition, and the emotions are considered likely only to infect it with confusion. This rationality is a hard, calculative, dehumanized, arid form of thought, inhospitable to myth, romance, and the body. What is lost or suppressed in this form of thought are the characteristics of Mythic and Romantic understanding, as well as of Somatic understanding (which we explore in chapter 5).

The initial excitement of Philosophic understanding comes from a belief that one's general schemes disclose the truth about reality, often in pellucid and simple forms that draw together everything one knows. It is as though the dark glass has been drawn away, and at last one really *understands*. To inquisitive creatures, this discovery can come with the force of revelation. As the years go by, we may forget the ardor of early Philosophic understanding, and, of course, it comes to some only partially, as a feeble glow rather than a lightning flash. But it can feel like what Faust sold his soul for. We don't see too much of the lightning flash or Faustian contracts in our schools and universities—but we do see some, and we could happily see more.

Philosophic understanding is not supported by ubiquitous features of Western daily life. But Mythic understanding *is* supported by ubiquitous oral-language use, and Romantic understanding is supported in the West by ubiquitous use of alphabetic literacy. Neither the Mythic nor Romantic kind of understanding is optimally developed by routine language and literacy uses, of course, and educational institutions can be helpful in systematically developing them. But the case of Philosophic understanding seems rather different. Without the self-conscious support of educational institutions, particularly colleges and universities, Philosophic understanding is likely to develop only fitfully and partially; the media and the general level of public discourse in the West do not provide the kind of community that can adequately sustain it.

In recent decades, the authority and permanence that Philosophic thinking has aimed at have been much criticized by "sociologists of knowledge" and others in the academic world, even if physical scientists do simply get on with their work as though the cacophony had nothing to do with them. My scheme, however, is a cumulative one; it does not chuck overboard Philosophic understanding and its ambitions, its excitement, its capacity to search out patterns and generate laws, and its distinctive construction and revision of general schemes. (In a book building a general scheme, you will not expect that.)

How Philosophic thinking is enfolded into Ironic understanding is the theme of chapter 5. There we will try to leave nothing behind; the child is father of the man, the child is mother of the woman.

Ironic Understanding and Somatic Understanding

Introduction

"All generalizations are false" might sum up the insight that leads to the decay of Philosophic general schemes. But that is a peculiar insight; it refutes itself. If I were to write it as a literal claim and argue for its truth, you would reasonably feel pity for my confusion and lack of reflexiveness. But if it is written and interpreted ironically, it establishes an odd kind of communication between us, taking on a somewhat humorous tone. We both understand that I do not mean what I have written literally but that I do mean something toward which the literal meaning points. You, subtle and ironic reader, will recognize my opening phrase as having something in common with, and as parodying, such assertions as "All meaningful statements are either verifiable empirical claims or conceptual truths" or "All knowledge is socially constructed." They are claims that seem to have a kind of validity but yet manage to refute themselves at the same time. My opening clause points you to the recognition that we will be dealing here with modern, and postmodern, problems concerning language and its referentiality.

If that is what I mean, why did I not simply write that and spare you the jokey digression? Because our primary topic is irony, and irony involves more than a perverse disguise of what might be better stated literally. Such an ironic opening leads to discussion in a number of directions, in all of which I would like to gallop at the same time. It leads to a discussion of the kind of   137 understanding that results from the breakdown or decay of general schemes. It leads to the nineteenth-century attempts to come to terms with the growing recognition that, as Victor Hugo famously pronounced it, "Tous les systèmes sont faux." It leads to the accumulating reflexiveness of language and consciousness and the ramifying consequences of this reflexiveness in modernism and postmodernism. It leads to Socrates, whom Thrasymachus irritatedly accused of habitual irony (*Republic,* I.336).

The story so far has concerned the development of language. Early attempts to express the nature of the world disclosed by human senses were oral, using vocabularies of at most a couple of thousand words. Literacy entailed a further development of language and increased vocabulary. The English grapholect now has available more than a million and a half words (Ong, 1977). Literacy promised more precision, complexity, security, and rationality in capturing experience and the world in words. In communities supportive of theoretic thinking, further linguistic developments promised a more systematic, comprehensive, and true account of reality. But the decay of belief in that promised truth, and the decay of belief that theoretic systems, expressed in however refined a language, could represent reality accurately has created problems about how language is supposed to represent reality at all. And if language doesn't represent reality, what does it do? And if our languages cannot give us access to reality, what, then, is reality? And if properly representing reality in language was what was meant by truth, then what is truth? Well, these are questions that have been asked before.

In the twentieth century, Western intellectual history has grappled with the recognition that language could not do what had previously been expected of it. Quite suddenly, and very widely in the late nineteenth century, our most intricate tool for grasping reality and truth began to seem inadequate for the job, and, worse, it began to seem like a self-generating, labyrinthine prison that offered no way out to reality.

More recently we have been urged to face up to the decay of earlier hopes that in language we would be able to establish foundations for our knowledge claims and secure the truth of our beliefs; instead we are to accept the "contingency of . . . our most central beliefs and desires," and abandon "the idea that those central beliefs and desires refer back to something beyond the reach of time and chance" (Rorty, 1989, p. xv). This recognition of the contingency of things is a requirement for living the undeceived life Richard Rorty recommends for what he calls "liberal ironists." Not that this ironic acceptance of contingency at the heart of things is a uniquely modern stance. It is a persistent theme of the Western intellectual tradition, dryly announced near the beginning of that tradition in Heraclitus's claim that "The cosmos, at best, is like a rubbish heap scattered at random" (Diels, frag-

138

ment 124). And the epitome of irony is expressed in what Vlastos calls "Socrates' renunciation of epistemic certainty" (1991, p. 4).

A more common theme in the Western intellectual tradition is that without some clear foundation, some bedrock of truth, human life and our sense of the natural world are chaotic and meaningless. The fear of raw contingency has long driven the pursuit of truth. But in this century, shockingly, ironic voices have suggested that nothing much happens if we give up looking for foundations to knowledge, and even for meaning; the sky holds in place, daily life goes on:

> "And so," Walter retorted sharply, "you think we ought to do without any meaning in life?" Ulrich asked him what he really needed a meaning for. One got along all right without it, he commented. (Musil, 1965, I, p. 255)

Such a recognition seems to disinherit the modern Western mind from the promised benefits of truth and secure knowledge; it suggests that "our desire for meaningful order may be meaningless; like letters written to a non-existent address" (Heller, 1959, p. 295). But the gods, or God, had guaranteed some kind of commensurability between the human world of meanings and the world of nature. So long as people conceived of the world as made and governed by God, then catastrophes, pain, diseases, death, and so on could all be accepted as meaningful parts of some design, however indecipherable to mere mortals. For those who contemplated Nietzsche's announcement of the death of God, the natural world became disturbingly incommensurable with the human world. What are we to make of our lot in this "heartless witless nature," as A. E. Housman put it, when "the more the universe seems comprehensible, the more it seems pointless"? (Weinberg, in Penrose, 1993, p. 82). What was so disturbing about Darwin's ideas was not descent from monkeys, with which the British magazine *Punch* and various clerics had such fun, but the mechanism of natural selection and its implication that we owe our precious consciousness not to God, framing our symmetry for some high purpose, but to blind chance, to raw contingency.

This weighty stuff does seem rather distant from the simple figure of speech we refer to as irony. "Bolingbroke was a holy man" is the example Dr. Johnson gives in his dictionary (1755) to accompany his definition of irony: "A mode of speech in which the meaning is contrary to the words." "Holy" is among the least appropriate descriptions for the brilliant but scheming, treacherous, abusive, egomaniacal rake Henry St. John, 1st. Viscount Bolingbroke. So why call him holy? Johnson's sentence exemplifies irony because most of Dr. Johnson's contemporary readers would have known that his claim could not be intended literally. Rather, it enables that odd communication that takes place between what is said and what is meant. Certainly   139 "an ironic utterance is not merely a statement about reality . . . but presupposes at least a tacit awareness of the disparity between a statement and the reality it is supposed to represent" (White, 1978, p. 208). The peculiar pleasure of irony seems sometimes to gain from there being readers or hearers who, knowing no better, could take the ironic statement at face value. Muecke also notes colorfully: "The golden eggs of irony could not be laid so abundantly if we were not knee-deep in geese" (1970b, p. 4), and "Until the ironic message is interpreted as intended it has only the sound of one hand clapping" (p. 39). And yet, it is commonly claimed, this odd figure of speech has become "the master trope of our age" (Conway and Seery, 1992, p. 3). The form of consciousness associated with it lies at the heart of both modernism and postmodernism.

Irony is notoriously multifaceted, and trying to characterize it has been likened to "gathering the mist; there is plenty to take hold of if only one could" (Muecke, 1969, p. 2). Even so, in this chapter I want to describe a further kind of understanding and explain why I think it is best called Ironic. It is well to go carefully with such a topic, remembering that "irony's guns face in all directions" (Enright, 1988, p. 110).

Irony and Socrates

When Thrasymachus referred to Socrates' habitual irony, he was not intending a compliment as someone might today. In Socrates and Plato's time, the most common meaning of *eironeia* was something like "dissembling," "shamming," or "pretending." The *eiron* was a person with generally unworthy motives, who never talked straight and was intent on deceiving or making a fool of someone. The term connotes rebuke and disapproval, reflected in Swearingen's suggested translation, "dissembling scoundrel" (1991).

Thrasymachus's particular complaint was aimed at Socrates' claim that he himself had no idea about the nature of justice and that he wished to question the others only so that he could learn about it from them. Thrasymachus clearly believed that Socrates did have a preferred conception of justice, which he was keeping to himself even as he deconstructed those of his companions. But, as the argument continued, what infuriated Thrasymachus was "not just [Socrates'] not saying what he means but his refusal to mean anything at all" (Bruns, 1992, p. 32).

In the early dialogues at least, and in the first book of the *Republic*, which houses Thrasymachus's complaint, Socrates lives up to his claim that he "knows nothing and is ignorant of everything" (*Symposium*, 216); he deconstructs others' claims to knowledge but offers nothing positive of his own in their place. He solves no problems, shows that all the proffered solutions are inadequate, and cheerfully leaves us to sort things out as best as we can.

What are we to make of Socrates' claim to know nothing? Clearly he means it in some sense. At his trial he told the court, "I am not aware of being wise in anything, great or small" (*Apology,* 21). And after painstaking arguments with Gorgias, Polus, and Callicles, he asserts, "But as for me, my position is always the same: I do not know how these matters stand" (*Gorgias,* 509). He concludes by observing, "In our present condition we ought not to give ourselves airs, for even on the most important subjects we are always changing our minds; so utterly stupid are we" (*Gorgias,* 527). To Thrasymachus, this is merely a cheap rhetorical ploy, ensuring for Socrates that he is never vulnerable in argument, that he cannot be caught in the contradictions in which he delights to catch others; but it is a ploy whose cost is often destructive and negative, establishing nothing, and as such is pointless and irritating.

But to the young men who gathered around Socrates, it was a part of what was so peculiarly fascinating about him. Alcibiades talks at some length in the *Symposium* about the great oddity of Socrates: "his absolute unlikeness to any human being that is or ever has been is perfectly astonishing" (*Symposium,* 221). In the course of this drunken panegyric, Alcibiades refers to Socrates' "ironical manner which is so characteristic of him" (*Symposium,* 218). While the claim to know nothing could hardly be taken literally, it nevertheless captured some genuine feature of Socrates' radical epistemic doubt that both bewildered and attracted those young men. Vlastos sums it up, romantically, by suggesting that Socrates was "a previously unknown, unimagined type of personality, so arresting to his contemporaries and so memorable for ever after, that the time would come, centuries after his death, when educated people would hardly be able to think of *ironia* without bringing Socrates to mind" (1991, p. 29).

Centuries after his death, the two writers who did most to give new definition to irony—Cicero and Quintillian—both refer to Socrates in doing so. The Greek disrepute attached to the term is removed, and it is now recommended as a subtle and sophisticated form of language connoting intellectual urbanity. This conception of irony carries over into modern Europe, helped by the finding of a filthy copy of Quintillian's *Institutio Oratorica* in 1415 in a tower in St. Gall, Switzerland. The Romans' elaborate discussion of the variety of forms of irony carried with it the echo of Socrates' curious stance in the world, and their enormous influence justified Kierkegaard's observation that "tradition has linked the word 'irony' to the existence of Socra-

FIVE

tes" (1965, p. 49). So we may look to Kierkegaard to see how that peculiar stance of Socrates was reinterpreted in more recent times and again tied to the concept of irony.

Kierkegaard begins his account by arguing that "it is in Socrates that the concept of irony has its inception in the world" (p. 47). In making this claim, Kierkegaard must have had something more in mind than the constant ironic comments Socrates sprinkles throughout the dialogues: as in, "one very small difficulty which I am sure that Protagoras will easily explain" (*Protagoras,* 328), just as he launches a devastating attack. These little ironies, sometimes falling into mere sarcasm, did not enter the world with Socrates; they seem to be a universal feature of language, like lying. Kierkegaard clearly agrees with Quintillian's observation of Socrates as the kind of person who does not use ironic quips just now and then, but who is somehow ironic through and through: "whoever has essential irony has it all day long" (Kierkegaard, 1965, p. 23); he sees the world constantly "*sub speciae ironiae*" (p. 67). What, then, is the character of this ironic perspective as exemplified by Socrates, according to Kierkegaard?

Kierkegaard reminds us how Socrates reacted to the Delphic oracle's pronouncement that he was the wisest of people: Socrates was surprised, as he thought he didn't know anything much, but concluded that the oracle might have considered him wisest because he was unique in realizing how little he knew. So he took it as a vocation from God, who alone is wise, to show in what sense the oracle was correct, by making clear that those who claimed most knowledge and wisdom were in fact ignorant and foolish. Thereby he would expose that "the wisdom of men is worth little or nothing" (*Apology,* 23). Socrates, Kierkegaard tells us, "traversed the entire kingdom of intelligence and discovered the whole realm to be bounded by an Oceanus of illusory knowledge" (p. 75). The overall result he likens to Samson's final achievement: "Socrates . . . seizes the columns bearing the edifice of knowledge and plunges everything down into the nothingness of ignorance" (p. 77).

The epistemological result of "essential irony" is the "infinite absolute negativity" (p. 278) that Kierkegaard takes from Hegel's commentary on irony. "It is negative because it only negates; it is infinite because it negates not this or that phenomenon; and it is absolute because it negates by virtue of a higher which is not. Irony establishes nothing. . . . It is a divine madness which rages like a Tamerlane and leaves not one stone standing upon another in its wake" (p. 278).

Well, this prospect is rather cheerless, not easy to advertise as an attractive component of a "fun" lifestyle, yet Socrates seems to have been buoyantly cheerful, even while facing death. If the "first potency of irony lies in formulating a theory of knowledge that annihilates itself" (p. 98), how is it that the annihilation leaves Socrates so jaunty?

Kierkegaard describes Socrates as a "dialectical vacuum pump" (p. 203) sucking away all claims to knowledge. We human beings seem instinctively compelled to construct representations of our world. Our psychological security seems to depend on our confidence that such representations correspond to reality. Socratic irony, therefore, threatens the very basis of our security, and certainly this is how many of Socrates' victims felt about his dialectical vacuum. But Kierkegaard argues that Socrates' jaunty self-confidence is somehow a result of his infinite absolute negativity. The fruit of Socratic irony, he tells us, is "merely to feel free" (p. 273).

Recognizing the insecurity of our knowledge and our feebleness and vacillation as knowers is not, for Socrates, disabling or constraining. Rather, such insights are a condition of genuine freedom: "it is by means of irony that the subject emancipates himself from the constraints upon him by the continuity of life" (Kierkegaard, 1965, pp. 272, 273). So the ironist can "cut loose" from the constraints of false knowledge that hold bound in their time and place those who fancy they have secure knowledge. Their knowledge, to the ironist, is simply a shared agreement about representing reality for local purposes at a particular time. To confuse these contingent forms with secure representations of reality is to be unable to pull free of local, temporary conditions. Kierkegaard uses numerous terms to indicate how Socrates "hovers" above the bondage of the nonironic; he is free, light, buoyant, for all time. Removing the burden of simplistic beliefs allows the ironic soul to rise "upward" out of local constraints and achieve autonomy.

Plato has been commonly represented of late as the grim, logocentric, patriarchal metaphysician who invented the kind of epistemology from which postmodernism is trying to save us. It is well to remember that he is also the mystical jokester and mythographer who constantly warned about the unreliability of words. Much must remain unsaid, he tells us; words *cannot* say what we mean. In the seventh letter, of probable authenticity, he explains the attraction of politics at Syracuse in preference to a life in which "[he] feared to see [him]self at last nothing but words." Even as he describes how the soul can come to perceive the essential forms—his arch-dogma—he cannot resist the ironist's shrug: "Heaven knows whether it is true; but this, at any rate, is how it appears to me" (*Republic*, VII, 517). However scholars distinguish between Plato and Socrates, the ironic Socrates exists for us only in Plato's construction of him. If Socrates is the arch-ironist, Plato, *il miglior fabbro*, is no less a one.

Plato is the ultimate exemplar of Cicero's *urbana dissimulatio,* even to the point of nearly always speaking through others. Recognizing the unreliability of words, and the double unreliability of written words to others—"He would be a very simple person . . . who should leave in writing or receive in writing any art under the idea that the written word would be intelligible or certain" (*Phaedrus,* 275)—Plato was hardly likely to write with literal simplicity. His arguments are crowded with jokes, myths, puns, and metaphors, and they tantalize with irony. The ironic reader will recognize the inadequacy of the literal words and look rather for the meaning they point toward. What else are these pages before your eyes, reader, but the shadow wall of Plato's cave? (Seery, 1992). The words, he insists, are uncertain shadows of meanings. "The point about Socrates"—one might say Plato's point—"is that we never know how to take him. . . . [H]is being . . . is playful, turning things upside down like a lord of misrule" (Bruns, 1992, p. 32).

The association with Socrates has given us, as part of the meaning of irony, a pervasive epistemic skepticism on the one hand and a psychological freedom from the constraints of particular times, places, and their conventions on the other. Whether the freedom leaves one buoyant or bereft may depend more on hormones than epistemology, but it is a freedom few ironists would swap for the illusory securities of the conventional mind. While we may seem to have come a long way from the simple irony of "Bolingbroke was a holy man," the journey helps us to understand why some people prefer to talk in this odd way. If nothing else, it signals knowledge of the unreliability of words and declares a kind of freedom. This freedom may not make one as cheerful as Socrates, but it is not insignificant.

"'TIS ALL IN PEECES, ALL COHAERANCE GONE"

Language, that endlessly fertile invention, gave us, among its early gifts, gods. Inherent in the idea of gods are two perspectives on our behavior and on the world; there is the everyday perspective from our entrammeled social lives and also that of the gods looking down on us with amusement, contempt, admiration, horror, or disinterest. Once we try to imagine what we might look like from a god's perspective—in the discourse of the gods—we may see any particular event or object as having more than one meaning, as playing distinctive roles in different narratives. Secular people pay less attention to the gods' narrative than to their own social narrative; religious people try to see their lives as far as possible in terms of the gods' narrative.

The ancient Greek theater mimicked a cosmos in which gods look down on human behavior. On the stage, Oedipus pursued Laius's murderer while the audience watched and listened from the towering tiers of seats, feeling the events both from Oedipus's perspective and from their own god-like perspective. Theater stimulated a peculiar consciousness, which one could perhaps apply to one's silent walk home afterwards, self-consciously feeling approved of or sneered at by the gods, who are as invisible to the walker as the walker had been to the Oedipus who had strutted and fretted his hour upon the stage earlier.

There are, of course, endless ways of dealing with the reflexiveness that gods' perspectives encouraged people to develop, and endless strategies for dealing with the threat of incoherence that insinuates itself in seeing events or objects from different perspectives. Multiple perspectives disclose multiple meanings—one may look at that stand of trees with aesthetic delight, or with calculations of what its timber would fetch in current markets, or with religious awe as the sacred resting place of an ancestor's spirit, or with determination to preserve it as the last sustaining habitat of an endangered species of moth, and so on. How are we to deal with a world in which multiple perspectives, meanings, and narratives throng for our acquiescence?

The fluent ironist can slip from perspective to perspective. The essential humor of irony is incongruity, applying in one perspective modes that are proper to another. One might take a TV advertisement as a philosophical proposition and respond accordingly. One might suggest that a wedding feast follows close upon a funeral for reasons of thrift with regard to the catering. One might recommend the eating of babies as an economical solution to a population outgrowing its food supply. One might transpose the kinds of arguments employed with a shifty used-car dealer about a defunct car to a pet shop about a dead parrot. But, more fundamentally, ironists' fluency in shifting among different perspectives opens up doubts about the security of what is seen from any one of them.

In premodern languages, to use MacIntyre's (1989) distinction, some canonical narrative determines which perspective is privileged, and the canonical narrative serves to suppress the others. In early modern Europe, Greek, Hebrew, and Roman narratives were made coherent within the canonical narrative of Christianity by the heroic intellectual activity of St. Augustine, St. Thomas Aquinas, and others (aided by the Inquisition for those less ready to accept the dominant metanarrative). But as the decades and the centuries passed, the further "annexation of Chinese, Sanskrit, Mayan, and old Irish texts, and . . . the bestowal of equal status upon texts in European vernacular languages from the thirteenth to the nineteenth centuries, [and] . . . the discovery of a wide array of preliterate cultures" (p. 196), led to an increasing strain on the canonical Christian narrative. The accumulation of texts and narratives, and the proliferation of perspectives these offered on the world, stimulated two general responses: an intensive search for the right perspective, the true narrative, on the one hand, and irony on the other.

The modern search for security among proliferating narratives is conventionally taken to begin with Descartes' claim that his thinking, however misguided, was irrefutable evidence that he existed, and this knowledge provided a secure foundation on which to build. The Enlightenment scientific project, in addition, seemed to discover a way of penetrating the cacophony of narratives to secure truths about the nature of things. But while this attempt to build increasingly secure epistemological foundations is one prolonged note in the Western tradition, it is accompanied by an even more sustained note made up of constant ironic voices saying in various ways that the search for secure truth is illusory.

The suspicion that all was not well with the optimistic Enlightenment project was voiced with energy even by some of those engaged in its scientific work. By the late eighteenth century, particularly among the German Romantics, it became commonplace to muse on the correlation between the increasing number of objective truths being established by the sciences and the decreasing sense of intellectual security people felt. Erich Heller summarizes Goethe's explanation of this metanarrative paradox: "every scientific theory is merely the surface rationalization of a metaphysical substratum of beliefs, conscious or unconscious, about the nature of the world" (1959, p. 26).

In a letter written in 1790, Benjamin Constant (1767–1830) suggested "God, i.e. the author of us and our surroundings, died before having finished his work. . . . [E]verything now finds itself made for a goal which no longer exists, and . . . we especially feel destined for something of which we ourselves have not the slightest idea" (Behler, 1990, p. 91). Such a scenario would at least explain some thinkers' bewilderment and uncertainty over an assertive program of positive science and a heterogeneous collection of cultural narratives, all of which in one way or another claim to offer a privileged perspective on the nature of things. The most insistent promoter of irony as the solution to this existential plight was Friedrich Schlegel (1772–1829). He took the limited sense of irony as given, for example, in Dr. Johnson's dictionary or Diderot's *Encyclopédie* ("a figure of speech by which one wants to convey the opposite of what one says," vol. 19, p. 86), along with the way the term had been developed in the study of rhetoric from the time of Cicero and Quintillian, and elaborated it into the stance we have since adopted.

"Irony," says Schlegel, "is the clear consciousness . . . of an infinitely teeming chaos" (1991, p. 100). His definition does not hold much hope for sense-making, but Schlegel's Romantic irony has among its resources a solution to the problem it recognizes. The ironic mind, especially that of the artist, can transcend the chaos of the world by harnessing together wild imaginativeness and deep seriousness, the artistic passion for life and sober scientific inquiry. This, anyway, is how Schlegel believed Socrates managed to be intellectually and psychologically buoyant while maintaining extreme epistemological agnosticism: "Socratic irony rises out of a union of the sense of life as an art and the spirit of learning and science" (p. 160). Irony, combining artistic imagination and scientific rationality, can enable us to make our way, using our artistic creations as stepping stones, beyond the chaos of this world.

What this transcendence requires in the individual is, in Schlegel's famous phrase, "transcendental buffoonery." The second half of Victor Hugo's proclamation about all the systems being false is, "la gènie seul est vrai!" So the Romantics' sense of irony discloses a chaotic world, but individual genius and its transcendental buffoonery provide a remedy for the distress infinitely teeming chaos might reasonably be expected to cause your average punter. Kierkegaard concurred at least with this view: Irony "is an excellent surgeon . . . its function . . . is of the utmost importance in order for the personal life to acquire health and truth" (1965, p. 338).

The trick of Romantic ironists' transcendence was to align their work with God's. After eloping with Dorothea Mendelssohn, Schlegel converted to Catholicism, so his sense of infinitely teeming chaos and the freedom of· irony fall within a theocentric scheme—one influenced significantly, in his case, by his sometime collaborator, the Protestant theologian, philosopher, and critic Friedrich Schleiermacher. By exposing, and associating with, God's work, the Romantic artist or imaginative scholar managed to overcome the constraints of the conventional world and escape the chaos that bound up those who could take no part in divine purposes. Whether through Hegelian philosophy, Rankean philosophic history, or the "primary imagination" that Coleridge held "to be the living power and prime agent of all human perception and . . . a repetition in the finite mind of the external act of creation of the infinite I AM" (Biographia Literaria, XIII), the Romantic ironist escaped from the threat of meaningless chaos that irony opened up.

The Romantics' sense of the role of "genius," and the association of genius with God's work, seems a tad overwrought today. Even in the nineteenth century more "modern" ironists found the divine connection not entirely satisfactory: "In our age philosophy has come into such an enormous result that all can scarcely be right with it. Insights not only into man's secrets but into God's secrets are sold at such a bargain that it all begins to look suspicious" (Kierkegaard, 1965, pp. 339–340).

The Romantics' contribution to our conception of irony has been, somewhat ironically, a kind of knowingness about epistemological uncertainty, perhaps resulting from increasing familiarity with radical doubt. But romantic irony has lacked the harder edges we will bump into below when   147 considering more recent conceptions, and it has been found too often hand-in-hand with belief in the relatively painless possibility of transcending irony's destructive implications. The nature of that Romantic transcendence has been usually expressed in vague terms, more like a hopeful gesture than a practical guidebook for the perplexed. That ineffectualness is what has given "romance" a bad name among the tough-minded to this day.

As I considered examples from historians' work in earlier chapters, it might be useful very briefly to observe the result of post-Romantic irony among historians in the later part of the nineteenth century. Hayden White describes how "the sensed inadequacy of language to the full representation of its object [came to be] perceived as a problem" (1978, p. 207). A response to this perception may be seen in the work of Jacob Burckhardt (1818–1897), one of Ranke's disaffected students. He concluded that the general schemes common to "philosophic" history writing could not be constructed from the study of the past alone. The historian cannot simply look at the past and describe what happened: "we are subject to the prejudices of our egoism (at best, to the predilections of our time)" (1965, pp. 27–28). The study of history, as he conceived it, "lays no claim to system"; it cannot disclose general truths about the historical process—it shows "mere reflections of ourselves" (1955, pp. 74–75). Burckhardt began his revolutionary work, *The Civilization of the Renaissance in Italy,* not with a Romantic concern with preventing some *mega ergon* from slipping away on the stream of Time into Oblivion, nor with a Philosophic desire to establish some metanarrative about the historical process, but with a more ironic observation:

In the wide ocean on which we venture, the possible ways and directions are many; and the same studies which have served for this work might easily, in other hands, not only receive a wholly different treatment and application, but lead also to essentially different conclusions. (1960, p. 2)

The Western tradition is commonly represented through the Enlightenment period and the nineteenth century in terms of an increasingly assertive rationalism accompanied by an inexorable scientific advance that dispensed world-changing technologies as its byproduct. The Western tradition also involves during this period a widening strain of irony that corrodes confidence, dissolves meaning, and undermines all claims to intellectual security. This epistemological subversion accompanied the self-representation of the physical sciences as bringing clarity, order, security, and law to our understanding of the world. This great scientific enterprise ground forward, unperturbed by skeptical or mocking ironic voices. It delivered early the message that the world accessible to our senses, and to those refinements of our senses that made up the tools of much scientific inquiry, is the only world there is. No gods are needed to explain how the world works, no mysterious forces or spirits exist, no transcendent state of affairs is running things, no Ideas or Forms lie behind the everyday particularity of the world. This message accompanied laws to account for the behavior of light, heat, sound, motion, acceleration, falling bodies, gases, fluids, solids, and so on. In some degree, then, science was an ally of irony, helping to dissolve the metaphysical realm.

In 1895 Wilhelm Roentgen discovered X-rays. In 1897 Joseph Thompson discovered the electron. In 1898 Marie Curie invented the term radioactivity and isolated pure radium in 1910. In 1914 Ernest Rutherford discovered the proton and, with Niels Bohr, proposed models of a subatomic world whose behavior required different laws from those earlier considered universally applicable to the physical world. And Einstein disrupted the common sense of such foundational notions as time and space. Louis Pasteur meanwhile had exposed a world of micro-organisms whose behavior accounted for everyday phenomena in souring, fermentation, putrefaction, and disease. The message of this new science was that the world was *really* quite *unlike* what it seemed to our senses. Our senses provided only a very limited perspective on a superficial level of reality; who could tell how many levels the world inaccessible to our senses might dissolve into, or even whether it might dissolve infinitely? The universe was turning out, as J. B. S. Haldane put it, not just to be queerer than we imagined, but queerer than we *can* imagine. In a formally similar way, Freud suggested that our conscious lives, our accessible selves, are mere illusions hiding a different but more real life that goes on in secret and that is the proper source for explanations of our behavior.

This new science, and its dissolution of so much of the common-sense framework of understanding that had dominated people's thinking, intermingled with and clearly encouraged some features of spreading irony. Presupposed verities were disrupted as, for example, the new geology and Darwin's new biology put flux and change where earlier there had been stability. For some, science was not dissolving the known world but, rather, constructing a new and more reliable account of reality. But the ironists doubted this no less than they had doubted the old "reliable accounts." And worse, as the structures of the new rational, scientific world, and its technologies, began to take shape, many felt confirmed in their conviction that rationality was delivering a nightmare.

The assertive confidence that accompanied "philosophic" rationality seemed to some ironic minds to be leading directly to new and more repressive societies, marked by the new, rational, totalitarian factories, prisons, and, some would add, schools. The great prophet of this view was Friedrich Nietzsche (1844–1900): "For some time now, our whole European culture has been moving towards a catastrophe, with a tortured tension that is growing from decade to decade: restlessly, violently, headlong like a river that wants to reach the end, that no longer reflects, that is afraid to reflect" (1968a, p. 3).

What was increasingly disturbing to some of the more agile minds was not that abuses of the rationally organized social systems were possible, but rather, more profoundly, that something inherent in them was at odds with human interests and aspirations. Alert observers began "rising up against civilization as a disease, and declaring that it is not our disorder but our order that is terrible." (Ah, no, that isn't Michel Foucault; it's Bernard Shaw expressing admiration for the insight of Charles Dickens's *Hard Times* [Cunningham, 1994, p. 6].) Nietzsche saw this terrible order involved in "our whole attitude toward nature, our violation of nature with the help of machines and the heedless ingenuity of technicians and engineers" (1956, p. 248).

Burckhardt's ironic sense of the insecurity, almost the arbitrariness, of historical knowledge found a more expansive and radical expression in the work of his admirer, Nietzsche. It was not just the general schemes inferred from the study of history that Nietzsche dismissed, but pretty well the whole furniture of the Western mind, from refined science to the "herd's" panoply of folk wisdom and beliefs. He attacked it all with dismaying plausibility, seizing, once again, the columns bearing the edifice of knowledge, collapsing everything into nothingness and ignorance. All claims to knowledge and truth are empty—"That there should be a 'truth' which one could somehow approach —!"(Nietzsche, 1968a, p. 249)—mere mythologies made up to comfort the weak and simple-minded; people forgot that these modern myths had been made up, then forgot that they had forgotten.

Nietzsche resolves the ancient quarrel between philosophy and poetry by pointing out that philosophy is no less fictive than is poetry. We are to discard the old distinctions between fiction and truth and recognize rather that there are two kinds of fiction: one that masquerades as truth and one that recognizes itself as fiction. It is that long masquerade that he wants to show for what it really is. The pretence that there is "an actual *drive for knowledge* that, without regard to questions of usefulness and harm, [goes] blindly for the truth" (Nietzsche, 1968a, p. 227; emphasis in original) or that there is a "will to truth" (p. 249), sickened him. These are nothing other than a mask for the desire to control, conquer, appropriate; the pursuit of truth is driven only by "wanting to be superior" (p. 249).

What makes the the pretence so difficult for the "herd" to recognize, and for Nietzsche to extirpate, is the way language has developed, taking up and carrying along even in its very structure a vast mythology of assumptions. The most basic features of language embody confusions even about cause and effect: "it is only the snare of language (of the arch-fallacies of reason petrified in language), presenting all activity as conditioned by an agent— the 'subject'" (Nietzsche, 1956, p. 178). So a sentence like 'The oak tree drops its acorns to the ground' falsely suggests a subject performing an action; it represents the world as operating according to sets of causes. Nietzsche unpicks causality, the cement of the rationalists' universe, as simply a product of grammar, not a constituent of the real world; causality is merely a part of one of our perspectives, of one of the stories we impose on reality. It is the simple-minded acceptance of how the world seems when seen through language that Nietzsche rails against: "We are not rid of God because we still have faith in grammar" (1968b, p. 483).

In *The Gay Science,* Nietzsche explores the kind of life that follows recognition that God is dead and that the intellectual cosmos that He had sustained is dead with Him. Recognition of those deaths is a precondition for the freedom of the individual and for the existence of the new kind of person who can live in a world without any guarantees of meaning, or *telos.* It is, of course, easier "to think 'I possess the truth' than to see only darkness around one" (1968a, p. 248). But one must face the abyss rather than accept the illusory comfort of "knowing the truth." In the face of the empty dark, the new undeceived superhumans will, like any artist, make their own meaning, sing their own songs, dance their own dances. Nietzsche wants "fellow revellers" to join him on the "mysterious dancing grounds" (1956, p. 6) and live human life as an artistic creation. If the meaning of life cannot be derived from some story, some narrative, some God's plans, then we must make it up ourselves. This sounds splendid, of course, and has sounded splendid to people of widely divergent views (cf. Ascheim, 1994), but it has never been entirely clear just what we should do tomorrow morning to realize Nietzsche's somewhat indeterminate vision of regeneration.

If Nietzsche is the archetypal representative of modernist irony, and we consider postmodernism a "radicalized, intensified version of modernism" (Behler, 1990, p. 5), it is not obvious what further radicalization of ironic epistemic doubt is possible for postmodernism. But as the line between modernism and postmodernism is vague and porous, one common solution is to enroll Nietzsche as a postmodern.

Since writing the preceding paragraph, I have spent a month lecturing and visiting schools in Australia and, on the way, Hawaii. At the University of Hawaii at Manoa I talked with a Scottish colleague who plays the bagpipes. He described a recent occasion when he had played, among other tunes, 151

"Scotland the Brave" and "The 79th's Farewell to Gibraltar," the latter composed, incidentally, by an ancestor of his. This particular performance was in a St. Patrick's day parade, during which the pipers marched along Kalakaua Avenue by Waikiki beach, in a procession watched mainly by Japanese tourists.

What sense do we make of this cultural event? Well, there are many senses, many perspectives, many meanings possible, many discourses into which it could fit. The Irish claim they gave the bagpipes to the Scots as a joke, and the Scots haven't seen the joke yet, but the Irish organizers of this parade clearly wanted the bagpipes for the drama and the note of exaltation they can provide. What sense would the ancestor who wrote "The 79th's Farewell to Gibraltar" make of it? It seems unlikely that he could have imagined the circumstances of this performance. (My colleague has since suggested he would have been utterly astonished, not least by witnessing women playing the pipes.) What did it mean to the honeymooning couples who took photographs of the event? What would it mean to their friends who looked at the photographs later in Kyoto? And what did it mean to the native Hawaiians watching this bunch of "haolis" and listening to the skirl of their alien pipes?

This event exemplifies an increasingly common experience in the Western world. No cultural metanarrative governs its interpretation; rather, it is left open to the multiple perspectives of its witnesses. It may variously invoke a profound connection with a cultural tradition forged long ago and far away in Scotland for some of its participants, recreational fun for others, a momentary amusing diversion, or perhaps even an ugly distraction. This makes for a mix 'n' match cultural construction, in which no one perspective has privileged status—though some might feel that the natives' view has a substance of dislocation, loss, and dispossession that accords it moral privilege. But the event has no *true* meaning apart from the meanings constructed by the witnesses or by those who heard or you who read about it.

Recognition that this kind of fragmentation of perspectives constitutes the only meaning or reality available to us is central to postmodernism. Postmodern irony is, again, tied up with the belief that the kind of truth long sought in Western intellectual activity is illusory, though postmodernism typically involves a playfulness with elements of this tradition for modern purposes, perhaps partly stimulated by relief at no longer having to carry on this hugely serious and portentous enterprise, and partly, no doubt, because the playfulness is tactically and rhetorically useful in breaking up metanarratives that work for some at the cost of others. Looking back, the postmodern thinker sees millenia of great intellectuals striving all their lives to "get it right," to hammer out a solid foundation on which to build secure knowledge, to articulate how the world really works, to mirror reality correctly in language. The frontispiece of the *Encyclopédie* is an elaborate engraving depicting the unveiling of Truth. This great event seems to be so consistently postponed that, at last, large numbers of postmodern thinkers have concluded something is fundamentally wrong with the whole enterprise, "that something (history, Western man, metaphysics—something large enough to have a destiny) has exhausted its possibilities" (Rorty, 1989, p. 101).

Each past generation has been particularly astute at pointing out the errors and inadequacies of its predecessors, and its errors and inadequacies are pointed out in turn by its successors. After endless philosophical work by the greatest Western thinkers, almost nothing is agreed, nothing is uncontested. If the enterprise were possible, surely *something* would be secured by now, and if Plato, Aristotle, Descartes, Kant, and Co. all have failed to get it right, what hope for thee and me? The idea that the Western intellectual enterprise has been a gradually progressive one, closing in on the truth, getting reality clearer, accumulating a comprehensive and accurate account of the nature of things, has been definitively given up in postmodernism. (Of course, postmodernism can be seen as just a slick and lazy way of claiming to have got it right at last.)

Irony is so pervasive in postmodernism that it might be easier to characterize postmodern irony by briefly sketching the sophisticated postmodern person Richard Rorty calls a liberal ironist. Terms that have been important in the Western intellectual enterprise, such as "truth," "objectivity," "knowledge," and "reality," take on new and somewhat different meanings for the liberal ironist. Because, as Rorty argues, we cannot get outside our conceptual schemes, we cannot reach a position from which to judge how adequately our conceptual schemes represent reality. Objectivity, in the old sense, is unattainable because we cannot determine whether our versions of the world and of experience capture how things are. The liberal ironist conceives of objectivity rather as a term useful to refer to those things about which it is relatively easy to achieve the widest intersubjective agreement. Knowledge is not discovered, Descartes-style, by sitting alone, working something out, and getting it right, but rather is constructed in dialogue and out of agreement. The old distinction between knowledge and opinion is redrawn to distinguish between those claims or perspectives about which wide agreement is easy to achieve and those about which it is hard to achieve. Truth is reconceived as a commendatory reference to beliefs that are widely and easily shared, not as corresponding with reality.

Liberal ironists do not construct theories so much as tell stories; they value the imagination more highly than the intellectual skills supposedly required for accurately representing reality. Rorty suggests there are two principal ways in which reflective people try to make sense of their world and of their lives in it:

> The first is by telling the story of their contribution to a community. This community may be the actual historical one in which they live, or another actual one, distant in time and place, or a quite imaginary one, consisting perhaps of a dozen heroes or heroines selected from history or fiction, or both. The second way is to describe themselves as standing in immediate relation to a non-human reality. (1991, p. 3)

The postmodern ironist believes that the second of these is illusory because it can be achieved only if one can escape the limits of one's community, with its "vocabulary" of concepts, beliefs, and cultural practices, and this is impossible—we are "incarnated vocabularies" (Rorty, 1989, p. 80). The first means that postmodern ironists accept radical and continual doubt about the reliability of the cultural "vocabulary" they themselves use, and they remain open to being "impressed" by other vocabularies—other ways of making sense of the world. They accept that arguments expressed in their present vocabulary cannot dissolve doubts and that their vocabulary is no closer to reality than are others. This position of radical epistemic doubt means that postmodern ironists are "never quite able to take themselves seriously because they are always aware that the terms in which they describe themselves are subject to change" (p. 74). And the ironist "spends her time worrying about the possibility that she has been initiated into the wrong tribe, taught to play the wrong language game" (p. 75).

The person still committed to the Enlightenment project of getting it right, of advancing rationally toward the truth, tends to question the utility of the postmodern enterprise. What's the point of making inquiries and arguments, trying to make sense and meaning, if one constantly doubts that the attempts are anything more than shifting stories? Well, the postmodern ironist replies, the point is to live well, or as well as possible, within the constraints of these contingencies. One can construct meanings, and so "solidarity," with others for purposes of living well and not causing pain. This is hardly a pointless use of intelligence, and it becomes less shocking as an aim for intellectual activity if only we recognize that this is the best we can hope for. Pointless, purposeless activity is, after all, how play used to be defined until its fundamental psychological and social importance became clear, and postmodernists happily adopt this sense of playfulness.

Postmodern irony is particularly hospitable to those who wish to disrupt some metanarrative by which they have been victimized. Some feminists, for example, recognize that "Irony is a particularly appropriate strategy for feminism" (Ferguson, 1993, p. 30) both because it disrupts patriarchal, hegemonic metanarratives and because through "the resources of irony we can think about how we do feminist theory and about what notions of reality and truth our theories make possible" (p. 35). Irony offers a flexibility and freedom from metanarratively-determined perspectives that "is an important resource for feminists (and others) struggling towards mobile subjectivities" (p. 163).

"And new Philosophy calls all in doubt," is one of John Donne's lines from "An Anatomy of the World: The First Anniversary," preceding that which forms the subheading of this section. Ironic philosophers have been calling all in doubt, since Socrates at least, and their postmodern successors in this long tradition continue to do likewise. Not that the Western cultural tradition has required philosophers in order to call all in doubt. Western poetry and drama have constantly explored the fragility of our sense-making and given voice to the anxiety or irony that often accompany it. The recognition of epistemic fragility has been one of the constants of Western intellectual life. Irony has been both a traditional product of this recognition in the West and a changing strategy for dealing with it.

Ironic Understanding as a More Inclusive Irony

The central constituent of irony is a high degree of reflexiveness on our own thinking and a refined sensitivity to the limited and crude nature of the conceptual resources we can deploy in trying to make sense of the world. That is, irony involves sufficient mental flexibility to recognize how inadequately flexible are our minds, and the languages we use, to the world we try to represent in them. Ironic, really. When Socrates cheerfully throws up his hands and says he knows nothing, he is recognizing the inadequacy of the language games we play to the ambitions we have had to know and express what is true. Ironic understanding involves the further reflexive recognition that our minds and languages have other games to play as well as trying to represent reality; particularly they can play the generative games we call art.

Now if this kernel of reflexiveness is enthroned in Ironic understanding, affecting everything that comes near it, how can we also take on board the general schemes of Philosophic understanding? Surely, the corrosive of irony is recognized in modern times primarily as it has gone to work dissolving general schemes and metanarratives? How can characteristics of Mythic and Romantic understanding also be absorbed into Ironic understanding and survive? To answer these questions, what we must do now is slog through some rather condensed, abstract material. So, let us push on into it.

The intellectual capacities that constitute Philosophic understanding enable us to bring very complex knowledge into coherent general schemes. The Philosopher tends to believe that general schemes can mirror reality and 155 deliver a true account of the nature of things. What Ironic understanding will absorb of Philosophic understanding are those abstract theoretic capacities that can bring intellectual order to complex phenomena. What Ironic understanding will not absorb is the belief that general schemes can uncomplicatedly mirror the truth about reality. The Ironist can, say, support a neoconservative or liberal or radical political initiative for its likely beneficial effects without becoming a neoconservative or a liberal or a radical; that is, without being a believer that one or other of those positions enshrines some general truth about how societies do and should function.

So far, so (relatively) uncontroversial, though that weasel word "uncomplicatedly" will need accounting for. Even a postmodernist will accept the use of intellectual capacities that generate metanarratives; the crunch comes in claims about the epistemological status of their products. What I want to retain in Ironic understanding is the corrosion not only of the belief that general schemes reflect the truth about reality but also of the belief that they cannot. That is, Ironic understanding avoids commitment to the credulity common in Philosophic understanding but also avoids commitment to the incredulity common in postmodernism. When a postmodern theorist, such as Lyotard (1979), expresses incredulity in the face of metanarratives and frames a theoretically elaborate manifesto of systematic incredulity, his work begins to take the shape of a new metanarrative, running the self-refuting risks of this chapter's opening sentence. Ironic understanding embraces the irony of postmodernism but not its dismissive certainties—an issue I will return to below when discussing the fifth kind of understanding. The weasel word "uncomplicatedly" is there to mark ironic bemusement about the possibility of reflecting the world accurately in words.

Absorbing characteristics of Philosophic understanding, then, means that Ironic understanders remain open to the possibility that the Enlightenment project might not be exhausted, that rationality might not be the deliverer only of nightmares, that knowledge, truth, and objectivity might not be confined only to contingent agreements, that Western science and rationality might be discourses more privileged than some others in terms of access to reality.

As reflexiveness is central to Ironic understanding, it might be ironically appropriate for me to illustrate the claim of the above paragraphs by reflecting on the general scheme of this book, and its Mythic, Romantic, Philosophic, and Ironic kinds of understanding. The overall structure of this theory is clearly a general scheme of the kind discussed in the chapter on Philosophic understanding. How, then, can I avoid being convicted of the inadequacies that Ironic understanders perceive in such general schemes? I have argued that Ironic understanding can absorb into itself the intellectual capacities generated in the development of Philosophic understanding while shucking off the disabling belief that such schemes uncomplicatedly reflect reality. The reflexiveness of irony is focused on the shadow realm between idea and reality. It makes problematic what had earlier not been considered problematic, making clear that generalized theoretic accounts of complex phenomena bear an uneasy relationship to the phenomena they seek to represent.

The contribution of Ironic understanding is to keep constantly to the fore the inadequacy of the categories and their characterizations to the reality they try to represent, and the contribution of Philosophic understanding is to attempt constantly to capture as much of the complexity of that reality as possible within some coherent general scheme. These two somewhat distinct perspectives, the one skeptical, the other striving to be ever more adequate, do not fit entirely clearly together, but they are far from incompatible. The trick is to keep one's irony pervasively skeptical without letting it undercut and disable the exercise of Philosophic capacities. Irony without Philosophic capacities is impotent.

I recognize that the terms and categories I have used, the forms of construction I have drawn on, are tied to a particular tradition and discourse, and that the language game I am playing, and the tribe I am playing it with, constrains the sense I can make (or fail to make). But I remain ironically doubtful about whether these constraints are as absolute as some assert. On the one hand I believe that my general scheme gives some useful purchase on the relevant phenomena in the real world out there, while on the other hand I remain ironically bemused about how such a crude scheme can represent the infinite complexity of that reality at all, let alone adequately.

Ironic understanding, then, gains the theoretic generalizing capacity of Philosophic understanding while keeping ironically in check the easy belief that truth resides in general schemes. Philosophic understanders' characteristic belief in the truth of some particular scheme most commonly leads to rigidity, making everything conform with the general scheme. Accomplishing this requires enormous intellectual activity, particularly in the face of increasing anomalies. Ironic understanding involves removing the commitment to the simple truth of general schemes, and so Philosophic capacities can be deployed by Ironic understanders with greater flexibility. A number of general schemes might be constructed from a particular body of knowledge, for example, without the Ironic understander's making a commitment to the truth of any of them, but rather selecting among them on aesthetic, utilitarian, or other grounds. The general schemes become alternative perspectives, some perhaps better or more useful for particular purposes than others, and no longer the sole residences of truth. Within Ironic understanding, then, Philosophic capacities survive and gain in flexibility of application and enlargement of their scope of operation.

W. H. Auden, in his poem "Numbers and Faces," distinguishes between lovers of small numbers who go "benignly potty" and lovers of large numbers who go "horribly mad." The person who is captive of some general scheme, lacking the irony that can make it a liberating tool rather than an enslaver, is constantly at the risk of going "horribly mad."

But what about Romantic understanding? How can romantic associations with the transcendent qualities of heroes, fascination with the extremes of experience and the limits of reality, and pervasive wonder coexist with irony? Modern and postmodern irony cast a cold eye on such extravagances, most commonly treating the enthusiasm of romance with condescension if not contempt. But the conception of irony in Ironic understanding is to incorporate romance. How?

To deal with this question, I'm afraid another must first be addressed. The prior question arises because Romantic understanding does not come directly to Ironic understanding but arrives "through" Philosophic understanding. So the prior question is, how can Romantic characteristics reach an accommodation with Philosophic understanding? This in turn might seem an unlikely accommodation when we recall that the characteristics of Philosophic understanding were forged by people who claimed that Philosophic kinds of thinking could come into being only by displacing Romantic kinds.

Let me try to indicate how an accommodation may be reached by revisiting the example of Marxism. Certain relatively simple forms of Marxism have involved straightforward Philosophic characteristics, in particular a clear general scheme. The survival of Romantic characteristics may be seen in the way that the convinced party member viewed Marxism not simply as a convincing analysis of social and historical processes but also as the object of a powerful affective commitment. Leading Marxists became imbued with more or less modified forms of heroic qualities. The idea of Marxism gathered around it in greater or lesser degree a modified sense of the transcendence earlier projected onto football teams or pop singers. But if romantic capacities are suppressed by, rather than encouraged to coalesce with, developing Philosophic capacities, the result will more likely be a doctrinaire, calculative, heartless, and arid ideology—as was too often the case.

The blending of Romantic characteristics with Philosophic general schemes is not confined to the great metanarratives like Marxism, of course. Nor are inadequately developed or suppressed Romantic characteristics evident only in grim ideologies. In *Middlemarch*, Mr. Casaubon, constructing his "key to all mythologies," perfectly embodies the desiccation, enervation, and impoverishment of life we commonly see when Philosophic capacities are developed at the cost of Romantic ones. The educational task is, of course, to develop each as fully as possible and to preserve as much as possible of each in the development of subsequent kinds. The persistence of Romantic understanding into Philosophic general schemes gives the latter energy, life, and an extended, affective meaning that the theoretic activity alone cannot provide. Reciprocally, Philosophic understanding gives direction, more general purpose, and focus to Romantic capacities.

Well, this is starkly schematic but, I hope, adequate to indicate how the capacities developed largely within one kind of understanding need not be simply superceded or suppressed by the capacities of the next. They can work together in varying ways and in varying degrees.

To return now to the earlier question: how do Romantic characteristics persist in Ironic understanding, and how are they modified by it? What kind of irony can accommodate romance? Consider the capacity to form Romantic associations with transcendent human qualities. Irony will corrode the enthusiasm of the Romantic association that generates for its object the sense of transcendence, but what can persist is the capacity to form associations. Whereas the commonest Romantic associations are formed with the wonderful, the extreme, the transcendent, irony can deploy this capacity to associate also with one's struggling neighbor, the person on skid row, the builder on that site down the street, or on mundane experiences. That is, irony can greatly enlarge the scope of operations of Romantic capacities by corroding their connection with characteristic Romantic objects.

The Ironic understander no less than the Romantic can form an association with the excellences of a football team or with exemplary compassion and dedication to others' needs, but will also be ready to recognize the excellences of opponents and recognize in the recipients of the exemplary compassion and dedication their own unique human qualities. So Ironic understanding can both absorb Romantic capacities and enlarge their scope of deployment.

The capacity to associate romantically with the heroic qualities that would best enable us to overcome the constraints that hem in our everyday lives can persist in Ironic understanding to fulfill much the same role. In Ironic understanding, that "overcoming" will be modified from the somewhat unfocused sense of transcendence common to the teenager yearning for the freedom or power of their pop-singing or football-playing heroes. But, however ironic we become, there persists the need to pull ourselves over everyday constraints, out of ruts, free from conventional thinking, and this Romantic capacity, modified by irony, provides the energy and power continually to haul ourselves up by our intellectual bootstraps.

The range of capacities that constitutes Romantic understanding, then,

159

can be absorbed into Ironic understanding. Their contribution is to give that energy, engagement, life, and affective meaning associated with romance without which irony is solipsistic and dryly alienating. (Irony's impact on romance is often assumed to produce cynicism. In this scheme, cynicism is inadequately developed romance, quite distinct from the richness of Ironic understanding.)

So let us take the enriching capacities of Romantic understanding on board the good ship Ironic understanding, ensuring that our Ironic under-stander will retain a "soul unsubdued with habit, unshackled by custom," as Coleridge recommended.

Some of the freshness and wonder to be taken on board will come from preserving and absorbing characteristics of Mythic understanding into Ironic understanding. How can irony coalesce with story-structuring and oppositional thinking? But before addressing that question, there is again the prior question of how Mythic characteristics can survive the develop-ment of Romantic and Philosophic understanding.

Consider the Mythic capacity for oppositional thinking. The starkness of those early oppositions, establishing conceptual categories in terms of the child's feelings, are reduced in Romantic understanding but are still com-monly used in exploring extremes of experience and the limits of reality. The Mythic oppositions become, as it were, confined within and adapted to the exploration of the external world. In Philosophic understanding, opposi-tional thinking is modified further; it is evident in the dialectical thinking that is characteristic of Philosophic understanding, and it is adapted also to the interplay of general schemes and particular anomalies. Even more sche-matically we can see how Mythic stories become modified to Romantic nar-ratives, which are further modified to Philosophic metanarratives. For example, the binary stereotypes of the Grimms' active males and passive fe-males leads to Romantic stories of heroic males righting wrongs and saving otherwise helpless damsels in distress, which in turn leads to Philosophic theories of the natural role of the male as the dominant partner in the human species.

But, surely, irony undercuts the constantly modifying utility of story-structuring and oppositional thinking? The reflexiveness of irony ensures that when some features of the world are represented in story forms or in terms of oppositions we recognize these as imposed on the world by our minds; we know that the world is not story shaped. These structures are imposed to make events meaningful in particular ways, determining how we feel about them. It is that construction of meaning that modern and post-modern ironists deconstruct, showing the role of the perceiving mind in what is perceived. To such ironists, this recognition puts a stop to such self-deceiving illusions and makes us face the unstoried contingency of things. Having faced the fact that reality is beyond the grasp of our stories, then, in Nietzsche's and Rorty's views, we may consciously make up our own contingent stories, constructing meanings that are good to believe for living well, but we must not suffer the confusion of thinking that these meanings derive from the reality on which we impose them.

Whether we accept a modern/postmodern view that the structuring and meaning-construction that stories and oppositions make possible may be deployed contingently, or whether we believe that some stories and some oppositions are better than others because they better reflect events, we can recognize how such Mythic capacities can be modified for continuing use in Ironic understanding.

Well, again, this is a schematic, somewhat ideal account of how Mythic, Romantic, and Philosophic characteristics can be incorporated in modified forms within Ironic understanding. Irony strips away beliefs that the earlier forms disclose the truth about reality, and it enables their deployment with greater flexibility than was possible within the constraints of earlier kinds of understanding. This schematic account is ideal in that it does not attend to the infinite pathologies that commonly disturb the educational process as represented by the gradual accumulation of the capacities of each kind of understanding. Inadequate development of any kind will ricochet through the educational process, yielding the range of failures, half-failures, and varied achievements we see around and within us.

The success of Ironic understanding is evident in the reflexiveness that not only yields doubt and "infinite absolute negativity" but also brings along with it Mythic, Romantic, and Philosophic thinking, thereby enriching one's ordinary everyday perceptions and transforming pervasive doubt and negativity into possibility. Elsewhere I have distinguished two responses to growing irony, which I unsophisticatedly called "alienating irony" and "sophisticated irony" (1979). The former results from the achievement of reflexiveness that undercuts and suppresses general schemes, romantic associations, and mythic stories. (The common suppression of earlier kinds of understanding that we recognize in ourselves and in other people echoes—recapitulates?—the common polemical attacks on intellectual predecessors in our cultural history; perhaps it is stimulated by a kind of shame at earlier unsophistication.) This alienating irony rejects the validity of any perspective, believes in no metanarratives, sees all epistemological schemes as futile; in short, it doubts everything

Sophisticated irony is different in that it succeeds in achieving reflexiveness without suppressing Mythic, Romantic, and Philosophic understanding. By preserving the earlier kinds of understanding as much as possible, we may develop a kind of irony that enables its users to recognize validity in all perspectives, to believe all metanarratives, to accept all epistemological schemes, to give assent to every belief. Well, that puts it simplistically, of course. This openness to possibility is not credulity or simplemindedness but, rather, the result of a flexible, buoyant recognition of a multivocal world, within and without. Put incautiously, as above, sophisticated Ironic understanding might seem cheerfully open to self-contradiction: committed to foundationalism on the one hand and antifoundationalism on the other; to traditional epistemology and the Enlightenment project as well as to Nietzschean insights and to the postmodern project. But the sophisticated ironist enjoys an abundant consciousness of varied ways of understanding, and can appreciate a varied spectrum of perspectives while concluding that some are better or more valid or more helpful or more beautiful than others in particular circumstances and for particular purposes. And if understanding is a primary purpose, some tools are better than others; science trumps magic, rationality trumps unreason. But, of course, we do have other purposes than understanding, and for some of the more exotic among them magic will trump science. The sophisticated ironist is adept choosing among and using the set of understanding tools we have considered.

The product of alienating irony is impotence; sophisticated irony is liberating and empowering. The aim of this educational theory is precisely to keep alive as much as possible of the earlier kinds of understanding in the development of irony.

SOMATIC UNDERSTANDING

Now, I have a number of times referred to a further kind of understanding, one most evident in pre-language-using human experience. The existence of this kind of understanding and its incorporation into Ironic understanding further enlarges the inclusiveness of this sense of irony, and seems to set it at odds both with the more radical forms of modern and postmodern irony and with alienating irony. Calling it Somatic understanding suggests a general embodied kind of understanding that is somewhat distinct from the languaged and conceptual kinds discussed so far. While I have little to say about it as a somewhat distinctive kind of understanding, it is important to discuss at this point because its persisting presence in Ironic understanding further distinguishes my conception of irony from those sketched earlier, and particularly from that of some postmodernists.

Somatic understanding is the first kind in the sequence, and persists through each of the other kinds and into the Ironic as well. (Discussing it here does not mean that it is only a part of Ironic understanding. This is just another case of the first being last.) The Somatic is a somewhat distinctive kind of understanding that sequentially precedes the Mythic, coalescing and accommodating with each subsequent kind of understanding as they develop on the Somatic foundation. Somatic understanding, then, is not something that exists only prior to language development but rather, like each of these kinds of understanding, it ideally remains with us throughout our lives, continuing to develop within, though somewhat modified by, other kinds of understanding.

Since drafting this book, I have come across Merlin Donald's remarkable *Origins of the Modern Mind*. Donald synthesizes a vast amount of data from anthropology, paleontology, linguistics, cognitive science, and, especially, neuropsychology into an articulate account of the major cognitive transitions in hominid prehistory and in the historical period, and of the new ways of representing reality and the new forms of culture each transition implied. The three most general tools that have effected these transitions he identifies as the body's mimetic skills, oral language, and external symbols, and these produce stages of cultural development which he calls Mimetic, Mythic, and Theoretic. His characterization of Mimetic culture is so like what I mean by Somatic understanding, I have junked my relatively impoverished account and will save space and add richness by referring to his characterization, summarizing the salient features here.

My recapitulation scheme is, of course, quite different from Donald's general argument, but it is noteworthy that his account of prehistoric Mimetic culture draws readily on the abilities of pre-language-using children today in its composition. He does this because of his argument that earlier cultural forms and mental characteristics survive into the present either by evolutionary coding or by fundamental forms of cultural transition. He contends, for example, that

Eibl-Eibesfeldt's evidence demonstrates how the mimetic layer of representation survives under the surface, in forms that remain universal, not necessarily because they are genetically programmed but because mimesis forms the core of an ancient root-culture that is distinctly human. No matter how evolved our oral-linguistic culture, and no matter how sophisticated the rich varieties of symbolic material surrounding us, mimetic scenarios still form the expressive heart of human social interchange. (1991, p. 189)

He notes further that "the use of patterns of mimetic representations in modern human society have remained distinct from the uses of our later cognitive acquisitions [like language and literacy]. In effect, there is still a vestigial mimetic culture embedded within our modern culture, and a mimetic mind embedded within the overall architecture of the modern human mind" (p. 163). Similarly, I argue that Somatic understanding survives both from its 163 prehistoric forms and from its recapitulated development in infancy into modern adult Ironic understanding.

Donald clarifies what he means by mimesis by distinguishing it from mimicry and imitation. Mimicry, he points out, seeks to reproduce exactly some event or action. It is a literal copying, such as many animals perform, duplicating expressions or sounds of others, as a parrot copies other birds or voices. Imitation is less literal, as in an offspring copying its parent's behavior; the offspring follows the general pattern of the parent's behavior but doesn't mimic it in literal detail. "Mimesis adds a representational dimension to imitation" (p. 169), as in adopting a gesture like covering the face to indicate grief. Mimesis is distinguished, then, by its involving "the *invention* of intentional representation" (p. 169, emphasis in original), and performance of such acts in front of an audience communicates intentions beyond what is possible for apes and other animals. "Mimetic skill or mimesis rests on the ability to produce conscious, self-initiated, representational acts that are intentional but not linguistic" (p. 168).

Crucial to the development of Mimetic culture, according to Donald, is "the way the *individual's own body,* and its movement in space, was represented in the brain" (p. 189, emphasis in original). The main constituents of Mimetic culture, which I want to borrow to fill out my characterization of Somatic understanding, are summarized by Donald as follows:

Intentionality: Within a few months of birth humans can shift their gaze to align it with that of a parent in a manner that attributes intention to the parent's gaze (Scaife and Bruner, 1975; Churcher and Scaife, 1982). Slightly older infants can point in order to draw others' attention to something. These are skills that chimpanzees lack.

Generativity: Motor actions can be broken down into components and then recombined for other purposes, either to represent a novel event or to communicate something new. There is a generative component in this ability in humans that is lacking in apes. Donald describes it in terms of young children's practice, rehearsal, and refinement of actions in play, in which the same basic actions, like lifting, smiling, hitting, falling, can be recombined into new sequences to represent events. "Human children routinely re-enact the events of the day and imitate the actions of their parents and siblings. They do this very often without any apparent reason other than to reflect on their representation of the event" (p. 172).

Communicativity: Mimetic acts are usually performed publicly, and even though communication might not have been their original purpose, they can be readily adapted to communicate within the social group.

Reference: Humans can very early in life distinguish between play-acting an event, such as a pretend fight, and a real event, a real fight. They can distinguish readily between representations and their referents.

Unlimited objects: Mimesis is limited to concrete, episode-bound representations, but there seem to be no limits on the events that can be represented or the physical modality of their representation.

Autocueing: "Mimetic acts are reproducible on the basis of internal, self-generated cues. This permits voluntary recall of mimetic representations, without the aid of external cues—probably the earliest form of representational 'thinking'" (p. 173). Exemplified in autocueing are an intellectual autonomy and generativity that are unique to humans and whose development has led to such odd consequences for us among the planet's animal species.

The social consequences of these skills becoming common in the prehistoric community would include "collectively invented and maintained customs, games, skills, and representations" (p. 173). These skills enable the sharing of knowledge without each member of the social group's having to reinvent it. Human children model their overall social structure in play, acting out their own roles or parents' or siblings' roles, and so on. Mimetic games, such as those with sticks and balls, are universal in the culture of young humans, and they commonly help to define social and gender roles without the use of language. Deaf-mute children who have not learned to sign, for example, play such games indistinguishably from other children. The games exemplify regular patterns of activity that also support ritual, cooperation in hunting, specialized social organization, toolmaking, and pedagogy—the Mimetic training of the young in society's repertoire of skills.

In the human past, Mimetic skills enjoyed considerable pragmatic success in socially coordinated activities such as toolmaking and hunting. "But its greatest importance would have been in the collective modelling, and hence the structuring, of hominid society itself. Mimetic culture was a successful and stable adaptation, a survival strategy for hominids that endured for over a million years" (p. 200). It is a survival strategy based on a set of cognitive tools developed and deployed long ago and adopted in somewhat different ways by young children today. Most of these tools develop in young children as a result of genetic action and, once developed, they yield a particular kind of distinctively human, nonlanguaged understanding, whose characteristics are intentionality, generativity, communicativity, reference, and so on.

Emphasizing the importance of Somatic understanding to this theory is awkward because it seems to conflict with what is taken almost for granted by many prominent philosophers. Much modernist and postmodernist theory is built on the assumption that human understanding is essentially languaged understanding. As Rorty puts it: "it is essential in [his] view that we have no prelinguistic consciousness to which language needs to be adequate, no deep sense of how things are which it is the duty of philosophers to spell out in language" (1989, p. 21). This is "the current *doxa* which unites the various schools" of advanced thinking (Norris, 1993, p. 289). It seems to me (and to many others) that we do have a prelinguistic consciousness and, worse, that this consciousness is not merely prelinguistic in a temporal sense but remains with us, as a part of our understanding, throughout our lives. As when we become literate we do not cease to be oral-language users, so when we become oral-language users we do not cease to be prelinguistic sense-makers. I do not mean that Somatic understanding constitutes some common "human nature," but simply that we also make sense of the world in a distinctively human way that is not linguistic.

The view that human experience is "essentially linguistic" (Gadamer, 1976, p. 19), that we are "incarnated vocabularies" (Rorty, 1989, p. 80), has drawn much from Wittgenstein's arguments about "language games" in his *Philosophical Investigations*. Those arguments are central to postmodernism, even if they do occasionally become scrambled and simplified in the process of being wrestled into place as foundations—a mixed metaphoric feat which Rorty accuses Lyotard of performing (Rorty, 1991, pp. 215ff.). Wittgenstein's related arguments support the view that language does not so much capture or describe reality as prescribe how we can see reality. So, for example, that short, hollow cylinder, closed at one end and with a ceramic loop on its side, you *see as* a coffee cup; you do not see a short, hollow cylinder, closed at one end with a ceramic loop on one side. We use things, we know things, as they are constructed for us by our language, by our concepts, by our cultural experience, by our socialization, by our history.

Now Ironic understanding is made up largely of Mythic, Romantic, and Philosophic characteristics, which in turn are determined by degrees in the development of language, so ideas about the importance of language in our understanding of the world are clearly already on board. What is at issue now is whether something else is to be taken on board that will require us to qualify that "essentially linguistic" conception of human experience— perhaps to something more modest, like "largely linguistic."

Important for my argument is the fact that very young, pre-language-using children have an understanding of the world. This is not an "animal" perception; it is a distinctively human "take" on the world. It is constituted of how we first make sense with our distinctive human perceptions, our human brain and mind and heart and whatever else our bodies can deploy in orienting themselves. Bernard Williams has argued against the view that human personhood comes only with language and socialization: "anyone who has lived with a six-year-old, or a two-year-old, has vivid reasons for thinking of them as persons" (1985, p. 114). I would add to this that anyone who has watched babies grow recognizes that language development does not mark some distinct beginning of that individual person; rather, language allows each individual a new kind of expression. This new expression is profoundly important, but its deployment by each individual is clearly continuous with that individual's earlier development; that is, language development does not mark some profound discontinuity in the development of individual personality. Rather, recognizable and distinct individuals adapt the common language they are initiated into to their distinctive, individual needs.

And you *can* see your coffee mug as a short, hollow cylinder, closed at one end, with a ceramic loop on its side. It takes some effort, but one can recapture the particularity of the artifact apart from its cultural purpose. Look for a long time at your coffee mug, or consider this book, not as a mug or a book but as the elaborately constructed artefact that it is. Consider the sheets of paper, from pulped wood, cleverly cut to equal sizes, fixed somehow at one edge and unattached at three, hinged, bearing ink stains in conventional shapes. Look at that "a" until it loses the association with the alphabet and sound and becomes, or reverts to, merely a shape. Consider the word "book," and say it aloud again and again until it loses its association with this artifact and becomes, or reverts to, a curious sound. Try Hamlet's "words, words, words," but maybe twenty or fifty times, until the odd sound is stripped of its associations and becomes just a peculiar noise human beings can make.

We are human beings before we are languaged human beings. (I recognize the Chomskian sense in which we have "from the beginning" a brain uniquely endowed with a "module" for language, but I am referring here to the sense of developed articulateness within a particular society and language group.) Beneath the layers of socialization we are each of us a unique individual consciousness. We are born alone and we die alone, and in the short interval between, underneath our languages, histories, cultures, and socialized awareness, we live alone. The sins we do by two and two, as Rudyard Kipling's devil reminded Tomlinson, we pay for one by one. This involves a recognition that along with our social being—"Humans are social animals"—we are also and ultimately alone. Our unique, individual consciousness can be vivid and clear or faint and suppressed.

Now, I recognize that some readers may want to deny that such an observation accurately describes their experience. Perhaps some may see this as a confessional passage and even be considering sending me a postcard of   167 condolence. But I am not describing some pathological condition; rather I am simply pointing to a feature of our existence that our socialized experience tends to suppress. Waking at night, one may turn and see the outline of one's spouse's head, and note the shadowed movement of an eye beneath the lid. Though one might have shared decades of the details of one's life with that person, one cannot begin to guess the images and emotions vivid inside that so well-known head as it lies asleep. And one settles back into the pillow in the dark and retreats to one's own private world. Our shared experience, our language, culture, and history constrain and socialize the activity of our brains, but the dramatic images of our dreams, or better the "hypnagogic hallucinations" that appear as flickering images that well up at the threshold of sleep (cf. Alvarez, 1995), are a kind of thinking produced by the brain's neurons firing away while the control of the perceptions' steadying grasp on the external world is shut down. This unique and private mental world is with us from the beginning; its imagistic, concrete, vivid forms of thought remain throughout our lives, endlessly active without, or "below," language. When steadied by waking perceptions of the external world, this private mental activity remains unique and provides us with a unique "take" on the world that the most energetic poetic intellects try to capture in language, always recognizing the inadequacy of language to the task. While one can exaggerate this unique "take" on the world, one can equally, as is currently fashionable, exaggerate the extent to which language mediates our understanding. Given the conception of education in this theory, which requires the fullest possible development of each kind of understanding, it becomes important to develop and preserve Somatic understanding, along with its sense of the uniqueness and loneness of our experience. The educational scheme requires that we seek ways to make this kind of understanding rich and vivid to ward off the anesthetizing socialization of the tribe.

The sense of a knowledge from the body, beyond human words, is of course a commonplace of poetry. It is also a commonplace of religious experience. As William James puts it:

Philosophy lives in words, but truth and fact well up into our lives in ways that exceed verbal formulation. There is in the living act of perception always something that glimmers and twinkles and will not be caught, and for which reflection comes too late. (1902, pp. 446–47)

That human beings have constantly tried to give voice to a consciousness they declare to be beyond language obviously does not refute Rorty's claim that there is no prelinguistic consciousness to which language needs to be adequate. But constant references to something people cannot put into words—"Nor mouth had, no nor mind expressed / What heart heard of, ghost-guessed" (Gerard Manley Hopkins, "Spring and Fall")—is in part what I want to encompass in Somatic understanding. In the case of Hopkins's poem, what the heart heard of, ghost-guessed, is the process of getting older announced in its own inexorable and irrefutable terms within the body. Consciousness of aging, as of toothache, goes all the way down, past language, concepts, and history, past multiple, decentered discourses. While language can indeed "mediate" even the most intractable experience, representing aging as an achievement, a triumph, or a state of continuing progress, to conclude that this power of language is indicative of its ultimate importance in human cognition seems simply to exaggerate. Certainly language tends to be given the paramount position in many modern models of human cognition. As Merlin Donald puts it: "Language is usually placed at the top of the cognitive pyramid; but language evolved in, and continues to be employed in, a wider cultural context. . . . In human culture . . . language is not used equally in all areas of activity, nor is it the only means of communication and thought. It is possible that language is a 'dedicated' system, that is, a specialized system for special applications, rather than a general-purpose device" (1991, p. 201).

When Vladimir Nabokov was interviewed in his later years, he insisted on a rather peculiar procedure. The interviewer had to submit in writing and in advance the questions that would be asked. Nabokov would then write his responses, and the interview consisted of the interviewer reading the questions and Nabokov reading his responses. If the interviewer deviated from the text, the interview was immediately concluded. Now, I am calling on a distant memory that I have been unable to verify: Robert Robinson interviewed him and the result was published in a British Sunday newspaper twenty-five or thirty years ago. One of the questions was something like, "Why do you insist on this peculiar interview procedure?" Nabokov's reply was something close to, "Because I think like an angel, I write like a competent craftsman, and I talk like a fool."

Many people clearly believe, most with less evident justification than Nabokov, that they think like angels; it's just that something goes wrong with the angelic thoughts as they are converted into language. This common notion that there is an ultralinguistic "angelic" consciousness that our language should strive to be honest to, to reflect truly, to correspond with, is obviously not in itself an adequate reason for disputing those who claim it does not exist. But the belief that we can have access to nothing below language that can constrain language, as Rorty claims, seems no less vulnerable to reasonable ironic doubt.

Somatic understanding provides to Ironic understanding something beyond language, something foundational to all later understanding. It is not the kind of metanarrative foundation sought in Philosophic understanding. The tension between the Somatic foundation of consciousness and the Ironic, flexible, linguistic superstructure allows to the Ironic language-user an understanding of ultralinguistic experience; this Somatic experience provides us with something below language that our language can strive to be true to, and that truth can be something more Rortyesque than agreements with fellow language-users.

> In general . . . the most crucial issues of irony reside in the area of self-conscious saying and writing and concern the problems of linguistic articulation, communication, and understanding in regard to truth. The ironic manner of expression can be described as attempting to transcend the restrictions of normal discourse and straightforward speech by making the ineffable articulate, at least indirectly, through a great number of verbal strategies, and accomplishing what lies beyond the reach of direct communication. This attitude, however, automatically constitutes an offense to common reason and understanding. . . . Socrates was the first example for that constellation. (Behler, 1990, p. 112)

The strategies for making the ineffable, including our Somatic understanding, articulate are those most popularly recognized as ironic. "Bolingbroke was a holy man"; there remains something mysterious about what such a simple, absurd assertion generates between speaker and hearer, writer and reader. It is the sense that there are features of our understanding that are beyond the possibility of articulating, even as we constantly try to articulate them, with which the reflexiveness of irony is entrammelled. And, incidentally, this crucial feature of irony seems largely lacking in Rorty's liberal ironist, who may be profoundly liberal but, in this crucial regard, seems to have given up on what the strategies of irony are designed for.

The intellectual tools of Somatic understanding do not go away as language develops. As Donald points out, language evolved, and continues to be employed, in a wider cultural context. A basic element of that wider cultural context for modern humans is the persistence within the architecture of our minds of a prelinguistic Somatic understanding or Mimetic culture. From this distinctively human understanding language emerged in the distant past and emerges every day in the lives of young children; the various forms of languaged understanding that we develop carry distinctive traces from this cognitive and cultural source.

CONCLUSION

There are many kinds of irony or, perhaps, many contexts in which the expression of irony takes varied forms. Within these kinds or contexts there are continua of degrees of irony, although I have largely ignored them in favor of reflecting on irony's central reflexiveness. This reflexiveness enables us to apply to our own sense-making, to our own understanding, to our own beliefs and opinions, the questions and doubts we may have about those of others. In this reflexive ability we can recognize, with Schlegel, that irony entails an ethical no less than an aesthetic and an intellectual dimension (cf. Handwerk, 1985). Ironic understanding thus requires expanding our sympathies and sensitivities even to those who seem quite unlike us. This is an educational aim shared with Rorty's liberal ironist; instead of identifying ourselves in terms of some excluded groups who are unlike "us," and who consequently can be treated with less sympathy, less sensitivity, less humanity, we will seek to include wider and wider groups within the category of "us."

Our initial understanding, according to this theory so far, is Somatic; then we develop language and a socialized identity, then writing and print, then abstract, theoretic forms of expressing general truths, and then a reflexivity that brings with it pervasive doubts about the representations of the world that can be articulated in language. But irony is a general strategy for putting into language meanings that the literal forms of language cannot contain; along with this, Ironic understanding involves abstract, theoretic capacities, plus the capacities stimulated by literacy, plus the winged words of orality, and also our bodily foundation in the natural world.

chapter 6

Some Questions and Answers

I have suggested that the three main ideas we have inherited about education—socializing, Plato's academic program, and Rousseau's developmentalism—are neither singly nor jointly adequate. Consequently, practical prescriptions for educating derived from them will be inadequate. In their place I have suggested a novel recapitulation scheme based on the development of intellectual tools that sustain somewhat distinctive kinds of understanding—somatic, mythic, romantic, philosophic, and ironic. How the scheme outlined so far can be elaborated into a comprehensive educational program remains to be explored. Some elaboration will take place in chapters 7 and 8, but a variety of objections to many features of the scheme may have already occurred to you. In this chapter, then, I would like to address potential objections and clarify some parts of the theory.

Because this scheme does nibble into a rather extensive acreage of academic real estate, the range of objections is, I imagine, extensive and varied as well. Instead of trying to organize a continuous narrative that addresses questionable features in some neat or rambling order, I will approach this by pretending that you have been a typically diverse but preternaturally patient conference audience that has listened to the previous chapters and now has the opportunity to ask questions, make comments, hurl abuse, or throw money. I will raise the questions for you and try to answer them. I will also intervene now and then on behalf of an imaginary skeptical reader ("lector") to raise further subsidiary questions to which I (as "auctor") will respond.

This procedure may generate in your mind the image of me running down into the audience, grabbing the microphone, asking a question, then scrambling back to the lectern to deliver the answer. But it provides as good a way as I can think of to raise a set of diverse questions.

Such a procedure will not be entirely satisfactory, especially to anyone whose objection is not even raised here because I am too dense or benighted to recognize it. But perhaps we can consider this chapter a preliminary discussion among those who find these ideas worth pursuing. We live, after all, in an electronic age, which is properly undermining the notion of the printed book as some kind of completed, definitive, authoritative statement. What we write in books are merely artificially extended parts of a conversation. Tomorrow or yesterday the author would have written something different. Books provide an inappropriate semi-permanence to the thoughts we put into words.

So I will put my Internet e-mail address at the end of this sentence, and invite anyone who wishes to send comments, questions, or related ideas to me at Kieran_Egan@sfu.ca. I will try to reply to each and also to build a file of comments and responses and responses to responses, and attach that to my replies to further messages. A better idea, however, is to see further questions and answers and contribute to the discussion on my World Wide Web home page. You can find it at http://www.educ.sfu.ca/people/faculty/kegan/.

In the following question-and-answer session, I will begin with easy questions designed to clarify some general features of the theory, and then I will move to some more challenging and diverse objections. So, where shall we begin?

Q: Ah yes. Sorry to jump up so fast. It's just that I've been listening carefully, but it's not been easy to take it all in, to see the overall argument and catch all the details together. What I'd find useful at this point would be a very short overview of the theory you're proposing. Just a very quick "recapitulation," you might say.
A: Quite. I begin with the assumption that all human minds everywhere are pretty much the same. That is, I take the general differences among the ways people make sense of the world and experience as stemming mainly from the various intellectual tools they are deploying rather than from their genetic makeup. Mythic understanding, for example, is not a product of genetically "primitive" minds or immature minds but a product of somewhat distinctive intellectual tools being deployed by genetically similar minds.

Lector: Just a moment! We seem to have problems at the very beginning here. First, what does "pretty much" mean? Hardly a precise   173 technical term, is it? And then there are "general differences" and "mainly."

Auctor: I am claiming that, given the phenomena of interest to this theory, the differences we note in people's thinking are sufficiently accounted for by differences in the intellectual tools being used. There may be differences because of age, gender, race, or whatever, but even if there were, these seem much less useful in characterizing kinds of understanding compared with the influence of the cognitive tools I have been considering.

Lector: I'm not sure you can mean what I think you are saying. You seem to imply that even age isn't significant in the development of these kinds of understanding. Do you mean this? You realize that we have a number of developmental psychologists here who would consider such a claim absurd.

Auctor: Of course one doesn't want to appear eccentric. It's not that I think that age has no influence but rather that whatever influence it has is very difficult, perhaps impossible, to assess apart from the sociocultural context into which the child grows. Whatever influence age has on children's developing understanding, I am suggesting, will be incidentally incorporated within the more comprehensive category of developing kinds of understanding.

Lector: I just can't let that pass. You are saying that age— maturation—can't be assessed whereas these language developments and kinds of understanding can? But surely you've got it the wrong way round; language developments are a function of age, of maturation!

Auctor: Maturation in some cultures does not lead to the language developments and the intellectual tools I have been describing. So it can't be a matter of maturation bringing about linguistic developments of the kind being considered here. What makes this theory interesting is its elaboration of a category—kinds of understanding—that is distinct from the psychological and epistemological categories we have been accustomed to use for cultural and educational development. This new category incorporates the influences of psychology and epistemology but does not try to separate them out.

Lector: So you are really claiming that we shouldn't consider maturation as influencing how people understand the world, and that there is no point studying maturation or psychological development separate from sociocultural contexts?

Auctor: No. First, I am claiming that if you want to grasp the most prominent differences among people's understanding of the world,

you would be better advised to look at the intellectual tools they use rather than at their age. To the degree the latter is relevant it will be incorporated in the former. As for studying some underlying maturational or psychological-developmental process, I am suggesting only that it will be very difficult to isolate it from sociocultural issues.
Lector: Well, I don't want to stop you from trying to answer the original question, so do carry on. But I should give notice of further questions on this issue.

OK. So, first, similar minds, different tools. Second, different cultures and environments have stimulated a great variety of intellectual tools to think with, but the ones that have had the greatest impact on general kinds of understanding are linguistic. Now I don't mean that all intellectual tools are linguistic, just that language is so influential that its major developments are clearly evident in the main distinguishable kinds of understanding.

We have seen that oral language develops from Mimetic activities, literacy develops from oral language, theoretic abstractions develop from literacy, and refined reflexiveness develops from theoretic abstractions. These developments are largely cumulative, but not entirely so; each cumulative addition seems to entail some loss. Each development is not simply of a set of skills; rather, each is tied into complexes of social behavior, and one acquires them primarily by growing up into or being initiated into communities that use them. Learning to use them involves, and requires, in diminished form the generative qualities of the minds of those people who first invented them. Literacy, theoretic abstraction, and refined reflexiveness rely on deliberate instruction, whereas somatic/mimetic and oral-language developments rely largely on evolutionary adaptations.

Each development of these language-based intellectual tools has ramifying implications for how its users can understand the world, and I have tried to spell out some of these ramifications. The kinds of understanding I have described have obviously been distinguished in various ways before. Differences between oral and literate cultures have been drawn many ways; "romance," for example, has long been recognized as a literary genre and as a stance in the world distinct from theoretic or scientific thinking. Irony has been distinguished from other tropes and discussed as a general form of consciousness. What is novel in my scheme, I think, is that I distinguish this set of understandings and tie them in with specific developments in language use.

I have also tried to show that these language developments stimulate similar kinds of understanding both in cultural history and in students to-   175 day. As students learn to use the intellectual tools involved in these language developments they recapitulate in their education a significant dimension of their cultural history.

I have further suggested that education might more fruitfully be thought of in terms of the acquisition of these kinds of understanding than in the traditional terms of some mix of socializing, academics, and psychological development.

Q: I don't see the connection between these stages and historical periods. You say they develop one after the other, in history and in the child, but you skip all over the historical map. You have Greek historians and nineteenth-century poets tossed together to build the picture of your Romantic phase, then we skip back to the Greeks again for the Philosophic layer, and Plato, who represents that one, also pops up representing Irony in the next stage. Your Philosophic examples come mostly from before the period of romanticism, yet you use some of the romantics to exemplify Philosophic thinking and others in describing the development of Irony. This seems a very odd notion of recapitulation. Also, the idea that these stages accumulate to some modern Ironic understanding just seems preposterous; a trip around your local supermarket should disabuse you of any fond notion about modern people being generally ironic.

A: The kind of order you recommend—relating historical periods neatly with students' ages—would conflict with some of the basic principles of this theory. Many nineteenth-century recapitulation theories specified the kind of orderly relationship between historical periods and students' ages that you seem to assume is a necessary feature of any recapitulation theory. But I argued that this theory is significantly different from those in identifying what is recapitulated.

Kinds of understanding are just the ways the mind works when using particular tools. All the kinds of understanding are potential or embryonic in all minds, along with an indeterminate range of other kinds of understanding that are so little evoked in our cultural environments that we hardly can recognize them. In oral cultures, for example, people will have access to Romantic, Philosophic, and Ironic ways of thinking because these are implicit in language use, but because there is generally little stimulus among the social practices of most oral cultures to sustain consistently those kinds of understanding, their use will be fitful and unsystematic.

Once a kind of understanding has been systematically developed and is sustained by communities using it, that kind of understanding will be accessible to anyone with adequate reasons or motivation to learn it within the appropriate community. This does not mean that everyone at any particular time in a society will "catch" it and will deploy the same intellectual

176

tools. Everyone in the supermarket you refer to has probably had some contact with, some stimulation of, and made some use of, all the kinds of understanding I have referred to. Probably most of us respond to the supermarket in a Somatic or Mythic manner. But running into a parent of a member of your child's soccer team may stimulate Romantic discussion of the excellences of your children's play, or a concern about the rising price of ginger might stimulate Philosophic reflection on world trade and politics, and so on. Among the people in the supermarket at any one time may be minds so consistently stimulated to Philosophic and Ironic thinking that these kinds of understanding predominate regardless of the task to be performed, even if such refined thinkers experience significant disadvantages in doing the weekly shopping. Jostling their elbows at the cereal shelves may be others who very rarely receive that kind of stimulation and have not acquired the intellectual tools that make Philosophic or Ironic thinking common or easy.

In describing kinds of understanding, I chose examples from the times in our lives when particular intellectual tools develop most energetically, and then from any historical periods when they were prominently used. My examples are supposed to indicate not that a particular kind of understanding represented "the spirit of an age" but that some people were using it for some clear purposes. So the notion that particular periods in general exemplify particular kinds of understanding is not what I mean.

In the case of children's minds, a parallel set of assumptions informs this theory. All children's minds in modern cultures will likely have experienced some stimulation of all these kinds of understanding early on. Even the Somatic peek-a-boo games a parent plays with a baby may include some irony. Kinds of understanding are products of the mind learning and using particular tools, and I have focused on the typical ages at which the particular tools are most commonly stimulated and developed.

Q: But if these kinds of understanding are potential in all minds and dependent on particular social forces evoking them, why the sequence? Even if you are not committed to particular historical periods, you suggest that the historical sequence of the development of these kinds of understanding is mirrored by the sequence in which students today can acquire them. What constrains the sequence? Why can't we just teach ironic understanding right off, and skip the preliminaries?

A: The sequence is determined by logical and psychological constraints working together. I think the psychological constraints are very hard to get at apart from the cultural forms in which they are realized. The logical constraints are similarly hard to isolate because they are always mixed with psychological factors.

177

Q: I need an example. Take the relationship between Romantic and Philosophic understanding. How do these logical and psychological constraints determine that one must develop significant Romantic understanding before one can develop significant Philosophic understanding?

A: Consider a couple of the examples of each that I used earlier. Is the kind of "Romantic" history written by Herodotus a necessary prerequisite to the kind of "Philosophic" history written by Thucydides?

The psychological constraints may be seen, a little murkily, in our development from a "mythic" and "egocentric" concern with the past as a means of glorifying oneself, one's family, and one's interests to a "Romantic" concern with the great achievements and exotic customs of others as well as of one's own social group, to a "Philosophic" concern with the laws that operate and determine the general process of historical change to which one's own group is subject just like others. The murkiness of this sequence is equaled by that of the constraining force of logic on historical understanding: first we note accumulation of information, establishment of procedures for deciding the relative reliability of various kinds of records, and an attempt to structure the information into some chronological scheme; then we see the "Romantic" coordination of diverse and engaging bodies of information into complex and coherent narratives; then the "Philosophic" search for regularities, theories, and laws derived from the various available narrative accounts.

Neither psychological nor logical constraints can be shown to compel us to learn history in such a way that significant Romantic understanding must precede significant Philosophic understanding, or to show compellingly why Herodotean history writing had to precede Thucydidean. But putting the two together, which is how they act after all, makes the sequence more plausible, I think. This is not a matter of two unconvincing explanations adding up to a convincing one, but rather two different kinds of constraints on a process working together to determine its sequence. So the sequential unfolding of Somatic, Mythic, Romantic, Philosophic, and Ironic understanding in cultural history and in the process of education is shaped by the joint operation of complex logical and psychological forces, such that significant development of a "later" kind is unlikely to occur unless some degree of preceding kinds have been developed. The same logical and psychological constraints apply to the initial invention and development of intellectual tools and to their acquisition by students today.

But cultural history cannot be ordered into somatic, mythic, romantic, philosophic, and ironic ages, as though everyone around "caught" and used more or less exclusively a particular kind of understanding. Similarly, though there are constraints on the sequence of their acquisition and on the time students take to develop a kind of understanding adequately to allow further kinds to become evoked and stimulated, we cannot talk about students being exclusively in Mythic or Romantic "stages." Rather a particular kind of understanding tends to assume prominence at particular times, and I have tried to indicate roughly the age ranges of the most intensive developments.

My outline suggests that heavy emphasis on a subsequent kind of understanding before prior kinds are adequately developed will be pedagogically ineffective. But the fact that preliminary stimulation of later kinds of understanding can begin very early also means that we would be unwise to eliminate all interactions that involve later kinds of understanding until students are assumed to be "ready" for them. So we will not try to eliminate theory and irony from our linguistic interactions with young children because precisely such interactions begin to evoke these tools for later development. I suspect that students who are exposed to theoretic and ironic discourse while most energetically developing their Mythic understanding will later find access to Philosophic and Ironic understanding easier.

Q: I don't have a clear image of how these layers or stages or kinds of understanding are supposed to work. You keep saying they are "somewhat distinctive." The first part of my question is, how distinctive is "somewhat"? The second part is how is that distinctiveness supposed to fit with your claim that they, " to some degree," coalesce? To what degree?

A: A problem for understanding intellectual development is that we have no adequate metaphors for it. You will perhaps recall Jonathan Miller's (1978) claim that it became possible to understand the function of the heart and the circulation of the blood only after the invention of pumps to clear mines of water. Everyone since the beginning of our species has felt that regular thump in the chest and has seen blood spurt when arteries are cut. Thinking of the heart as a pump enabled us to understand its function. But we have no similarly useful metaphor to help us understand intellectual or cultural or educational development. The nearest processes are biological, and certainly these have been exploited during this century to try to get some clearer image of what goes on in the intellect as we learn and experience new things. Piaget's is perhaps the best known elaboration of a biology-based metaphor of development, and John Dewey elaborated a conception of education drawing on "growth."

I have tried to adhere to a nonbiological and rather vague use of "development." These kinds of understanding are only "somewhat" distinctive in that they are not wholly different forms of thought, mutually incomprehensible; they are not so much like different computer programs as like modules of a well-integrated program, focusing on different tasks but each able to comprehend the others. Well, that's not a great metaphor either; tempting though computer metaphors are for mental operations, they always seem to confuse as much as they clarify. So I can't be very clear about how distinctive "somewhat" means. I can only refer you back to the characterizations of the kinds of understanding and say that the differences described there are what I mean by "somewhat."

The "distinctive" part of my too-frequently used phrase "somewhat distinctive" constrains the degree of coherence we manage to achieve by combining the various kinds of understanding, whether they are derived from evolutionary adaptations or from invention and learning. The notion of a holistic cognition seems to me an illusion supported by the plasticity of our mental operations. That is, I think kinds of understanding do retain some degree of autonomy, and so our thinking in general is more incoherent than we allow ourselves to recognize. Some tasks differentially evoke and stimulate different kinds of understanding, and we can and do move from one to another in response to particular challenges. Sometimes two different kinds of understanding will yield perspectives that create conflicts about how we should perform a task or how we should behave in particular situations. The earlier example of taking a Romantic or Philosophic stance with regard to a forest rather crudely illustrates an aspect of what I mean. We have, you might say, a fivefold mind, or, more dramatically, we are a five-minded animal, in whom the different kinds of understanding jostle together and fold in on one another, to some degree coalescing, to some degree remaining "somewhat distinct."

I talked earlier of mixed forms, using the example of the Romantic Marxist, whose thinking mixes a Philosophic general scheme with Romantic "heroizing" of Marx or Lenin. Perhaps an appropriate image for this limited coalescence is partially scrambled eggs, in which one can "somewhat" distinguish the yoke from the albumen, but in some areas they are indistinguishably mixed, and one certainly cannot unscramble them. But coalescence is a concept metaphorically derived from the behavior of gases and liquids, and perhaps we might better draw images from that source.

Q: Are all your answers going to be this long?

A: No.

Q: Your presentation seems removed from the daily life of the school I work in. Your notion of clarifying a conception of education that would give schools a defensible position against the good-willed but rampantly inconsistent demands of the various "stakeholders" just seems to me . . . well, irrelevant. Who pays the piper, calls the tune; academics' voices are offstage squeaks and bleats when it comes to calling the tune schools must dance to. Schools are used as societal mop-up institutions—keeping youths off the streets in times of high unemployment, providing day care and basic economic training for children of working parents, reproducing social class distinctions, and so on. Educational ideas don't cut much of a swath through the urgent economic pressures that drive the demands that parents, businesses, and politicians make on schools. These contingent realities are the brutal forces that eat general theories for breakfast. You asked for comments as well as questions.

A: Yes, yes. My meek academic soul trembles before your stark vision of reality, and I fear you may be right. It may be that the prospect for education holds neither joy, nor love, nor light, nor certitude, nor peace, nor help for pain; education may continue always to be a darkling plain where ignorant armies clash by night. But I suppose one has to hope there will be voices who demand of education that it should help people to understand something of whence our lives come and whither they go. Well, perhaps Matthew Arnold is not the most popular ally to echo at present, but I wonder whether your attentiveness to one kind of power doesn't lead you to underestimate another. I suppose consciousness of your cynical realism and its occasionally overwhelming plausibility persuaded me early on to enlist Keynes's observation about the power of ideas. People behave in response to what they think is the case.

Q: You have built this theory largely on developments in language use. But we are now in an electronic age when visual media and oral discourse are the sources of so much of what students know about the world and experience. Doesn't this new electronic world, in which one has access to information via iconic rather than alphabetic symbols, make your ideas hopelessly old-fashioned, tied into a visibly dying high-literate culture? The new media are breeding a new kind of consciousness, and perhaps a new understanding outside your scheme.

A: Writing systems store information, ideas, and experience in coded forms outside the body in such a way that they can transform how one understands the world. What the new electronic media, and computers in particular, can do, and promise to do more of, is give easier and faster access to greater stores of coded information, ideas, and experience. Computers do not access these coded sources in such a way as to eliminate the need for traditional reading and writing skills, especially as, in the short term anyway, the information, ideas, and experience are mostly coded in alphabetic text.

The computer on my desk will read to me, in any of a range of machine voices, any text I convert into the program that it can recognize and transfer into sound. The advantages of visual access to text won't be signifi-   181 cantly undone by the conversion of text back into oral forms. Certainly some tasks might be managed better and faster orally, but the advantages of visual access to text for any contemplative task still seem abundant. The history of cultural developments so far has involved accumulating cognitive tools, not discarding them. The later kinds of understanding are not alternatives to the earlier; they incorporate the earlier in significant degree. What makes new visual technologies most potent is carrying into them what has been gained in older technologies. Literacy was a sterile tool for keeping records until the oral achievements of Homer and his kin were added to it. The cyberworld of the cyberjockeys will remain similarly utilitarian and sterile until we bring along into it what we have gained through literacy and begin to expand its possibilities. The fullest use of new tools comes to those who have most fully developed the earlier ones. I can't see any reason why we should expect this principle to be changed by electronic media—but who knows? I should not be so glib, but in my limited experience, students who spend huge amounts of time with interactive computing and TV and little time reading seem to be on not a cutting edge so much as a zonked-out edge. The excited leaders of the expedition into cyberspace are not going far if they leave the food behind. But, again, who knows?

Q: You talk about "children" as though there is some generic child that is the same everywhere in all societies. I don't think this is so. I work with aboriginal children in Australia, and their stories are not at all like "Peter Rabbit," or the other middle-class English stories you have built your Mythic stage on. Those are leisured, self-indulgent productions, stimulating an idle, effete "imagination." You talk also about that self-indulgent "imagination" as though it, too, is something generic rather than the class-based, limited thing that it is. The stories my children learn are pragmatic introductions to important realities of their environments. Their imaginative activity is similarly tough and pragmatic as well as vivid and powerful. What you have to say about Mythic understanding might have some relevance to the leisured middle classes of wealthy Western countries, but it is irrelevant to aboriginal children and, I would expect, to immigrant children and also to working-class children in the West. The important social construction of narrative in oral societies has led to their members saying of Western schooling that "they teach you to read and make you stupid."

A: I do not refer to a generic child but to generic cognitive tools, like oral language. Languages are indeed different from one another. Perhaps some are so distinctive that the kinds of understanding they stimulate vary with regard to the very general implications I have drawn—images, stories, binary opposites, and so on. So much I'll concede to the Whorfian hypothesis (Whorf, 1956), though I am clearly more impressed by the similarities among all languages as argued by Pinker (1994). But I would be surprised if all the implications drawn in chapter 2, say, were not equally evident in the children you work with as in the most pampered middle-class English child. Indeed, I'd be very surprised because the categories of Mythic understanding were arrived at mainly from studies of children in cultures other than in the West; the challenge was to find western exemplars. And I don't see why middle-class western children should be so disparaged. It is easy to underestimate how stories like "Peter Rabbit" help children deal with the pragmatic realities of life and death, nature and culture, human and animal.

Growing up is rarely without its horrors, whether in the Australian outback or in north Oxford, in Winnipeg, Wigan, Wabash, or Wollongong.

Also I think this description of Mythic understanding and the transition to the kind of literacy that supports Romantic understanding can be of use to teachers of aboriginal, immigrant, and working-class children because it points up the positive intellectual tools with which these children commonly come to school. Too often, literacy is taught without much regard for the richness of children's oral-culture background. With this in mind, the educational task becomes a matter not of ignoring or even suppressing those oral tools but of stimulating and developing them in the first place, and then of introducing literacy and its associated intellectual tools in coordination with the oral. The fact that middle-class children, coming from homes heavy with "literacy-based discourse," learn to read more easily can deceive teachers about what is being lost in their gain. I hope my observations about Mythic understanding help improve the education of middle-class children who suffer inadequate development of "oral" intellectual tools as well as immigrant, aboriginal, and working-class children, whose oral intellectual tools are often suppressed in favor of a narrow literacy (and who are thereby rendered "stupid").

Q: Jerome Bruner talks of two distinct kinds of thinking, which he calls narrative and paradigmatic. These reflect, as I understand it, what might be called story-like and theory-like thinking. There are many such distinctions that recognize an important difference between everyday thinking in which we make sense of the events that impinge on us and the disciplined, objective thinking of science. Merlin Donald's account has a mythic stage, which yields to a theoretic stage resembling your Philosophic understanding. How does your Romantic form fit between these two more readily recognized forms of thinking? Could your Romantic kind be just a transition rather than a distinctive kind of understanding itself?

A: How one slices up the developmental continuum is in part a strategic   183 matter, determined by your particular interest. My sense is that mythic and theoretical thinking are sufficiently distinctive to merit the separate treatment I have given them. And, of course, I am not the first to recognize a somewhat distinctive kind of thinking in the process of educational development appropriately called Romantic. Elsewhere I have discussed the similarities and differences between this sense of Romantic understanding and A. N. Whitehead's category of "romance" in education (Egan, 1990, ch. 8), and acknowledged a debt to Northrop Frye's discussion of the "romantic" among his other *mythoi* (Egan, 1979, p. 169).

Perhaps my focus on education has brought out the distinctiveness of Romantic understanding, and that then points up examples of such thinking in cultural history. I suspect this greater attention to "Romantic" intellectual tools may be welcomed by those who are only too aware of how many students seem to lose their way in schooling during the intermediate years. Piaget's theory, for example, deals only with logico-mathematical tools and has no equivalent between concrete and formal operations. Little is offered to help the teacher recognize the affective characteristics, the fascination with extremes and the exotic, the formation of "romantic associations," and so on, that are central to Romantic understanding.

Equally important, those characteristics of Romantic understanding become a part of Philosophic understanding. That is, the usual characterizations of paradigmatic or theoretic thinking represent it as somewhat desiccated and sterile, lacking the richness that is contributed by the Somatic, Mythic, and Romantic characteristics from which it emerges. I think the Romantic element in this continuum should make my scheme attractive to those who are uncomfortable with the attenuated conception of abstract theoretic thinking commonly offered as a paradigm of the most sophisticated kind of human thought.

Q: I'm still concerned about these binary opposites you began with. I see them as perpetuating all kinds of stereotypes that we are struggling to overcome. I thought it exposed something about your scheme that you began the next chapter casually mentioning telling the story of Cinderella to five-year-olds. Stories like "Cinderella" perpetuate stereotypes of the good, passive, housekeeping girl who needs the dashing active prince to make her life worthwhile. Cinderella is a part of a stereotype of female passivity encouraged by a whole history of white male oppression in Western culture, and you begin with something that supports and perpetuates it.

A: No doubt stories like Cinderella, and Peter Rabbit, embody stereotypes
184 that can be and have been harmful. But the principle underlying the use of

binary opposites in this theory supports your view of the dangers of stereo-typing. The problem with stories or informal discourse or social practices that set in place destructive stereotypes is that they are implicit, unex-amined; they are represented not as cultural contingencies but as facts of nature, the way things are. The most basic principle of this theory is that educational development moves forward by bringing to consciousness what had earlier been operations of the mind. Particularly this is the case with forms of language use. The point about binary sets is not that one teaches them, but they are already in place because of the way our language works at a fundamental level. What I recommend is two related things: first, mediating between the opposites, and thereby elaborating them, and second, making them explicit. That is, instead of such oppositions sliding into the child's mind under the story or the story-form lesson, they become explicit and objects of thought and inquiry.

For this reason I don't think we make educational progress by banning "Cinderella" because it is built on inappropriate stereotypes. And banal re-writings to reflect current sentiments simply undermine the point of telling the story at all. "Cinderella" is more than a collection of crude stereotypes. The educational and aesthetic values of the story can be preserved first by telling it and then by explicitly considering the stereotypes on which it is based. This does not mean that the story needs to be followed by an aca-demic discussion, but that in talking about stories such issues can be casually raised. One mediates the oppositions by critical discussion of them and one furthers the process of bringing operations of thought into consciousness and so under conceptual control (Hoogland, 1994).

"Stereotype" has degenerated into the name we give to concepts we don't like, but stereotypes are actually necessary for thinking. Indeed, all concepts are simplifications we make for particular purposes, to fit into and build particular views of the world. So we can't get rid of stereotypes. At particular times for particular groups, some stereotypes will seem either useful or socially destructive ("female passivity," "white male oppression"); the educational solution, it seems to me, is not to get rid of all expressions of those stereotypes from our culture and its historical records, but rather to bring them explicitly into consciousness for critical examination. One might well conclude, of course, that new and different stories might be in-troduced to displace the old canon, but the displacement, I am arguing, following Hoogland, should involve aesthetic and psychotherapeutic crite-ria as well as social and ideological ones (recognizing the problems of distinguishing these).

Q: I am surprised that you have written so much about education without   185 any mention of morality. It is as though you see education as a purely intellectual process with "intellectual tools" much in evidence but no moral sensitivity encouraged.

A: I cannot easily distinguish the kinds of understanding I have been dealing with from morality; that is, morality and education seem not to be discrete categories. One of the things Plato is said to be plainly wrong about is his belief that virtue and knowledge are tied up together—that the pursuit of truth is properly a moral enterprise. Plato is supposed to have made a simple category mistake, which later philosophers have pointed out, but I have a sneaking sympathy for Plato's view. He sees selfishness and egotism and various other moral inadequacies breeding illusions and confusions whose result is the impossibility of attaining *episteme*. While the love of truth is perhaps, as A. E. Housman put it, the faintest of human passions, one can see the kind of connection I mean in Iris Murdoch's observation that "'Truth' is not just a collection of facts. *Truthfulness,* the search for truth, for a closer connection between thought and reality, demands and affects an exercise of virtues and a purification of desires. . . . Thought, goodness and reality are thus seen to be connected" (1992, p. 8). Well, that connection may not be quite so easily seen, especially by an ironist, but its potential suggests why I think this book is about moral education as much as intellectual education.

Q: Any scheme that requires children today to recapitulate their cultural history must be essentially conservative, even reactionary. Basil Bernstein and Michael Apple have written at length about how a society selects, classifies, distributes, transmits, and evaluates the knowledge it puts into the school curriculum and how this process reflects the distribution of power in society. Yours is clearly a very elitist scheme, with your Ironists at the top determining the curriculum that will ensure their reproduction. I realize you claim that what is to be recapitulated are intellectual tools, but these tools are to be stimulated and developed by specific content. Your constant references to the ancient Greeks, and the high-culture story of Western "development" you have laid out, make it clear that we are in for a content-heavy, neoconservative program. Why not say so?

A: It is true that development of these kinds of understanding will require learning a lot. The assumption that those who require students to learn a lot are conservative or traditional grows out of the progressivist/traditionalist dichotomy that this scheme is designed to mediate, or transcend. You might equally well have observed that people like Vygotsky, Bakhtin, Kristeva, and Habermas have emphasized the role of the community and the culture in the formation of individuals' understanding, and so this scheme should be associated with their more radical positions. I think this

186

scheme doesn't fit well with the old, stale ideological conflicts that center on the school, but no doubt that blithe claim may be questioned.

You recognize that this scheme describes the intellectual tools as being recapitulated, not the particular knowledge of the culture associated with their initial development.

Q: You identify as one of the dysfunctional features of the currently dominant conception of education the conflict within it of the Platonic program and socializing. But we usually talk about this as a necessary tension between our educational ideals and everyday social utility. How do you imagine this tension can be eliminated by your scheme? Surely there will always be a tension between our everyday social needs and our academic ideals? I mean, the content of the curriculum will always be in significant part determined by particular social needs, and these will have to reach an accommodation with subjects like Latin that may have educational value but no social utility. Today we consider it more important that all kids become familiar with computers than that they all learn Latin.

A: You are raising a number of complicated issues. My point was that considering socialization and Plato's academic program as both necessary components of education creates that particular tension—one can't do both adequately without their coming into conflict and undermining each other. In my scheme, what we have is a conception of education in which we have the clearer task of stimulating and developing the different kinds of understanding. That is, socialization is no longer a part of education; Plato's academic program is no longer a part of education; Rousseau's developmentalism is no longer a part of education.

> *Lector:* Now hang on a minute! I recall your saying that these were all necessary elements and that you were going to show how we could preserve the best bits while shucking off the mutually incompatible and dysfunctional bits.
>
> *Auctor:* That's right. I am suggesting that educationalists do not have to wonder how best to socialize children, or decide what knowledge is of most worth so they can build their curricula from the best that has been thought and uttered in the world, or work out how to make our teaching cohere with and support some proper, natural developmental process. The educationalists now have to work out only how to further the development of these kinds of understanding. In doing this we will incidentally be achieving what is salvageable of the old ideas.
>
> *Lector:* No, no. You don't seem to understand the question. Societies will still want to shape children to their needs, values, prejudices, and stereotypes, and these agendas will sometimes conflict with your ideal

development of some particular kind of understanding. The question is, how is your scheme supposed to be able to overcome this tension?
Auctor: It isn't. What it does is remove this as a tension within education or for educational institutions. We are no longer in doubt how far we should socialize, how far to pursue an academic program, how far to attend to individual development, and how much time to allot to each. Societies socialize; schools stimulate and develop kinds of understanding.
Lector: No, no, no. Look, if the school's development of understanding conflicts with some important social value, or with some social prejudice, if you will, then the conflict remains between society and schools dedicated to your conception of education.
Auctor: Yes. This scheme will not solve all society's problems, but it can, I think, solve some of education's. What it offers to the school is a greater clarity of purpose and a more manageable task. Compare schools, for example, with hospitals; hospitals have a much less contentious conception of "health" than we currently have of "education." Of course, potential conflicts will remain between society at large and schools whose purpose is realizing this conception of education. It's just that if schools do adopt this conception of education, they will know where they stand, and what they stand for, in such conflicts. They stand for greater understanding. If societies don't want that, then they won't fund schools that adhere to this conception of education.
Lector: But *that's* the point! Most societies, in the form of their politicians at least, are not much interested in Plato's or Rousseau's ideas; they want to produce kids who can read, write, do mathematics—students who will be able to do a productive job and not cause trouble.
Auctor: Yes, and students who are educated according to this scheme will very likely be able to read, write, do mathematics, and work better than the "products" of our current systems of schooling. "Not causing trouble" can mean being a conformist drone or not being a psychotic, disaffected aggressor. A system dedicated to developing the kinds of understanding we have been dealing with would not produce many conformist drones, and its output of psychotic, disaffected aggressors would likely be low. That is, the things Western multicultural societies are willing to pay for—their basics, their bottom line—are pretty easily achieved if we are not constantly embattled over our very aims for the institutions engaged in the task.

Also, of course, "society" is not exclusively concerned with the crudely utilitarian in education. We hear so much about "basics" because even the most utilitarian skills and knowledge are achieved at lower levels than seems reasonable given the time and money expended. If we can achieve these basics routinely, "society" will welcome the more refined kinds of understanding this scheme proposes.

The tension between socialization and education will no doubt survive the imminent galactic implementation of this conception of education, but it will not survive as a tension within education, confusing its aims and so its practice at every level. The point of a more coherent theory is better practice.

Q: You argued that Plato and traditional liberal educators see the dynamic of the educational process primarily in accumulating particular forms of knowledge, and that Rousseau and progressivists see it primarily in some internal developmental process. You did say that no one holds exclusively to one position or another, but you also suggested that both of them are wrong because they identify the dynamic in what you call constraints on the process. So what about your scheme? What is the dynamic here? And what happens to accumulating knowledge and psychological development?

A: I'm glad you asked me that; I wrote a chapter about it but then junked it as too much to the side of the central theme of the book. (It is available on my home page, under the title "Omitted Chapter," should anyone be interested.) Put simply, in this scheme the central dynamic is imagination—that generative feature of the mind involved both in the invention of intellectual tools in cultural history and in their acquisition in education. What the imagination can grasp is enabled and constrained by the logic inherent in the various forms of knowledge and by the psychologic inherent in the process of human development. So the dynamic of this scheme is a troika of a generative imagination guided and constrained by epistemological and psychological forces.

Lector: That took a chapter?
Auctor: Well, it wasn't a *very* long chapter.

Q: You have avoided being clear about whether you think these are stages that represent progress. Is Ironic understanding better than Mythic? You seem cautious not to commit yourself, constantly pulling back from where your argument is leading.

Auctor: Which is?
Lector: That this *is* another of those developmental schemes that covertly assert the superiority of white male Western thinking, that

189

asserts that Mythic thinkers are inferior to Ironic thinkers, that cultures in which Ironic thinking is emphasized are superior to Mythic cultures. This is just another cultural imperialist scheme in which you've tried to make reassuring, patronizing noises about how "orality" has positive features and how one loses some things when one becomes literate. But you obviously think literacy and its sophistication are better than orality. Irony is the aim of your educational process.

Auctor: But I think Mythic understanding is better if you live in a mythic culture and Ironic is better if you live in a modern high-literate culture. I don't think there is any point trying to educate someone who lives in an oral culture to consistent high-literate Ironic understanding.

Lector: That's simply avoiding the issue. In your scheme Romantic understanding is made up of Somatic understanding plus Mythic understanding plus the additional characteristics of Romantic understanding, and Ironic understanding is made up of all the other kinds plus the Ironic. That is, each kind is higher, fuller, more sophisticated, better than those preceding it. The Ironic mind is therefore simply better than the Mythic mind according to this scheme. It's what we call a hierarchical integrative model, in which later stages include the earlier and add something new. So, no more fudging. When you say "development" don't you mean "progress"?

Auctor: Well, perhaps you'll understand my reluctance to give any simple answer here. You may recognize how your question fits into a curious modern inquisition, such that acknowledging that one sees "progress" in such a scheme ties one into a vast trail of associated guilts; immediately one is convicted of privileging Western ways of knowing and so one is held guilty of endless atrocities performed throughout history and around the world by Westerners who justified their actions because of their superior minds. An ideologically nimble inquisitor denies that there can be any qualitative differences among minds and so associates with and appropriates the voices of victims of injustice around the world, and so feels huge moral self-righteousness in convicting one of . . .

Lector: What *are* you muttering about?

Auctor: Oh, sorry. Just preparing to deal with a sticky question.

Lector: About time!

Auctor: OK. There are two general approaches to the nature of the relationships among the somewhat distinctive kinds of thinking identified in schemes like this. We can see them as simply hierarchical, in which the later forms are superior to those that precede them; if they weren't superior, after all, why would we want to try to develop them? Alternatively, we can see them as somewhat distinctive ways of thinking, none of which is inherently superior to any other; they are just heterogeneous, but equally valuable and useful for somewhat different purposes in somewhat heterogeneous social and environmental conditions. In this alternative view, the later kinds do not provide any better access to truth or reality, but are simply fitted, in a Darwinian sense, for different environments; their value turns on their fitness for their sociocultural niche. Systematic development of Philosophic understanding in a traditional oral culture would ensure that the culture wouldn't remain oral for long, and so we might conclude that Philosophic understanding is maladapted for that sociocultural niche.

Whether we conclude that the hierarchical-progressive conception is more correct, or better, than the heterogeneity conception turns on, among other things, whether we think there is something inherent in the human mind that inclines it toward some particular direction for greater fulfillment. That is, Ironic understanding is not simply a continuation of aimless evolution, no "better" than anything that preceded it and just better fitted to certain wholly contingent sociocultural conditions. Rather, Ironic understanding provides a fuller realization of the mind's potential than preceding kinds of understanding. Evolution might aimlessly have produced human minds, but human minds can now consciously control their own development; they are no longer subject to the adaptive controls that govern fitness for niches. The development of language has taken over from evolution in the driver's seat of change in human minds. Rather than adapting to our environment, we change it to suit our mind's wishes and desires. In that sense, we have broken free of evolutionary pressures. So the question is whether Ironic understanding allows a richer, more abundant human experience.

It is now commonplace to condemn earlier hierarchical classifications of kinds of thinking and minds as racist, sexist, and, more recently, ageist. That is, the "primitive" thinking of aboriginal peoples in parts of the world colonized by Europeans was considered confused, simplistic, and emotional and was associated with the thinking of women and children. In place of that earlier dogma, and in significant part as a result of shrinking with horror from what it was used to justify, has come the modern dogma that diverse kinds of thinking simply relate to diverse kinds of tasks in diverse sociocultural environments—and that none is better than any other and none is worse than any other. This is a comfortable position to hold as it releases one from any association with racist, sexist, and ageist views.

191

But it is not clear that either dogma helps us sort out how to make sense of the differences in kinds of thinking we have been considering; the former is indeed racist, the latter is irresponsible.

Lector: But the Ironic is made up of the other kinds of understanding plus some additional things, so this scheme must surely favor the hierarchical rather than the heterogeneity view?

Auctor: There are two things that prevent me from simply saying "yes." First, there are those losses. As one kind of understanding is partially coalesced with a subsequent kind, it seems that something of the former is lost. I used Wordsworth's very vivid description of the losses that commonly come as we move from what I call Mythic to Romantic understanding. One part of what fades involves a vividness of participation in the natural world and an enriching imaginative power to embody that world in our emotional experience; this power seems unable to survive in subsequent kinds of understanding as it can exist for children and in traditional oral cultures. In an ideal education, we would seek to preserve as much of this as possible in Ironic understanding, but what we would preserve seems at best only an ever-fading vision of what was once so bright. This scheme, then, is not hierarchical-integrative in the sense that Piaget's is. Rather, this scheme strives to be hierarchical-integrative, but cannot integrate all of the characteristics of its previous kinds of understanding. These losses are not trivial, and, as I suggested earlier, it seems to me quite easy to lose more in the way of alienation, desiccation, and pedantic rigidity than one gains in the way of aesthetic delight and insight. One can, in W. H. Auden's words, fairly easily become "horribly mad" or "benignly potty."

Another reason why this scheme can't simply be fitted into the hierarchical-progressive slot is the limited coalescence that takes place as new kinds of understanding develop. Limited coalescence results in increasing fragmentation as kinds of understanding accumulate. "Fragmentation" is perhaps too dramatic a term, but each kind of understanding deploys somewhat different principles of sense-making, and even when we develop significant Ironic understanding, other principles remain constantly in play. Our thinking, I mean, is more heterogeneous than we seem willing to recognize. The richness and abundance that Ironic understanding offers comes at a price, like many complex systems, of vulnerability to instability and fragmentation.

Is the Ironic mind better than the Mythic? There is perhaps no sensible general answer. Given the changing world we have in the West, and increasingly everywhere else, the most sophisticated intellectual tools for understanding the world seem, despite their losses and vulnerabilities, Ironic. This scheme is not one of constant "progress" to Irony, which is why I want to persist in using a rather vague nonbiological sense of "development."

Q: I don't think the stages you have sketched exhaust the kinds of understanding. You should add a sixth stage, based on spiritual understanding, beyond Irony.

A: No, no. *You* should add a sixth. I've done my bit. Perhaps I'd be prudent not to add that most of the candidates I have seen for a further "spiritual" kind of understanding seem to me straightforwardly Romantic. Though, I *should* add, there are other forms of spiritual experience, evident in Buddhist and Christian meditation traditions, in which one aim is the suppression of the ego self. The spiritual aims of these traditions connect, it seems to me, with my discussion of Ironic understanding's ability to see the coffee cup as a ceramic object stripped of its association with our conventional purposes. Various spiritual traditions teach us to see the world stripped of our stories, metanarratives, and philosophic schemes and released from the perspective contructed by the ego self (Bai, 1996). I do not consider this kind of spiritual experience a distinctive kind of understanding; rather, I see it as a fruit of Ironic understanding when a richly developed Somatic understanding is preserved within it.

Q: I'm at a loss to express my embarrassment, but I was registered for the dental technician's conference also scheduled in this hotel, and I seem to have confused the room. I've a twisted ankle, too, and anyway didn't like to get up and leave once you'd begun, especially as it would have meant waking those between me and the aisle. But I did catch various things you said, between reading the papers from the bicuspid panel. I recall some Greek who said that if horses had gods, they would look like horses. A bit of a leap, perhaps, but I thought the model of the ideal educated person you present looks just like a liberal academic, someone like yourself, perhaps. You don't think this is just a defensive way of asserting that you and people like you are the best kind of human being? I mean, I wonder about me and my colleagues who aren't academics, and don't have these communities for developing Philosophic and Ironic understanding, and about those people in oral cultures you keep going on about. Are we inferior to you people, then?

A: This theory isn't about superiority and inferiority as people; it's about intellectual tools that affect the ways minds make sense of the world and experience. Also I don't see why dental technicians should be cut off from the communities that support Philosophic and Ironic thinking. These com-   193 munities exist today in the books and journals we read and in media with which we interact. My experience of academic discourse suggests that Irony is not much a part of those routine exchanges any more than it probably is at conferences of dental technicians.

But having made all the appropriate apologetic noises, I am forced to say that it would be a bit odd if the institutions we have set up and maintain at great expense in order to educate didn't provide more hospitable environments for education than institutions with more limited and utilitarian purposes.

Q: You suggested that the educated person in your scheme is the one who preserves most of the various kinds of understanding as she or he goes along. But as you point out, each of the pre-Ironic kinds of understanding has problems. Why should we want to preserve Mythic binary thinking, which is at the root of simplistic categorizing and has contributed to racism and sexism, and why preserve Romantic hero worship, and Philosophic crazy ideologies? Why should we try to recapitulate these?

A: The fact that a hammer can be used to break vases does not immediately suggest that we should ban hammers as vase-smashing instruments; they do other things, too. The fact that binary thinking has been complicit in racist and sexist thinking does not mean that this is its only and inevitable use. Romantic heroizing may have been used to glorify aggressive males' being destructive, but it can equally glorify the patient, the compassionate, the loving, the quietly courageous. In an educational program we will want to emphasize each tool's best use.

The preservation of characteristics is, it seems to me, crucial to education. The imaginative energy of childhood, the romantic engagements of early adolescence, the search for regularity and generalizations of later adolescence, are all qualities that enrich the Irony of educated adulthood. This preservation of characteristics proper to earlier periods of life has been noted before, of course. G. Stanley Hall observes: "Gifted people seem to conserve their youth and to be all the more children, and perhaps especially all the more intensely adolescents, because of their gifts, and it is certainly one of the marks of genius that the plasticity and spontaneity of adolescence persists into maturity" (1904, I, p. 547). G. K. Chesterton, expressing his great admiration for George Wyndham, described Wyndham's most remarkable and admirable quality as being that his "life had left in him so much of himself; so much of his youth; so much even of his childhood" (1937, p. 122). When we suppress Mythic and Romantic characteristics as "childish things"—a suppression that seems to have been endemic to traditional academic schooling in the West—the too common result, as described by Hall, is that "we are prematurely old and senile of heart. . . . What we have left is second-hand, bookish, shopworn, and the heart is parched and bankrupt" (II, p. 59). Rhetorically a tad over the top perhaps, but expressing the educational disaster of assuming we can somehow make young children "rational" before furthering the development of the intellectual characteristics out of which and along with which a rich rationality properly emerges.

Q: You have been critical of Piaget's theory, or at least of how it has been applied in education. How is this theory different from his?

A: Piaget claims to have described an underlying process of psychological development that is genetically programmed into us such that, in interaction with appropriate environments, it will spontaneously develop. I am claiming that particular kinds of understanding develop as a result of our learning to deploy particular intellectual tools in societies that support the development of those tools. Piaget's is a scientific theory aiming to expose something about the nature of human beings' development; mine is a critical study aiming to expose how sociocultural contingencies in combination with logical and psychological constraints shape the development of kinds of understanding. As far as education is concerned, Piaget has adopted the Rousseauian belief that the dynamic of the educational process lies in the internal psychological developmental process he describes; the curriculum must conform to that process if it is to be meaningful to the child and support the child's "operative" development. If Piaget was correct and his theory, or the emendations made to it in recent years, did adequately describe an internal psychological development, it would form one of the constraints on the development of kinds of understanding I am describing.

Q: So what are we to make of the ages you give for each of these kinds of understanding? Are they the result of the underlying developmental process or of the way we teach, or what?

A: As I keep saying, psychological development or maturation clearly influences the ages at which these kinds of understanding become most energetic. But so does logic influence the time it takes to acquire the component tools that constitute each kind of understanding. At present we can say that it simply takes a certain amount of time to work through and bring under conscious control the various forms of language use that are basic to this scheme. The ages I indicate are rough estimates based on observations of how long it typically takes students to develop and become fluent in the relevant uses of language. Current studies of psychological development provide no greater precision that I can see than these estimates. The problem for trying to be more precise is manifold: variety in the extent and kind of stimulation of the relevant intellectual tools individual students achieve; the adequacy of development of prior kinds of understanding to support   195 subsequent kinds; the adequacy of community support and sensitive teaching that individual students receive; and the usual range of individual differences among students.

Q: OK. I've sat through enough of this earnest, self-satisfied crap. Just look at the rhetoric if you want to see what this theory's really about. The pseudo-wit and effete irony and all this frigging lector/auctor shit. You're up to the elbows in it, in this Greek and Latin and the Western frigging intellectual tradition. What turns your crank are those twittering bits, like a copy of Quintillian's whatever it was found in a tower in St. Gall whenever it was. Jeez! That sums it up. Romantic nostalgia over the rotting corpse of the Western imperial knowledge-industry. You're just one of the deodorizers, sprinkling "kulture" on the corpse machine, which is in the basic business of exploiting, disempowering, and devoicing anyone who gets in the way of its drive for total power. You try to skip around Nietzsche, but you don't even understand what you quoted. He was talking about people like you "trying to be superior," trying to get it right, capturing "the truth"! Ha! As if! Earnestly trying to be clear, not able to recognize that clarity in this arid rationality tradition is just a part of the business of fascist oppression. You are an unwitting agent of a nasty cabal in a power struggle. Academia is complicit in the system of imperialist oppression, providing the tools and manufacturing the "morality" that enslaves the poor, the illiterate, the world's laboring masses, and academia allows the enslavers to feel good about it. They're spreading "Western enlightenment," after all, to those they enslave! It's by rejecting this whole frigging discourse, as Nietzsche said, that we can become free of its oppression.

A: Ah yes, Nietzsche and freedom. He says, "freedom means that the manly instinct which delights in war and victory dominates over other instincts, for example, those of 'pleasure.' The human being who has become *free*—and how much more the *spirit* that has become free—spits on the contemptible type of well-being dreamed of by shopkeepers, Christians, cows, females, Englishmen and other democrats. The free man is a warrior." That's the freedom Nietzsche promotes in *Twilight of the Idols* (1888). You overthrow the king—but first you get the Terror and then you get the emperor. Perhaps Edmund Burke's perspective is unlikely to impress you.

I can't deny you have an argument that is hard to evade, but it is one that rebounds on you, of course. In the end, I think my frigging discourse will do less hurt and harm than yours.

Q: I don't think you are off the hook with that response. You might try to dismiss my colleague's—if I may?—objection by pointing to the Darth Vader side of Nietzsche, but no part of your answer addresses the concern that has arisen in various ways already. Your notion of development is the

2

old Western-privileging conception of "progress." Irony is trumps, and the other stages are just more or less cute; Philosophic types are stuck in their general schemes, Romantics have succumbed to some dream of transcendence, Mythics don't realize their binary stories aren't reality, and the Somatic types are, what, chasing butterflies? This is the old story, valorizing the white male and his position at the peak of evolution with his terrific rationality, protected by his irony. You can't go on about those Greeks so much and not give the show away—what about the rest of the world? And a token paragraph about feminist uses of irony only makes it all the more blatant.

A: I've tried to show why this scheme seems not to fit the category that you have sketched again. You ignore my point about the characteristics of each kind of understanding being preserved in the later ones. If the "Somatic types" are chasing butterflies, then so will the Ironist. The male-privileging seems also unfair, a hangover by association from other developmental theories. Valorizing rationality makes this no more male oriented than female oriented. The sense of Philosophic rationality I recommend incorporates Somatic, Mythic, and Romantic characteristics that have commonly been suppressed in the more harsh and calculative kind of rationality promoted particularly by positivists. My sense seems to cohere with what Kristeva calls for when she discusses how women may appropriate "the logical, mastering, scientific, theoretical apparatus" in becoming scientists, but that they run the danger of suppressing thereby "the expression of the particularity belonging to the individual as a woman. On the basis of this fact, it seems to [her] that one must try not to deny these two aspects of linguistic communication, a mastering aspect and the aspect which is more of the body and of the impulses, but try, in every situation and for every woman, to find a proper articulation of these two elements" (1984, p. 123). But I would want to make the same point for men, too, and I have tried to show in some detail how this articulation (of more than two elements) can occur.

But having responded this way, defensively, I concede that a privileging of the Western intellectual tradition remains; from whose tradition of constant self-criticism, of course, your questions come.

Q: I'm interested in the comments you've made about all these kinds of understanding being somehow implicit in language, and I suppose implicit in the kind of mind that developed language, and so, I suppose, implicit in the end in life itself. That is, these unfurl, first evolutionarily and then somehow they unfurl out of language, so that Irony is somehow implicit in language from the beginning. I'm not getting at the teleological issue you responded to earlier. I was wondering, rather, whether you would agree with Father Ong when he writes in his *Interfaces of the Word* (1977, p. 288) that "Irony is almost as old as speech itself. Perhaps it is in some way even inherent in speech." I mean, as soon as speech allows one to describe something, it equally allows one to describe things that are not, and to say things such that the obvious sense or description or claim is not to be trusted: "Look out, Urg! Here comes a mastodon!" when no mastodon is in sight. We recognize irony in that space where an unreliable narrator is addressing an unknowable reader, playing with the conventions of sincerity. I often think irony is rich in young children but is short-circuited by schooling—don't you?—where literalness in various shapes is impressed on them, often by teachers who assume that's all they can deal with. And your theory involves the claim that the early evocation of Irony is a prerequisite to its later more abundant unfolding, am I not correct? Also, given your theory's looking both ways, I mean at children and at cultural history, I was reminded of Seth Schein's book on *The Mortal Hero: An Introduction to Homer's Iliad,* which I do recommend if you aren't familiar with it. He talks about Homer's style, the mythological context, the heroic themes, and the values of the poem all being traditional, but that the *Iliad* "generates its distinctive meanings as an ironic meditation on those traditional themes and values" (1986, p. 42). I like your observation that irony is not something alien that only appears late, in history and in life. It exists sporadically and sometimes vividly in childhood and in the earliest records of Western intellectual life, so it is far from a stranger when it unfurls in the more widely supported forms we are familiar with today. It is "adumbrated"—I think that's the fashionable term—earlier in life. I am also reminded of Father Ong's general view of how the "reflectiveness of writing"—the fact that it slows language production down by ten times, allows revision, and occurs, most unnaturally, in isolation—well, all this "encourages growth of consciousness out of the unconscious" (1982, p. 150) in a way that sounds like your kinds of understanding adding one layer of self-consciousness of language—or "operations of the mind," as you have called them, drawing on Hayek—one layer on top of another. Though Father Ong doesn't suggest the losses of consciousness dribbling out the other end that your theory emphasizes. In his view—perhaps you are aware?—"In its evolution, consciousness does not slough off its earlier stages but incorporates them in transmuted form in its later stages" (1977, p. 49). Now you don't entirely agree with this—do I infer correctly?—but I have noted in Richard Rorty's discussion of irony . . . well, perhaps this question has gone on rather longer than I intended. You have a response?

198   A: No, no. I wouldn't presume.

Q: You have said nothing much about kids who might find they can't achieve, say, Philosophic understanding, to say nothing of Ironic. This reads like Plato's blithe dismissal of the less able. I know you aren't responsible for the distribution of intellectual ability among the population, but if you are proposing an educational theory, you owe us an account of the fate of those who are less "developmentally able" in terms of your scheme. Are they to be Mythic all their lives, or even, as my colleague put it, just left somatically to chase butterflies?

A: I haven't addressed differences in abilities to develop these kinds of understanding because I'm not sure this theory implies anything particularly useful about the unequal distribution of intelligence(s)—whatever is meant by that word. I would like to make two points. First, current schooling tends to place an undue emphasis on the importance of a particular logico-mathematical facility, and the rewards of our systems go disproportionately to those children who have this particular ability in high degree. The kinds of understanding I am outlining, emphasizing imaginative and affective capacities, will be more hospitable to a significantly wider range of children than are the kinds of intellectual activity most rewarded today. Second, differences in ability to learn will no doubt affect the speed, the degree, and the richness of understanding different children will attain, but none of this implies dismissal of students who are least able to develop Ironic understanding. Because these kinds of understanding are not in some simple sense hierarchical, and because one can continue to develop any kind even as subsequent kinds are being marginally stimulated, this scheme offers some useful guidance for the continuing education of students who may have difficulty developing in significant degree the intellectual tools of Philosophic and Ironic understanding.

Nothing in this scheme can guarantee that everyone will be successfully educated in all kinds of understanding. But it does offer some positive suggestions for how to continue the educational development of the least able students even if they find Philosophic and Ironic understanding largely inaccessible. Also, incidentally, I don't think Plato was blithely dismissive; he simply concluded that the intellectual tasks that constituted his educational scheme were beyond the majority of students. Our current systems of schooling draw much the same conclusion, but usually refuse to acknowledge what in practice they do; thus we have a mealy mouthed rhetoric whose primary purpose is to disguise the crude practice that dismisses most students from any serious educational engagement.

Q: How can one be happy in a condition of sophisticated Irony?

A: As I suggested earlier, I suspect happiness has more to do with hormones than education. The only relevant point that comes to mind is that Ironic understanding seems to allow one to appreciate more jokes—even the cosmic ones.

Q: I've been listening carefully, but I have heard you cite no empirical support for your theory at all. Have you done no research in schools or with children? How on earth do you expect people to take this theory seriously if it is totally without empirical research backing?

A: You are raising issues I can't adequately deal with except at book length (though, by chance, they are issues that I have inadequately dealt with at book length; see Egan, 1983). This theory is unlike those that commonly receive empirical research attention in education. It represents a species of general theory construction that seems to me a necessary part of any vigorous area of study, but a species of which we have seen very few examples in education in recent decades. Assuming that one can run tests that will produce "empirical research backing" for such a theory suggests a confusion. It is not clear what kind of empirical test you might run to determine whether this is a better or worse general conception of education than those it seeks to displace. Perhaps it might help to think of this new theory of education as more like what T. S. Kuhn (1962) calls a paradigm than the small-scale theories common in educational research today. Now, this kind of general theory isn't what Kuhn had in mind, though it might fit one of the twenty-two different senses of "paradigm" one of his critics identified in his book. Paradigms and this kind of general theory do present the empirical researcher with similar problems. The person doing what Kuhn calls "normal" research is working within a paradigm that determines what counts as appropriate questions to ask, what will suffice as appropriate methods of answering questions, what will serve as acceptable answers, and so on. That is, normal research activity will not affect the paradigm because the paradigm represents the set of presuppositions that are the rules determining normal research activity. This general theory is aiming to change the conception of education people hold, and thus affect the set of presuppositions that determines what kind of research is appropriate.

> *Lector:* Just a moment! You are telling us there is no way we can test your theory? Are we supposed to accept it on faith?
> *Auctor:* As I said, that is not as easy to answer as you seem to suggest. The main test you can perform is to accept provisionally this general theory, understand it as clearly as possible, and then look at education "through" it. The test comes from judging whether the field of education makes more sense conceived according to this new theory than according to the old theory. If one tries this test, familiar features of ed-

ucation will appear at unfamiliar angles (like uses of story forms) or in unfamiliar relationships with other features (like generating anomalies for students' ideological beliefs); some prominent features will almost disappear (like the principle of "expanding horizons") and other features that were little noticed before will appear very prominent (like "romance"). To give it a fair test one will have to perform the difficult feat of giving up, if only provisionally, the assumptions and presuppositions that go with one's current conception of education. (This is the feat Keynes thought was rarely achieved by anyone over thirty, but perhaps he was feeling neglected and pessimistic the day he wrote that.)

Lector: So basically you are admitting you have no empirical research backing?

Auctor: Not at all. The book is clogged with the stuff. The theory is composed from the products of empirical research in education and critically analyzed empirical observations from history. The problem is that the question exemplifies an approach to evaluating this theory that seems to me confused and inappropriate. To look at this theory through the presuppositions of the current conception of education it seeks to displace is pointless. It is those criteria, those presuppositions, the currently dominant conception that I am arguing are inadequate to the phenomena of education. You can't run some empirical tests to see which is better because their aims are different, their means are different, the phenomena from which they are built are different. I'm afraid you have to rely on the very hard task of thinking if you want to give this theory a fair test. Call it a "thought experiment."

Q: My question refers to your opening chapter where you talk about the three educational ideas. I was brought up, professionally I mean, in the context of John Dewey's social reconstructionist ideas, in which psychological development, schooling, and social change are all linked. I found your picture of the dominant conception of education to be unlike anything I recognize. The terms you use seem to me fanciful; you seem to have little idea about current educational discourse and its concerns. Your three ideas simply don't fit current discussions about key educational issues. Yours is an eccentric picture, so your "solutions" to the problem of incoherence you identify are simply irrelevant to our real-world concerns.

A: I think my discussion is not irrelevant but may be couched in unfamiliar terms. What the unfamiliar terms do, however, in characterizing the three educational ideas is help to explain why current educational discourse has been so unproductive for a long time, and why it seems so arid   201 to anyone outside it. I think you are right in identifying the dominant form of educational discourse in North America, and also quite generally in the West throughout this century, as a mixture of the psychological developmental, the pragmatics of schooling, and a concern with social change. In my terms, you are describing a conception of education that privileges Rousseau and socialization at the expense of Plato. I recognize that the social improvement dimension of progressivism isn't simply socialization; that's why I gave Rousseau pride of place. Dewey seems to me, despite his comments on the inadequacy of Rousseau's ideas, to be very much a Rousseauian thinker about education. For Dewey the "ultimate problem of education is to coordinate the psychological and the social factors" (1972, p. 228). The dominant educational discourse throughout this century has focused on this task. Its difficulties have been compounded because no equivalent driving principle has coordinated the academic curriculum with the psychological and social factors. This coordination has nevertheless been recognized as a task to be fitted in somehow, even without any adequate principles to guide it.

Q: You have argued that each kind of understanding is susceptible to particular dangers if it isn't developed properly, yet if developed properly it is then susceptible to losses of capacities belonging to prior kinds of understanding. I'm not clear about either of these problems. As far as I can see, inadequate Somatic development leaves one susceptible to difficulties constructing meaning and seeing patterns and rhythms in events; inadequate Mythic development leaves one susceptible to uncritical and simplistic beliefs; inadequate Romantic development leaves one susceptible to sentimentality and cynicism; inadequate Philosophic development leaves one susceptible to know-all, imagine-nothing general schemes; and inadequate Ironic development leaves one susceptible to alienation.

In addition, you observed that the early energetic development of each kind of understanding in cultural history seemed to involve an attack on, or suppression of, the most prominent characteristics of the previously dominant kind. You associated this with the way, in individuals, the energetic development of a new kind of understanding led to losses of characteristics of the previous kind. You didn't mention losses with the development of Somatic understanding, but you have implied that the development of Mythic understanding cut away indeterminable intellectual possibilities. You didn't quote, but you might have made your point clearer if you had, Robert Graves's poem about the "cool web of language" that "winds us in" and is responsible for our "Retreat from too much joy or too much fear" ("The Cool Web"); this web is our first conceptual anesthetizer. The development of Romantic understanding, you suggest, implies losses to our sense of magic, our sense of involvement in the natural world, and creates a barrier between our conceptions and the reality they try to capture and represent. The development of Philosophic understanding implies a loss of vividness and personal association with knowledge. The development of Ironic understanding implies loss of a holistic conception of one's self and of one's universe, some loss of integrating intellectual power.

I'm summarizing the occasional phrases you use. Can you flesh all this out more clearly?

A: I don't think so. I've done my best earlier.

Q: Your scheme seems to me just another of those reductive stage theories you criticized at one point. We have Frazer's magical, religious, and rational stages, which you mentioned, or Compte's theologic, metaphysical, and positive. Hayden White, drawing on Vico, elaborates a scheme of metaphor representing the "age of the gods," metonymy representing an age of heroes, synecdoche representing integrative thinking of parts to whole, and irony representing negation and decadence. Then there's Northrop Frye, on whom you clearly drew at some point, with his mythic, romantic, tragic, and ironic stages. Hegel's phases of history are birth and early growth, maturity, old age, and dissolution or death—like the organic spring, summer, autumn, and winter seasons. Freud's four mechanisms of dreamwork provide more echoes—condensation, displacement, representation, and secondary revision. Then there are Piaget's stages, of course, and Marx's elementary, extended, generalized, and absurd phases. And Wunt's . . . and I should mention Stephen Pepper's world hypotheses of . . . and . . . Well, I could go on. These reductive schemes all share the ambition of putting complex, seamless processes into discrete boxes. How is yours any less inadequate than the worst and most reductive of such schemes?

A: Well, of course they are reductive and create artificial lines in complex processes. The trick is to find a way of representing the relevant phenomena adequately *for a particular purpose*. The breaks between different kinds of understanding are not represented as discrete in this scheme and the kinds of understanding are not discrete boxes, but I don't think the process is seamless. I think there are some periods of greater and faster change than others—an extension of "punctuated evolution" into the process of cultural development. We can't think without reductionism, as we can't think without stereotypes. The trick is to reduce and stereotype only in ways that help illuminate rather than the opposite.

Q: Well, we seem to be out of time. People are hungry and tired, and some are bored out of their skulls. Any last words?

A: I confess that this theory still seems to me like an engine with bits falling off, steam coming from inappropriate joints, oil dripping, some gleaming pieces attached insecurely to scavenged old bodywork—but it does seem to chug forward a bit, better at least than the traditional-conceptions-of-education engine with its massive crew and smartly uniformed technicians, which hums and clangs admirably but doesn't actually go anywhere, or at best zooms round in ever-diminishing circles. Ah well, another metaphor out of control. Plato did all this so much better—prisoners in caves, divided lines, the myth of Er, and funeral pyres at dawn.

c h a p t e r 7

Some Implications
for the Curriculum

INTRODUCTION

Theories about the curriculum, as about education in general, can be divided into two categories. Before the middle of the nineteenth century the theories were largely concerned with the moral virtues, human excellences, and knowledge that should be inculcated in a small group of males who would become the social and political elite. After the mid-nineteenth century they have been largely about what skills and knowledge are required to prepare the masses, female and male, for productive work, good citizenship, and satisfying leisure. The difference between the two categories is tied up with literacy. In the former period, the masses were illiterate, and the accumulating culture coded in writing was uncomplicatedly seen as irrelevant to them; they were left to their oral-Mythic-folk cultures. In this century, we, the masses, have become more or less literate and are equipped to access the accumulated lore of the Western tradition. A crucial problem for the school curriculum, and increasingly for the college and university curriculum, has thus become the relevance of that quondam elite culture to the lives of the masses. Discussion of this problem has been, and continues to be, attended by intense polemics, particularly when claims for curriculum time to develop this elite culture seem to clash with the time needed to prepare people for productive roles in the modern economy.

And that is just one of a number of contentious problems with which the curriculum designer has to deal. It intersects with a multitude of other social, ideological, technical, prudential, and moral issues. Each of the three old educational ideas implies prescriptions for the curriculum that suggest solutions to that impendent array of issues.

The socializing idea implies a curriculum aimed at preparing children as adequately as possible for the life they are likely to lead; it focuses on developing the skills and knowledge that are relevant to "real life" outside the school. This curriculum is responsive to changes in society and addresses topics such as family life, consumer education, hygiene and diet, sex education, and other conspicuous features of the social life students are entering. Plato's idea today implies a curriculum aimed at initiating students into the forms of disciplined knowledge, and into some forms at a significantly deeper level; it focuses on developing familiarity with the culture that has accumulated in the Western literate tradition. This curriculum is attentive to what Matthew Arnold called "the best that has been thought and said in the world"; the "best" is perceived to be stable, beyond considerations of immediate utility, and likely to change only very slowly as a result of new attainments in the various disciplines. Rousseau's idea today implies a curriculum aimed at the fullest development of each person's potential; it focuses on extending, elaborating, reorganizing, reconstructing, and transforming the student's individual experience. This curriculum is more attentive to procedural skills than to any specific privileged content; the content is selected largely on the basis of what is required in extending the student's everyday experience.

The current "common sense" approach to the curriculum, typical of state-run institutions, tries to balance these three schemes. The trouble is, each of them has significant problems separately, and together they do not blend into a coherent curriculum. We are so used to mangled curricula, however, that their fundamental incoherences are accepted as necessary "tensions" produced by the competition of "stakeholders." Consider for a moment how we should resolve competing claims on curriculum time between Latin and consumer education. A socializing scheme would have no difficulty resolving this, nor would a Platonic scheme. But when we try to deploy both, as is commonly the case, the mind can only boggle—and leave it to a fight between the forces that give greater weight to socializing or academic criteria. We have come to accept these political fights as the proper way to compensate for incoherent concepts.

The problems with each of the three ideas with regard to the curriculum are well documented by proponents of the other two. The socializing curriculum attends too much to current social conventions and is consequently inclined to narrow-minded provincialism, to accepting the contingent forms of contemporary society as privileged, and to seeing other societies and other conventions as inferior to the degree that they are different. The Platonic curriculum tries too hard to secure for students a reliable image of reality, at the expense of wisdom, compassion, and skills relevant to managing in current society. The Rousseauian curriculum is insensitive to how far individual development is a social matter and how far intellectual skills are tied in with disciplined knowledge, and so inclines towards superficiality and ill-founded confidence.

The alternative offered in this chapter is a curriculum that can develop the set of intellectual tools discussed earlier. I will have nothing much to say about the curricula for Somatic understanding and for Ironic understanding, assuming that the former is constrained in ways that do not leave much room for curriculum content choices and the latter is unconstrained in ways that leave so much room that prescription would be pointless. I will focus, then, on implications for the curriculum that will support development of Mythic, Romantic, and Philosophic understanding and restrict my comments mainly to curricula appropriate for typical schools, and for colleges and universities.

I do not promise to detail and justify a whole curriculum from the early years to adulthood, all in a single chapter. What I will do is outline the principles that this theory generates for constructing a curriculum that will encourage development of these kinds of understanding. I will focus on features of this curriculum that differentiate it most clearly from those that currently dominate schools, colleges, and universities. Perhaps elsewhere these broad brush strokes can be elaborated into a detailed specification of curriculum content. For now, I will consider some content by way of example.

Please prepare, then, for a change of pace from the more theoretical discussions of the previous chapters. We are now ready to explore how the theory might be implemented within current schooling conditions, and to consider changes that could be made tomorrow without serious disruption.

MYTHIC UNDERSTANDING

The characterization of Mythic understanding identified metaphor, rhythmic language, images generated from words, abstract and affective oppositions, story structures, and so on as among its constituent intellectual tools. What curriculum content can best stimulate development of these tools?

A couple of general principles will come into play in considering each kind of understanding; one derives from the requirements of the kind of un-

207

derstanding, the other from the requirements of the direction in which we want the student to develop. I will discuss these principles in terms of Mythic understanding, and leave it as understood that the same points refer to Romantic and Philosophic understanding, even though I will not repeat them later. The first general principle that can help our selection of curriculum content involves reflection on the cultural forms common to oral-language users, as we will be recapitulating the intellectual tools that they developed. The second principle involves reflection on the direction, toward Romantic, Philosophic, and Ironic understanding, in which we want the curriculum to take students.

These might seem conflicting principles, more likely to bemuse than to help us; reflecting on the kaleidescopically rich variety of cultural forms in oral societies may seem to draw us in opposite directions from the path of Western disciplined inquiry toward which our further kinds of understanding beckon us. We can, I think, be attentive to both of these general principles, looking backward and forward, as it were, and still construct a coherent curriculum. Being attentive to both means that the Mythic understanding we will aim to develop will be constrained by our sense of the direction in which it is to develop, but that we will not be so attentive to the intended direction that we will neglect the distinctively Mythic forms from which the later developments must grow. So, for example, Mythic understanding can be stimulated by any of a large range of kinds of stories referring to the past—oral cultures suggest rich examples from the most fantastic to very accurate accounts of past events. These oral stories have a number of common features that we will draw on. But because we aim to support students' development of Romantic, Philosophic, and Ironic understanding, we will select Western-style historical accounts of the past for our elementary curriculum, but frame them in Mythic terms. So our two general principles can work together; the one directing us to the oral foundations of our understanding, the other directing us toward the forms of their development we want to stimulate.

Perhaps I should not leave the example of history hanging. I meant it only to illustrate that one can draw on both general principles and come up with a curriculum that honors both. History does not commonly appear in the elementary curriculum these days, as it has been replaced by social studies with its outdated "expanding horizons" basis. In chapter 2 and elsewhere (Egan, 1988) I have given reasons for abandoning social studies, but I do not want to replace it with the old-style history that attended not at all to Mythic principles. So, the question becomes, What kind of history will find a place in the elementary curriculum?

The first general principle directs us to the oral foundations of any area of study we want to include in the curriculum. The oral foundation of history is myth. We need to reflect not only on the endless variety of mythic references to the past but also on their common features and on the psychological and social functions they performed. All oral cultures have traditional tales about the past, some embedded in sacred myths recited as parts of rituals, others more informal and variable in content and in their social uses. All are in a story form and all serve to fit present experience into an extended and more generally meaningful context.

Drawing on some of the other characteristics of Mythic understanding, we could begin our history curriculum with the cosmic story of the struggle of life against extinction. (Virginia Lee Burton's *Life Story* [1962] exemplifies one way to dramatize it.) More recent history can be structured in terms of the struggle for freedom against oppression, with the dramatic incidents of that extensive and ongoing story forming the lessons over many weeks. We can see history also in terms of the struggle for security against the danger of arbitrary violence. We could devise many such overarching stories that would serve the psychological and social purposes of myths or traditional tales in oral cultures, and would use similar structural techniques in their presentation.

It would be easy, for example, to design a yearlong history program based on the story of the human struggle for freedom against oppression of various kinds. My brief examples here will be Western-oriented only because that is what I am familiar with; in designing such a program in detail one would select examples of different kinds of oppression and various struggles for freedom from around the world. One might include slavery in the ancient world, drawing on vivid incidents such as Spartacus's revolt against Rome or the struggles of Queen Bouddacea against the invading legions; one could look at the treatment of Jews in medieval and modern Europe, of captives in early North and Central American cultures. One could study Gandhi and Martin Luther King, and so on. None of this need involve falsification. We will simplify, but even the most sophisticated history-writing involves simplification. The aim is to tell a vital part of the human story that will help students make sense of the world and the society into which they are growing. I have already argued that such a curriculum, focused on the triumphs and defeats of men, women, and communities in varied places down the ages, could be of more educational value than the typical social studies focus on the role of the mailman and the structure of the local environment. Introducing children to their world in terms of its powerful and dramatic events, rather than through idealized, ordered routines of their   209 local customs, presents them with images of struggles and accommodations that are analogous to the struggles and accommodations they are themselves going through in their early years. History is one of the major tools we have for making sense of experience in a changing world. Historical understanding does not simply "develop" in later years (as argued by some Piagetians, see, e.g., Hallam [1969]); its later forms develop on the basis of prior and prerequisite developments.

With regard to the "languages and literatures" segment of the curriculum, the general aim will be the stimulation and development of the student's Mythic language. One of the principles discussed earlier as central to language development was the growth in consciousness of language, or "metalinguistic awareness." I would like to begin with something that seems to me important in this development but that is commonly neglected in education: the sense of humor. While we may recognize that sophisticated irony inescapably involves a kind of humor, its prerequisite developments are little attended to in education.

It is hard not to become grim and dull discussing humor, but its educational value seems to me considerable, both because of its role in language development and because of its related role in stimulating and enlarging these various kinds of understanding. Again, I will not discuss this topic in the two later sections of this chapter, but, in changing forms, humor will continue to play an equally important educational role in developing Romantic and Philosophic understanding as in stimulating Mythic understanding.

At the simplest level, jokes can extend vocabulary and begin the crucial process of making language explicit and itself an object of reflection. "When is a door not a door?" "When it's ajar [a jar]." Ho, ho. Getting the point of this simple word-joke, and the hundreds like it, provides mediation between open/closed, adding a tiny bit to the child's ability to describe the world and experience more articulately. Even more important, it fosters the realization that identical sounds can take different forms when written and can mean different things.

Metaphoric play can be encouraged by jokes such as those in Bill Keane's popular "Family Circus" cartoons. The child standing on the lawn observes: "The grass is flossing my toes," or the frayed shoelace is said to have "lost its claw," or the approaching storm is announced with "The sky's grumblin'." Children can be encouraged in class to engage in the deliberate confusion of categories that makes metaphor work and that makes it funny.

Further consciousness of language, or, in Hayek's terms, bringing operations of the mind into consciousness, can be encouraged by parody, which children commonly delight in almost as soon as they have learned the convention being parodied. One sees it in the rather mysterious "You know what?" "What?" "That's what!" which caused my three-year-old daughter endless mirth, or in "Why did the turtle cross the road?" "I don't know. Why?" "Because it was the chicken's day off," which similarly reduced my four-year-old son to paroxysms of glee ten or twenty times a day.

The jokes that Lewis Carroll builds into the Alice books exemplify a form that increases consciousness of the contingency of categories and playfully threatens to undermine the normal conventions of reason: "'Take some more tea,' the March Hare said to Alice, very earnestly. 'I've had nothing yet,' Alice replied in an offended tone, 'so I can't take more.' 'You mean you can't take *less*,' said the Hatter: 'it's very easy to take *more* than nothing.'" (*Alice in Wonderland,* ch. 7); "They draw all manner of things—everything that begins with an M-.' 'Why an M?' said Alice. 'Why not?' said the March Hare" (ibid.); "'There's nothing like eating hay when you're faint.' . . . 'I didn't say there was nothing *better,*' the King replied. 'I said there was nothing *like* it.'" (*Through the Looking Glass,* ch. 7).

I don't mean these examples are somehow paradigmatic kinds of jokes for stimulating the intellectual tools of Mythic understanding, but rather that they exemplify ways in which the joke can be a fertile means of building awareness of language and of developing increasingly sophisticated language use. Another value of jokes, of course, is that they are fun; they are a form of language whose use carries an immediate reward.

Language also has its own rhythms, which can give delight apart from their sense or meaning, as the nonsense verses of Edward Lear or Dr. Seuss attest. The pervasive pleasure children get from rhythmic language is evident from such massive compilations as the Opies' (1969, 1985). The favorite "Knock, knock" joke among local preschoolers went: "Knock, knock." "Who's there?" "Mickey Mouse's underwear." Rolling-on-the-floor mirth followed this one, the rhythmic appeal no doubt reinforced by the hint of approaching a taboo. Exploration of jokes might sensibly be added to the elementary language curriculum, not in the sense of meticulous analytic study, but as encouraging awareness of how language works and how the students can make it work in their own invention of jokes. The child developing language is, at the most basic level, learning to shape sound so that it can affect others. Response to the child's efforts is crucial; the teacher or parent has the somewhat delicate task of encouraging what may be chaotic exploration while also encouraging the selection of meaningful patterns and the discipline required to refine them.

These activities are developments of somatic explorations and patterns finding their way beyond the body through language. We can move readily from this linguistic exploration back to the body, furthering its rhythmic development, by combining words and music in song. This continuing somatic development can be encouraged further in more sophisticated exploration of the varied sounds our bodies can make in addition to those we shape into words; we can click (incorporated into some languages in South Africa), squeak, clap, stomp, and, surely sadly neglected, we can whistle. We are instruments of music and its manner of communicating meaning. Thus the exploration of how to construct pattern and meaning in human sounds plays a part in the languages curriculum.

Exuberant word-play in poetry can encourage children's sense of how words can make meaning and images, and can delight by its sheer sound even when meaning and images are not easily grasped. I have mentioned the Edward Lear and Dr. Seuss rhymes. Robert Southey's "The Cataract of Lodore" is a perfect example of verbal exuberance—a challenge for the reciter no less than the listener.

Literatures would include the rich variety of stories from around the world that incorporate the features characterized in chapter 2. The more these "folk" tales can be told rather than read the better, probably, and the more that can be told by people from whose cultures the stories come the better, especially if some cultural context for the story can be provided. More contentiously, perhaps, there is a class of stories that should also be made very familiar to children. These are the great mythic or religious stories of the world, and particularly those of the child's own culture and of the dominant culture(s) into which the child is growing. Without knowledge of such stories, children will find it harder, maybe impossible, to make sense of the cultural experience that surrounds them. Sometimes these stories will be from a central religious text, such as the Jewish Torah or Christian Bible; sometimes they will be sets of exemplary social tales, such as the Nasrudin stories in Islamic cultures; sometimes they are bodies of textualized myths, such as the Greek or Norse stories of gods and mortals.

The set of foundational Western stories, mainly from the Bible, from Greek and Norse myths, from those long ago absorbed from Islamic sources, and from the folk cultures of western Europe, cannot be taken simply as any other stories in the curriculum. They are important because, first, they have become intricately connected with Western languages and, second, because they give rise to literary developments that we want students to absorb.

To pick up that first point, these stories are important because their rhythms of expectation and satisfaction, of hopes and fears, of courage and action, of belief and behavior, have helped to shape our categories of understanding and our conceptions of virtues and vices; they are implicated in profound ways in the sense of the world delivered to us in our languages.

Without knowledge of these stories, students will be less equipped to make sense of the world.

Northrop Frye elaborates the second point when he writes: "If we don't know the Bible and the central stories of Greek and Roman literature we can still read books and see plays, but our knowledge of literature can't grow, just as our knowledge of mathematics can't grow if we don't learn the multiplication table" (1963, p. 28). Perhaps he slightly overstates the point, but our general principle of selecting curriculum content that will direct us toward subsequent kinds of understanding clearly prescribes this set of stories as central to our elementary literatures curriculum. I realize this focus raises problems in a multicultural society, but if our primary concern is education, the issue to address is the strategic one of how to present these stories in an acceptable way, not how to negotiate their disappearance from the curriculum. We will sensibly be flexible and sensitive to particular situations, and be prepared to let our decisions turn on courtesy and kindness rather than on narrow logic or ideology.

Writing is language made visible, but it allows us to do things with language that were not possible in oral cultures. Initiation into writing might well explore the techniques it initially made possible. So, along with the usual early writing activities, we might encourage children to make lists, draw up tables, make recipes, design flowcharts, and so on.

What kind of introduction to science will we provide in the curriculum by applying the two general principles? We will probably find it easier to apply the second principle, of setting in place prerequisites for Romantic, Philosophic, and Ironic scientific understanding, than to apply the one that requires us to devise a Mythic form of science. 'Mythic science' sounds like an oxymoron. Our first principle requires us to ask what is the oral foundation of science. Well, the oral foundation of science seems to be what was dismissively called magic. Oral cultures certainly observed the world and formulated schemes of classification as a result, but the schemes are, from a scientific point of view, idiosyncratic, often weirdly incomprehensible, and often metaphorically tied to the objects classified rather than to some rational abstract scheme that can provide control over them. For example, at the simplest level, many cultures have no general system of counting. If you ask members of many oral cultures to count, they will reply "Count what?" (Goody, 1977). We see the traces of such object-tied counting in English— twin, brace, pair, deuce, yoke, dual, couple, binary, and mates all refer to twoness with regard to different things.

When we look at oral cultural inquiry into the natural world we see something rather different from science, something more intimately partici-   213 patory in the objects of the natural world that seems alien and uncomfortable to the scientific mind. How are we to accommodate both of these and construct an elementary science curriculum? The beginning inquiry, reflecting that of oral cultures, is less an attempt to know *about* nature as to *know* it in some participatory way, to know it as something we are an intimate part of, not set off from. One component of our early science curriculum might involve each student "adopting" something in the natural world—say, a tree, a patch of grass, a spider's web, rain, a dog or cat, or clouds. Students would be expected and helped simply to observe their adopted piece of the natural world, not in the sense that is currently common in which students have checklists, learn the names of the object and those of its parts, have drawing equipment or make notes, and deliver reports of a kind appropriate to their ages. In the Mythic curriculum they would observe silently for sustained periods of time with no other aim than to feel their way into the nature of what they are observing. They will feel how the tree stretches its leaves out to the sun, how the rain trickles down it, and how the branches move in the various winds. Obviously this will require support and training, but perhaps less than many may assume; this kind of absorption occurs quite commonly and without tutoring in many children. A little ingenuity should enable us to encourage it in many more. The aim is a kind of dreamlike absorption into the object being observed or rather being participated in. The dreamlike mind will tie the object into emotions and half-formed stories. I recognize that this may seem decidedly odd, but I think the decisiveness of our break with the natural world has given us a science that has forgotten its foundations in full human participation in the natural world. A deliberate introduction to science of the kind recommended here might go some way toward encouraging a greater sensitivity to the natural world. We might seek guidance for such a curriculum from cultures that have excelled at combining absorption with attentive observation. The native cultures of North America, for example, excelled at this.

Forms of classification of phenomena are also to be encouraged in our elementary science curriculum. The dominant Piagetian scheme has encouraged an image of young children's classification as prerational, with intellectual progress being seen as the gradual "development" of rational classification. These assumptions direct our attention away from the "confused," "chaotic," or "egocentric" ways young children classify. In this scheme, however, we are encouraged to see young children's classifications as no less complex, sophisticated, and orderly than the rational forms that are represented as correct. But we need to attend to the metaphoric connections that underlie young children's "confused" ordering schemes; these are often tied in with unsuspected qualities of the objects being classified. Again, a look at

214

the kinds of schemes common in oral cultures can provide ways of enabling children to explore variety in the ordering and classifying of phenomena (see, for example, Lévi-Bruhl, 1985).

Where, in these two brief examples, is the influence of the second general principle—the sense of direction toward rationality and scientific ordering? In both cases, intellectual engagement is the necessary precursor of rational ordering. Most students, especially children who live in the city, have the rational ordering thrust on them *before* they have engaged the natural world in any significant, meaningful way. Often the rational ordering displaces the meaningful mythic engagement; in the common elementary science units on The Child as Observer, for instance, the child observes only to order, classify, and learn in a simplified rational mode. The future direction is evident in my examples because they introduce a constituent of a mature scientific understanding that is currently, and destructively, neglected. That is, this sense of intimate participation in the natural world is not a primitive confusion that rational, positivist science conquered, but is a foundational constituent of a proper scientific understanding.

And what is the oral foundation of mathematics? Mathematics grows out of our number sense, which we share with many animals and insects; our number sense is about as good as that of blackbirds but less good than that of some species of wasp. How to move from our number sense to the trick of counting and then to the tricks counting can be elaborated into, is the challenge with which our two general principles present us. Tobias Danzig's *Number: The Language of Science* (1967), which Albert Einstein described as the "best book on mathematics I have ever read," presents us with some clues for making this early development. Our number sense is evident in our ability to distinguish the number of things we see at a glance, which humans can manage up to about six or seven. But this is not adequate to people who herd cattle or sheep and who need to keep an accurate count. So what means did people in oral cultures use, and how can we draw on those while moving in the direction of Western mathematics?

The structure of the current curriculum represents mathematics as a series of "skills," or as sets of increasingly complex algorithms, that the child has to master. This most common approach—however "fun" the lessons are made—can obliterate the sense of magic that early counting systems reflected. Our early mathematics curriculum has to focus on recreating, or recapitulating, the magical ingenuity of the inventions and discovery that make up the subject. We will want to teach counting systems and various patterns and manipulations evident in mathematics so that children become competent and confident, recognizing the external manipulations as simply expressions of their internal human ingenuity. Some of this can be achieved by embedding the "skills" in story structures such as exemplified in chapter 2, whereby the child is encouraged to associate affectively with the cleverness of the character who succeeds in calculating what would be impossible for the number sense to deal with.

Many early counting systems used rhyme and rhythm, and echoes of these are still heard in the number rhymes that survive from "folk" work songs. Not only can such rhymes help to teach counting and simple arithmetic, but they can also help to embed counting and arithmetic in meaningful contexts that expose their original purposes. Number-based puzzles and tricks, magic-number games, and so on encourage the development of the number sense in the ingenuity and magic of counting. None of these activities, which are attentive to Mythic understanding, will obviate the need for some hard work and repetition to ensure fluent mastery of the basic mathematical skills. The development of these skills is not intrinsically difficult if we bear in mind the intellectual tools the Mythic child brings to them. Ignoring those tools, on the other hand, sets us back on the path of the largely meaningless accumulation of little understood external algorithms that buries for most children any sense of the ingenuity and wonder of even elementary mathematics.

The disciplinary divisions toward which we will be moving in the curriculum are reflected in the manner I have touched on history, languages and literatures, science, and mathematics here. The first general principle invoked above would, however, encourage us not to put very much emphasis on those divisions. All manner of "interdisciplinary" topics can readily be incorporated in the Mythic curriculum (see Armstrong, Connolly, and Saville, 1994). (I recognize that many people think the choice between an interdisciplinary curriculum as distinct from one divided up into traditional disciplines is of crucial importance. No doubt it makes some difference, but I can't get excited about this as an issue of much educational significance. And, anyway, any sensible curriculum will incorporate both principles at different times.) An arts segment of the curriculum would focus on encouraging students' exploration of the range of sensations and patterning possibilities available to ear, eye, taste, touch, and movement. But that arts curriculum will clearly overlap considerably with those I have discussed briefly above, as the exploration of rhyme, rhythm, and counting suggest.

Mathematics, science, language, and music are often taught as having a nature to which the child has to conform. Educational success is then measured in terms of the degree of conformity achieved. I am recommending a rather different approach here, one that seeks an accommodation between the "nature" of those disciplines and the intellectual tools by means of which the young child can engage them. These tools, in Vygotsky's sense, mediate the child's grasp and understanding of them. Designing the Mythic curriculum, then, is a matter of selecting that content within these disciplines that the mediating tools of Mythic understanding make accessible, meaningful, and engaging.

ROMANTIC UNDERSTANDING

The characterization of Romantic understanding identified engagement by the extremes of experience and the limits of reality, association with transcendent human qualities, the personalizing of knowledge, and a distinctive romantic rationality as among its constituent intellectual tools. In what follows I will look, first, at what kind of curriculum can best stimulate and develop the intellectual tools of Romantic understanding and, second, what curriculum comes into focus by looking at the world through the mediation of those tools. I think we should have a distinctive transition-year between the Mythic and Romantic curriculum, dedicated very largely to stimulating development of Romantic understanding, but it will be easier to describe the transition curriculum after outlining what it is a transition to.

If students are to explore the scale of reality and the limits of experience, the content that will most readily support this kind of inquiry will be the *mega ergon*—the great achievements, the most terrible disasters, the most exotic features of human experience and of the natural world. Taking this *mega ergon* as a criterion for selecting curriculum content, we can apply it in two somewhat distinctive ways. First, whatever topic is being studied, we will search within it for content with these characteristics. Second, we can create a slot in the curriculum for the direct exploration of extremes and limits. We might call it something like Human and Natural Records. It would not be intended for extensive study, but rather for sharp, intensive, limited views on varied topics. Such a curriculum slot might be scheduled for two or three sessions each week, perhaps at the end of the day, and for no more than ten or fifteen minutes. It would be a kind of *Guinness Book of Records* segment, though with somewhat richer elaboration and context and, if available, illustration. Through the year, students individually or in small groups could prepare presentations. The accumulation of hundreds of these "records" over the years, overlapping as they will with topics being studied in greater depth or in other ways, will provide a significant body of diverse knowledge about the limits of the world and of human experience.

In chapter 3, the exploration of the scale of reality was related to students' fascination with hobbies, collecting, and other activities, which involved exploring something as exhaustively as possible. This in-depth method of inquiry also yields a criterion for selecting a curriculum that has two uses. First, it encourages the teacher to provide students with some opportunity for exhaustive exploration in whatever topic is being studied. Second, as the previous item advised making room in the curriculum for brief "records" segments, so this criterion suggests a one- or even two-year extensive project, in which students individually or in small groups focus on thoroughly exploring something—eels' life cycles, the mendicant orders in the Middle Ages, light and its sources, beetles, the contents of the solar system, eggs, or whatever they choose. Perhaps, on a monthly basis the students could discuss with the class as a whole their ongoing projects.

Forming romantic associations with transcendent human qualities suggests another twofold criterion for selecting curriculum content. First, the criterion can be used in selecting the content that the teacher will emphasize in teaching any topic. In studying eels we may foreground the ingenuity, persistence, and heroism of Johannes Schmidt in tracking down their breeding grounds in the tangled Sargasso Sea, or in studying the Industrial Revolution we may foreground the daring and near-reckless drive of an engineer like Isambard Kingdom Brunel. Second, we can create another brief segment of curriculum time that will focus directly on transcendent human qualities and their expression in varied circumstances. Each quarter-hour segment, two or three times a week, could focus on an exemplification of a particular transcendent human quality—in the world of sports, in the news, in history, or in the world of entertainment. We could call it Human Qualities or Overcoming, and focus in each segment on cases that vividly exemplify compassion, courage, power, patience, genius, hope, strength, tenacity, persistence, and so on.

Another Romantic characteristic that can be converted into a criterion for the selection of curriculum content is the ready engagement by whatever stimulates wonder and awe. As with the characteristics I have already identified, this criterion provides guidance in two directions. First, it directs us to select within any topic we might be studying—whether earthworms, division of fractions, or the Treaty of Vienna—whatever features of that topic seem best able to stimulate the sense of wonder or generate a feeling of awe. The clauses of the Treaty of Vienna alone might do little to inspire awe or even wonder; in that case we could "humanize" the Treaty, or look for transcendent human qualities that led to its framing, or find some other Romantic approach to it.

Second, it encourages us to include in the curriculum the content that seems best able to stimulate students' senses of wonder and awe. This suggests another short, fifteen-minute curriculum segment, in this case dedicated to small but constant stimuli to students' sense of wonder. One trick is to bring out the strange and wonderful in what seems routine or taken for granted. Another is to focus on the odd and strange. This curriculum segment could be organized around varied, random, questions, such as: How can birds fly? Why are some people colorblind? What good are mosquitoes? What is plastic and how is it made? Why are there so many stones around? What is soil made of? Awe is more complicated and more difficult to evoke, but might be encouraged by a further set of questions: Must all things end? What is life? How many stars are there? How do we learn language?

This quarter-hour curriculum segment cannot, of course, answer any such questions adequately. The point is to raise questions and provide as much of an answer as possible that brings out the wonder of the topic. The aim is to raise interesting or odd questions and answer them as well as possible without any pedagogical fuss. By pedagogical fuss here I mean we will have no "inquiry methods" or "discovery processes" that might have value elsewhere. "What is soil made of?" may elicit for a few moments T. S. Eliot's "fur, flesh, and feces" answer. Along with information about how long it takes how much decaying fur, flesh, and feces to lay down an inch of soil, we could consider the rate of soil erosion, and so on.

The pedagogical skill required here consists of selecting questions that have surprising or wonder-inducing answers, and not getting tied down in systematic, detailed coverage of an issue. Perhaps ten minutes might be a safer amount of time to allot. As with the other small curriculum segments, students can become involved in framing questions and researching answers, always ensuring that their presentations focus on the strange, wonderful, and awe-inspiring. The aim is to build gradually and randomly a particular level of knowledge about the world that stimulates, bit by bit, wonder and awe at being alive in this world at this time.

A further characteristic of Romantic understanding, which yields another criterion for selecting curriculum content, is the ready access to knowledge that is "humanized." Again we have two ways of deploying this principle. First, it provides us with a criterion for selecting content within any topic we are teaching. It directs us to bring out those aspects of the topic that make it accessible in terms of human emotion, and to bring out conceptions of causality seen largely in terms of human agency. All events, objects, and processes, whether physical or historical, can be made Romantically accessible if they are represented as analogous at some level to the way in which human emotions are seen as causing things to happen. To repeat an earlier point, this does not require us to falsify. Rather, the Romantic manner of conceiving of events, objects, and processes is one way of trying to make sense of them. They are ultimately ineffable; even our most sophisticated forms of representation and explanation are inadequate. Shunning this Ro- 219 mantic approach as simplistic is merely a hangover from the polemics that accompanied promotion of Philosophic approaches; the Romantic is properly a constituent of later kinds of representation and explanation.

Second, the "humanizing" principle directs us to select curriculum content that can best stimulate and develop this particular tool of Romantic understanding. In chapter 3 I mentioned various popular tabloids and magazines (*National Inquirer, People,* and *Entertainment Weekly,* to name a few) that exemplify the results of aggressively applying this criterion. Such stories are Romantic in the sense that they focus on individual people or groups of people, and on exotic or extreme behavior or achievements. Causality in these stories works through the will, which acts in direct response to an emotion; luck and chance are usually represented as due to good or bad behavior or character, however indirectly.

Like the previous principles, this one would support a quarter-hour segment; we could call it "Brief Lives." Two or three times each week, teachers or students could prepare and present the story of someone's life, or some part of someone's life, emphasizing the Romantic characteristics. The presentations should come in random order—Hildegard of Bingen today, Jesse Owen yesterday, Edward G. Robinson tomorrow, then Ramon Lull, Mary Wollstonecraft, Henry the Navigator, Joan of Arc, someone's great-aunt or great-uncle, and the last Tasmanian aborigine. One of the related characteristics of Romantic understanding was the revolt against constraining conventional forces, so some of our brief lives might include agonistic accounts of St. Teresa of Avila against the church hierarchy, of Gandhi against the British army, of Martin Luther King against the Washington establishment, of Chief Seattle against an earlier Washington establishment, of Maria Montessori against the Italian medical powers-that-be, or of someone's mother or father against some unjust social regulation.

This principle also supports activities that are becoming quite common, such as having students compile oral histories from their recorded interviews with elderly people in the community, tracing their lives, their adventures, exotic incidents, and memories of how things were and how things changed into the present unpredicted, peculiar world.

So far, then, by considering how characteristics of Romantic understanding can become principles for determining curriculum content we have some new chunks of curriculum time and some topics to fill them. Implementing these ideas would give us, perhaps twice a day, brief segments devoted to people's lives, to stimulating wonder, to forming associations with transcendent qualities, to recording limits of experience and of the natural world. Over the longer period of one or two years, students would also be pursuing some topic in exhaustive detail, and they may be involved in the topic by playing a role—a sheep trader in Australia, a Franciscan friar in medieval slums, a particular kind of egg or beetle, or one of the contents of the solar system. This set of activities is designed both to stimulate students' active engagement with the world and also to contribute to the unsystematic but intensive accumulation of detailed knowledge about it.

These brief, frequent exposures to Romantic bits and pieces will probably do little toward the systematic development of disciplined understanding. We must also attend to putting in place the Romantic constituent of later forms of understanding of mathematics, history, and science, focusing systematically on the stimulation and development of students' Romantic language. Earlier I discussed how our most sophisticated understanding is built layer by layer. Scientific understanding is not simply Philosophic, as it is often represented, but is properly also Somatic, Mythic, Romantic, and Ironic. The principle used to explore science in the Mythic section above involved reflecting in two directions; first, on what form proto-scientific inquiry took in oral cultures and, second, in what direction we were to stimulate and develop it. Here we will ask an analogous, twofold question: What Romantic form did science take in cultural history and which features of science are particularly important to the development of the most sophisticated modern scientific understanding? We will want to raise this dual question in all disciplines.

In the study of history we will look for dramatic narratives driven by human emotions and intentions. A chronological scheme should be in place after Mythic studies, refined by the various narratives selected for study. An increasingly confident sense of what is possible in human affairs can be encouraged by focusing on the extremes of human experience. Thomas Carlyle (1795–1881) suggested that history be seen as composed of innumerable biographies; we will want to incorporate a sense of this Romantic principle in our curriculum. We will also build our narratives on strong metaphors, such as those Gibbon (1737–1794) used in *The Decline and Fall of the Roman Empire* to describe the empire's passage from vigorous youth to tired old age. The further Romantic principle of engagement by the strange and different would support, along with other reasons, a much wider inclusion of events and people in varied cultures from around the world than is currently common.

Given these criteria, it is clear that no specific historical topics are more appropriate or more valuable than others. We will select topics from countries around the world and across time because of their amenability to such Romantic treatment. The aim will be to build up somewhat unsystematic historical knowledge. It will be both extensive and intensive, and will focus on vivid events, characters, institutional rises and falls, and so on. There will 221 no doubt be constant overlaps with the smaller curricula segments discussed above, particularly the Brief Lives segment, but this overlap seems all to the good.

History can also play a role in making the science curriculum more accessible to students during these Romantic years. This is not to collapse science to history, but rather to suggest a way of embedding scientific achievements in their historical setting, particularly through discussing the passions, hopes, fears, and intentions of those who developed the scientific knowledge in the first place.

So what does science look like when we view it "Romantically"? It is, first, a contextualized science, one in which theories, experiments, and facts become meaningful within narratives of human lives and intentions, one which draws on such transcendent qualities as persistence, ingenuity, patience, accuracy, and so on, in pursuit of the nature of things. This peculiar adventure—the tools forged to aid in it, the personalities and emotions that have driven it, and the wonder of what has been exposed by it—will form our science curriculum. TV programs and books such as James Burke's *Connections* and *Connections*[2] show how science can be presented in a Romantically engaging way. The average teacher with the supplies available to the average school cannot be expected to compete with the quirky showmanship of Burke, but they can learn from his construction of engaging narratives and his personalizing of inventions and discoveries.

None of this need change significantly the content of the science curriculum. Theories, laws, factual knowledge, and the systematic investigation of nature will not be ignored; the usual purposes of the science curriculum will not be discarded. Central place will, however, be given over to the Romantic engagement with the exotic and the wonderful, because this focus is prerequisite to, and the route toward, Philosophic understanding of science. Romantic principles will yield criteria of selection that will effect *some* changes in the science curriculum, favoring those topics that are more amenable to this Romantic treatment. No doubt to the distress of purists, implementation of such criteria would increase the more spectacular and dramatic features of scientific activity and reduce the logical sequence of systematically accumulating knowledge. This would result because these kinds of understanding see the growth of human knowledge less in terms of the regular logical sequences we impose on it later and more in the discontinuous forms shaped by the somewhat distinctive intellectual tools we develop over time. Emphasizing narrative structures, the drama, the mystery, and the human dimension undercuts the dulling influence of premature and simplified Philosophic principles of selection and organization in the science curriculum.

Many of the same general observations can be made about the mathematics curriculum. We need to embed the sequence of skills and algorithms to be learned into an historical and human context. We need to see the human purposes for which different forms of mathematics were developed and, as far as is known, who invented or discovered each theorem, algorithm, technique, or advance in mathematical understanding. The curriculum would be rich in historical figures, particularly the Egyptians, Greeks, Arabs, and Jews to whom we owe so much.

Clues to the form a Romantic mathematics curriculum might take can be found, again, if we focus attention on the early period of literacy, between myth and the systematizers. There we find figures like Pythagoras, whose intoxication with numbers catches the Romantic sense of what is exotic and wonderful about mathematics. To Pythagoras, being able to manipulate numbers and mathematical relationships and find that their results could be applied to the world was a discovery close to magical. In teaching Romantic mathematics, we must begin by excavating what is wonderful about each skill, each technique, each algorithm. This is not a call for massive research for each element of the curriculum, but for an alertness to the romance of numbers. In teaching long division or long multiplication, we might introduce the topic by showing how the Greeks or the Romans performed it. The daunting complexity becomes immediately clear. But how else might one go about it? The wonderful ingenuity of the Arab invention of a number for nothing, zero, and the elegant ease it permits in handling what were immensely difficult calculations, can be made dramatically clear.

So, again, Romantic principles of selection will not significantly change the content of the mathematics curriculum, but they will introduce historical and human dimensions that tend to be largely ignored at present; and they will focus less on students' gradual accumulation of a logical sequence of algorithms and more on the wonder of puzzles, mathematical tricks, and games, the peculiarities one can discover in number relationships, and so on.

The formation of romantic associations via transcendent human qualities and the continuing development of linguistic tools will both support a prominent place in the curriculum for languages and literatures. Recall William Empson's description of literature as the chief means by which we come to understand what it is like to have feelings and beliefs different from our own; this will aid in our selection of appropriately Romantic literature. I should emphasize that, perhaps paradoxically, "Romantic" literature does not immediately direct us to literature of the Romantic period. The writings of Wordsworth, for example, include features of Mythic, Philosophic, Ironic, and Romantic understanding, and there are many other past and modern writers whose work is more purely "Romantic," in the sense characterized in chapter 3. The poetry of Coleridge or Poe, say, can be made more accessible, engaging, and meaningful if it is introduced with details of the lives of the poets.

Poetry no less than science can gain by being seen as a part of a person's life. Literature that involves strong and clear narratives, that deals with transcendent human qualities such as courage, love, and persistence, that focuses on some extremes of human experience, that examines something strange and exotic and that highlights other characteristics of Romantic understanding, will help do the educational job for us. These principles provide criteria that can be used relatively straightforwardly to select appropriate literature for the Romantic curriculum.

Exploration and experiment with burgeoning literacy are crucially important in developing the tools of Romantic understanding. Each area of the curriculum can contribute something distinctive to this, of course, but it will be useful also to dedicate a segment of the curriculum precisely to appropriate exploration of and experiment with literacy. The general aim is gradually to increase students' awareness of language and their conscious control of it. Many activities can contribute toward this aim, but I will mention just three that seem not very common—etymology, rhetoric, and "exotic" languages.

The value of etymology as a stimulant to linguistic self-awareness has been well made before (e.g., Temple and Gillet, 1989), but here I want to add the ways in which etymology can both appeal to and support Romantic understanding. The trick is to focus on the romance of etymology rather than on the Philosophic, systematic study of word origins. (Again, this is not to dismiss the latter but rather to put in place the understanding that will better lead to it.) If we think of words as like people, whose biographies are made up of growth and change, with occasional dramatic conversions and confused adventures, then we can discover the romance of etymology. I do not imagine etymology as a distinct curriculum segment so much as a relatively common visitor to the languages and literatures curriculum.

Not every word has an adequate "biographical" background to engage the Romantic mind, and choice of words will be based on those with a sufficiently interesting life story to tell. The manner should be less like the condensed listings of the major library dictionaries of etymology and more akin to the extended tales of a book like *The Private Lives of English Words* (Heller, Humez, and Dror, 1984). Students can be asked to solve puzzles, such as to discover why "money" is connected with "memory" and "muse," or what "gossip" has to do with God, or, indeed, where the word "god" comes from. Alternatively, during each lesson teachers can focus on a word or two or ask students to research a word for a future class. Stimulating interest depends partly on the selection of words with vivid, dramatic, and entertaining life stories. The story is important here. There is not much value in teaching about the gods after whom the days of the week are named; one has to show the historical reasons why those gods won out in English, why we have a mix of cultural deities, why the week is made up of seven days, and so on.

Rhetoric is usually described as the art of using language to influence the emotions or, relatedly, the beliefs of others. Rhetoric is valuable here, in part because it represents the preservation and elaboration within literacy of techniques of language use largely worked out in oral cultures (Ong, 1982). That is, if we look at early literacy to help us decide on forms appropriate in education, rhetoric is indicated as important. Earlier I emphasized the common discontinuity between the oral culture with which children come to school and the training they then receive in literacy. More prominent attention to rhetoric encourages us to tie early literacy to the students' already well-developed oral skills.

Rhetoric is increasingly recommended in schools and at college level and offers rich suggestions for the curriculum. I would add only that when selecting topics we should look at the needs of Romantic students. One useful topic not much mentioned is exploration of the various dialects available in the student's native language. In English, for example, the range of dialects is enormous. Exploring them means learning their distinctive forms and expressions, learning to speak in appropriate accents, and becoming familiar with the distinctive vividnesses, force, and subtlety of other dialects, especially those that are less represented in the student's native dialect or in standard English. Similarly, students can be encouraged to explore what Walter Ong has called different "grapholects," forms of written expression different from conventional standard forms. These explorations will all help to develop awareness of language and extend control over it. They will also help to resist the repressive conventionalizing that is so common and destructive. (I realize that these suggestions will seem themselves exotic to teachers who struggle to achieve even basic literacy in their pupils. But I am writing here for what can be expected of students who have been through an adequate Mythic curriculum and appropriate teaching and who have made a successful transition to Romantic understanding. I should add, as well, that these explorations of dialects and grapholects will make mastery of standard forms easier to accomplish.)

Students can also study the variety of rhetorical forms around them as they appear in political arguments and speeches, advertising, newspaper reporting, conversations at school and at home, comic strips, prayers, and so on. The central aim is constantly to increase awareness and develop control   225 over the various forms of language. More common tasks, like keeping a journal, can be encouraged to develop awareness of, and elaborate on, the distinctive, private "I" who is doing the writing.

I mentioned "exotic" language-learning. I mean that in addition to the second language students might be learning—and at least one modern language is important, if only to provide perspectives other than those that come with the native language—students should also make some progress in learning a language very different from their own, say, in a different orthography. For native English speakers, Sanskrit, Chinese, Thai, even ancient Egyptian hieroglyphs would suffice. The aim is not to achieve fluency but simply to get some insight into how a very different language delivers a representation of the world.

Another feature of the languages curriculum suggested by Romantic principles concerns developing and elaborating students' sense of humor from its Mythic forms. This is important because vivid and flexible understanding and deployment of metaphor are crucial to imagination, creative thinking, and intellectual freedom. Nelson Goodman suggests that a "metaphor might be regarded as a calculated category mistake" (1979, p. 73); we could look at some of the classic "Monty Python" sketches as characteristically Romantic because their humor tends to rely on taking a metaphor literally and creating a world that is, as a result, consistent but madly at variance with the everyday world. Monty Python-ish skits also involve other features, of course, that make their brand of humor a matter of taste; when we fail to appreciate them, however, we might wonder if our dulled metaphoric flexibility is such that we cannot see the fun in creating worlds based on calculated category mistakes. This dulling represents an educational failure to develop linguistic tools, and it is a failing we will want to avoid by encouraging students' playful manipulation of metaphors and calculated metaphoric crimes. The aim is to develop the sense of humor and metalinguistic awareness at the same time.

A general observation concerning the Romantic curriculum follows from the need to prepare for the development of Philosophic general schemes. One important feature of those schemes is that the degree of their sophistication turns on the amount of knowledge they have to organize. The problem created by too little or too narrowly focused knowledge, to put it in crude terms, is that almost any general scheme can order it. This means that the student is easy prey for any ideological or metaphysical scheme. With too little knowledge, the process of recognizing anomalies and making the scheme more sophisticated can get going only in the most rudimentary way. Similarly, Ironic understanding requires development of a sense of the contingency of the conditions one finds oneself in. This sense of contingency cannot come about as a product of relative ignorance; that breeds credulity, not irony. In other words, besides the Romantic reasons for learning a lot of diverse knowledge, the sense of direction toward Philosophic and Ironic understanding adds a further requirement on the curriculum of the Romantic years to ensure that students master a lot of knowledge. This principle seems lost in a climate where many argue that accumulating knowledge is of small importance compared with learning procedural skills, or "critical thinking," or where to locate knowledge when it is needed. These procedural skills are often promoted as important aids in sifting a body of knowledge so large that no one can "know" everything. But the mind and the imagination cannot do anything with knowledge that is in the library; they require knowledge to be in the memory. Now this puts it too crudely, of course, but I want only to emphasize the somewhat unfashionable idea that the Romantic curriculum will be rich in detailed and varied content that students will be required to learn.

Sketching these principles, I have been conscious of trying to defend my position on the one hand against those who want the curriculum to be devoted to "job-ready skills," to quote a local catchphrase, and on the other hand against academic purists who are suspicious of anything Romantic as too like entertainment to involve serious academic work. But I think that the curriculum I have begun to sketch will do a better job of teaching useful knowledge and skills and will also better prepare for sophisticated academic work. Single-minded devotion to "job-ready skills" is a recipe for vocational redundancy in a decade or so, at a terrible cost to the intellectual resources of the individual. Single-minded devotion to academic study engenders narrowness of mind, dullness of soul, and what Whitehead called "the shadow of the crammer" (1967, p. 21).

Early adolescence is commonly a time of intense and vivid emotional life, and also a time of deepest boredom and depression. Contemporary schools are often least sure in knowing how to deal with the middle school years, when the clear socializing and basic information-providing that drives the early curriculum fades and the urgency of vocational preparation does not yet give precise direction. This lack of inspiration for the curriculum can be overcome in significant degree by recognizing the importance of what I am calling Romance to students' developing understanding. Romantic understanding can give shape to the intermediate curriculum and offer the students a world that is rich, complex, varied, and as intense and vivid as their own emotional lives.

At the beginning of this section I mentioned that students at about age eight experience a transition year between Mythic and Romantic understanding and suggested that their curriculum be designed to stimulate and assist that transition. I can now indicate briefly what that year's curriculum might look like. The major curriculum segments of the Mythic curriculum would remain in place, though their teaching would increasingly conform with the Romantic model. The smaller segments discussed in this section would be introduced, so the Brief Lives segment, the focus on transcendent qualities and on stimulating wonder, on presenting extremes of experience and limits of the natural world, would each have a quarter-hour or so of class time a couple of days each week. Throughout the curriculum the focus will be on Mythic understanding being brought, as it were, within the constraints of reality.

Philosophic Understanding

One implication of this theory is that the curriculum of the last two years or so of secondary schooling and the undergraduate years at college or university should have something in common. Having something in common implies not that the last years of secondary schooling are simply a preparation for college or university but rather that the characteristics of Philosophic understanding will be recognized in both curricula.

One evident hurdle to Philosophic understanding is the inability of so many students to grasp the point or significance of abstract ideas. This is not considered a problem, however, by those who see themselves as practical people engaging in practical things; they tend not to place any value on acquiring the abstract languages framed to deal with an order that underlies surface diversity. When such people are powerful in government, education departments, and legislatures, pressures mount for an increasingly down-to-earth, real-world curriculum. Abstractions and theories are seen as idle, ivory-tower indulgences removed from the gritty reality of sensible life. Yet inadequate development of Philosophic understanding leaves students not only unaware of the practical power of abstract theoretic thinking but also pretty well defenceless against any appealing Philosophic scheme, whether it be Nazi or Marxist or modern variants thereof. Inadequately educated minds are vulnerable to simplistic ideas; such vulnerability is improper in the citizenry of a democracy.

A curriculum that embodies Philosophic principles may well seem alien to the needs and backgrounds of many students who have no plans for further education. I realize that I focus on developing familiarity with ideas at a time when many educational institutions, and interested others, including parents and the students themselves, are looking to more deliberate vocational preparation. While I might be able to get away with the claim that the

Romantic curriculum and teaching methods will be better able to deliver the skills and knowledge the everyday working world requires, it would seem implausible to suggest that intensive Philosophic study will better prepare one for routine work. How then do I justify its place in the curriculum of those going directly into jobs requiring only basic literacy and some common sense?

First, this curriculum is proposed not for the typical senior secondary student of today but rather for the student who has already followed a systematic Mythic and Romantic program of study. Second, effective citizenship in a democracy requires some Philosophic understanding, even if such understanding is not necessary for the bulk of lower-paid service and manufacturing jobs; that is, education for democratic citizenship must involve more than vocational preparation, while it nevertheless supports vocational preparation (a point Dewey makes elaborately [1966]). Third, it may well be that many students can develop only rudimentary Philosophic understanding in the final years of secondary schooling; some is better than none, and education need not stop with school. Fourth, the development of kinds of understanding is not restricted to advanced academic students. Finally, education is not merely about preparing for jobs.

Even if these justifications are grudgingly allowed, the main obstacle to Philosophic understanding for most students today is how few are able to have the intensive contacts with Philosophic communities that are necessary to stimulate, develop, and support it. Individual teachers will here and there provide some hint of such a community, but the ethos of the typical secondary school is not animated by much in the way of Philosophic excitement. And even for those students who do attend colleges and universities, a large proportion seem motivated to do so because these are assumed to be the routes to better jobs. Whatever Philosophic community may be alive in those institutions is commonly avoided by such students, who are also inclined to complain that their studies are not directed precisely enough to the practical aspects of the jobs they are aiming for and are "too theoretical."

I suspect, and hope, that a clearer sense of Philosophic understanding might make it easier for us to create the appropriate kinds of communities, both in senior secondary schools and in colleges and universities. The problem, I think, is that these institutions are not theoretical enough. Now, I realize that is a dangerous way to put it. What I mean is that, at present, the rather haphazard introduction of theoretical abstractions leaves students bewildered; they are inadequately prepared for theoretic thinking because they have experienced no systematic Romantic understanding, and they consequently fail to recognize how flexible theoretic abstractions can provide the mind with the greatest and most powerful tool for practical activity. It is the 229 vague, half-grasped, undeveloped "theory" that is inert, enervating, and removed from practical reality.

The energetic combatants in colleges and universities debating the relevance of the Western "canon" are reluctant to recognize that for most students whatever result emerges is largely irrelevant. Most students, collecting their C and B and even A grades, make so little contact with the animating ideas that undergird their studies that the actual content hardly matters, except for purely practical and vocational purposes. Pierre Bourdieu et al. (1994) make a similar argument in *Academic Discourse;* while the academic left and right bicker over whether the curriculum is too traditional or too radical, they fail to recognize that most students absorb so little of academic culture that the bickering is largely irrelevant. The malaise of higher education is that so few students see the point of it. This scheme is designed to make the point a bit clearer to those involved in the enterprise and to enable them to design curricula and teach so that more students can more easily come to see the point of Philosophic understanding.

I will begin with the transition year, dedicated to the stimulation and early development of Philosophic understanding. This should be offered at around age fifteen and will be somewhat distinct from the Romantic curriculum that precedes it and the Philosophic that follows. In general, it will involve a shift in focus away from the wonderful and toward the systematic; students will come to recognize themselves as agents constrained by the processes that determine the workings of the world. The Romantic quarter-hour focus on transcendent qualities will shift over the year to a focus on ideas. Whereas students earlier learned about some human quality through dramatic events of people's lives, now the central focus becomes the nature of the quality itself; from seeing dramatic examples of courage or compassion we turn to consider the nature of courage or compassion. We might change the name of the segment from Human Qualities to Ideas to signify this shift in focus.

Similarly, the segment devoted to Brief Lives might be changed to People and Their Theories. Whereas at the beginning of the year we might consider Bentham and his remarkable career and achievements (not to mention his mummified body moldering very gradually till the 1960s or 1970s in its display case in the University of London), by the end of the year we will consider Bentham's theory of Utilitarianism. A quarter-hour account of Utilitarianism might seem absurd, but the purpose is dramatic presentation of the main features of the theory rather than systematic study of the theory itself. Such segments should retain a tie to the theoreticians' lives, preserve some sense of narrative, and capture the dramatic nature of a very wide range of theories—social, physical, cosmological, weird, utopian, you name it. As earlier, the teacher might present some theories, and students either individually or in small groups might research and present other theories, and other teachers, parents, visitors, might describe or advocate yet other ideas. Sometimes, of course, segments may revisit and discuss previously presented theories or ideas, or to present countertheories or conflicting ideas. The aim is to present theories clearly and dramatically so that they will be accessible even to the less intellectually gifted students.

The gradual move toward theoretic abstraction will characterize the whole curriculum of the transition year. If students are to study transportation during this year, for example, we will use many Romantic principles in organizing the topic, but we will also deliberately introduce a number of very general ideas. If we are considering developments in transportation over time, we might liken the earth to a kettle heating up, on which things begin gradually to pick up speed and various forms of transportation, allied to growing populations, enable more and more people to travel faster and faster around the globe until they bubble and boil off into space. Well, not the greatest idea, but an example of how even a simple theory-like simile can introduce a dimension of general ordering to varied and complex phenomena. Study of forms of life might move to introduction of the Gaia hypothesis —the idea that the whole earth should be considered a single living organism. This is the point in a student's life at which one might get the maximum intellectual mileage out of such theories.

Teachers for the subsequent years can then assume that students will be disposed to engage knowledge presented in this way, as well as in Mythic and Romantic ways, and that students will be open increasingly to Ironic hints and doubts. The gradual move indicated above, from people and humanized events to ideas and theories, is one that will be mirrored in all curriculum areas; in some cases it will result in a change in focus, as in choice of appropriate literature, but in others, such as science, both the topics and their treatment will undergo a more radical shift through the year toward the kind of curriculum I will describe below.

The most general Philosophic principle that will serve as a criterion for selection of curriculum content is the search for general laws that operate "behind" phenomena. The Philosophic curriculum will be shaped by two divergent impulses resulting from this principle. One will lead to more discipline-oriented content than in previous years because most theories and general organizing schemes have been worked out in the particular disciplines; if that's what we want, there's where we'll find them. The second will point toward general schemes that reach across disciplines, looking always for more general theories, complex causal networks and connections among theories located in particular disciplines. We will want to respond   231 both to increased disciplinary inquiry and to an increased impulse to inter-disciplinary inquiry.

One response to this latter impulse is to introduce a new and substantial curriculum segment called something like Theory of Knowledge—to choose a term used in the current International Baccalaureate program—or Metaknowledge. It would be dedicated to very general, interdisciplinary inquiries, as well as metalevel questions about particular disciplines and their theories. That is, it would encourage a level of reflexive inquiry about all the other things the students are studying. This segment might be introduced during the transition year but would play a more central role for the remainder of the secondary school years.

Metaknowledge would obviously overlap with the brief segments on Ideas and Theories but it would differ from them in that it would involve a systematic and detailed exploration of fewer ideas. The danger of calling it simply Philosophy is that it would be influenced by university philosophy courses that do not routinely explore the most general ideas in psychology, sociology, cosmology, morality, anthropology, and connections among them. The aim is not a careful analytic study of past philosophers' arguments—though these may occasionally be relevant—but rather is to open up the world of ideas at its most general and, dare I say, intoxicating level. This engagement, after an adequate Romantic curriculum, should indeed carry with it an excitement not common in schools today.

The training feature of this curriculum segment is one that has been long established in French senior secondary schools, where one of the rites of passage has involved a four-hour essay to be written on a philosophical question; some recent examples include: Is passion compatible with wisdom? Can a work of art be considered immoral? Does knowledge inhibit the imagination? To be able to perform this daunting task, French students are trained largely in rhetorical skills, such as how to construct and present an argument about abstract ideas. They learn how to use such formal organizing techniques as thesis—antithesis—synthesis and others that should help political discourse in a democracy. I am far from proposing wholesale adoption of the French model, though it has obvious virtues—philosophy students all remember the question on which they wrote their "bac-philo" essay. The subject for Metaknowledge, though, would not be techniques for dealing with abstract questions, which can stimulate a precocious virtuosity, so much as chewing on the thesis of general arguments such as Karl Popper's *Open Society and its Enemies* or Allan Bloom's *The Closing of the American Mind* or Giambattista Vico's *The New Science*.

I should emphasize again that the purpose of this kind of abstract study is not to carry the mind away from concrete particularity—quite the opposite. Recall Hayek's argument that abstractions are necessary for identifying concrete particulars. These general thematic abstractions bring into recognition and under control a wider and more varied range of concrete facts, events, and phenomena, and it will be in terms of these that most of the discussion and inquiry goes forward.

The languages and literatures curriculum would focus on development of appropriate Philosophic language, not simply in the sense of vocabulary development but also in the elaboration of ideas through engagement of the imagination. A writer who exemplifies this is Jorge Louis Borges, whose *Inquisitions, Labyrinths,* and other works show how a literature of ideas brings sharply into recognition vivid concrete events and objects, whether Argentinian gauchos or mythical lotteries that determine history. Perhaps influenced by their philosophic studies, French and German authors commonly write fiction animated by ideas; one thinks immediately of Camus as an example accessible to students.

The study of literature is in danger when its quarrelsome old antagonist, philosophy, is around. The danger is that the literature will be displaced by the ideas. Certainly this has tended to be common in universities, where reading enjoyable books and talking about them seems so unlike anything one could justify being paid for. In fact, upon its introduction in the university curriculum in the nineteenth century, literature was promptly displaced by a rigorous philology on the desks of the more hard-minded professors. It is commonly displaced today by any number of ideological interests, by various forms of deconstruction and postmodernism, and by something generally and quaintly called "theory." The fashionable displacers will change and literature will survive, but the call for a Philosophic understanding of literature might seem to support these kinds of displacement. No, what I am calling for is a study of literature that helps to develop ideas, not a study of ideas that helps to displace literature. "Great" literature will be useful because, as I noted earlier with respect to Wordsworth, one dimension of greatness is the involvement of all kinds of understanding. As students develop Philosophic understanding, we might note a shift of focus from the drama and events of Hamlet, to give another example—will Hamlet kill his uncle before the uncle kills him?—to the ideas and motives that animate Hamlet, or from the tensions Jane Austen creates among her characters to the ways in which social conventions undergird the relationships. The shift involves the addition of a dimension of understanding that can enrich one's experience of the text.

The way in which development of theoretic abstractions brings a wider range of concrete particulars into sharp focus may be made evident also in the history curriculum. Philosophic understanding will not only draw us toward metahistories and the potent generalizations that bring some order and 233 meaning across as wide a range of events as possible, but it thereby returns us to detailed events, facts, and concrete particulars that further support or undermine generalizations and metahistorical schemes. When studying, say, medieval knights and the crusades, we will constantly seek to set the details in wider contexts. Elaborating these will require gathering further detailed knowledge: about armaments and therefore metallurgy at the time, about inheritance laws that survive into this period of increasing food production and population growth and their influence on the prospects and behavior of younger sons, or about the early development of capital accumulation. That is, what the drive to form general historical schemes does is bring into meaningful recognition a range of concrete detail that would have had little Romantic appeal. Whatever the historical topic being studied, the Philosophic principle will direct us to the content that allows us to construct potent generalizations.

If we use the principle to select the most appropriate topics for the history curriculum, we will turn to those that already have been organized by some strong and clear general scheme. A book like Tawney's *Religion and the Rise of Capitalism* (1926) might alert us to include such a topic for study, beginning with Tawney's dramatic argument (that the individualism and work ethic fostered by Calvinist Protestantism led to the development of an efficient workforce, industrial growth, and capitalism in northern Europe). The purpose is to stimulate a Philosophic understanding of history and imaginative engagement with the details. The thesis of Tawney's book, and of many like it, may be wrong in all kinds of ways, but they are right for students at this age as stimulants to a further dimension of historical understanding. In building support or doubts about some general scheme, students will have to engage in studying details and weighing their significance in light of some more general meaning. We may regret the immense generality and drama of the theories to be focused on, particularly in the first couple of years of Philosophic engagements, but these form the route to increasingly precise and supportable claims, to seeing just what the problems are with these metahistorical schemes, to development of analytic rigor in research, and to making more sophisticated sense of history. To try to skip what some academic historians consider as a regrettable kind of historical study is to neglect development of a level of historical understanding that leads to more general meaning than that x or y happened.

Through college and university years, the history curriculum will gradually focus on increasingly particular topics, though students will persistently be challenged to form, defend, and undermine general schemes. None of this leads to prescribing particular eras or arenas of history. The main superficial difference from typical history curricula today might be the choice of which general ideological schemes or metahistories are prominent. A segment of the history curriculum might be devoted to ongoing discussion about general trends in history. Are we studying a Thucydidean tragic process or an organic rise and fall of civilizations? Are we driven by economic forces working themselves out through class or national competition, or have we come to "the end of history"? Does history consist of just one damn thing after another? Are the patterns we see our own constructions in hindsight or are they reflected from historical events themselves?

Science is the "natural" Philosophic subject. Science grew in the historical program of developing Philosophic understanding and has remained its ideal embodiment, dedicated to capturing the nature of things in a theoretic language. But given the pedagogical rule that universal dullness buries all, one of the peculiarities of the science curriculum and teaching when students are in their the late teens is the common rejection of theoretic excitement in favor of the accumulation of facts. This is particularly evident in universities, where the first couple of years of most science programs are taken up with cramming basic knowledge seen as prerequisite to approaching the realm of general and disputed theories. The more general and speculative theories in any discipline are treated like an unconventional and disreputable relation who, even though the children find her exciting and entertaining, must be kept hidden from view, her very existence denied as long as possible. So the main pedagogical engine for engaging the late teenager with science is shut away, and allowed to peek out only later when the conventionalized and dulled students who remain may be assumed to be inoculated against her wiles. A common result is that the more imaginative students, who might enormously enjoy scientific study and contribute significantly to the enterprise, are disenchanted and repelled.

Well, that's maybe a too jaundiced view, but it is one supported too commonly by the programs I have seen and by undergraduate students who say they are waiting for all the details to make sense but who for now must continue to cram in the details. Perhaps stimulated, too, by memories of a Physics teacher who would carefully steer us away from anything interesting to the class, with a pursed-lipped smile that suggested these were matters to be approached by initiates only after years of grim toil. So the dramatic, speculative, and contentious theories will be up-front in the early years of our Philosophic science curriculum. Investigation of the contentious questions will carry the students to the detailed studies that are currently presented in a contextless fashion.

Similarly in the social sciences, the first university courses in psychology, sociology, and anthropology are not the forums for getting the basic tools and facts in place; rather, they provide the opportunity to deal with the   235 most general theoretical disputes in those disciplines. Psychology programs often begin by teaching about human behavior in a way that presupposes the appropriateness of the cognitive science program or, a little while ago, the behaviorist program. I suggest, on the contrary, that raising the problems with these programs provides the way in to the study of the psyche. What are the competing theories about how to understand the psyche, or society, or human behavior? What evidence supports these different theories? How can one assess this evidence? What further information would help one theory or another?

These comments are obviously not designed to fill out a detailed curriculum but to show how the characterization of Philosophic understanding yields principles that direct us to one kind of curriculum rather than another. For the natural and social sciences, they point toward a curriculum that will begin with the most general and contentious theories and work from them to expose in a meaningful way a range of new concrete particulars. As the years go by, we can assume that students will have the range of theoretical understanding well developed so that new, detailed content can be introduced without undue concern about its being located theoretically. Students will absorb content into increasingly sophisticated theoretical positions or will see it as anomalous and, as such, particularly valuable in requiring adjustments to accepted theories and in stimulating the development of Ironic understanding.

Our Philosophic curriculum, then, will start from the most general theoretic dimension of any area of study—whether that be molecular biology or selling real estate. The engine of theoretic understanding is fueled by the interaction between general theory and the range of particulars it opens up— the facts, events, and experiments that support or challenge it. The product of Philosophic understanding in any area is flexibility and power in dealing with particulars, and this applies to real estate no less than to molecular biology.

Philosophic understanding has been discussed here largely in utilitarian terms, but as with each of these kinds of understanding, it has what is perhaps best described as a spiritual dimension. The distance is usually quite large between the interests of the paymasters of the educational system and the spiritual culture that education at its best cultivates. The problems this distance creates for educators, insofar as the Philosophic curriculum is concerned, is well put by George Elder Davie: "a consumer society . . . is interested in science only for its material fruits, and . . . has neither patience with, nor understanding of, the spiritual activity responsible in the last resort for the thing which gives rise to the useful inventions, i.e. the disinterested research and the detached play of mind which criticizes ideas" (1986, p. 87).

Organizing curricula and teaching for examinations, and the everyday business of school, college and university work, can cause us to neglect this spiritual aim no less than can the narrow interests of a consumer society. Disinterested study and the detached play of mind are fruits of Philosophic understanding and of the engagement with theoretic abstractions. They may not be absolutes, and we may not expect students to be absolutely disinterested and detached, but we can encourage greater or less disinterest and detachment in our choice of curriculum and in the manner of teaching; greater seems better.

It may seem odd to touch on university curricula without engaging the virulent arguments about the "Western canon." I am suggesting that questions like these are exactly what the curriculum should include. In order to assess the merits of the arguments, students will have to sample the literature of the Western canon in detail and consider other literatures as well—this goes for the African-American or Asian-British student no less than for the Anglo-Saxon. The energy stimulated by the general argument is what fuels pursuit of relevant details and careful reading.

I can hardly pretend that the canon Kulturkampf is irrelevant to the Philosophic curriculum. In general, it seems to me inevitable, if one wants to develop Philosophic and Ironic understanding, that the inquiries and their products that generated these kinds of understanding in the first place form a significant part of the curriculum, which means that the Western tradition and its disciplines are inescapable. Now, clearly, there are many ways of being, and becoming, educated, and the neoconservative insistence on replication of a traditional canon is, in terms of the arguments in this book so far, unjustifiably narrow. But radical assertions of the irrelevance of the Western canon to adequate education are also, in terms of my argument, unjustifiably arbitrary.

CONCLUSION

Critics of the presently dominant curriculum often hark back to a better past—presumably the one that produced them or their own greatly admired teachers. Gary Wills, a conservative American journalist, notes with anguish and something like anger or despair the rise of such subjects as women's studies and black studies, and points out that at African-American universities, such as Fisk in Nashville, the curriculum at the beginning of the twentieth century included Tacitus and Horace in Latin, and Sophocles and the Bible in Greek. He wonders how it can be considered progress to change 237 from this to current vogues like "ecological ethics" and other fashionable discipline-less topics.

Gerald Graff has investigated what the old classical curriculum so prized by conservatives actually involved. Students studied only "a small portion of any text, dwelling in class on minutiae of pronunciation, etymology, moods and tenses, and points of classical philology" (1987, p. 28). He evokes many witnesses to the mindlessness of the classics as usually taught. It is unfortunate that the classics curriculum was justified in terms of faculty psychology, Latin and Greek being valued as hard subjects because hard intellectual work was supposed to develop faculties of the mind much as hard exercise developed muscles of the body. We might recall Hazlitt's comment again: "Anyone who has passed through the regular gradations of a classical education, and is not made a fool by it, may consider himself as having had a very narrow escape" (1951, p. 147).

But while it might seem easy to scoff at the educational value of Latin and Greek for a microtechnologized world awash with drugs and plagued by violence, even the most radical cannot avoid a nagging doubt that the progressivist program that made the curriculum increasingly "relevant" to students' lives has been profoundly unsatisfactory. In fact, the more urgently "relevant" the curriculum has been made, the more generally clueless seem its products.

What I am taking from the classical curriculum is the recognition that, in some significant degree, knowledge forms the mind, but I am arguing that it does not do so in the simplistic way assumed by traditionalist educational thinkers who draw on Plato. From the more radical curriculum, I am taking the recognition that the mind is also formed by the intellectual procedures developed in the process of learning. We cannot, however, rely on some developmental regularities to support this process as assumed by progressivist and radical educational thinkers who draw on Rousseau. The curriculum I have outlined here draws on principles derived from the distinctive kinds of understanding. It leads students by a somewhat unconventional route to, what seems to me, a more abundantly educated life.

8

Some Implications
for Teaching

INTRODUCTION

If education is reconceived as the process of developing each of these kinds
of understanding as abundantly as possible, how should we reconceive the
role of the teacher and the practice of teaching to accord with this new conception?

Each of the three old educational ideas considered in the first chapter
implies a somewhat different sense of the proper role of the teacher and of
the practice of teaching. Inherited from the socializing tradition is the sense
of the teacher as an initiator and role model whose primary responsibility is
to guide the students into the norms, values, skills, and knowledge that will
enable them to approximate the ideal of adult citizenship. Inherited from the
Platonic tradition is the sense of the teacher as an authority in some area of
disciplined knowledge whose primary responsibility is to instruct and inspire students to achieve intellectual mastery with regard to that privileged
knowledge. Inherited from the Rousseauian tradition is the sense of the
teacher as a solicitous facilitator whose primary responsibility is to support
each student's individual development. The general conception of the
teacher's proper role today is made up of a mixture of these three overlapping
senses, the mix commonly varying depending on whether primary, intermediate, or secondary students are in mind. The mix will also vary, of course,
depending on the commitment of the conceiver to one or another of those
three traditions. As with the general conception of education from which
they are derived, there are problems with each of these three senses sepa-

rately, and they do not fit well together. Trying to implement all of them in some degree makes for a very tough and frustrating job.

If one considers teaching as primarily responsible for evoking, stimulating, and developing kinds of understanding, how does this sense of teaching differ from the three above? That is what I will try to convey in this chapter. The somewhat different kinds of understanding also imply differences of their own for teaching; trying primarily to develop Mythic understanding, for example, will involve one in some different approaches, emphases, and activities than if one is trying primarily to develop Philosophic or any other kind of understanding. I will, then, discuss teaching in five sections, focusing on each of the kinds of understanding in turn.

As formal education has been a prominent concern in this book, I will again emphasize Mythic, Romantic, and Philosophic teaching, and will consider these from the point of view of teachers in typical educational institutions. I will assume that the implications mainly to be teased out here are those that apply to an adult who has responsibility for educating thirty children in a class. Except for the first short section on Somatic understanding, I will deal only briefly with those implications that might be drawn from the theory for the parent concerned with educating one or a few children, though I trust a number of implications will be fairly clear. I will also touch only briefly on implications for continuing and elaborating one's own education in the various kinds of understanding, though, again, I trust that a number of these will be clear.

The trick here, then, is to move from the level of theory to principles for teaching and from there to the level of practical technique. In each of the three central sections I will begin with the technique, constructing a planning framework for teaching from the characteristics of each kind of understanding proposed by the theory. I will then discuss the principles that undergird the framework, and give an example of how the framework can be applied to some particular topic. This chapter is not intended to be an extensive exploration of the theory's implications for teaching practice, but rather a demonstration that it does have clear and distinctive practical implications.

One general principle is that the best kind of teaching will always be "outward looking." That is, if we bear in mind that these kinds of understanding are not discrete stages but coalesce in a significant degree, then, while primarily teaching to develop, say, Mythic understanding, we should try also to include some stimulus to Romantic, and even Philosophic and Ironic, understanding. For example, in chapter 7 I discussed the value of humor in the development of language and Mythic intellectual tools. I drew on some of the jokes Lewis Carroll uses in the Alice books. These are jokes with clear Mythic appeal, but they also have Romantic, Philosophic, and

Ironic resonances. These "outward" resonances—the dimensions of meaning below the surface—make them more educationally valuable than other equally funny but "dimensionless" jokes. I am not suggesting that the more constrained focus on developing a particular kind of understanding is inadequate, but simply that this general principle recommends that the teacher be alert to introduce resonances of subsequent kinds of understanding in teaching any topic.

This general principle might be clarified by relating it to another of Vygotsky's rich ideas: that of "zones of proximal development" (Vygotsky, 1978, pp. 84–91). Vygotsky distinguishes between the developmental level a student seems to be at measured by the tasks the student can successfully perform alone, and the developmental level that is evident when the student performs tasks with the assistance of others. The zone between these two measures, Vygotsky argues, needs to be taken into account when assessing students' development, and teachers should focus much of their effort in this zone so that students' learning can draw forward their development. The "outward looking" teaching that is implied by the theory in this book shares with Vygotsky's idea the importance of engaging students in intellectual activity in their zones of proximal development. My principle differs, however, in two ways: first, the image of the zone is not so much a distance on a linear scale as a space for expansion in all directions outward from a central node; second, I call for a deliberate teaching effort to *extend* the zone, even if only sporadically and tenuously, into the most advanced kinds of understanding. Students may grasp only the haziest hint of the more distant resonances set off by such teaching, but that does not matter. Its purpose is to create a dimension toward which the student's understanding may grasp. Ah, these inadequate spatial metaphors.

Somatic Understanding

The infant's development of Somatic understanding largely recapitulates evolutionary adaptations, but, of course, this recapitulation, to be most adequately achieved, needs to be supported by parents and other caregivers. The significant difference between the modern infant's recapitulation and the historical evolutionary adaptations is that we now have a sense of the direction in which we want the infant to develop intellectually. It may just have been a set of cultural contingencies that led to high literate irony, but in interacting with the infant we will attend selectively to stimulate and support the development of capacities that will optimally prepare the infant for an Ironic destiny. This observation needs the immediate qualifier that we must   241 not attend to literacy-directed developments to the exclusion of the range of capacities proper to Somatic understanding. A balance is to be sought, rather than a shallow and febrile precocity.

Somatic understanding primarily results from the infant's mind discovering its body. In the process, the infant learns to use the body to carry out his or her purposes; reciprocally, the infant discovers through the activity of the body and of the world's responses to its actions what range of purposes can be formed and carried out, and, relatedly again, discovers the body as a source of purposes. This Somatic exploration sets the foundational development of understanding, particularly by building the framework of space, time, causality, effort and response, the rhythms of hunger and satiety, pleasure and pain, and so on. Prominent, too, is the discovery of one's social nature through the patterns of communication, care, and affection that recapitulate evolutionary adaptations and become shaped into particular cultural patterns. These foundations of all future understanding are in significant part laid in activities commonly referred to as play. Play has sometimes been described as a rehearsal, preparing for real and serious learning later on, but it might better be seen as the most serious learning in which we engage, on whose success all later learning depends. (Huizinga, in *Homo Ludens* [1949], represents civilization as play prolonged into adult life.) This is not a call to bring earnest pedagogies to bear on infants' play; my point simply reflects an ironic recognition of the proper association between the serious and the playful in place of the common confusion of the serious with the grim.

Somatic understanding develops most typically and abundantly till about two and a half years, at which time it cedes some of its energy to Mythic developments. But Somatic understanding does not properly cease to develop at that point. While it diminishes after the early years, though perhaps experiencing a resurgence in puberty, it can be deliberately extended in small ways throughout life. The fifty-five-year-old who learns to somersault when diving from a low springboard into a pool (see your physiotherapist before, or after, attempting this), or, less dramatically, decides to begin using his or her nondominant hand for eating, brushing teeth, cleaning, occasional writing, etc., or learns at last to whistle melifluously will continue to extend Somatic understanding in some degree.

Let me indicate briefly how one might support Somatic development while attending to the direction of subsequent kinds of understanding. "Rhythm is a uniquely human attribute; no other creature spontaneously tracks and imitates rhythms in the way humans do, without training" (Donald, 1991, p. 186). Rhythms in sound are fundamental to language use, and some of the more subtle rhythms, even to the time taken in breathing in and out, are intricately involved in the grammar of human languages. We are evolutionarily programmed for language, and the grammars of all human languages have much in common, so much, indeed, that a visiting alien would conclude we all speak dialects of a basic Earthspeak (Pinker, 1994). Very early, we begin to track the rhythms of our local speech community, attending to them even in the womb. So, while learning a language is supported by predispositions, parents can enrich the process by frequent and varied vocal interactions with infants. Everyday grammatical speech can play a prominent part in such interactions, but so can rhythmic language-play, songs, clicks, squeaks, whistles, and occasional harmonizing with the infant's own sounds. Counting is another rhythmic use of language that parents can use in creating rituals, like counting the steps going upstairs or removing toys from a box. The infant follows the rhythmic sounds related to certain actions, preparing already for later consciousness of abstractions.

The fascination of people like Victor, "the wild boy of Aveyron" (Itard, 1962; Lane, 1976), or "feral children" who spend their early years cut off from language-using environments, lies in part in our wonder at what human consciousness is like without being shaped by language. Whatever intellectual tools feral children develop, they do not include the post-Somatic set discussed in this book, except perhaps in the most embryonic way. In contrast, it would seem that the richer the linguistic environment in which Somatic understanding develops, the better the young mind is prepared for the further kinds of understanding available in high literate cultures. This early emphasis on the rhythms of language should not displace energetic exploration of the body and its purposes, nor is it aimed at precocious verbalization approximating adult norms as early as possible. Given the direction in which we are particularly concerned to stimulate development, an environment that is rich and varied in the sounds humans make to build meanings is educationally important.

As rhythm is to the ear, so pattern is to the eye. The two interact, of course, but "visual thinking is now seen as largely autonomous from language" (Arnheim, 1974, p. 167). By the age of two months, the infant will shift its focus of visual attention to follow that of an adult, looking across a room, for example, in the direction the adult is looking (Scaife and Bruner, 1975; Churcher and Scaife, 1982). This indicates something of how early we recognize other people's distinct deployment of vision. The one-year-old can begin with colored markers on paper or card, leaving a record of bodily movement. A parent can begin to introduce patterns, letting the infant explore shapes and colors and whatever patterns can be constructed. All man- 243 ner of gesturing and pointing games can enlarge the infant's grasp of how to coordinate bodily movement and vision to communicate and interpret meaning.

The parent can provide stimuli as rich as possible for the infant's exploration of the body, its possibilities and purposes. Coordination of the senses into patterned behavior can be encouraged by relating, say, rhythms of sound with bodily movements, beginning with moving arms to a song and leading to dance, or by introducing rituals—regularities of behavior that have significance and impose meaningful patterns on time.

I concluded the earlier discussion of Ironic understanding by emphasizing that it is grounded in Somatic understanding, that all our understanding is ultimately rooted in our material being. Our body, then, is where we start from in our exploration of the world and experience. We begin, as it were, by our minds expanding throughout our bodies and then from our bodies out into the world. Later teaching success, therefore, should be sought not so much in getting knowledge into the student's mind but rather in enabling the student's mind to expand into the knowledge. This is perhaps a trite way of condensing the point, but teachers who recognize that difference can transform their practice. Let us go on to consider how.

Mythic Understanding

This section focuses on how teachers of children from preschool years to about age eight can shape and present knowledge so that it is meaningful and imaginatively engaging and so that it stimulates and develops Mythic understanding. I will begin with the set of intellectual tools discussed in chapter 2—such as abstract and affective binary opposites, metaphor, images, and story-structuring and draw from these some principles for teaching. From these principles I will then construct a framework that could be used to plan a lesson or set of lessons on a topic. The framework is designed as a set of questions whose answers should produce an effective lesson or unit plan. I will exemplify the use of this framework in planning some lessons on "The Properties of the Air," which a local curriculum recommends as an appropriate science topic for the first years of schooling.

I will start with the struts of the framework and briefly discuss the principles on which they rest, and then work through the example. Organizing the topic in this way will, no doubt, be more formal than a parent's thinking 244 about how to explain something to a child, and perhaps more formal than many experienced teachers might prefer, but the underlying principles can be drawn out and used more informally and casually by those who wish.

Mythic Planning Framework

1. Identifying Importance

What is important about this topic? What is affectively engaging about it?
The difficult part here, or at least the unfamiliar part for many teachers, is the requirement that one identify what one finds moving about any given topic oneself. We are not so much to think about the topic as to dwell on it with our emotions alert. Commonly, when we think about what children will find interesting, we can fall into a patronizing view in which we neglect what is emotionally important about the topic for us. Remember that Mythic understanding is not something we leave behind as we grow older; it remains properly a part of our understanding. So when we locate something with a significant affective tug for ourselves, we have a good starting point from which to teach the topic to children. We do not, after all, want to introduce trivial features of the topic to them; the most important features will better engage their imaginations and develop their Mythic understanding of their world. (By going for what we find truly important about a topic, we can at least counter the insidious trivialization of childhood and of early childhood education, in which a sanitized and prettified conception of the world and human experience is considered all that children can and should understand.) This first step is the hardest of the planning process, but if it is done well, the rest will follow relatively easily.

How can we apply this principle to the topic of "Properties of the Air" for a class of six-year-olds? What is important about the air we breathe and walk through unhindered. The point is not to find some "correct" answer or even the best answer, but to find something that has some affective charge for you and is a good answer. That the air sustains our lives is, of course, an obvious point of importance to us, but, put that way, we are reaching a rather simple logical conclusion, not locating an affective core. If we were to take a "chunk" of air, such as that which fills the classroom, what have we got? The air is full of noises, somehow, of waves and particles, smells, living things, and decayed flakes of skin. If we could just change the scale of things or what the eyes can see, instead of empty, featureless air we could show children that the air is full of wonders with seemingly magical properties. In the contrast between its apparent emptiness and its actual fullness of wonders we can locate an affective charge that will provide us with our starting point.

245

2. Finding Binary Opposites

What binary concepts best capture the affective importance of the topic?
This is usually easier to answer than the previous question, though it may take a little practice to become fluent in finding appropriate oppositions. Binaries are easy to find because they should follow fairly directly from the reflection on what is affectively important about the topic. The trick here is to locate something dramatic inherent in the topic. Not drama in the sense of blood and gore, but a sense of tension, of contrasting perspectives perhaps, that can be opened up and become immediately accessible to children. This principle follows from the earlier theoretical discussion about children's intelligence and understanding being different from adults' primarily in terms of the intellectual tools being used. So this principle further disturbs the common conception of children's thinking as simple, concrete, and, as a result, trivial. Instead, the theoretical discussion emphasizes a conception of children's thinking as characterized by complexity, by powerful affective and abstract concepts, and by a likeness to adult thinking with regard to the intellectual tools of Mythic understanding. The search for the binary concepts should not be a search "out there" for logical divisions one can make in the topic but should, rather, continue the internal search of the teacher's own emotional organization of the topic.

In the case of our example, the initial feeling about what was important leads us fairly easily to the binary set empty/full, "empty" here carrying the affective sense of dull, without interest, an undifferentiated lack, an absence of content in the air, and "full" carrying affective associations with richness, variety, and magical plenitude.

3. Organizing the Content into a Story Form

3.1 First Teaching Event

What content most dramatically embodies the binary concepts, in order to provide access to the topic? What image best captures that content and its dramatic contrast?
We now need to clothe our conclusions to the previous stages of the framework in the content of our topic. The first part of story-shaping the content of our topic involves locating some dramatic incident, character, or idea that provides immediate access to the topic by making vividly clear at the beginning some aspect of its basic affective meaning. This story-shaping does not require us to find some fictional story to convey the point of the lesson. I mean by "story" what the newspaper editor means when she or he asks "What's the story on this?" We want to know its affective meaning within a

narrative context that orients our understanding to the content—whether it is a "story" involving incidents and people, or a scientific discovery, or a natural phenomenon.

Our lesson or unit will be a narrative in a causal sequence, beginning with a conflict or problem that is elaborated or complicated in the middle and concluding with some resolution of the initial conflict or problem. Making the lesson or unit a story rather than a logically structured presentation of knowledge implies that the meaning to be conveyed has an affective component. Our first teaching event follows from the teacher asking not what are his or her objectives but rather what is the dramatic true story to be told—be it about earthworms, the weather, decimalization, or punctuation. Obviously this does not exclude the possibility of using a fictional story to introduce our topic, if that satisfies the requirements of this principle, but my concern here is with teaching academic content using some story ingredients rather than telling stories about academic content.

We might begin teaching about properties of the air by switching on a radio in one corner of the room and listening for a moment to voices. Then, turning the radio off, the teacher could carry it to another part of the classroom, change the channel, and switch it on again, listening for a few moments to music. How do the music and voices get into the radio? Where do they come from? A number of the children will likely have asked their parents such questions, and the teacher can begin by harvesting and clarifying the answers. Then the teacher might ask, what does the air in the room look like to the radio that can only see radio waves? The teacher at this point might switch on the radio again and move it around while changing from channel to channel. The air must be full of different radio waves. To the "eye" of the radio, the walls of the room are not very significant—it can "see" through them. Alternatively, if conditions make it easy, the teacher can darken the room and shine a powerful flashlight or allow a beam of sunlight to enter, gleaming on the endless dust particles in the room. They seem to be constantly in drifting motion, and while they are usually invisible, they seem to fill the air. What are they made of? Well, 60 percent of the dust in a typical classroom is made up of decayed flakes of human skin. (We commune with each other more fundamentally than we sometimes realize.) The teacher might ask the students where they think flies defecate, and wonder what that was that just floated by. In a few minutes, the empty air can be seen to be full of a huge variety of particles of things that make up the undifferentiated dust. In both cases we underline the contrast between the assumed emptiness of the air and its actual repletion with varied, complex, and wonderful things.

3.2   Structuring the Body of the Lesson or Unit

What content best articulates the topic into a clear story form?
This section involves organizing the bulk of the content. Having sorted out
our organizing principles above, this should be relatively straightforward.
Our sense of what is affectively important and our binary concepts become
the criteria for deciding what content about the topic should be included.
The other criterion that will work with these is derived from a central principle of good storytelling. Fictional stories, if they are to be effective and
engaging, include nothing that is not relevant to working out the conflict
or problem introduced at the beginning. The state of the weather or a character's eye color or clothing are mentioned only if they contribute in some
way to building the affective meaning of the story. To the degree that irrelevant material is included, the story becomes flaccid and interest is dissi-
pated. Describing the eye color and clothing of every character, for
example, would quickly bog most stories down: each character is no doubt
clothed and has eyes of some color, but the criterion that determines
whether these should be mentioned comes from whether they advance the
plot in some way. If a novelist leaves off developing the plot when the central characters meet for the dénouement in a disused factory and begins to
describe what the factory produced, where its raw materials came from,
what the workers were like and what tasks they performed, the reader's interest will quickly wane. Similarly, in building our story-form lesson or
unit we must use as a criterion of selecting for content whatever is relevant
to elaborating and developing the binary concepts set up by our beginning;
they are to provide the basic and clear structure. So we will not include everything of relevance to the topic; "relevance" in a story-form lesson is determined by the binary concepts that catch what is affectively important
about the topic.

If the teacher thinks of the lesson or unit as more like telling a good story
than conveying a body of information, then the need to focus on how to tell
the story as crisply and vividly as possible comes to the fore rather than the
attempt to meet sets of knowledge, skills, and attitude objectives. If the story
is told well, such objectives will be met in a more meaningful context. I
should perhaps add that when I mention telling a story, this does not mean
simply that the teacher will be unvaryingly talking at the students. Trips to
museums, interviewing people in the community, building models, and so
on can all be tied into the developing storyline. What makes the lesson or
complex unit story-structured is not some fictional component but its narrative development of the central binary concepts. This makes it clear why it

matters to identify a centrally important aspect of the topic in the beginning and find sturdy binary concepts that bring out a conflict or problem: everything in the lesson or unit is going to be tied precisely to them.

How, then, will we story-structure our lessons on the properties of the air? Well, I think that is already clear. We can deal with a range of properties following the pattern of the introductory teaching event. We can find ways to help the students form images of other entities that fill the air of the classroom, focusing on, say, microbial life, gases, subatomic particles from the sun and from outside our solar system, pollutants, pollens, and perhaps even an exploration of the history of the chunk of air currently in the classroom from earliest times to the present.

4. Conclusion

What is the best way of resolving the conflict inherent in the binary concepts? What degree of mediation is it appropriate to seek? How appropriate is it to make the binary concepts explicit?

As with any story, the conclusion has to resolve or satisfy something set up in the beginning. In the case of story-form teaching, a primary focus for the concluding teaching activities will be on the binary concepts that have given structure to our lesson or unit. Sometimes the conclusion can be used to mediate the binary set, or, if one concept has been emphasized at the expense of another, the conclusion can involve switching the perspective to the neglected concept. If we bear in mind the general theoretical observation that educational development proceeds by means of the mind becoming more explicitly aware of what earlier had been implicit structural features of thinking, it will always be appropriate to reflect on whether and to what degree children should be aware of the binary concepts that have given shape to their exploration of a topic. One might retell in brief the narrative that has been followed, exposing its structural features.

The conclusion, then, is not simply where we stop because we have covered the required material; rather, it needs to have, like the ending of a good story, a quality such as James Joyce describes as an "epiphany"—in the case of our teaching, that means revelation of something about the topic that takes one's understanding further, reveals some deeper meaning, perhaps a mystery, that cannot easily be conveyed in the body of the lesson or unit. I recognize that this might seem to border on the exotic, or even to be over the border, but it punctuates what might otherwise be routine teaching with moments of rich intensity. One way of achieving such intensity might be to combine this search with the push toward some Romantic, Philosophic, or Ironic understanding.

So how might we conclude our exploration of the air? In this case the   249 empty/full binary concepts will have been quite close to the surface, if not explicit, through the unit. But the dimension of richness and wonder in the "fullness" of the air might usefully be focused on. Ask the children to sit still and close their eyes and imagine themselves shrinking and shrinking, like Alice in Wonderland. And when they have become as small as a mote, the teacher can describe the senses that will allow them to "see" and feel the air in their classroom quite differently. Either the teacher can prepare a "guided discovery" tour around the huge viruses and bacteria, the swirling winds that carry the varied and multicolored boulders of dust around, the particles flashing by, the waves of radiation from light sources, fly feces, heat from bodies, radio waves, and so on, or, alternatively, the children can describe what they can "see" after some preparation and rehearsal. If time has been spent in groups working to represent the various properties of the air, the conclusion of the unit could be the celebrous presentation of each group's "property"—bacteria, dust, gases, pollutants—to the class. The point of such an exercise is to emphasize that this amazing wonderland of unfamiliar thronging objects, life forms, and forces is the very classroom they are sitting in; unlike Alice's, it is a real wonderland.

5. Evaluation

How can one know whether the topic has been understood, its importance grasped, and the content learned?

Evaluation in this framework will focus on seeking evidence for the child's Mythic understanding of the topic. We will be looking for such things as affective engagement, imaginative involvement, and the deployment of the intellectual tools that constitute Mythic understanding. How does one measure these? Most experienced teachers would have little difficulty in most cases identifying which students experience these at varying degrees of intensity. It might be useful to develop an instrument, perhaps a simple checklist, that would help teachers to attend to the behaviors and qualities of engagement that would give some evidence of students' Mythic understanding. The instrument might alert teachers to such things as the amount of continuous time a child spends engaged in a project, the kinds of questions and comments made, the originality of the work and its evidence of metaphoric connections, the degree of commitment to a project, the recognition of the role of the binary structuring of the unit and use of it in their own work, competence and confidence in written, oral, and pictorial presentations, and the vividness, originality, and relevance of images used in oral language, in writing, and in pictorial displays. More traditional forms of evaluation and the newer qualitative procedures can be used, of course, to give evidence of the degree and extent of children's knowledge of the content.

In the case of our unit on properties of the air, the teacher might observe the ways in which children reflect their understanding through their role-playing, discussions, and their final presentations; assess the degree of understanding by their implicit or explicit deployment of the dominant binary concepts and their recognition of the richness of the "full" air; their contributions to the group project and their ability to cooperate in the process of jointly conceiving their aim; originality in their written, oral, and pictorial presentations; imaginative involvement and affective engagement in roles, in the group project, and in the final presentation; a simple test of knowledge of the properties of the air. All but the last of these can be conducted during the normal teaching/learning process of the unit.

The example given above is a sketch of a plan that might be used by a single teacher presenting a traditional subject area to a class of students. I chose this kind of example because this remains, according to extensive surveys (Goodlad, 1984), the most common style of teaching. That is, this example, and the others that will follow, do not reflect curriculum preferences, but are common topics taught routinely at these ages and help to clarify some principles of this theory for teaching. Before moving on, though, I would like to make two points. First, I should acknowledge that the most urgent affective issue concerning properties of the air these days might be its quality and its ability to suspend and distribute pollutants of varied kinds. One might, therefore, organize the unit on a pure/polluted binary set, or, more dramatically yet, on a life/death structure. These choices would, in turn, influence the content selected and the kind of story one would tell about the air.

Second, I should describe briefly the way this framework has been used by teachers who have worked most intensively with it. Much the same has occurred with the other frameworks, to be described in the rest of this chapter, so I will make this point just once here, though it refers equally to the following kinds of understanding, too.

The principles and framework seem to incline teachers to cooperate in designing integrated units of study lasting from a month or so to a whole term or semester. Between two or three to as many as seven or eight teachers plan together developing a "story" that may involve three or more classes of students. All the prescribed curriculum content will be accommodated within the overarching story structure.

In Melbourne, for example, a group of teachers prepared a term-long unit on the early Australian sheep business. The teachers and students   251 worked together to transform the classrooms, using all kinds of craft and art skills. In one room, a platform about knee height was built around two walls. When I visited recently a computer sat on a desk near one end, and other structures were in the process of going up. This room was the loading dock, from which the wool would be exported around the world. The computer operators kept track of quantities, prices, and destinations. An adjoining room was a small town, made of old milk cartons that rose to about eye level, leaving space for twisting narrow streets between offices, shops, and school. A bemused visitor to this wonderland, I was surprised as a class of children arrived, squeezing past, tossing their bags into their "office" or "shop," and getting on with the work of the day, dealing with some aspect of the social economy of the sheep. Elsewhere, no doubt, the farmers were busy with their activities.

In Winnipeg, six teachers combined their classes for a "Romantic" story of the 1920s for students of about ten and eleven years. In a section of the library the teachers performed a play, which opened with an old woman leafing through the contents of a trunk from her attic. As she takes out the objects and photographs, culled from the students' parents' or grandparents' attics and old junk shops, her reminiscences are brought to life by the other teachers. In 1920s life, the main character appears as an impetuous young woman whose adventures give rise to much worry in her family. The "play" becomes a way for the teacher-actors to recapture the spirit of the 1920s and to engage the student audience in the project of recreating what life back then was like. The students then play roles in groups, learning some aspect of 1920s life—business speculation, music, manufacturing growth, inventions, and so on—and presenting their discoveries to the other groups and to the school as a whole. Their story tells of the confident expansion of the economy, then overconfidence, then the stock market crash of 1929.

Extensive units such as these provide opportunities for teachers' own engagement and enlarges their energies; the influence of such projects also tends to spread to the rest of the school. At the same time, the students become involved with their learning in a way not common in school experience. Most of the Melbourne children will remember aspects of the wool trade throughout their lives, and most of the Winnipeg children will retain a strong association with the 1920s.

How can parents encourage the development of Mythic understanding? As oral language is central, continuing to talk with children is clearly indicated! The characteristics of Mythic understanding suggest ways to structure the conversation. Parents might practice telling their young child or children the most important thing that happened to them each day. If this narrative involves the child, so much the more engaging. Appropriate, powerful, binary concepts can build the narrative, and vivid metaphors and images can enrich its meaning and promote accessibility. A good starting point is an incident that creates an expectation that can then be confirmed or undermined by subsequent incidents. These need not be polished performances; short and simple will do. And then, parents should be prepared for questions that show surprising incomprehension on the part of children. But persistence is essential, and with the child's guidance parents can become experts quite quickly. Soliciting the child's equivalent narrative about his or her day is useful, particularly if parents ask the right questions. It can become a pleasant and easy habit.

The other range of stories that parents have to tell are about the social and natural world. If we think of the knowledge we have accumulated over millennia as conceivable in a variety of ways, and recall that it can be constituted as a set of great stories as well as a store of academic disciplines, then parents can shape knowledge about galaxies and dinosaurs or anything in the world into brief, engaging narratives.

And, of course, there are fictional stories. Which stories should we tell young children? Those with the characteristics described in chapter 2. Children's taste is no less varied from child to child than is adults', so we should explore a range of stories. Let the children's response—as well as our own sense of what is affectively important and valuable—be our guide.

A story time each day, perhaps at bedtime, clearly has many benefits in addition to the educational ones. We tend to be so dependent on books and TV that few of us have confidence that we *can* tell a story. But I encourage every parent to try. Perhaps read a story to yourself first, and run through it in your head. Then, cuddled in the dark perhaps, tell it in your own words, following your own, perhaps stumbling rhythms. This recommendation follows the earlier observations that a crucial part of the development of the imagination involves the child's *generation* of images from words. Illustrated storybooks in part, and TV all the time, supply images that reduce or suppress this vital intellectual capacity. Also, parents might be surprised by how much more powerfully the child responds to the oral telling of a story over the polished reading. As Northrop Frye put it: "The art of listening to stories is a basic training for the imagination" (1963, p. 49).

Mythic understanding, like Somatic, is not something only for the childhood years, when it tends to be most energetic. Our fifty-five-year-olds can continue to enlarge their Mythic understanding of the world and experience. A more energetic and imaginative intellectual life will follow from the effort to see particular experiences in varied, perhaps competing story structures, to persist in constructing vivid, perhaps deliberately weird mental images

253

from the words of friends or TV characters, to cultivate in our own oral and written discourse vivid images, fresh metaphors, and concrete particularity (he writes abstractly). A greying woman chatting on the phone, sitting on a red chair in the kitchen, looking through the doorway to the room where her overweight husband's brown-slippered feet are stretched out toward the TV, on which a football game is being shown, can imagine that the feet are in control of the man and they have stretched him out so they can watch from close up the exciting antics of the football players' feet. (This is just an example, not a fetish being exercised.) Or perhaps she can imagine that the TV is watching him, its active eye presenting him with different images so that it can study his response—a frustrating piece of empirical research as the husband half-dozes through everything.

Lively metaphoric "seeing as" is crucial to an imaginative mind able to do original thinking. Very quickly the early energetic "seeing as"—seeing the cylinder open at one end as a cup—becomes a set of fixed and rigid concepts, the products of frozen metaphors. We might make a habit of disrupting this habit of the dulling mind by constantly "unseeing as," by unfreezing the metaphors. See the table as cut and treated wood, or laminated particleboard and plastics and metal. See the familiar garden as it once was—waving grassland or forest. See the school as bricks and glass and bureaucratic structures.

Mythic understanding grows with flexible use of oral language, and we can, after extending and elaborating our vocabulary, constantly work toward precision, clarity, simplicity, and vividness in our oral delivery.

Romantic Understanding

In this section I will focus primarily on how teachers of students from about eight to fifteen can shape and present content so that it will be meaningful and engaging and will stimulate and develop Romantic understanding. I will work from the set of characteristics discussed in chapter 3. These include a fascination with the limits of reality and the extremes of experience; an attraction to those things, people, ideas, qualities that transcend the constraints of our everyday lives; a ready engagement by knowledge represented as a product of human emotions and intentions; and a detailed interest in something. The role played by narrative structuring, affective meaning, and images will continue, if at a somewhat reduced level.

Let us see how we can infer from these characteristics of Romantic understanding another planning framework, one appropriate for students who are prominently deploying Romantic intellectual tools in their learning.

Again, I will organize the framework in terms of a set of questions whose answers should yield a lesson or unit plan, then briefly discuss the principles that undergird each section of the framework, and conclude each strut with an example. In this case, given that "literacy" has been a central feature of Romantic understanding, I will try to sketch a "romantic" unit on the improbable topic of punctuation. I will again stick to a restricted topic in a particular teaching area—language arts or English—because this seems to conform with the way most teaching is organized, but teachers might find the framework helps them design more elaborate, integrated units.

The Romantic Planning Framework

1. Identifying Transcendent Qualities

What transcendent qualities can be seen and felt as central to the topic? What affective images do they evoke? What within the topic can best evoke wonder?
As with the Mythic framework, the most difficult part is at the beginning. This first strut of the framework asks teachers to begin planning a topic by searching within themselves for the transcendent qualities that can give life, energy, and meaning to the topic. A part of this task might involve running through the content in one's mind, searching for affective images, for something heroic or wonderful about the topic. It might help to look for examples of qualities like courage, compassion, energy, ingenuity, and tenacity.

It should be emphasized that this first step requires teachers to think about the topic until they are *moved* by something in it. That emotional engagement provides the key to the student's imagination. Again, it is not a matter of working out what will "Romantically" move the students but rather what "Romantically" moves the teacher or parent. This emotional engagement, this *moving,* needn't suggest images of teachers in tears or in the throes of passion while planning. Rather, it suggests that they think about the topic with their emotions alert and home in on whatever engages their Romantic sensors. As always, the more one knows or finds out about a topic, the easier this will be. Once the transcendent quality is identified, the rest of the planning should be relatively easy.

How, then, do we think about punctuation in such a way that we can find something moving about it? What transcendent quality can we build the lessons on? We might begin by reflecting on the purpose of punctuation and how it developed. Early alphabetic texts had no punctuation—just letters, one after the other, filling the space on the tablet, stone, or parchment. Reading was consequently difficult, and, to make sense of a text, one would have to read it aloud. Indeed, silent reading seems to have been a very rare accomplishment in the ancient world. Julius Caesar apparently mastered the   255 skill so that he could read letters about military or political affairs without being overheard, and St. Augustine notes St. Ambrose's ability to read silently as unusual. Punctuation, then, consists of simple, elegant, and ingenious inventions that have been added to texts for easier reading. These inventions democratized reading, making it no longer the exclusive skill of an elite eager to protect the power, privileges, and social benefits that went with it.

This brief history suggests one area in which we might find something moving: the new accessibility of reading has brought about incalculable revolutions in human history and cultural life, influencing more people more profoundly than all the conquerors, warriors, and egomaniacal politicians in the world. Our sense of wonder might be readily engaged by the discrepancy between the invention of these tiny marks and their vast social and cultural consequences—a little like chaos theory's example of the movement of a butterfly's wing in South America leading to profound changes in weather conditions in the northern hemisphere.

An alternative transcendent quality we might have picked out of this reflection is courtesy. Had we selected that one, we would have seen punctuation as an act of courtesy from writer to reader. But let us take simple, elegant ingenuity.

2. Organizing the Topic into a Narrative Structure

2.1 Initial Access

What aspect of the topic best embodies the transcendent qualities identified as central to the topic? Does this expose some extreme of experience or limit of reality? What image can help capture this aspect?

We might again approach shaping the topic into a narrative with our newspaper editor's question "What's the story on this?" in mind. The story-structuring need not be as tight as in the earlier framework, but the basic principles of the story will still be important to provide access, ensure clear communication, and encourage affective engagement with the content. To begin with, we need to find some aspect of the topic that clearly embodies our chosen transcendent quality. Commonly, this will be clear as a result of the reflection that yielded the transcendent quality in the first place, but sometimes it might require a separate reflection and research. The aspect we begin with also should suggest an image that is vivid and exposes something central about the topic. We should also seek out something that might seem strange, bizarre, wonderful, and show something extreme about experience or some limit of reality. Overlapping criteria are suggested here, and the teacher should not think it essential to satisfy all of them for every lesson.

Think of them as hints about the direction one's thinking should take when looking for the initial teaching event for a unit.

How can we find some aspect of punctuation that will satisfy these criteria? The overall narrative line suggested by earlier reflection on the topic concerns the impact on cultural history, political history, and even our sense of ourselves brought about by these simple, elegant, and ingenious marks in text. The story describes a momentous shift from reliance on the ear to reliance on the eye in accessing knowledge. It is part of the adventure of moving from an oral to a literate culture with all that that has entailed. In this story, punctuation plays a decisive role in transforming text so that it can be read easily. Our exploration of punctuation will involve spaces between words, paragraphs, headings, uppercase and lowercase letters, commas, periods, quotation marks, exclamation points, and question marks. Each element helps to break up text for easier understanding; they permit us to engage relatively easily in such curious silent communication as you and I now share. Try reading this punctuation-less text:

INITIALACCESSTHENMIGHTBEPROVIDEDBYGIVINGTHESTUDENTSAPIECEOFTE
XTWITHOUTANYPUNCTUATIONSIMPLYALLTHEWORDSFLOWINGTOGETHERAUSEFU
LINTRODUCTIONDOYOUTHINKSONOBREAKSCOMMASORPERIODSORANYOTHERSI
MPLEANDELEGANTINTENTIONSTHATPROVIDECUESTHATMAKETEXTSSOMUCHMOR
EACCESSIBLETOTHEEYEAREYOUSTILLSTRUGGLINGTOREADTHISJUSTSEEINGHOWM
UCHMOREDIFFICULTTOREADTEXTLIKETHISWILLGIVESTUDENTSSOMEIMAGEOFT
HEVALUEOFPUNCTUATIONDONTYOUTHINKPERHAPSYOUMIGHTHAVETHESTUDEN
TSREADTHISINITIALTEXTALOUDNOTTHISONEOFCOURSEBUTSOMETEXTYOUCHOO
SETHATCANBEPRESENTEDLIKETHISBETTERTOSELECTSOMETHINGMADEESPECIALL
YHARDDUETOITSLACKOFALLKINDSOFPUNCTUATIONBYREADINGITALOUDTHEYWI
LLDISCOVERWHYTHEEARREMAINEDIMPORTANTTOREADINGUNTILPUNCTUATIONT
RANSFORMEDTEXTTHATISONEWAYOFBRINGINGOUTTHEIMPORTANCEANDIMPACT
OFPUNCTUATIONOK

2.2 COMPOSING THE BODY OF THE LESSON OR UNIT

What content best articulates the topic into a clear narrative structure? Sketch the main narrative line and fit the content to it.

The task now is to use our transcendent quality to select appropriate content that will be articulated on a clear narrative line. The transcendent quality becomes our principle of selection, our criterion of relevance, ensuring that the affective point runs from beginning to end of the lesson or unit. A Romantic perspective on a topic can disturb some people; it is not qualified enough or not precise enough; it seems to grab for the exotic and showy rather than the cautious and correct. But Romantic planning is not a license for glitter and sparkle at any cost, especially at the cost of accuracy; it never licenses falsification, even if it does encourage highlighting certain aspects of a topic at the expense of others. This feature of Romantic understanding is found regrettable by those who have been schooled not to trust their own, perhaps suppressed sense of romance. But it seems to me necessary for adequate development of understanding of any topic: more proportionate views may follow, but engagement is necessary first.

The central task here is to reflect on the whole unit or lesson and think of it in terms of some overall narrative structure. That is, one needs to select and highlight content that will make clear to students that one is not simply relating a sequence of facts or events but that one has a story to tell them, and that the set of facts and events constitute a unity of some kind. As Richard Feynman described his approach to teaching: "I wasn't only worried about the content of each lecture, but also each lecture had to be self-contained, complete in itself. It had to be a dramatic production—which had a dramatic line, with an introduction, a development of the theme, and a dénouement" (Regis, 1994, p. 18). Another scientist who is a master of such narrative structuring is Carl Sagan. His *Cosmos* series for TV and in book form (1980) have been much criticized by "sophisticates," but it is brilliantly organized to engage the Romantic mind.

Our punctuation example arrives at this point with the general principle of its narrative structure worked out. The transcendent quality of simple, elegant ingenuity provides our criterion for selecting content, and the connection between the tiny textual marks and their massive social and culture consequences is the source of wonder that we will highlight as we demonstrate punctuation's help in the momentous move from ear to eye. Given our narrative line, we could decide to take each punctuation mark that we want to consider either in the sequence of historical appearance or, which turns out to be not very different, in the degree of its impact on making texts hospitable to the eye. This narrative line, incidentally, properly brings into the topic items sometimes not considered in lessons on punctuation, such as separation of words by spaces. We could begin with that dramatic invention, showing in the introductory block of text what an enormous impact it has on the eye's ease of access to meaning. Then we might consider the use of uppercase and lowercase letters, then the effects of the period or full stop, and the comma, and so on. Each item needs to be shown in terms of its simple elegance and ingenuity and its contribution to moving away from the use of the ear to the independence of the eye. Such a narrative might lead to instances of concrete poetry or to other modes of using text so that the ear contributes very little and meaning relies almost entirely on the eye.

One could use the initial block of text, showing how each new punctuation adds to easy scanning; in addition, the students could be asked to compose texts that are particularly ambiguous, hard to interpret, or funny without a particular punctuation mark. The teacher could initiate this latter activity with some examples, along the lines of the message sent by Tyrone, a character in one of Donald J. Sobol's *Encyclopedia Brown* stories (1986). Tyrone wanted to send a loving message to his sweetheart that read, "How I long for a girl who understands what true romance is all about. You are sweet and faithful. Girls who are unlike you kiss the first boy who comes along, Adorabelle. I'd like to praise your beauty forever. I can't stop thinking you are the prettiest girl alive. Thine, Tyrone." But Tyrone phoned the message to Adorabelle's younger sister, Lulubelle, and neglected to read the punctuation. So the message Adorabelle received was this: "How I long for a girl who understands what true romance is. All about you are sweet and faithful girls who are unlike you. Kiss the first boy who comes along, Adorabelle. I'd like to praise your beauty forever. I can't. Stop thinking you are the prettiest girl alive. Thine, Tyrone."

2.3 HUMANIZING THE CONTENT

How can the content be shown in terms of human hopes, fears, intentions, or other emotions? What aspect of the content can best stimulate a sense of wonder? What ideals and/or revolts against convention are evident in the content?

This strut of the framework directs us to think about the content in terms of its human dimensions—what our newspaper editor might call "digging out the human-interest angle." While this technique can lead to journalistic trivia, when properly used it can also identify an important element of Romantic engagement in a topic. The point is not simply to "put people into the lesson" but rather to focus on what it is about the content that can be grasped in terms of emotions. Recall from chapter 3 how the Romantic understanding of causality begins with emotions initiating events. Emotions are most easily identified when we focus on the hopes and ideals of proponents in conflict with the conventional forces that oppose them. But we can also identify emotions in unlikely topics, by describing, say, weeds on a rock face in terms of tenacity or earthworms slithering through damp soil in terms of aesthetic joy.

Teachers recognize that an illustrative anecdote that deals with some extreme of human endurance, foresight, ingenuity, compassion, or suffering immediately grabs students' attention. What this strut involves is the extension of the engaging force of such narratives to the whole lesson or unit. Often we can achieve this by locating content in the context of hopes, fears, passions, and intentions of people's lives. What makes others' lives interesting to us is the degree to which we can imaginatively grasp them in terms of the emotions, hopes, fears, and intentions we can share. This principle does not refer to our finding some introductory "hook" to the topic but directs us rather to locate its human importance.

How can we apply this principle to punctuation? Well, we have already articulated the topic in a narrative of a set of tiny but revolutionary inventions, so we might very easily focus wherever possible on some of the inventors. We can find useful material in Illich (1993) and Olson (1994). We might dwell on Hugh and Andrew of St. Victor, say, and those monks who transformed the appearance of a typical page of text during the eleventh and twelfth centuries in their drive to capture a more literal sense of Biblical texts. It was a drive that Smalley, writing about Hugh of St. Victor, compared with "that curiosity which set explorers in quest of Eldorado and led to the discovery of a continent" (1941, p. 72).

2.4 PURSUING DETAILS

What parts of the topic can students best explore in exhaustive detail?
This strut directs us to focus on encouraging students to build their own areas of genuine expertise. By discovering *something* exhaustively, students can gain security that the world is knowable and is not infinite.

We can incorporate this principle into our unit on punctuation fairly easily. Students, individually or in small groups, can research the comma, the question mark, paragraphing. The teacher will need to ensure that the library or a study area contains sufficient resources so that students can, indeed, learn perhaps as much as is known about the topic. In some cases, the origin might still be little known, and so exploration might focus on changed usage through the centuries or in different countries.

3. Conclusion

How can one best bring the topic to satisfactory closure? How can the student feel this satisfaction?
Our narrative line through the lesson or unit should not simply run out when we have covered the content. As with any story, we need to find some satisfactory ending; the sense of an ending may be felt in a satisfying way if it provides both the kind of epiphany mentioned earlier and some glimpse of Philosophic and Ironic understanding of the topic.

We might conclude our unit on punctuation by bringing together the variety of indications that students will have encountered about the imprecision of rules of punctuation. At the pragmatic level, this may help alleviate some frustration caused by the difficulty in understanding clearly the proper use of the comma, say, or the apostrophe. Drawing on the alternative transcendent quality indicated in the beginning, our attempted epiphany might occur if we emphasize that punctuation is not so much a set of precise rules to be mechanically mastered as simple, elegant, and ingenious inventions used in somewhat unstable ways as acts of courtesy between writer and reader. The sense of punctuation as courteous convention also stimulates a Philosophic general scheme about *the* proper way to understand punctuation while hinting at an Ironic sense of the ultimate arbitrariness of these ingenious inventions.

How can we manage such an epiphany in practice? At the simplest level, if the unit has prepared students for such an understanding by means of the various practical exercises and research projects they will have done, the teacher could simply bring it about by talking about punctuation as courtesy. Alternatively, we could give out blocks of text again, this time of lowercase text in which the words are separated. The students, in small groups, could be invited to invent their own punctuation marks in order to make the text easier to read and understand. The only rule would be that none of the conventional punctuation marks could be used in their usual ways. (If computers are available with "dingbat" fonts, the students might find it easier to work on screen.) When finished, students could look at as many of the newly punctuated texts as they can. If the whole set can be made available to each student, the class might vote on the innovations they find most helpful, constructing an agreed-upon convention. A few things should become clear in this exercise: the arbitrariness of the conventions that are currently dominant; their simple elegance and ingenuity; the difficulty of coming up with new punctuation ideas (in that most of the students' innovations will likely be simple substitutions for current conventions); the recognition that punctuation marks are meaningless and confusing unless there is agreement about their use and meaning; that acceptance of someone's innovation is a recognition of how it helps one's interpretation of text. These lessons can be underlined by the teacher's accompanying them with the courtesy narrative.

4. *Evaluating*

How can one know that the content has been learned and understood and has engaged and stimulated students' imaginations?
Evaluating the development of students' Romantic understanding involves ensuring that they understand the material, but we will not measure that understanding solely in terms of what details they can recall. Rather, we will focus on whether the students can use the knowledge in contexts other than those in which they learned it. We will seek evidence as well of Romantic engagement with the knowledge, attending to students' pursuit of further related knowledge beyond what is required by classroom assignments.

Teachers can use the qualitative approaches popularized in recent years, and familiarize themselves with the practices of connoisseurship as described by Elliot Eisner (1985).

How can parents encourage the development of Romantic understanding? I argued that this kind of understanding is a product of a particular kind of literacy, largely elaborated in ancient Greece, which stimulated and supported a distinctive inquiry into the nature of reality. What is distinctive about the initial stages of that inquiry is that they are not the kind most typical of much (prematurely) theoretic schooling but are rather more keenly directed to whatever exposes dramatic details about the extremes or limits of reality. Details from the *Guinness Book of Records,* the *mega ergon,* the outrageous behavior of pop stars, film stars, sports stars, and "personalities" in general, the most terrible suffering, the greatest achievements, ashes and diamonds but little in between, are what stimulate the Romantic mind.

The easy seductiveness of television has made dinnertime reading almost obsolete, it would seem. Instead, parents—and perhaps children, too, depending on their fluency—could spend the dinner hour reading aloud from a romantic book (a practice one reader of the manuscript thought I might promote as a dieting technique). By themselves, of course, children can read appropriate books as well, from sensational stories of exotic and bizarre events and behavior to more exemplary accounts of people exhibiting extremes of behavior that are outside the range of children's everyday experience. Dramatic biographies can be very appealing; children might enjoy learning about people such as Gandhi, Marie Curie, Martin Luther King, Helen Keller, and Florence Nightingale. In addition, there is a vast range of books with the characteristics sketched in chapter 3 that "Romantic" children can launch into; for those who become absorbed, there are also major literary works with prominent Romantic qualities (such as Dickens's novels). Dickens's writings, of course, also have Philosophic and Ironic qualities that can elaborate the young person's understanding in ways that more popular novels will not. Many materials, from comic books to Dickens and beyond, can stimulate and develop Romantic understanding.

This theory is largely about language developments, not so much in terms of vocabulary growth and grammatical sophistication—though they obviously play a role—but in terms of the kinds of concepts, the focus of discourse, the everyday content that surround and seek responses from the child. Parents can stimulate and develop Romantic understanding by talking with their children about those things that conform with the characteristics mentioned in chapter 3, such as heroic acts, amazing events, new discoveries about the cosmos, the outrageous behavior of "personalities," dramatized accounts of friends' behavior, interesting gossip, or the children's particular hobby or obsession.

Our fifty-five-year-old can continue to develop Romantic understanding by seeking out experiences or reading that will stimulate awe and wonder. He or she might choose one of those "exploration holidays" into unusual places to witness strange and exotic customs and behavior, or more simply decide to become knowledgeable about a particular subject, be it spiders, women philosophers of the Middle Ages, or jungle warfare in Malaya. Any such Romantic exploration will lead to increasing one's sense of the limits of reality and the extremes of behavior, and make life more abundant.

PHILOSOPHIC UNDERSTANDING

In this section I will focus mainly on how teachers of students in senior high school or college might shape and present material to students so that it will be meaningful and imaginatively engaging and will also stimulate and develop their Philosophic understanding. I will begin with a planning framework again—not that I expect teachers to follow it slavishly—because it is a convenient way of laying out the set of principles derived from the theory for teaching at this level. Teachers can then select whichever features they think might be useful.

At this teaching level, the logic of the content often determines its presentation. As with the psychological models that currently dominate thinking about instruction of younger pupils, this seems inadequate.

I am assuming these students will have been educated according to the principles outlined for each of the previous kinds of understanding. In the real world of current high school, college, and university classrooms, a significant proportion of students will have only very partial access to Philosophic understanding. My general recommendation would be to combine elements of the Romantic framework with the Philosophic, perhaps even providing a Mythic introduction. Both Feynman and Sagan provide this mix, and, particularly in the high school years, mixing of modes is probably the most sensible way to proceed. In a later section of this chapter I'll explain how to manage this fairly easily.

The characteristics of Philosophic understanding discussed in chapter 4 include the formation of general schemes and a language of theoretic abstractions to support them; the sense of oneself as an agent (or, more fashionably, a victim) within complex social, psychological, metaphysical, and historical processes; the lure of certainty; the search for authority and truth within general schemes; the dialectical play between general schemes and anomalies; and the flexibility theory gives to the mind's ability to deal with the world.

Let us, then, move from these characteristics to a planning framework. The high school teacher, whose students may only be beginning to construct their Philosophic understanding, needs to emphasize the first couple of struts of the following framework. The college and university teacher might want to emphasize the later struts, which encourage elaborating and disturbing general schemes. After setting each strut in place, I will discuss the principle on which it is based and then give a couple of examples of its use. Driven by Ironic reflexiveness again, I will use the topic of this book as one example and will consider as well the more routine academic topic of the Industrial Revolution.

Philosophic Planning Framework

1. *Identifying Relevant General Schemes*

What general schemes seem best able to organize the topic into some coherent whole? What are the most powerful, clear, and relevant theories, ideologies, metaphysical schemes, and metanarratives?

For the average teacher, this beginning should seem less difficult than those required in the previous two frameworks. Even though we might not usually think of a topic to be taught in terms of the general schemes used to organize it, such schemes are usually closer to the surface of our thinking at this level of education. A useful guide for identifying general schemes is to consider what are the main controversies surrounding the topic, what ideological sides are taken on it. Among these, one can look for the more dramatic and powerful general schemes. In this context, "powerful" refers to the generality of the scheme in terms of how much of the relevant content it can organize and give meaning to.

In the earlier frameworks teachers are asked to reflect on the topic until they locate something within it that moves them affectively. Similarly, in beginning to plan Philosophic teaching it is important to locate something that stirs the teacher, something that he or she cares deeply about. What we will be dealing with at this Philosophic level are the schemes that we and others have developed for composing meaning in our lives and in our world. So, again, our reflection must not be of a purely intellectual kind, assessing which of a range of schemes students might find engaging, but must begin in the rag-and-bone shop of our own hearts, turning up those things that matter to us affectively and aesthetically.

The teacher's job here is to think about the topic Philosophically and present it to the students Philosophically. To do this, some general scheme will be required. This does not mean that the teacher should continually supply the students with general schemes. Indeed, students will already have their own that are only too ready to absorb the topic. What the teacher can offer in such cases is an alternative that students might consider or seek to displace with their own preferred scheme. While nothing may matter to the student more than his or her particular general scheme, from a pedagogical point of view what particular general scheme is used doesn't matter at all so long as it can make some comprehensive sense of the topic.

If I were to teach the topic of this book, I would begin by locating what seem to me the main theories used in representing the process of educational development. I would likely conclude that Plato's and Rousseau's theories were largest on the landscape, along with a rather diffuse conception of socialization, and, little regarded now but clearly a distinct theory, recapitulation. The modern forms these theories take, and the ways they have mixed together, awkwardly produce what seems to me a dominant and somewhat incoherent ideology of education. That this matters to me has less to do with some abstract idea of improving educational practice, I suppose, than with a personal sense of opportunities lost, aesthetic pleasures denied, abundant possibilities diminished by an education the recollection of which brings to mind fear, humiliation, conviction of stupidity, numbing boredom, and a belittling bewilderment at not being able to make some sense of what schooling was supposed to be about. What it is about clearly connects with the peculiar cultural development of the West, which raises a set of related theories. I would also, of course, have in mind the new idea of this book, contrived with the help of recapitulation, and other bits and pieces. This general scheme seems to me more coherent and aesthetically more satisfying than the unsteady mélange of theories for which it is proposed as a replacement, and it seems to have the potential to lead to better educational practice. It also aims to follow Bruner's (1960) recommendation of contriving a scheme of education courteous enough to represent the world and experience to children in ways they are best able to understand.

The Industrial Revolution, for another example, might be represented in either of the two main metanarratives used to organize history—comic or tragic. Comic metanarratives represent events within an overall historical scheme of improvement; the most common has been a liberal progressive scheme of gradual amelioration: enlargement of freedoms and knowledge, restriction of arbitrary violence and despotic power, and so on. Marxism is another of the great comic metanarratives, in which history is represented as the dialectical struggle of classes, each new one generating its own antithesis on the way to a better and classless society. Tragic general schemes have included Thucydides' vision of decay being tied in with flaws in human nature 265 and, in recent times, Foucault's accounts of diminishing freedoms. Let us take the liberal progressive scheme as our organizer for the content about the Industrial Revolution.

2. Organizing the Content into a General Scheme

2.1 INITIAL ACCESS

How can the general scheme be made vivid? What relevant content best exposes the general scheme and shows its power to organize the topic?
These questions direct us to think about what will be our first teaching act as we introduce the topic. We have our general scheme in mind and now begin clothing it by finding the most dramatic content that is representative of the topic as a whole. The beginning of the unit has both to engage the students' Philosophic imagination by its dramatic representation of what is centrally important about the topic and also to stimulate their desire to learn more about it in order to see whether or to what degree the suggested general scheme is True.

In teaching about development, I would begin with brief accounts of the main general schemes that have been used to organize the topic in the past (such as socialization and the schemes of Plato and of Rousseau), indicate why they are separately and jointly inadequate, and then offer grounds for thinking that a new kind of recapitulation scheme might do the trick.

The Industrial Revolution might be introduced with a sketch, using whatever media the teacher chooses, of the "advance of civilization" meta-narrative. Western history is thus represented as a process in which knowledge, reason, and individual freedoms from oppression and for personal choices have been gradually increasing. In this metanarrative the Industrial Revolution, in the fag end of which we are living, may be seen as the greatest contributor to an ameliorating process. During the revolution mechanisms were developed for generating freedom from drudgery, for the establishment of legal and political institutions to protect enlarged freedoms for the individual, for the invention of technologies of knowledge production and dissemination, for the rapid increase in wealth that greatly enhanced cultural and educational opportunities, and so on. Although far from utopian, these can be represented as significant advances from the nasty, brutish, and short lives that had been the lot of the bulk of humanity. The current state of these products of the Industrial Revolution will thus be represented in the general scheme as all subject to continuing improvement in the future, and students' proper social roles, suggested by this metanarrative, will involve their struggling to further these progressive social and cultural developments.

2.2   ORGANIZING THE BODY OF THE LESSON OR UNIT

What content can be used to articulate the topic into a general scheme? What metanarrative provides a clear overall structure to the lesson or unit?

Here the teacher needs to reflect on how the selected general scheme can best organize the content into a coherent whole. This planning strut is an extension of the story and narrative structuring of the two previous frameworks (it is helpful to keep this in mind). The story feature moves in this case from the level of individuals, motives, and events to that of ideas; even so, similar structural principles need to come into play—think of the story as a metanarrative that emphasizes the narrative.

In the case of my first example, the developmental scheme of Somatic, Mythic, Romantic, Philosophic, and Ironic kinds of understanding suggests a fairly simple metanarrative structure. The underlying narrative would focus on developments in language and in related intellectual tools that are in turn tied in with this sequential unfolding of human understanding. Some dramatic tension could come from contrasting this scheme with those it is proposed to replace—which is, of course, the metanarrative of this book.

For the unit on the Industrial Revolution, the teacher could use the liberal progressive scheme as the criterion to select the content. We will look at the inventions in terms of release from drudgery and the enlargement of possibilities for most people, at child labor laws and the progressive legislation aimed at improving the conditions the revolution created for the laboring masses, at increases in population and food supply, at antislavery activities and legislation, at cultural activities and increased scope for their enjoyment by greater numbers, and at the gradual growth of education and democracy.

3.   *Introducing Anomalies to the General Scheme*

What content is anomalous to the general scheme? How can one begin with minor anomalies and gradually and sensitively challenge the students' general schemes so that they make the schemes increasingly sophisticated?

The aim here is not to destroy students' general schemes by confronting them with major anomalies. Rather, teachers must be sensitive to the degree to which students are committed to their general schemes and aim to make these more sophisticated. The longer-term aim is to change students' perceptions of the *status* of their general schemes—not exchange one general scheme for another—so that they see them eventually as not simply true or false but as more or less useful. The teaching task may be seen initially as providing aliments—to use Piaget's term—to the scheme, enlarging its scope and potency as an explanatory device, and then sensitively introduc-   267 ing facts or events or ideas that are anomalous. Teachers must then help students elaborate the scheme in order to accommodate anomalies. Perhaps only a few anomalies can be dealt with by a full class of students; others might need to be addressed to individual students in response to written work or in small group discussions. Teaching needs to move each student forward between the Scylla of overconfident belief in the truth of general schemes and the Charybdis of undermined schemes leading to a general cynicism and alienation. The trick is to kickstart the dialectical process of anomalies that cause revision of the general scheme, which then demands further knowledge to deal with the anomalies, which in turn suggests further anomalies.

It may seem that teaching at these higher levels is only peripherally concerned with specific content and is intently conscious of general schemes and anomalies to them. Obviously, that is an inappropriate picture. The usual focus on the content to be taught should continue, but here we should add a dimension of learning that seems rarely to be considered.

In the first example, the development of kinds of understanding, I find it relatively easy to raise some anomalies to the three old theories I plan to displace. During the presentation of my alternative scheme, I would probably prefer to lay out the Somatic, Mythic, Romantic, Philosophic, and Ironic kinds of understanding first, and then give voice to some of the anomalies that remain—as in chapter 6. In some cases I would suggest ways in which the scheme could be elaborated to respond to anomalies, and in other cases I would simply have to acknowledge that this general scheme cannot accommodate all the evident anomalies. The final defence would be that it can accommodate a lot of what might appear as anomalies and that it organizes more of the phenomena it deals with in a comprehensible order than any other theory or scheme

In the second example, we might suggest anomalies to the liberal progressive scheme used to organize the Industrial Revolution by asking some very general Philosophic questions: Is industrialization fundamentally at odds with human nature? Has industrialization, Frankenstein-like, taken on a life of its own, which now threatens its creators? Why should this rational process of ameliorization have led, in advanced countries, to Hitler, Mussolini, Franco, and Stalin with widespread and enthusiastic support? Do we continue to face such dangers in our country now? Why or why not?

It does not matter that students do not have enough data to formulate adequate answers. No one has. What such questions achieve is stimulation, even, perhaps, irritation; students are invited to apply their general scheme to new, very general data and to try to impose shape and pattern on further historical phenomena. Once students show some flexibility and control over the general scheme and some commitment to it, then the teacher may begin the introduction of increasingly anomalous particulars, to kick into self-sustaining life, as it were, the engine of Philosophic inquiry.

Students who have adopted the liberal progressive scheme might be asked to study the forces that led to legislation to improve working conditions and consider whether it was enacted only when it was seen as supporting rather than threatening increased production. Or they might be asked to study the constraining and disciplining practices of factories, the new prisons, and the new schools, and consider how these can fit a progressive ameliorating scheme. Students who have adopted a Marxist general scheme might be asked to study the movement to abolish slavery to see how the scheme needs to be elaborated to accommodate what the student learns, or to study the reforms of factory owners such as Robert Owen to see how their scheme can deal with these. The aim here is not to propose destructive objections to the schemes but to focus them on material that is in some degree anomalous to their simple forms.

4. Presenting Alternative General Schemes

What alternative general schemes can organize the topic? Which can best be used to help students see the contingency of such schemes?
The principle suggested here is that somewhere in our teaching of a topic, we should provide students with alternative general schemes to the one we, or they, have most prominently used. In some subject areas and with some topics this will be easier than with others, of course. An historical event, for example, can usually be seen in a number of ideological contexts or philosophical schemes. The final years of the Chinese Empire can be taught from the perspective of a liberal Westerner, an archconservative Mandarin, or a Marxist. Each of these, and perhaps others, can be seen to highlight particular features of those years; none of them needs to falsify anything, and none of them represents some objective truth. Each perspective in turn can be evaluated as more or less satisfactory in conveying an understanding of the relevant events and in determining what events should be considered relevant. It should become clear that considering a variety of general schemes contributes to a richer understanding of the topic.

In the case of my first example, I would begin with some alternative educational theories, only to point up their inadequacies. I would also consider alternative recapitulation theories, showing again how they were unable to accommodate to large-scale anomalies. In writing this book, of course, I have a persuasive purpose, so I have not tried to highlight the virtues of alternative general schemes, but in teaching this to a university class I would

269

explore in particular other developmental schemes, such as those of Piaget, Vygotsky, Erikson, and Donald, drawing attention to the dimensions of cultural and/or individual development about which they enhance our understanding. I would try to make clear that these varied attempts to represent human development, and to seek educational implications from them, should be seen not so much as to-the-death competitions for the truth but rather as comparatively useful aids in understanding the processes to which they refer.

In dealing with the Industrial Revolution, it would be useful to offer a Thucydides-Foucault tragic scheme for students' consideration. The purpose would be to see more or less the same content from a quite different perspective. Contrasting schemes should help students recognize that the schemes themselves are not right or wrong so much as more or less adequate in accounting for the data. One or other of the schemes might be assessed as more powerful in accounting for most of the data, but it might need to be pointed out that they also serve as criteria for deciding what counts as data, and that the more powerful scheme is often seen as such only because it focuses too little on what would otherwise be anomalous data. The clash of general schemes may raise more general questions, such as whether the true dynamic of liberal progress derives from self-interest rather than selflessness. If a student's general scheme resists accommodating the conclusion that self-interest is the dynamic, that student might be assigned to study in detail various inventions, their adoption, and their dissemination to determine whether any dynamic other than self-interest is able to explain the facts. If the opposite conclusion is held, that student might be assigned to study in detail the activities of Robert Owen, Elizabeth Fry, and middle-class supporters of labor organizations and consider whether there is no useful distinction to be made between their behavior and that of the most ruthless factory owners.

5. *Conclusion*

How can we ensure that the student's general schemes are not destroyed or made rigid, but are recognized as having a different epistemological status from the facts they are based on? How can we ensure that the decay of belief in the truth of general schemes does not lead to disillusion and alienation? How can we lead students toward a sophisticated Ironic understanding of the topic?

The objective here is to ensure that students recognize that their general schemes have potential utility rather than objective truth. Now, when students are just beginning to develop general schemes, we will obviously not want to emphasize the undermining features. But in concluding any unit or lesson it will be appropriate to seek out some way of at least hinting at the difference between the very general schemes and the facts they are based on, letting the teacher's sense of students' Philosophic development determine the degree of support or challenge the teacher offers.

A point I will return to later, but which is particularly pertinent here, concerns the importance of the teacher's own development of Ironic understanding. "Philosophic" teachers, committed to their own general schemes, tend to see their teaching task as bringing students to recognize the truth of those schemes. Too often they count success as the creation of disciples, and students with whom they are not in this way "successful" are dismissed as hopeless or as ideological enemies. It is true that such learning can generate great fervor and energy in students, but it also commonly results in personal conflicts, and it can be dramatically confrontational. Often, the most zealous Philosophic teachers use the intellectual seduction of students to compensate for their own suppressed doubts about the adequacy of their general schemes. None of this helps students recognize the difference between the epistemological status of detailed factual claims and the claims of general schemes. This is not to assert that such claims are entirely distinct but only that they are not the same, and that recognizing the difference is important to a rich development of Ironic understanding; it is in that distance between details and scheme, between reality and idea, that the shadow of irony lengthens.

In my first example, I could conclude by returning to the three general schemes I began with and give each of them a more generous reading, showing how each one might be interpreted more liberally or be extended to address material I claimed my general scheme dealt with in a superior fashion. As a result, I would expect students to recognize that each of these schemes helps to enlarge our understanding of cultural or individual development. While I wouldn't expect much fainting despair as students come to recognize that the general scheme that undergirds this presentation of my theory is something less than the ultimate word on its subject matter, I would want to ensure that they recognize its utility. The recognition of utility as separate from objective truth provides appropriate preparation for Ironic understanding.

In the increasing sophistication of general schemes, I argued earlier, lies the seeds of their own destruction. The conclusion of the unit on the Industrial Revolution seeks to elaborate students' understanding while exposing in greater or lesser degree the difference between the general scheme and the facts, events, and other detailed knowledge they have learned. It may be that this purpose has been largely fulfilled by the previous activity of looking at 271 the revolution through the lenses of three or four general schemes, comparing their adequacy, utility, and even aesthetic appeal. A concluding activity might be to consider what promises are implicit in the different general schemes for the postindustrial world. For example, if a Marxist scheme is adopted, students could be asked to consider whether the inherent promise of equality—generating a proletariat whose increasing power is prerequisite to the classless society—does not presage the eclipse of freedoms as a condition of achieving that equality. If a liberal progressive scheme is adopted, the students could be invited to consider the likely social consequences of allowing individual possessiveness such a free rein, and whether private wealth, public squalor, and a large underclass of powerless, unhealthy, uneducated, frustrated, and bitter people is not inevitable. Both scenarios—and others—underline the extent to which the same body of data can be organized in different ways and disrupt in lesser or greater degree the sense that the truth lies in the general scheme.

6. *Evaluation*

How can we know whether the content has been learned and understood, whether students have developed a general scheme, elaborated it, and attained some sense of its limitations?

We will, of course, want evidence that students have learned the content that has made up the lesson or unit of study; this can be achieved through traditional techniques. We will also want evidence about how adequately students have developed some general scheme and used it in organizing the content. This can be evaluated by examining students' written or oral discussions to see whether the theoretic language appropriate to the topic is deployed flexibly and correctly. The teacher can also examine the written work for evidence of increasing elaboration of general schemes in light of anomalies. Either casual cynicism about or committed devotion to the truth of some scheme indicates failures of teaching and learning, though unqualified commitment during the early period of Philosophic understanding should not be a cause of much worry. From the students' writings it may be relatively easy to gauge their fluency in and commitment to abstract ideas as a means of gaining a flexible understanding of the world, but it is difficult to be precise in scoring such readings. Perhaps the teacher could use rather gross categories, like "easy and flexible," "adequate," "inadequate," to evaluate students' performance. Such scales are also useful in encouraging the teacher to value such characteristics in their students' performance.

For the first example, that of the topic of this book, the teacher should see whether students recognize the characteristics of each kind of under-standing and have a flexible sense of how one kind leads on to the next, how they partially coalesce, how the dynamic of the process works, and so on; again, these can be evaluated with traditional techniques. The teacher could also look for evidence that students recognize the limits of this scheme.

In the Industrial Revolution example, we would want to know at the most basic level whether and how adequately students have mastered the content, recognizing that what counts as appropriate content will change somewhat depending on the general scheme. We will want to know from their written work how flexibly and fluently they can use the abstract lan-guage through which general schemes can be developed, deployed, and elaborated. We will want to ensure that they can consistently deploy a partic-ular general scheme in making sense of the details of the revolution. And, particularly as students develop more sophisticated general schemes, we can examine their written work and oral discussions for evidence of recognition that all is not well in the realm of general schemes, that truth is not as easily attainable there as had been thought, that the worm of irony is beginning to wriggle and chew into the grand edifices of the general schemes.

Parents of well-educated children at around fifteen or sixteen years can stimulate and help the development of Philosophic understanding by increas-ingly using theoretic language while dealing with abstract ideas. This should not involve droning disquisitions; rather, a chat about sport or fashions or a pop star can be made more interesting to the incipiently Philosophic adoles-cent by referring to the social functions of sport, the exploitation of the fashion impulse or what drives changing fashions, or the cult of celebrity, illustrated perhaps by some of Marshall McLuhan's snappy and Philosophically rich ob-servations. The point is not to change the topic of conversation but to enrich it with a philosophic dimension that will readily engage students at about this age.

The parents themselves, and our fifty-five-year-old, might be the ones trying to keep up with the Philosophic understanding of late adolescents. There are many communities—including "virtual communities," which one can join via computer—that support and develop the language of theoretic abstractions crucial to this kind of understanding. The subject does not mat-ter so much as the language in which it is framed, expressed, and under-stood. "Intellectual" journals such as *Scientific American, New Society, Harper's,* the *New York Review of Books* and the *London Review of Books,* and the *Times Literary Supplement* are significant components of the public Philo-sophic community, providing commentary on Philosophic research, ideas, and books. There is also a range of literature aimed particularly at, and supportive of, Philosophic understanding; Jorge Luis Borges exemplifies a focused Philosophic discourse that involves contstant Ironic elements.

Our interactions with Philosophic communities will constantly mix features of Mythic, Romantic, and Philosophic kinds of understanding. We should keep this in mind, since their separation in this book for purposes of description may lead some to expect them to be used distinctly. I mentioned earlier that Philosophic understanding of any topic might be eased by providing a Mythic and Romantic path of access to it. Consider, again, this book as an example. It opens with a trio of inadequate ideas in binary contrast to a new and adequate idea; the reader is encouraged to feel that the traditional behemoths' lumbering dominance should be challenged by a nimble and cheerful newcomer. The reader's Romantic association is attracted toward the underdog, first by exotic bits and pieces from recapitulationists and Vygotsky, and then from the worlds of myth and fantasy, Herodotus and ancient Egypt, central Asian peasants and their inability to manage syllogisms, and so on. These elements ease the reader through the lengthy characterization of the new idea, which keeps an open door to the Ironic while working largely in a Philosophic vein.

Similarly, the teacher can provide access to a Philosophic treatment of a topic by means of a Mythic and Romantic introduction. A unit on plate tectonics might begin with "static/dynamic" binary concepts, presenting images of the earth as static, stable, and working through its reliable cycle of seasons. Such a view has an obvious intuitive appeal because, in terms of the tiny human life span, the earth does appear stable. The teacher can indicate that this view dominated thinking in the West until the nineteenth century, when people's imaginations became accustomed to much longer stretches of linear time. The competing image of a dynamic earth can then be introduced. The teacher could encourage Romantic association with the dynamic as crucial to understanding a constantly changing planetary surface. The teacher could also focus on the drama of relatively recent events. The spill of Atlantic water over the Straits of Gibraltar, filling the low-lying basin of what is now the Mediterranean, is a good example; for years and years there poured one of the largest waterfalls that could even have been witnessed by early humans. The explosion of Krakatoa is another dramatic event; its massive destructive force, its sound, and the violence of the waves it generated, were detected thousands of miles away. None of this introductory material need be labored or very time consuming, but it should ease access to the topic, increase engagement, and enrich understanding.

As I mentioned earlier, the teacher of Philosophic students should have already developed significant Ironic understanding himself or herself. Now, this kind of observation is sometimes construed as implying that the teacher is supposed to talk down to or patronize students. This interpretation strikes me as a peculiar way of looking at an inevitable feature of adequate teaching. If the teacher has no greater understanding than the student, it is hard to see how the role can be justified. The central sensitivity and skill of teaching consists in presenting knowledge to students in a manner that is most accessible and most stimulating to their developing understanding. What some represent as patronizing might more properly be seen as a matter of courtesy.

IRONIC UNDERSTANDING

Teaching people who are already engaged in Ironic understanding and who deploy the appropriate intellectual tools might be seen as a conversation between one who knows more about a topic and one who knows less. But this teaching will not involve the disparities assumed above, in which the Ironic teacher courteously accommodates students' kinds of understanding. Ironic teaching will casually use all of the kinds of understanding, moving from one to another as seems best to enrich and deepen understanding.

CONCLUSION

This somewhat new conception of education requires that teachers be sensitive to the kinds of understanding and the intellectual tools their students are deploying. This sensitivity obviously needn't be in the terms of this theory, with its unfamiliar categories and unconventional manner of characterizing children's thinking and learning; many teachers exemplify remarkably well-attuned sensitivity to their students and would no doubt characterize students' thinking in terms that are quite different from mine. But I hope even such expert teachers would recognize an echo of their insights in this theory, and see its value in its provision of at least one way of alerting preservice teachers to a crucial dimension of educational practice. I think it might also be valued as offering some new strategies for planning and teaching; these are sketched only in outline here but can be elaborated in a number of ways (e.g., Armstrong, Connolly, and Saville, 1994).

Initially, it may seem daunting that one has to develop some new pedagogical refinement and precision in recognizing arcane "kinds of understanding." I don't think the call is for something extraordinary. I have tried to provide concrete, descriptive help to support and direct that sensitivity, and the rough age guides given earlier can limit what one has to focus on. So-   275 matic characteristics will likely predominate up to two and a half years, then Mythic until about eight years, Romantic until about fifteen, Philosophic until the early twenties, and Ironic thereafter. This scheme describes ideal circumstances, of course, but these kinds of understanding are not the precise on/off conditions suggested by some Piagetian stages, for example. Teachers can relatively easily appeal to more than one kind of understanding at a time. Addressing students in a "higher" kind than their most energetic zone of development doesn't make the material incomprehensible; it may just be less engaging and less meaningful than it could have been, but that seems the normal course of events in many classrooms. If one is teaching, say, a class of twelve-year-olds, one can introduce a topic in a Mythic way, using binary concepts in a dramatic story opening, and then move on to a Romantic exploration of extremes and limits, exposing the binaries to critical examination, and showing the human dimensions of the content through a narrative structure, in the process providing some glimpse of general schemes that undergird the topic. While the main focus will be Romantic, one can set up the topic to provide as clear access as possible for the more Mythic and the more Philosophic students, too. This flexibility of presentation may seem to require superhuman intellectual nimbleness, but we actually do this kind of shifting routinely when addressing diverse groups and in conversation. When a scheme like this makes differences in understanding explicit, however, it provides some practical guidance for those who lack experience of, or an intuitive feel for, such differences.

A clear implication of this conception of education is that, in order to teach effectively at any level, the teacher must be familiar with the appropriate kind of understanding and have themselves abundantly and flexibly developed it, and must consequently feel and clearly recognize its affective tug in their own lives. This central principle challenges most directly the disinterested dispensing of knowledge that has no affective tug on the teacher. What does not engage the teacher produces dreariness for both teachers and students; the students being younger can often bear it better, but it erodes the souls of both.

(Teachers who would like copies of the Mythic, Romantic, and/or Philosophic planning frameworks will find them on my home page, whose address is in chapter 6, page 173.)

Afterword

The idea of education in this book is that we recapitulate the kinds of understanding that have developed in cultural history. We begin with the Somatic and Mythic kinds, whose basic forms are genetically programmed as a result of our evolutionary history; they come with the human body, in its senses and brain, and with the development of an oral language. Thereafter our general learning capacity comes increasingly into play, enabling us, more laboriously, to develop Romantic, Philosophic, and Ironic kinds of understanding by recapitulating the cultural inventions of literacy, theoretic thinking, and extreme linguistic reflexiveness.

The educational process is shaped by evolutionary developments in the distant past and by cultural developments in the more recent past. There were clear advantages to early societies if their younger members learned language very quickly and used it to build workable images of the society and the cosmos—images to which they also developed strong emotional commitments. The reproductive success of such groups led to the uniqueness of human childhood in the animal world. An advantage also was to be gained in preserving throughout life, even if in diminishing degree as individuals aged, a relatively undifferentiated learning capacity. Such a capacity would allow a degree of adaptability and flexibility in learning the particular skills and lore required within the complex cultural societies that language created; these societies might be indeterminately varied, and the individual had to be intellectually equipped to adapt to any particular set of norms. 277

Today, as a result, young children quickly learn a language and generate images of their immediate society and of their cosmos. This early learning is rapid and typically so successful that it remains fixed throughout life, providing a template of presuppositions on which future learning is fitted. By ages four or five this incisive learning—directed, in plausible accounts, by a differentiated mental module—diminishes significantly and, during the next few years, the dynamic language-learning and society-orienting drives gradually give way to the less urgent general learning capacity.

Evolution has not equipped us ideally for the educational tasks required by advanced literate societies. We are equipped intellectually for the condition of small nonliterate social groups sharing unquestioned ideologies and images of the cosmos. Our preparation for such groups is only too evident despite our educational assaults on our young, and helps to explain why we have such difficulty and pain in expanding our understanding into and through adulthood. We have to adapt our undifferentiated learning capacity to deal with much more complex and flexible learning than it has been evolutionarily shaped to handle. We cannot tinker with the "hardware" supplied to us by evolution, so we have to adapt the "software" of educational programs in order to subvert the natural constraints on our intellectual flexibility. The weak, undifferentiated learning capacity is not designed to disturb and reshape the early intellectual conditioning we experience. The challenge for education is to work out how we can nevertheless manage to do this.

All major educational thinkers have recognized the problem created by the influence of evolutionary pressures to adapt to conditions that are no longer those with which we are faced in modern, highly literate societies. The theorists did not put it in these terms, of course. Plato offered a fifty-year curriculum of increasingly abstract, disciplined knowledge. While that certainly seems a part of the solution, by itself it seems too fragile, too rigid, and ultimately an act of insufficiently warranted faith. Rousseau offered the more radical recommendation of trying to starve the early rapid learning of anything to work on—by keeping the child away from society and away from words, words, words as much as possible—thus leaving the later learning capacity with nothing to undo. While this is an acute suggestion, it seems in the end simply unrealistic—the child deprived of so much early learning would not likely develop the later richness of understanding Rousseau assumes will be possible. John Dewey characterized the problem in terms of "natural" or "incidental" and "formal" learning (1966, pp. 6–9), and proposes as a solution making the latter as much like "natural" learning as can be contrived. This, too, is an important insight, but it seems in the end inadequate because it does not recognize that the dynamic of "natural" learning is available to us in significantly diminishing degrees after about age five.

My proposal for dealing with this fundamental problem draws on that greatly underestimated educational thinker who foolishly expressed his ideas in verse, William Wordsworth. His sense of the character of early "modular" learning and its diminution at around five led him to conclude that the best hope for keeping that educational energy alive in the later years was to stimulate the imagination. This would preserve some flexibility of the intellect that would enable people to deal more effectively with the complex demands of modern changing social conditions. I have tried to draw on and develop this idea. For each of the "literate" kinds of understanding— Romantic, Philosophic, and Ironic—I have emphasized the particular intellectual tools that support imaginative flexibility. My characterization of these tools has been drawn from observations of their development, refinement, and use in cultural history.

Ideas about evolution transformed understanding in nearly all areas of human inquiry. Even as they began to take shape in the late nineteenth century they foundered in education because of inadequate conceptions of what aspects of human evolutionary and cultural history were being recapitulated. Since the abandonment of recapitulation, educational thinking has persisted in a manner uninfluenced by the seismic paradigm shift that Darwin's ideas effected in modern thinking. It may seem a lame boast to have devised a theory that manages to bring educational thinking into the late nineteenth century—but there we are.

bibliography

Alvarez, A. (1995). *Night: An exploration of night life, night language, sleep and dreams.* London: Cape.

Applebee, Arthur N. (1978). *The child's concept of story.* Chicago: University of Chicago Press.

Armstrong, Miranda, Connolly, Ann, and Saville, Kathy. (1994). *Journeys of discovery.* Melbourne: Oxford University Press.

Arnheim, Rudolf. (1974). *Art and visual perception.* Berkeley: University of California Press.

Ascheim, Steven E. (1994). *The Nietzschean legacy in Germany, 1890–1990.* Berkeley: University of California Press.

Ashton, Elizabeth. (1993). Interpreting children's ideas: Creative thought or factual belief? A new look at Piaget's theory of childhood artificialism as related to religious education. *British Journal of Educational Studies, 41* (2), 164–73.

Bacon, Francis. (1965). The great instarvation. In S. Warhaft (Ed.), *Francis Bacon: A selection of his works.* London: Macmillan. First published, 1620.

Bai, Heesoon. (1996). *Moral perception in the nondual key: Towards an ethic of moral proprioception.* Unpublished Ph.D. thesis, University of British Columbia, Vancouver, Canada.

Bakhtin, M. M. (1986). *Speech genres and other late essays* (Caryl Emerson and Michael Holquist, Eds.; V.W. McGee, Trans.). Austin: University of Texas Press.

Banks, M. S., and Salaparek, R. (1983). Infant visual perception. In M. M. Haith and J. J. Campos (Eds.), *Handbook of child psychology* (Vol. 2). New York: Wiley.

Barzun, Jacques. (1961). *Classic, romantic and modern.* Boston: Atlantic–Little, Brown.

Behler, Ernst. (1990). *Irony and the discourse of modernity.* Seattle: University of Washington Press.

Bennett, JoAnn, and Berry, John W. (1991). Cree literacy in the syllabic script. In David R. Olson and Nancy Torrance (Eds.), *Literacy and orality.* Cambridge: Cambridge University Press.

Bernstein, Basil. (1975). *Class, codes, and control: Vol. 3. Towards a theory of educational transmission.* London: Routledge and Kegan Paul.

Bertelson, P., and DeGelder, B. (1988). Learning about reading from illiterates. In S. Galaburda (Ed.), *From neurons to reading.* Cambridge: MIT Press.

Bettelheim, B. (1976). *The uses of enchantment.* New York: Knopf.

Black, Max. (1962). *Models and metaphors.* Ithaca, N.Y.: Cornell University Press.

Bloom, Alan. (1987). *The closing of the American mind: How higher education has failed democracy and impoverished the souls of today's students.* New York: Simon and Schuster.

281

Booth, Wayne C. (1974). *A rhetoric of irony.* Chicago: University of Chicago Press.

———. (1979). Metaphor as rhetoric: The problem of evaluation. In Sheldon Sacks (Ed.), *On metaphor.* Chicago: University of Chicago Press.

Borges, Jorge Luis. (1968). *Other inquisitions 1937–1952.* New York: Simon and Schuster.

Bourdieu, Pierre, et al. (1994). *Academic discourse* (Richard Teese, Trans.). Oxford: Polity. First published in France, 1965.

Brainerd, Charles J. (1978). *Piaget's theory of intelligence.* Englewood Cliffs, N.J.: Prentice-Hall.

Brett-Smith, H. F. B. (1921). *Shelley's Defence of Poetry.* Oxford: Blackwell.

Brown, D. E. (1991). *Human universals.* New York: McGraw-Hill.

Bruner, Jerome. (1960). *The process of education.* Cambridge: Harvard University Press.

———. (1986). *Actual minds, possible worlds.* Cambridge: Harvard University Press.

———. (1988). Discussion. *Yale Journal of Criticism, 2* (1).

———. (1990). *Acts of meaning.* Cambridge: Harvard University Press.

Bruns, Gerald L. (1992). *Hermeneutics: Ancient and modern.* New Haven, Conn.: Yale University Press.

Burckhardt, Jacob. (1955). *Force and freedom: An interpretation of history* (James Hastings Nichols, Ed.). New York: Meridian Books.

———. (1960). *The civilization of the Renaissance in Italy* (S. G. C. Middlemore, Trans.). London: Phaidon Press.

———. (1965). *On history and historians* (Harry Zohn, Trans.). New York: Harper Torchbook.

Burke, James. (1978). *Connections.* Boston: Little, Brown.

Burkert, Walter. (1985). *Greek religion* (John Raffan, Trans.). Cambridge: Harvard University Press.

Burton, Virginia Lee. (1962). *Life story.* Boston: Houghton Mifflin.

Butler, Marilyn. (1981). *Romantics, rebels, and reactionaries.* Oxford: Oxford University Press.

Carey, S., and Gelman, R. (1990). *The epigenesis of mind.* Hillsdale, N.J.: Erlbaum.

Case, Robbie. (1985). *Intellectual development: Birth to adulthood.* New York: Academic Press.

———. (1991). *The mind's staircase: Exploring the conceptual underpinnings of children's thought and knowledge.* Hillsdale, N.J.: Erlbaum.

Cassirer, Ernst. (1946). *Language and mind* (Suzanne K. Langer, Trans.). New York: Harper.

Chesterton, Gilbert Keith. (1937). *Autobiography.* London: Sheed and Ward.

Churcher, J., and Scaife, M. (1982). How infants see the point. In G. E. Butterworth and P. Light (Eds.), *Social cognition: Studies of the development of understanding* (pp. 116–36). Brighton, Sussex: Harvester.

Cochrane, C. N. (1929). *Thucydides and the science of history.* London: Oxford University Press.

Coe, Richard. (1984). *When the grass was taller.* New Haven, Conn.: Yale University Press.

Coles, Robert. (1989). *The call of stories: Teaching and the moral imagination.* Boston: Houghton Mifflin.

Cole, M., and Scribner, S. (1974). *Culture and thought: A psychological introduction.* New York: Wiley.

Collingwood, R. G. (1946). *The idea of history.* Oxford: Clarendon Press.

Comnena, Anna. (1969). *The Alexiad of Anna Comnena* (E. R. A. Sewter, Trans.). First published in Greek, ca. 1150.

Conway, Daniel W., and Seery, John E. (Eds.). (1992). *The politics of irony.* New York: St. Martin's Press.

Cornford, Francis MacDonald. (1907). *Thucydides mythistoricus.* London: Edward Arnold.

———. (1912). *From religion to philosophy.* London: Edward Arnold.

———. (Trans., Ed., Intro.). (1941). *The Republic of Plato.* Oxford: Oxford University Press.

———. (1952). *Principium sapientiae: The origins of Greek philosophical thought.* Cambridge: Cambridge University Press.

Cunningham, Valentine. (1994, February 18). Fight, fight, and fight again. *Times Literary Supplement.*

Dale, Peter Allan. (1989). *Science, art, and society in the Victorian age.* Madison: University of Wisconsin Press.

Danzig, Tobias. (1967). *Number: The language of science.* New York: Free Press. First published, New York: Macmillan, 1930.

Darling, John, and Van de Pijpekamp, Maaike. (1994). Rousseau on the education, domination and violation of women. *British Journal of Educational Studies, XXXXII*(2), 115–32.

Davie, George Elder. (1986). *The crisis of the democratic intellect: The problem of generalism and specialization in twentieth-century Scotland.* Edinburgh: Polygon.

de Castell, Suzanne, Luke, Allan, and Luke, Carmen. (1989). *Language, authority and criticism: Readings on the school textbook.* London: Falmer.

Dewey, John. (1911). Culture epoch theory. In P. Monroe (Ed.), *A cyclopedia of education* (Vol. 2) (pp. 240–42). New York: Macmillan.

———. (1966). *Democracy and education.* New York: Free Press. First published, 1916.

———. (1972). Plan of organization of the university primary school. In J. A. Boydsen (Ed.), *John Dewey: The early works, 1882–1898: Vol. 5. Early essays, 1895–1898* (pp. 224–43).

Dodds, E. R. (1951). *The Greeks and the irrational.* Berkeley and Los Angeles: University of California Press.

Donald, Merlin. (1991). *Origins of the modern mind.* Cambridge: Harvard University Press.

Donaldson, Margaret. (1978). *Children's minds.* London: Croom Helm.

Durkheim, Emile. (1956). *Education and sociology* (Sherwood D. Fox, Trans., and Intro.). New York: Free Press.

Egan, Kieran. (1978). Thucydides, tragedian. In Robert H. Canary and Henry Kozicki (Eds.), *The writing of history: Literary form and historical understanding.* Madison: University of Wisconsin Press.

———. (1979). Progress in historiography. *Clio, 8*(2), 195–228.

———. (1983). *Education and psychology: Plato, Piaget, and scientific psychology.* New York: Teachers College Press.

———. (1986). *Teaching as story telling.* London, Ontario: Althouse Press; Chicago: University of Chicago Press, 1989; London: Routledge, 1989.

———. (1988). *Primary understanding: Education in early childhood.* New York: Routledge.

———. (1990). *Romantic understanding: The development of rationality and imagination, ages 8–15.* New York and London: Routledge.

———. (1992). *Imagination in teaching and learning: The middle school years.* Chicago: University of Chicago Press; London, Ontario: Althouse Press; London: Routledge.

Eimas, P. D., et al. (1986). Speech perception in infants. *Science, 171,* 303–306.

Eisenstein, Elizabeth. (1979). *The printing press as an agent of change: Communications and cultural transformations in early-modern Europe* (2 vols.). New York: Cambridge University Press.

———. (1983). *The printing revolution in early modern Europe.* Cambridge: Cambridge University Press.

Eisner, Elliot W. (1985). *The educational imagination.* New York: Macmillan.

Elkind, David. (1976). *Child development and education: A Piagetian perspective.* New York: Oxford University Press.

———. (1981). *The hurried child: Growing up too fast too soon.* Reading, Mass.: Addison-Wesley.

Ellis, A. K. (1986). *Teaching and learning elementary social studies.* Boston: Allyn and Bacon.

Enright, D. J. (1988). *The alluring problem: An essay on irony.* Oxford: Oxford University Press.

Erikson, Erik H. (1963). *Childhood and society* (2nd ed.). New York: Norton.

Favat, André. (1977). *Child and tale: The origins of interest.* Washington, D.C.: National Council of Teachers of English.

Feldman, Carol Fleisher. (1988). Symposium contribution on "Literacy, reading, and power." *Yale Journal of Criticism, 2*(1), 209–14.

———. (1991). Oral metalanguage. In David R. Olson and Nancy Torrance (Eds.), *Literacy and orality.* Cambridge: Cambridge University Press.

Ferguson, Kathy E. (1993). *The man question: Visions of subjectivity in feminist theory.* Berkeley: University of California Press.

Fischer, Kurt. (1980). A theory of cognitive development: The control and construction of hierarchies of skills. *Psychological Review, 97,* 477–531.

Fodor, Jerry. (1983). *The modularity of mind.* Cambridge: MIT Press.

Fornara, Charles William. (1983). *The nature of history in ancient Greece and Rome.* Berkeley: University of California Press.

Fox-Keller, Evelyn. (1986). How gender matters, or, why it's so hard for us to count past two. In J. Harding (Ed.), *Perspectives on gender and science.* Brighton: Falmer Press.

Frye, Northrop. (1963). *The educated imagination.* Toronto: Canadian Broadcasting Corporation.

Gadamer, Hans-Georg. (1976). *Philosophical hermeneutics* (David E. Linge, Trans. and Ed.). Berkeley: University of California Press.

Gardner, Howard. (1983). *Frames of mind: The theory of multiple intelligences.* New York: Basic Books.

———. (1991). *The unschooled mind.* New York: Basic Books.

———. (1993). From conflict to clarification. *Linguistics and Education, 5*(2), 181–36.

Gardner, Howard, and Winner, Ellen. (1979). The development of metaphoric competence: Implications for humanistic disciplines. In Sheldon Sacks (Ed.), *On metaphor.* Chicago: University of Chicago Press.

Gluckman, M. (1949–50). Social beliefs and individual thinking in primitive society.

Memoirs and Proceedings of the Manchester Library and Philosophical Society, 91, 73–98.

Gombrich, E. H. (1960). *Art and illusion.* Princeton: Princeton University Press.

Gomme, A.W. (1954). *The Greek attitude to poetry and history.* Berkeley and Los Angeles: University of California Press.

Goodlad, John I. (1984). *A place called school.* New York: McGraw-Hill.

Goodman, Nelson. (1979). Metaphor as moonlighting. In Sheldon Sacks (Ed.), *On metaphor.* Chicago: University of Chicago Press.

Goodman, Paul. (1962). *Compulsory mis-education and the community of scholars.* New York: Vintage Books.

———. (1970). *New reformation.* New York: Random House.

Goody, Jack. (1977). *The domestication of the savage mind.* Cambridge: Cambridge University Press.

———. (1987). *The interface between the written and the oral.* Cambridge: Cambridge University Press.

Goody, Jack, and Watt, Ian. (1963). The consequences of literacy. *Contemporary Studies in Society and History, 5,* 304–45.

Gordon, Daniel. (1994). *Citizens without sovereignty: Equality and sociability in French thought, 1670–1789.* Princeton: Princeton University Press.

Gould, Stephen Jay. (1977). *Ontogeny and phylogeny.* Cambridge: Harvard University Press.

Graff, Gerald. (1987). *Professing literature: An institutional history.* Chicago: University of Chicago Press.

Guthrie, W. K. C. (1962). *A history of Greek philosophy.* Cambridge: Cambridge University Press.

Hall, G. Stanley. (1904). *Adolescence: Its psychology and its relations to physiology, anthropology, sociology, sex, crime, religion, and education* (2 vols.). New York: D. Appleton.

Hallam, Roy. (1969). Piaget and the teaching of history. *Educational Research, 12,* 1, 211–15.

Hallpike, C. R. (1979). *The foundations of primitive thought.* Oxford: Clarendon Press.

Handwerk, Gary J. (1985). *Irony and ethics in narrative: From Schlegel to Lacan.* New Haven, Conn.: Yale University Press.

Hardy, Barbara. (1968). Towards a poetics of fiction: An approach through narrative. *Novel, 2,* 5–14.

Harris, R. (1986). *The origin of writing.* London: Duckworth.

Havelock, Eric A. (1963). *Preface to Plato.* Cambridge: Harvard University Press.

———. (1982). *The literate revolution in Greece and its cultural consequences.* Princeton: Princeton University Press.

———. (1986). *The muse learns to write.* New Haven, Conn.: Yale University Press.

———. (1991). The oral-literate equation: A formula for the modern mind. In David R. Olson and Nancy Torrance (Eds.), *Literacy and orality.* Cambridge: Cambridge University Press.

Hayek, F. A. (1970). The primacy of the abstract. In Arthur Koestler and J. R. Smythies (Eds.), *Beyond reductionism.* New York: Macmillan.

Hazlitt, William. (1951). On the ignorance of the learned. In W. E. Williams (Ed.), *A book of English essays.* Harmondsworth, Middlesex: Penguin.

Heath, Shirley Brice. (1983). *Ways with words.* Cambridge: Cambridge University Press.

Heller, Erich. (1959). *The disinherited mind.* New York: Meridian Books.

Heller, Louis, Humez, Alexander, and Dror, Malcah. (1984). *The private lives of English words.* London: Routledge and Kegan Paul.

Hicks, Deborah. (1993). Narrative discourse and classroom learning. *Linguistics and Education, 5,* 127–48.

Hirsch, E. D. Jr. (1987). *Cultural literacy.* Boston: Houghton Mifflin.

Hirst, Paul. (1974). *Knowledge and the curriculum.* London: Routledge and Kegan Paul.

Huizinga, Johan. (1949). *Homo ludens: A study of the play element in culture.* London: Routledge and Kegan Paul.

Hoogland, Cornelia. (1992). *Poetics, politics and pedagogy of Grimm's Fairy Tales.* Unpublished Ph.D. thesis, Simon Fraser University, Burnaby, British Columbia, Canada.

———. (1994). Real "wolves in those bushes": Readers take dangerous journeys with Little Red Riding Hood. *Canadian Children's Literature, 73,* 7–21.

Hudson, W. H. (1918). *Far away and long ago.* London: Dent.

Illich, Ivan. (1983). *In the vineyard of the text.* Chicago: University of Chicago Press.

Inhelder, Bärbel, and Piaget, Jean. (1958). *The growth of logical thinking* (Anne Parsons and Stanley Milgram, Trans.). New York: Basic Books.

Itard, Jean-Marc-Gaspard. (1962). *The wild boy of Aveyron.* (George Humphrey, and Muriel Humphrey, Trans.). Englewood Cliffs, N.J.: Prentice Hall. Compiled from two reports, first printed in 1801 and 1807.

Jarolimek, J. (1982). *Social studies in elementary education* (6th ed.). New York: Macmillan.

Jowett, Benjamin. (1937). *The Dialogues of Plato.* New York: Random House.

Joyce, James. (1964). *A portrait of the artist as a young man.* New York: Viking.

Kant, Immanuel. (1952). *Critique of judgement* (J. C. Meredith, Trans.). Oxford: Oxford University Press. First published, 1790.

Kearney, Richard. (1988). *The wake of imagination.* London: Hutchinson.

Keil, F. (1989). *Concepts, kinds, and cognitive development.* Cambridge: MIT Press.

Kenyon, John. (1989, December 15–20). The outcome of energy and conflict. *Times Literary Supplement.*

Kermode, Frank. (1966). *The sense of an ending.* Oxford: Oxford University Press.

Keynes, John Maynard. (1936). *General theory of employment, interest and money.* London: Macmillan.

Kierkegaard, Søren. (1965). *The concept of irony: With constant reference to Socrates* (Lee M. Capel, Trans.). Bloomington: Indiana University Press. First published, 1841.

Kittay, Jeffrey. (1991). Thinking through literacies. In David R. Olson and Nancy Torrance (Eds.), *Literacy and orality* (pp. 165–73). Cambridge: Cambridge University Press.

Kleibard, Herbert M. (1986). *The struggle for the American curriculum: 1893–1958.* Boston: Routledge and Kegan Paul.

Knapp, M., and H. Knapp. (1976). *One potato, two potato.* New York: Norton.

Koestler, Arthur. (1964). *The act of creation.* New York: Macmillan.

Kolakowski, Leszek. (1989). *The presence of myth.* Chicago: University of Chicago Press.

Kozol, Jonathan. (1967). *Death at an early age.* Boston: Houghton Mifflin.

Kristeva, Julia. (1984). Two interviews with Julia Kristeva by Elaine H. Baruch and Perry Mersel. *Political Review,* 1.

Kuhn, Thomas S. (1962). *The structure of scientific revolutions.* Chicago: University of Chicago Press.

Lane, Harlan. (1976). *The wild boy of Aveyron.* Cambridge: Harvard University Press.

Leach, Edmund. (1967). Genesis as myth. In John Middleton (Ed.), *Myth and cosmos.* New York: Natural History Press.

Lévi-Bruhl, Lucien. (1985). *How natives think* (Lilian A. Clare, Trans.; C. Scott Littleton, Intro.). Princeton: Princeton University Press. First published, 1910.

Lévi-Strauss, Claude. (1964). *Totemism.* London: Merlin.

———. (1966). *The savage mind.* Chicago: University of Chicago Press.

———. (1970). *The raw and the cooked.* New York: Harper and Row.

———. (1978). *Myth and meaning.* Toronto: University of Toronto Press.

Lloyd, G. E. R. (1988). *The revolutions of wisdom: Studies in the claims and practices of ancient Greek science.* Berkeley: University of California Press.

———. (1990). *Demystifying mentalities.* Cambridge: Cambridge University Press.

Luria, A. R. (1976). *Cognitive development: Its cultural and social foundations.* Cambridge: Harvard University Press.

———. (1979). *The making of mind: A personal account of Soviet psychology* (Michael Cole and Sheila Cole, Eds.). Cambridge: Harvard University Press.

Lyotard, Jean-François. (1979). *The postmodern condition: A report on knowledge* (Geoff Bennington and Brian Massumi, Trans.; Fredric Jameson, Foreword). Minneapolis: University of Minnesota Press.

MacIntyre, Alasdair. (1981). *After virtue.* Notre Dame, Ind.: University of Notre Dame Press.

———. (1989). Relativism, power, and philosophy. In Michael Krausz (Ed.), *Relativism: Interpretation and confrontation.* Notre Dame, Ind.: University of Notre Dame Press.

Malinowski, Bronislaw. (1954). *Magic, science and religion.* New York: Anchor. First published, 1926.

Matthews, Gareth B. (1993). Childhood: The recapitulation model. In Matthew Lipman (Ed.), *Thinking children and education.* Dubuque, Iowa: Kendall/Hunt.

———. (1980). *Philosophy and the young child.* Cambridge: Harvard University Press.

———. (1984). *Dialogues with children.* Cambridge: Harvard University Press.

Mayr, Ernst. (1963). *Animal species and evolution.* Cambridge: Harvard University Press.

McClure, J. Derrick. (1989–90, December 29–January 4). Wars of the word. *Times Literary Supplement.*

McFarland, Thomas. (1985). *Originality and imagination.* Baltimore: Johns Hopkins University Press.

McLuhan, Marshall. (1962). *The Gutenberg galaxy: The making of typographic man.* Toronto: University of Toronto Press.

Mehler, J., et al. (1988). A precursor to language acquisition in young infants. *Cognition, 29,* 143–78.

Miller, Jonathan. (1978). *The body in question.* New York: Random House.

Modgil, Sohan, and Modgil, Celia. (1982). *Jean Piaget: Consensus and controversy.* New York: Praeger.

Momigliano, Arnaldo. (1966). The place of Herodotus in the history of historiography. In *Studies in historiography.* London: Weidenfeld and Nicolson.

More, Hannah. (1777). *Essays on various subjects, principally designed for young ladies.* London: Wilkie and Cadell.

Morgan, L. (1877). *Ancient society.* Chicago: Kerr.

Muecke, D. C. (1969). *The compass of irony.* London: Methuen.

———. (1970a). *Irony.* London: Methuen.

———. (1970b). *Irony and the ironic.* London: Methuen.

Müller, Max. (1873). The philosophy of mythology. Appendix to his *Introduction to the science of religion*. London: Murray.

Murdoch, Iris. (1992). *Metaphysics as a guide to morals*. London: Chatto.

Musil, Robert. (1965). *The man without qualities* (Eithne Wilkins and Ernst Kaiser, Trans.). New York: Capricorn Books. First published as *Der Mann ohne Eigenschaften*, 1930–43.

Narasimhan, R. (1991). Literacy: Its characterization and implications. In David R. Olson and Nancy Torrance (Eds.), *Literacy and orality*. Cambridge: Cambridge University Press.

Nelson, Katherine. (1977). Cognitive development and the acquisition of concepts. In R. C. Anderson, R. J. Spiro, and W. E. Montague (Eds.), *Schooling and the acquisition of knowledge*. Hillsdale, N.J.: Erlbaum.

Nietzsche, Friedrich. (1956). *The birth of tragedy and The genealogy of morals* (Francis Golfing, Trans.). New York: Doubleday Anchor. *The birth of tragedy*, first published, 1872; *The genealogy of morals*, first published, 1887.

———. (1962). *Philosophy in the tragic age of the Greeks* (Marianne Cowan, Trans.). Chicago: University of Chicago Press.

———. (1968a). *The will to power* (Walter Kaufmann, Ed.; Walter Kaufmann and R. J. Hallingdale, Trans.). New York: Vintage. First written c. 1883–88.

———. (1968b). Twilight of the idols. In *The portable Nietzsche* (Walter Kaufmann, Trans. and Ed.). New York: Viking. First published, 1889.

Norris, Christopher. (1993). *The truth about postmodernism*. Oxford: Blackwell.

Nyberg, David. (1993). *The varnished truth: Truth telling and deceiving in ordinary life*. Chicago: University of Chicago Press.

Oakeshott, Michael. (1991). *The voice of liberal learning: Michael Oakeshott on education* (Timothy Fuller, Ed.). New Haven, Conn.: Yale University Press.

Ogden, C. K. (1976). *Opposition*. Bloomington: Indiana University Press.

Olson, David R. (1977). From utterance to text: The bias of language in speech and writing. *Harvard Educational Review, 47*, 257–81.

———. (Ed.). (1987). Understanding literacy. Special issue of *Interchange, 18*(1/2).

———. (1993). How writing represents speech. *Language and Communication, 13*(1), 1–17.

———. (1994). *The world on paper*. Cambridge: Cambridge University Press.

Olson, David R., and Torrance, Nancy (Eds.). (1991). *Literacy and orality*. Cambridge: Cambridge University Press.

Ong, Walter J. (1958). *Ramus and Talon inventory*. Cambridge: Harvard University Press.

———. (1971). *Rhetoric, romance, and technology*. Ithaca, N.Y.: Cornell University Press.

———. (1977). *Interfaces of the word*. Ithaca, N.Y.: Cornell University Press.

———. (1978). Literacy and orality in our time. *ADE Bulletin, 58*, 1–7.

———. (1982). *Orality and literacy*. London and New York: Methuen.

Opie, Iona, and Opie, Peter. (1959). *The lore and language of schoolchildren*. Oxford: Oxford University Press.

———. (1969). *Children's games in street and playground*. Oxford: Oxford University Press.

———. (1985). *The singing game*. Oxford: Oxford University Press.

Osborne, John. (1992, May 2). Final victory to the silk dressing gown. *The Spectator.*

Paley, V. G. (1981). *Wally's stories*. Cambridge: Harvard University Press.

———. (1984). *Boys and girls: Superheroes in the doll corner.* Chicago: University of Chicago Press.

———. (1990). *The boy who would be a helicopter.* Cambridge: Harvard University Press.

Pattanayak, D. P. (1991). Literacy: An instrument of oppression. In David R. Olson and Nancy Torrance (Eds.), *Literacy and orality.* Cambridge: Cambridge University Press.

Pearson, Hesketh. (1948). *The Smith of Smiths.* Harmondsworth, Middlesex: Penguin. First published, 1934.

Pearson, Lionel. (1939). *Early Ionian Historians.* Oxford: Clarendon Press.

Penrose, Roger. (1993, October 21). Nature's biggest secret. *New York Review of Books.*

Philips, Denis, and Kelly, Maevis. (1975). Hierarchical theories of development in education and psychology. *Harvard Educational Review, 45*(3), 351–75.

Piaget, Jean. (1973a). *To understand is to invent* (George-Anne Roberts, Trans.). New York: Grossman.

———. (1973b). *The child and reality* (Arnold Rosin, Trans.). New York: Grossman.

———. (1975). *The development of thought: Equilibration of cognitive structures.* New York: Viking.

Piaget, Jean, and Inhelder, Bärbel. (1969). *The psychology of the child.* New York: Basic Books.

Pinker, Stephen. (1994). *The language instinct: How the mind created language.* New York: Morrow.

Popper, Karl. (1945). *The open society and its enemies.* London: Routledge and Kegan Paul. (1963, 4th rev. ed. by Harper Torchbooks.)

Postman, Neil. (1982). *The disappearance of childhood.* New York: Delacorte Press.

Postman, Neil, and Weingartner, Charles. (1969). *Teaching as a subversive activity.* New York: Delacorte Press.

Quine, W. V. (1979). A postscript on metaphor. In Sheldon Sacks (Ed.), *On metaphor.* Chicago: University of Chicago Press.

Ranke, Leopold von. (1956). Preface to Histories of the Latin and teutonic nations from 1494–1514. In Fritz Stern (Ed.), *The variety of histories.* Cleveland: Meridian. First published, 1824.

Ravitch, Diane. (1983). *The troubled crusade: American education 1945–1980.* New York: Basic Books.

Ravitch, Diane, and Finn, Chester E. (1987). *What do our 17-year-olds know?* New York: Harper and Row.

Rawson, Claude. (1988, December 2–8). Quandaries of the quotidian. *Times Literary Supplement.*

Read, C., Zhang, Y., Nie, H., and Ding, B. (1986). The ability to manipulate speech sounds depends on knowing alphabetic writing. *Cognition, 24,* 31–44.

Regis, Ed. (1994, May 26). Swami. *London Review of Books.*

Richards, I. A. (1936). *The philosophy of rhetoric.* Oxford: Oxford University Press.

Richards, Robert J. (1992). *The meaning of evolution.* Chicago: University of Chicago Press.

Ricoeur, Paul. (1991). *From text to action: Essays in hermeneutics, II* (Kathleen Blaney and John B. Thompson, Trans.). Evanston, Ill.: Northwestern University Press.

Roldão, Maria do Céu. (1992). *The concept of concrete thinking in curricula for early educa-*

tion: A critical examination. Unpublished Ph.D. thesis, Simon Fraser University, Burnaby, British Columbia, Canada.

Rorty, Richard. (1989). *Contingency, irony, and solidarity.* Cambridge: Cambridge University Press.

————. (1991). *Objectivity, relativism, and truth.* Cambridge: Cambridge University Press.

Rosenbluth, Vera. (1990). *Keeping family stories alive.* Vancouver, British Columbia: Hartley and Marks.

Roszak, Theodore. (1969). *The making of a counter culture.* New York: Doubleday.

Rousseau, Jean-Jacques. (1911). *Émile* (Barbara Foxley, Trans.). London: Dent. First published, 1762.

Sagan, Carl. (1980). *Cosmos.* New York: Random House.

Scaife, M., and Bruner, J. S. (1975). The capacity for joint visual attention in the infant. *Nature, 253,* 265–66.

Schein, Seth L. (1984). *The mortal hero: An introduction to Homer's Iliad.* Berkeley and Los Angeles: University of California Press.

Schlegel, Friedrich. (1991). Ideas, 69. In *Philosophical fragments* (Peter Fichow, Trans.). Minneapolis: University of Minnesota Press. First published, 1800.

Scholes, Robert J., and Willis, Brenda J. (1991). Linguists, literacy, and the intensionality of Marshall McLuhan's western man. In David R. Olson and Nancy Torrance (Eds.), *Literacy and orality.* Cambridge: Cambridge University Press.

Scribner, S., and Cole, M. (1981). *Psychology of literacy.* Cambridge: Cambridge University Press.

Seeley, L. (1906). *Elementary pedagogy.* New York: Hinds, Noble and Eldredge.

Seery, John A. (1992). Spelunkers of the world unite! In Daniel W. Conway and John A. Seery (Eds.), *The politics of irony.* New York: St. Martin's Press.

Shattock, Joanne. (1989). *Politics and reviewers: The "Edinburgh" and the "Quarterly" in the early Victorian age.* Leicester: Leicester University Press.

Shaw, George Bernard. (1965). *Collected letters 1874–1897,* Vol. 1 (Dan H. Laurence, Ed.). London: Max Reinhardt.

Shepard, R. N. (1975). Form, formation, and transformation of internal representations. In R. L. Solso (Ed.), *Contemporary issues in cognitive psychology.* Washington, D.C.: V.H. Winston and Sons.

Siegel, Linda S., and Brainerd, Charles J. (Eds.). (1978). *Alternatives to Piaget: Critical essays on the theory.* New York: Academic Press.

Smalley, B. (1941). *The study of the Bible in the middle ages.* Oxford: Clarendon Press.

Snell, Bruno. (1960). *The discovery of the mind: The Greek origins of European thought.* New York: Harper Torchbooks.

Sobol, Donald J. (1986). *Encyclopedia Brown and the case of the mysterious handprints.* New York: Bantam Skylark.

Spacks, Patricia Meyer. (1981). *The adolescent idea: Myths of youth and the adult imagination.* New York: Basic Books.

Spence, Jonathan. (1984). *The memory palace of Matteo Ricci.* New York: Viking Penguin.

Spencer, Herbert. (1861). *Education: Intellectual, moral and physical.* London: G. Manwaring.

Sprat, Thomas. (1958). *History of the Royal Society of London for the improving of natural knowledge* (J. I. Cope and H. W. Jones, Eds.). St. Louis: Washington University Press.

Stock, Brian. (1972). *Myth and science in the twelfth century.* Princeton: Princeton University Press.

————. (1983). *The implications of literacy.* Princeton: Princeton University Press.

Street, Brian V. (1984). *Literacy in theory and practice.* Cambridge: Cambridge University Press.

Sutton-Smith, Brian. (1981). *The folktales of children.* Philadelphia: University of Pennsylvania Press.

————. (1988). In search of the imagination. In Kieran Egan and Dan Nadaner (Eds.), *Imagination and education.* New York: Teachers College Press; Milton Keynes: Open University Press.

Swearingen, C. Jan. (1991). *Rhetoric and irony: Western literacy and western lies.* New York: Oxford University Press.

Tambiah, Stanley Jeyaraja. (1990). *Magic, science, religion, and the scope of rationality.* Cambridge: Cambridge University Press.

Tawney, R. H. (1926). *Religion and the rise of capitalism.* London: Murray.

Taylor, Charles. (1985). *Human agency and language.* Cambridge: Cambridge University Press.

————. (1991). *The malaise of modernity.* Concord, Ontario: Anansi Press.

Temple, Charles, and Gillett, Jean Wallace. (1989). *Language arts* (2d ed.). Glenview, Ill.: Scott, Foresman.

Trilling, Lionel. (1950). *The liberal imagination.* New York: The Viking Press.

Tulviste, Peter. (1979). On the origins of theoretic syllogistic reasoning in culture and the child. *The Quarterly Newsletter of the Laboratory of Comparative Human Cognition, 1*(4), 73–80.

Turner, F. M. (1974). *Between science and religion: The reaction to scientific naturalism in late Victorian England.* New Haven, Conn.: Yale University Press.

Tyler, Ralph. (1949). *Basic principles of curriculum and instruction.* Chicago: University of Chicago Press.

Vernant, Jean-Pierre. (1982). *The origins of Greek thought.* Ithaca, N.Y.: Cornell University Press.

Vico, Giambattista. (1970). *The new science* (T. G. Bergin and M. H. Fisch, Trans.). Ithaca, N.Y.: Cornell University Press. First published, 1725.

Vlastos, Gregory. (1991). *Socrates: Ironist and moral philosopher.* Cambridge: Cambridge University Press.

Vygotsky, Lev. (1962). *Thought and language* (Eugenia Haufmann and Gertrude Vakar, Trans.). Cambridge: MIT Press.

————. (1978). *Mind in society: The development of higher psychological processes* (Michael Cole, Vera John-Steiner, Sylvia Scribner, and Ellen Souberman, Eds.). Cambridge: Harvard University Press.

Warner, James H. (1940). The basis of J.-J. Rousseau's contemporaneous reputation in England. *Modern Language Notes, 55,* 270–80.

Warnock, Mary (1976). *Imagination.* London: Faber.

Watts, Isaac. (1741). *The improvement of the mind: Or, A supplement to the art of logick.* London: James Brackstone.

Weber, Alfred. (1946). *Theory of location of industries* (Carl Joachim Friedrich, Trans.). Chicago: University of Chicago Press.

Weber, Max. (1975). *Roscher and Knies: The logical problem of historical economies* (Guy Oakes, Trans.). New York: Free Press.

————. (1978). *Economy and society: An outline of interpretive sociology* (G. Roth and C. Wittich, Eds.). Berkeley: University of California Press.

Weinberg, Steven. (1993). In Roger Penrose, Nature's biggest secret. *New York Review of Books* (1993, October 21), 82.

Wertsch, James V. (1985). *Vygotsky and the social formation of mind.* Cambridge: Harvard University Press.

———. (1991). *Voices of the mind: A sociocultural approach to mediated action.* Cambridge: Harvard University Press.

White, Alan R. (1990). *The language of imagination.* Oxford: Blackwell.

White, Hayden. (1973). *Metahistory: The historical imagination in nineteenth-century Europe.* Baltimore: Johns Hopkins University Press.

———. (1978). *Tropics of discourse: Essays in cultural criticism.* Baltimore: Johns Hopkins University Press.

Whitehead, Alfred North. (1967). *The aims of education.* New York: The Free Press. First published, 1929.

Whorf, Benjamin Lee. (1956). *Language, thought, and reality.* Cambridge: MIT Press.

Wilde, Alan. (1981). *Horizons of assent: Modernism, postmodernism, and the ironic imagination.* Baltimore: Johns Hopkins University Press.

Williams, Bernard. (1985). *Ethics and the limits of philosophy.* Cambridge: Harvard University Press.

Winch, Peter. (1970). Understanding a primitive society. In Bryan R. Wilson (Ed.), *Rationality.* Oxford: Blackwell.

Winner, Ellen. (1988). *The point of words: Children's understanding of metaphor and irony.* Cambridge: Harvard University Press.

Wittgenstein, Ludwig. (1969). *On certainty* (G. E. M. Anscombe and G. H. von Wright, Eds.; Denis Paul and G. E. M. Anscombe, Trans.). Oxford: Blackwell.

Wood, Michael. (1985). *In search of the Trojan War.* London: British Broadcasting Corporation.

Wolpert, Lewis. (1993, September 24). Know how to know. *Times Literary Supplement.*

Yates, Frances. (1966). *The art of memory.* Chicago: University of Chicago Press.

Young, Michael. (1971). *Knowledge and control: New directions for the sociology of education.* London: Collier-Macmillan.

index

abstract thinking, 81, 106, 184, 232; in young children, 47–53. *See also* theoretic abstractions

academic disciplines, as foundation of education, 13–15, 20, 20–25

Adams, Richard, 71

Addison, Joseph, 112

affective, component in thinking, 61, 64, 245; images, 62, 246, 255; meaning, 63–65, 246

Alcibiades, 141

alienation, 98, 102, 160; "alienating irony," 161, 162

alphabet, 75, 76

Alvarez, A., 168

Anaximander, 79

Anaximines, 79

anomalies to general schemes, 129–31, 134, 135, 157, 267–69

Apple, Michael, 186

Applebee, Arthur, 45

apprenticeship, 49

Aquinas, St. Thomas, 145

Arian, 108

Aristotle, 55, 75, 79, 105, 110, 111, 113, 116, 124

Armstrong, Christopher, 133, 134, 135

Armstrong, Miranda, 133, 216, 275

Arnheim, Rudolf, 243

Arnold, Matthew, 181, 206

arts, in the curriculum, 216

Ascheim, Steven E., 151

Ashton, Elizabeth, 50

Auden, W. H., 158, 192

Augustine, St., 145, 256

Austen, Jane, 233

autobiographies of childhood, 101

awe, 218, 219

Bacon, Francis, 88, 111, 112

Bai, Heesoon, 193

Bakhtin, M. M., 65, 186

Banks, M. S., 39

Barzun, Jacques, 96

behaviorism, 117

Behler, Ernst, 146, 151, 170

Bernstein, Basil, 66, 186

Bertelson, P., 75

Bettelheim, Bruno, 38–40

binary structuring, 37–44, 86, 160, 184, 185, 246, 248, 249

Black, Max, 55

Blake, William, 96

Bloom, Alan, 31, 232

Bodin, Jean, 1

Bohr, Niels, 149

Booth, Wayne C., 56

Borges, Jorge Luis, 92, 274

Bourdieu, Pierre, 230

Brainerd, Charles J., 50, 122

Brett-Smith, H. F. B., 115

Brown, D. E., 34, 38, 44, 59

Bruner, Jerome, 44, 79, 96, 164, 183, 243, 265

Bruns, Gerald L., 144

Burckhardt, Jacob, 148, 150

Burke, Edmund, 196

Burke, James, 222

Burkert, Walter, 86